SELF-NARRATIVES
The Construction of Meaning
in Psychotherapy

HUBERT J. M. HERMANS
ELS HERMANS-JANSEN

THE GUILFORD PRESS
New York   London

© 1995 The Guilford Press
A Division of Guilford Publications, Inc.
72 Spring Street, New York, NY 10012

Printed in the United States of America

This book is printed on acid-free paper.

Last digit is print number: 9   8   7   6   5   4   3   2   1

Library of Congress Cataloging-in-Publication Data

Her   , H. J. M.
   elf-narratives : the construction of meaning in psychotherapy /
H   ert J. M. Hermans, Els Hermans-Jansen.
   p.   cm.
   ncludes bibliographical references and index.
   ISBN 0-89862-878-4
   1. Psychotherapy.   2. Self-evaluation.   3. Self-perception.
I. Hermans-Jansen, Els.   II. Title.   III. Title: Construction of
meaning in psychotherapy.
   [DNLM: 1. Psychotherapy—methods.   2. Self Assessment (Psychology)
3. Motivation.   WM 420 H552s 1995]
RC480.5.H38   1995
616.89'14—dc20
DNLM/DLC
for Library of Congress   95-8249
                                                 CIP

These are opposites: Two moments, each undeducible, untransportable, and unmixable, that still are, in an insoluble way, united with each other.
—Romano Guardini, 1925

Acknowledgments

We thank our colleagues who have given their support during the preparation and writing of this work: Wim Bronzwaer, Erik Dyckhoff, Jan van den Eeden, Hans Hoekstra, Harry Kempen, Engelien van Lokven, Jim Lamiell, Mikael Leiman, Karel van de Loo, Dan McAdams, Michael Mahoney, Piotr Oleś, Miel Otto, Theodore Sarbin, Tjeb Toornstra, Cees van der Staak, Rob van Woerden, Danielle Verstraeten, and Lenie Verhofstadt-Denève.

Margreet Poulie and Rens van Loon commented on the manuscript as a whole. Willem van Gilst gave advice on methodology and devised computer programs for the various versions of the self-confrontation procedure.

Brigit van Widenfelt made detailed editorial remarks, and Wies Cloosterman worked on the layout of the text with great care.

We thank Toby Troffkin, Wendy Ross, and the editorial and production staff of Guilford as a whole, who have done excellent work in the final stage of the preparation of the book. Finally, we are indebted to our colleagues all over the world who have commented on the articles we wrote for professional and scientific journals that preceded this publication.

Preface

This book is the product of a 20-year cooperation between a personality psychologist, Hubert Hermans, and a psychotherapist/counselor, Els Hermans-Jansen. How did this cooperation start and how did it develop? In 1967, Hubert did his dissertation on achievement motivation and fear of failure, for which he developed two psychological tests, one for adults and one for children. Over the years, however, he felt a growing dissatisfaction with test construction and its underlying premises. Three basic issues led him to redirect his work. First, he questioned how achievement motivation or fear of failure can change when they are based on the concept of traits and relatively stable dispositions. Second, he questioned the emphasis by psychology in Western society on the construct of achievement motivation, recognizing that when this emphasis is exaggerated, it seriously restricts the range of possible values and human potential. Third, and most fundamental, psychological tests, like so many other products of psychology, seemed to him to be based on an objectifying relationship between psychologist and subject in which the subject is studied by the psychologist. Considering the far-reaching implications of the basic relationship between psychologist and subject, Hubert felt a strong need to continue his research activities on the cooperative relationship between the two parties. On the basis of these three considerations, he formulated a valuation theory and a self-confrontation method that has the following characteristics: (1) a gradual and theory-guided transition between assessment and change; (2) a broadening of the valuational scope so that people can express a great diversity of meaning units that play or might play a significant role in their daily lives; and (3) a cooperative relationship in which clients or subjects are invited to act as the investigators of their own self-narratives and challenged to take initiatives to change their situation.

Els Hermans-Jansen worked in the '60s in several institutions where she was confronted by the serious behavioral problems of adolescent boys and girls that had typically led to the decision to place them in a juvenile institution. Els discovered that although these young people had personal histories filled with bad and frustrating experiences, they were never entirely closed off from contact with others and a willingness to cooperate. The observation that young people could behave entirely differently depending on the nature of the relationship they were in stimulated her interest in psychology and education. After finishing her studies, she became qualified in several psychotherapeutic and counseling techniques, particularly client-centered therapy. At the same time, she became acquainted with the self-confrontation method, which she began to include in her own practice as a method for assessment and change. She discovered that this method was both open and structured. It was open to the specific stories clients told about themselves and structured to the extent that it brought order and direction to an often chaotic experiential world.

The subject of this book was thus a common project of two authors who entered it from quite different perspectives, one as a researcher and personality theorist interested in the psychology of motivation and the other as a practitioner interested in the question of how to motivate people to explore their own life in greater depth and bend it into a more fruitful direction.

Contents

Introduction

This book addresses three levels of understanding: theory, method, and practice. The theoretical framework, valuation theory, is rooted in the metaphor of the person as a motivated storyteller, that is, as someone who has a story to tell about his or her own life. In telling this story the person gives special significance to particular events (or groups of events), which function as "units of meaning" or, using a more dynamic term, as "valuations." The term *valuation* suggests that a person attributes positive, negative, or ambivalent values to the events of his or her past, present, and future. The various valuations are organized into a system that depends on the nature of person–situation interactions and is reorganized over the course of time. It is supposed, moreover, that basic motives influence the organization and reorganization of the valuation system. Two motives are particularly salient: the striving for self-enhancement (self-protection, self-maintenance, and self-expansion) and the longing for contact and union with something or someone else. Together these elements (basic motives influencing the way people give value to their life events) form the constituents of the metaphor of the person as motivated storyteller.

The organization and reorganization of the valuation system, reflecting a telling and retelling of one's self-narrative, is systematically investigated in the self-confrontation method, a form of self-investigation performed in cooperation with a psychologist. This method focuses not only on the content and organization of the different valuations but also on their latent motivational basis. The motivational characteristics of the valuation system are made explicit and used in such a way that a smooth transition between assessment and change is realized. The nature of the change process is evaluated in a second self-investigation so that the direction of the process may be continued or corrected.

Over the years, the self-confrontation method has resulted in a great variety of practical ideas, procedures, guidelines, and routes to change, which we present in this book together with illustrative cases.

The valuation approach was developed through a series of alternating phases of theory construction and exploration of methodological devices and practical procedures. We never constructed a complete theory, which was later applied in practice. Rather, we sketched out the theory and then continuously modified, expanded, and enriched it by frequent feedback from practice. This feedback was given not only by the professionals who assisted the clients but also by the clients themselves, who offered their impressions, ideas, and advice. There were periods, sometimes several years in length, when we did not feel a need to develop the approach further despite our daily conversations about clients; at other times there was a sudden surge of new ideas, often stimulated by a finding that we did not expect at all, that opened our eyes to new possibilities for assessment, change, or evaluation.

After all these years, we see our approach, including our successes, failures, and frustrations, as strong support for the scientist–practitioner model as it was originally promulgated at the Boulder Conference in 1949 (Raimy, 1950), a model that caused so many pains and discussions in our field (e.g., Barlow, Hayes, & Nelson, 1984). We were therefore delighted to see that more than 40 years after the model's inception the fertile ideas of the Boulder Conference were again articulated at a national conference, held in Florida, of leaders in the field (Belar & Perry, 1992).

The general support by attendees of the Boulder and Florida conferences of a scientist–practitioner interaction agrees with Mahoney's (1989) criticism of "the regrettable schism within modern psychology." It is also in agreement with Hoshmand and Polkinghorne's (1992) conclusion that a revised conception of the relationship of science and practice is needed "in which there is a productive interplay rather than elevation of one form of knowledge above the other" (p. 63). A similar view marks our position as well: "A dialogical relationship is required among scientists and practitioners, moving from an asymmetrical relation in which one of the parties is intrinsically dominant over the other towards a more symmetrical relation, in which both scientists and practitioners function as co-constructors of psychological reality" (Hermans & Kempen, 1993, p. 135).

We have become increasingly convinced that the prevailing concept that a theory should first be developed and later applied in practice is not a very productive one for counseling and therapy. We have learned that practice is not some technical set of behaviors that is received from theoreticians or researchers but, rather, a highly dynamic and complex system in which action alternates with theoretical reflection, a system well described by Schön (1983, 1987) as "reflection in action." When theory and practice function as interdependent parts of a dynamic system, the traditional psychological subdisciplines still have a role to play and may feed the scientist-practitioner interaction in a variety of ways. However, all these inputs have to be checked, adapted, or reformulated to adjust them to the theory, methodology, and practice that result from scientists and practitioners working together. This suggests that counseling and therapy represent specific fields of practice open to contributions from psychological subdisciplines and other disciplines.

The approach presented in this book can best be characterized as ecumenical. Although the valuation approach has a specific theory and methodology, therapists and counselors of different orientations will recognize a number of phenomena and discover a variety of assessment and change procedures that can be integrated into their own conceptual maps and practices. The metaphor of the person as storyteller is highly adaptable and more or less basic to practitioners working in a variety of traditions. For example, cognitive behavior therapists will recognize both the powerful role of valuations as narrative interpretations of one's behavior and the role specific actions play in changing ("invalidating") ineffective behavior, workers in the tradition of Freudian psychoanalysis will be interested in the importance of defenses and in the analysis of dreams and myths, and Jungian psychoanalysts will note the great importance attached to the "coincidence of opposites" in the affective life of the individual and to the integration of the self. Therapists and counselors working along client-centered lines may be interested in the organization and lifelong development of the self and in the working of the person's self-knowledge; psychologists interested in personal construct psychology will recognize the constructive and imaginative nature of valuation as well as the affect matrix that has the form of a grid; and therapists who follow Frankl's logotherapy will see that "meaning of life" may be studied by the approach proposed here (for a specific treatise, see Hermans, 1989). Finally, psychologists working with subselves or subpersonalities (for a review, see Rowan, 1990), will find a concrete procedure to assess and reorganize the valuation system in such a way that suppressed or neglected subselves are made explicit and developed.

The self-confrontation method has three functions: assessment, process promotion, and evaluation. As an assessment procedure it provides, in the form of a thorough self-investigation, a narratively structured overview of concerns, problems, and goals. This structured overview of personal meanings (valuations) referring to the past, present, and future gives direction to a change in these meanings, reflecting the process promotion or psychotherapeutic function of the method. This process promotion is realized through a number of specific strategies that challenge the client's personal responsibility and action potential. The behavioral change is then evaluated in a second self-investigation, one in which the meaning of this change is examined, thus providing a starting point for a new round.

The three functions of the method can be used by therapists and counselors who want to assess and change the personal meaning of clinical problems and their specific associated behavior, by school counselors who want to address identity problems or problems in social relationships, by career counselors who want to contribute to their clients' career decisions and to the establishment of directed movement into the future, and by researchers who are interested in the idiographic analysis of individual meaning processes.

It is certainly not our intention to present the valuation approach as a system that is closed to rival approaches and fixed forever. On the contrary, readers may read the book as an example of a view that invites them to construe alternative possibilities. This volume comprises many examples of specific assessment techniques, guidelines for change, and evaluation devices that may stimulate the psychologist to develop new and even better ones in the light of the basic metaphor and the theoretical framework. Ideally, the methodology invites the reader to learn to play it as an instrument. Note, however, that this requires not only good ideas but also training and practice.

The book contains nine chapters, the last of which is a manual for how to conduct this method. Chapter 1 presents the metaphor of the person as a motivated storyteller in comparison with other metaphors used in psychology. Chapter 2 discusses valuation theory as a conceptual framework for the narrative construction and reconstruction of meaning units, with special attention to basic motives underlying these units (i.e., striving for self-enhancement and longing for contact and union). Chapter 3 is entirely devoted to the self-confrontation method as a concrete procedure for self-investigation; the three functions of the self-confrontation method—assessment, process promotion, and evaluation—are discussed. Chapter 4 offers an overview of different, and opposite, valuation types (e.g., success, aggression, unity, unfulfilled love) and discusses some routes for change from one type of valuation to another. Because imagination is central to the narrative metaphor and to the process of valuation, the role played by imaginal figures and interactions is assessed and discussed. The implications for psychological health are formulated in terms of differentiation, integration, and flexibility of the valuation system. Chapter 5 focuses on dreams as routes for investigating less conscious valuations. Some stories from Greek mythology are selected as exemplifying valuation types in collective stories. At the end of this chapter an investigation of the Narcissus myth results in a specific affective profile that is typical of Narcissus desperately gazing at the water; it is demonstrated that this profile can be used for identifying valuations from individual clients that reflect the so-called *fugit amor* experience (unfulfilled love). Chapter 6 gives an extensive treatment of forms of dissociation (defenses) and dysfunctional valuations. Special attention is devoted to depression, suicide, grandiosity, hostility, overdependence, and limitlessness. Psychosomatic complaints are discussed as "somatic symbolizations." An extensive case study is presented of a woman who split off her hostility in the form of a separate self, the witch; the content and specific organization of her self system and the self system of the witch are discussed, with special emphasis on changing the two systems in the direction of integration. In Chapter 7 the lifelong development of the self is discussed. It is demonstrated how the same basic motives return in each period of life but in different ways. In fact, the presented model combines developments of a linear and a circular kind. Chapter 8 summarizes and integrates the ideas in the preceding chapters.

Finally, we have included a manual offering a variety of practical guidelines corresponding to the several phases in the self-confrontation method presented in Chapter 3. A series of guidelines are provided for the psychologist who wants to develop the necessary skills. The final part of the manual is devoted to several adaptations and extensions of the self-confrontation method for clinical, therapeutic, and research purposes.

CHAPTER 1

The Person as Motivated
Storyteller: Basic Metaphor

The basic metaphor underlying the approach to the self as presented in this book is that the person is a *motivated storyteller*. Let us briefly focus on the components of this metaphor, "story," "telling," and "motivation," in order to understand its full significance.

HOW THE STORY REFLECTS
THE METAPHOR OF CONTEXTUALISM

People from all times and cultures have used story telling as a basic way of organizing experiences and giving meaning to their lives. Within psychology *story* or *narrative* has a somewhat specialized meaning. Sarbin (1986), one of the main advocates of the narrative approach, views narrative as a way of organizing episodes, actions, and accounts of actions in time and space. He also suggests that narrative organizes our fantasies and daydreams, our unvoiced stories, our plans and memories, even our loving and hating. In line with Pepper's (1942) seminal work on root metaphors, Sarbin discusses four basic metaphors that order our world: Formism, mechanicism, organicism, and contextualism.

    Formism stresses the organization of the world on the basis of the form of objects, that is, on the basis of their perceivable similarities and differences. A common sense example of formism is found in the work of the artisan, who fashions products according to the same plan. The plan or form of the product is revealed in categories more than in particular instances. The concept of formism also underlies psychological and psychiatric models. Personality trait theories and classifications of dysfunctions—for example, the *Diagnostic and Statistical Manual of Mental Disorders*, 4th edition (DSM-IV; American Psychiatric Association, 1994)—provide categories for studying similarities and differences among people. Classifying people is a typical activity flowing from formism.

The root metaphor of *mechanicism* is characteristic of the dominant worldview in Western civilization. Its main representative is the machine—a clock, a steam engine, a computer, even a municipal water system. The mechanistic worldview considers events as the products of the transmittal of forces. The relationships between events are determined by efficient causality. Mechanistic theories can be found in the tradition of behaviorism and radical empiricism. Not only orthodox S-R models but also the more liberal S-O-R models, which allow cognitive interpretations to play a role as intervening variables, are in essence based on a mechanistic root metaphor (see Hultsch & Plemons, 1979; Rychlak, 1988).

Organicism considers the world as an organism rather than as a machine or set of forms. Organicism locates parts within organic wholes, like organs in a functioning body. A fully developed organic structure is the end of a process of progressive steps or stages of maturation. In psychology, organicism plays a significant role in the theories of Maslow and Rogers. In these humanistic theories, personality, or the self, grows through progressive stages to ever-higher levels of development. Organicism has been a most influential metaphor not only for humanistic psychology but also for developmental psychology. Widely known examples of this approach are Erikson's (1963) eight stages of development and Havighurst's (1972) developmental tasks. Also Kohlberg's (1969) and Loevinger's (1976) theories, too, are examples of the organismic view.

The root metaphor for *contextualism* is the historical event. Contextualism provides the basis for a story or narrative. The central element is the historical event that can only be understood when it is located in the context of time and space. As Sarbin (1986) argues, contextualism presupposes an ongoing texture of elaborated events, with each being influenced by preceding episodes and influencing following ones and with each being affected by multiple agents who engage in actions. There is a constant change in the structure of situations and in the positions occupied by actors who are oriented to the world and toward one another as intentional beings. Often these actors have opposite positions, as if functioning on a stage as protagonists and antagonists, as they enter relationships of love, hate, agreement, or disagreement. The thoughts, feelings, and actions of the protagonists can only be understood as emerging from their relationships with antagonists, who are coconstruing reality in often unpredictable ways.

As Sarbin (1986) argues, there is a basic similarity between the historian and the novelist. Although their emphases are different, both the historian and the novelist can be considered narrativists. The historian relates stories about presumably actual events influenced by reconstructed people who have their intentions and purposes. Since history can only be written on the basis of incomplete data, historical reconstruction is not possible without imagination. The novelist, on the other hand, writes about fictive characters in a context of real-world settings and with a certain degree of comprehensibility. Fiction makes use of elements derived from observed reality and is only possible by new or unusual combinations of realistic elements. Historical and novelistic narratives make use of both "facts" *and* "fictions." Not surprisingly, *story* and *history* are etymologically related.

Examples of contextualism in psychology can be found in the groundbreaking work of such divergent figures as James, Mead, and Freud. These thinkers have in common an interest in the distinction between *I* and *Me* (and their equivalents in other European languages) precisely because of the narrative nature of the self. Whereas the uttered pronoun *I* stands for the author, *Me* stands for the actor or narrative figure. The person is able not only to imagine himself or herself traveling to a place or visiting somebody but, as an author, to describe himself or herself as an actor. In this configuration, the I can imaginatively construct a story with the Me as the protagonist and with another person as the antagonist. Such narrative construction is possible because the I can imagine the Me in the future and can reconstruct the Me in the past (Crites, 1986; Sarbin, 1986).

These root metaphors not only influence the theoretical views of psychologists and psychotherapists but are reflected in the self-narratives of people in their daily lives. Typical of formism are trait descriptions such as "I'm a very open person" or "Other people see me as emotional" or self-classifying statements such as "I'm a depressive type" or "I'm an alcoholic." A mechanistic view underlies statements like "My problems were caused by the early death of my father" or "My illness changed my life forever." Organicism is expressed in sayings like "He has not grown far enough to take responsibility for this task" or "When she is mature enough, we will give her this opportunity." Contextualism is found in statements like "It is the first time in my life that I have the courage to talk about this problem" or "When my husband's opinion differs from mine, I find it difficult to keep my own stance."

The specific nature of contextualism can be clarified by comparing it with the other root metaphors. Formism classifies events in such a way that they result in general traits, types, or characteristics (e.g., a person who is always asking for help from others is labeled "dependent"). Contextualism, on the contrary, is sensitive to the particulars of time and space and will therefore highlight a particular event in the context of other events and will understand a particular actor by considering him or her vis-à-vis other actors (e.g., a person thirsting for revenge is understood to be responding to an insult made by an opponent). Mechanicism orders events in antecedent–consequent relationships, with the antecedent event working as a cause. From the perspective of contextualism, it would be an oversimplification to select two events and place them in a cause–effect relationship even if the mechanistic model acknowledges the workings of intermediate factors that may modify the cause–effect relationship. Contextualism presupposes a multiplicity of events (referring to the past, present, and future and to the relationships with other actors) that together form an interconnected totality. Moreover, contextualism does not suppose efficient causation but final causation. The person as a storyteller does not react to stimuli but is oriented to the realization of purposes and goals and is involved in a continuous process of meaning construction.

As already described, the most typical feature of organismic theories is the supposition of the existence of a predictable sequence of stages or tasks. Contextualism acknowledges the importance of predictable, or expected, events but differs from organicism in that it is also sensitive to unexpected events. Contextualism emphasizes that lives change over time in ways that are not necessarily predictable. Longitudinal studies have resulted in an increased appreciation of the influence of historical factors on human lives (Elder, 1974, 1979) and, moreover, have made clear that lives are much less predictable than was formerly recognized (Clausen, 1972; Gergen, 1980; Kagan, 1980; Riegel, 1975). Changes in collective and personal history require narrative construction and reconstruction. These changes may result from such divergent events as economic recession, a job change, relocation to another place, an encounter with a significant other, the sudden loss of a friend, divorce of parents, and a life-threatening operation. All these events are to some degree already invested with collective meanings inherited from our cultural tradition. At the same time, the individual as an agent of meaning has the capacity to interpret these events in his or her own way, and this interpretation may coincide or contrast with any collective meaning.

TELLING AND RETELLING ONE'S SELF-NARRATIVE

When there is a story, there is always someone who tells the story to someone else. It is the reciprocity between teller and listener that makes storytelling a highly dynamic interactional phenomenon. This reciprocity leads to a concept that plays a significant role in this book, namely, dialogue.

In his book *Problems of Dostoyevsky's Poetics* (1973), originally written in Russian in 1929, the literary scholar Mikhail Bakhtin makes a sharp distinction between logical and dialogical relationships. He explains the difference by using as an example two phrases that are completely identical: "Life is good" and, again, "Life is good." When we consider these phrases from the perspective of Aristotelian logic, they are connected by a relationship of identity. From a logical point of view they are, in fact, one and the same statement. From a dialogical perspective, however, they can be considered as two sequential remarks following each other in time and coming from two spatially separated people in communication, who in this case happen to be in agreement. The two phrases are identical from a logical perspective but are different as utterances, the first being a statement, the second a confirmation. Similarly, one may compare the statements "Life is good" and "Life is not good." In a logical sense one is a negation of the other. However, as utterances from two different speakers, a dialogical relation of disagreement between the two phrases can be seen to exist. In Bakhtin's view, the relationship of agreement and disagreement are, like question and answer, dialogical forms.

There are two forms of dialogue that together structure our daily experiences: imaginal and real dialogues. In the lives of normal people these forms of dialogue are certainly not separated. On the contrary, side by side and interwoven, they structure the process of intersubjective exchange. In her book *Invisible Guests,* Watkins (1986) argues that imaginal dialogues constitute an essential part of our narrative construction of the world. Even when we are outwardly silent, we find ourselves communicating with our critics, our parents, our consciences, our gods, our reflection in the mirror, the photograph of someone we miss, a figure from a movie or a dream, our babies, or our pets. When we plan to visit our friends we see and hear them in our imagination before we actually meet them, and when we have left them, we rehearse parts of the conversation. Imaginal interactions certainly have a pervasive influence on real interactions.

Caughey (1984), a social anthropologist, has also considered the role of "imaginary social worlds" both in Western and in non-Western communities. He did fieldwork on Fáánakker, an island in Micronesia, and in the Margalla Hills of Pakistan and compared these cultures with North American culture. One of his main conclusions was that imaginal interactions are in no way restricted to non-Western cultures. According to Caughey's estimations, the "real" social world of most North Americans includes between 200 and 300 people (e.g., family, friends, acquaintances, colleagues). Moreover, a swarming throng of other beings enters their world, beings with whom no face-to-face contact exists. Caughey divides these into three groups: (1) media figures with whom the individual engages in imaginal interactions (Caughey describes a suburban grandmother who had a lifelong "affair" with Frank Sinatra despite 40 years of marriage); (2) purely imaginary figures produced in dreams and fantasies; and (3) imaginal replicas of parents, friends, or lovers that are treated *as if* they were really present. Caughey argues, as Watkins (1986) did, that imaginal dialogues and interactions exist side by side with real interactions (e.g., "If my mother could see me now . . .") and may or may not have a direct link with reality. Caughey (1984), moreover, criticizes the exclusive identification of the expression *social relationships* with actual social relationships, an identification that he considers "an ethnocentric projection of certain narrow assumptions in

Western science" (p. 17). He also proposes to speak of an imaginal social world rather than a purely inner world, in order to emphasize the imagined interaction with other people or beings.

In sum, two suppositions underlie the narrative approach to be presented in this book. First, stories acknowledge both the perception of reality and the power of imagination (e.g., in filling the gaps in one's memory and in anticipating future events); whereas stories combine fact and fiction (Sarbin, 1986), the telling of stories involves real and imaginal dialogues (Caughey, 1984; Watkins, 1986). Second, space and time are basic components of story telling. Stories always imply a temporal organization of events and a plot structure that relates past, present, and future in a meaningful way. At the same time, stories are organized around actors who, as protagonist and antagonist, have opposite positions in a real or imaginal space.

MOTIVATION, PLOT STRUCTURE, AND STORY THEMES

Stories are populated by motivated actors who are purposefully oriented to the world. Hermans and Kempen (1993) give the example of a detective story: Confronted with a murder, the detective sets out to find the reasons or motives behind the deed. The discovery of a meaningful relationship between the events and the intentions of the actors reveals the point or the theme of the story. When the detective begins the investigation and does not yet know the guiding theme behind the actions of the suspect, many observations may seem incoherent or even confusing; the detective is not yet able to see if a particular observation is relevant. In the course of time, however, the imaginative detective learns that certain hitherto incomprehensible observations provide insight into an elaborate pattern of events that together form the plot.

With the example of the detective story we touch a more general feature of narratives: the dialectic relationship between event and plot. Polkinghorne (1988) has convincingly argued that the meaning of a particular event is produced by a recognition of how event and plot interact, each providing form for the other. Events do not dictate any plot, and not every plot is appropriate to order a given set of events. In order to arrive at a meaningful plot structure, it is necessary to move back and forth between plot and events. According to the principle of "best fit," a proposed plot structure is compared to the events at hand and is revised accordingly. In this comparative process a particular theme is guiding the selection of the events and the organization or revision of the plot. The theme allows the gathering together of events as interrelated parts of a story. The theme, moreover, functions as a guide for the selection of certain events as relevant and other events as irrelevant. The construction of a guiding theme may even lead to the generation of new events: The detective may set a trap for the suspect in order to further validate his or her reading of the facts; if the suspect behaves as anticipated, the detective has additional support for the hypothesized plot.

Stories as we know them from novels, movies, fairy tales, myths, and program music may be organized around a variety of themes, such as jealousy, revenge, tragic heroism, injustice, unattainable love, the innocence of childhood, inseparable friendship, and discrimination. In spite of this thematic variety, however, our culture provides us with a limited number of basic themes that function as organizing frames for the understanding and interpretation of life events. Let us consider some examples of themes that offer a structure for understanding the events in our life.

A well-known classification was developed by Frye (1957), who argued that themes in narratives are rooted in the experience of nature, particularly in the cycle of the seasons. Spring gives inspiration to comedy, expressing people's joy and social harmony after the threatening winter. Summer, representing abundance and richness, gives rise to romance, which depicts the triumph of good over evil and virtue over vice. (Note that for Frye romance is not restricted to attraction between people.) Autumn, representing the decline of life and the coming death of winter, gives rise to tragedy. In the winter, satire is born because in this season people become aware of the fact that they are ultimately a captive of the world rather than its master. In satire, people find an opportunity to criticize their own fate.

Whereas Frye's classification of story themes is based on the cyclical movements of nature, Gergen and Gergen's (1988) reflects an interest in developments of a more linear type. In their classification a progressive narrative relates changes over time toward a desirable end state. An individual telling a progressive narrative might say, "I am learning to overcome my shyness and be more open and friendly with people." A regressive narrative, on the other hand, is focused on decrements in the orientation toward a desirable end state; the storyteller of such a narrative might say: "I can't control the events of my life anymore." Finally, in a stable narrative the individual remains essentially unchanged with respect to the valued end point; here the storyteller might say, "I am still as attractive as I used to be."

Classification of basic story themes may also be based on the psychological motives of the actors. Murray's (1938) system of needs and his use of the Thematic Apperception Test (TAT) is a classic example. In the TAT one and the same picture elicits from subjects stories with different themes (achievement, affiliation, dominance, sex, etc.). The underlying assumption is that the themes expressed in the stories reflect the subject's more or less unconscious needs. Later investigators used TAT procedures to assess particular motives or needs, such as the achievement motive (McClelland, Atkinson, Clark, & Lowell, 1953), the power motive (Winter, 1973), the affiliation motive (Boyatzis, 1973), and the opposing needs for power and intimacy (McAdams, 1985).

In line with research on psychological motivation, our own work (Hermans, 1988; Hermans & Van Gilst, 1991) relates basic themes on the collective level to psychological motives on the individual level. The assumption is that there are two basic themes in collective stories—heroism and love—and that these themes are reflected in the psychological motives of individual people. Two motives are distinguished: the striving for self-enhancement (i.e., self-maintenance and self-expansion) and the longing for contact and union with the environment or other people. In a study of Goya's serial painting *The Capture of the Bandit El Maragato* (Hermans, 1988), it was observed that the painting expressed the polarity of winning versus losing, representing the theme of self-enhancement. It was found that the same theme was present in the self-narratives of individual clients, with the experience of winning being expressed in such statements as "My status position is acceptable but not enough; I want to go a few steps further" or "My achievements were mine; they were valued." The experience of losing was expressed in statements like "I have the feeling that John can be strong by keeping me weak" or "Violence and aggression have knocked me down."

A similar approach was used in an investigation of the Narcissus myth (Hermans & Van Gilst, 1991). The central part of the myth, Narcissus looking into the water, represents the experience of unfulfilled love and can be considered an expression of an existential longing for contact and union with other people and with oneself. We explored whether patterns similar to the affective patterns derived from the central part of the myth exist in the individual narratives of clients. It was found that the theme of unfulfilled longing was also present in specific statements in clients' self-narratives. The Goya study and the Narcissus study suggest that basic themes, expressed in collective stories, are present in the self-narratives of individual people as well.

In sum, both in individual and collective stories the plot transforms a purely chronological listing of events into an organized whole. The theme of a narrative functions as an organizing principle in structuring the plot and serves as a criterion for highlighting certain events as more relevant than others. Story themes, and psychological motives, bring coherence and direction to events that are otherwise fragmented and dispersed over time and space.

CHAPTER 2

The Self as
an Organized Process
of Meaning Construction

In this chapter we outline valuation theory as the conceptual framework underlying the methodology and practices discussed in the following chapters of this book. Valuation theory helps us understand the personal meaning of events in people's past, present, and future, how these meanings are organized into a system, and what their motivational characteristics are. Let us start with a presentation of the theory.[1]

VALUATION THEORY

Valuation theory (Hermans, 1987a, 1987b, 1988, 1992a) is a theory of the self developed to study individual experiences, their ordering into a meaning system, and their changes over time and space. The theory's view of the person is inspired by earlier philosophical–phenomenological thinking (James, 1890; Merleau-Ponty, 1945). The self is conceived of as an "organized process of valuation." The process aspect refers to the historical nature of human experience and implies a spatiotemporal orientation: A person lives in the present and is therefore oriented from a specific point in time and space to the past and to the future. The organizational aspect emphasizes that the person, by orienting to different aspects of his or her spatiotemporal situation and through self-reflection, creates a composite whole in which experiences are differentially weighted.

The theory's central concept, valuation, includes anything people identify as a relevant meaning unit when telling their life narrative. A valuation is any unit of meaning that has a positive (pleasant), negative (unpleasant), or ambivalent (both pleasant and unpleasant) value in the eyes of the self-reflecting individual. It can include a broad range of phenomena: a precious memory, a difficult problem, a beloved person, an unreachable goal, the anticipated death of a significant other, and so forth. Through the process of self-reflection, in dialogue with oneself or another person, valuations are organized into a single narratively structured system. Depending on the individual's orientation in time and space, different valuations emerge. In this changing orientation the valuation system changes: New valuations enter the system, old ones are deleted. In this way the organization and reorganization of the system reflects the simultaneity of stability and change.

The concept of valuation can be described as an interplay between the I and the Me, the two components of the self (James, 1890) whose distinction, according to Rosenberg (1979), can be regarded as classic in the psychology of the self. In James's view the I is equal to the "self-as-knower" and continuously organizes and interprets experience in a purely subjective manner. The Me is identified by James as the "self-as-known" or the "empirical self." Because he was aware that there is a gradual transition between Me and Mine, James concluded that the empirical self is composed of all that the person can call his or her own, "not only his body and his psychic powers, but his clothes and his house, his wife and children, his ancestors and friends, his reputation and works, his lands and horses, and yacht and bank-account" (p. 291). As we mentioned in the introduction, Sarbin (1986) translated the I–Me distinction into a narrative framework by proposing that the uttered pronoun I stands for the author whereas Me stands for the actor, the character of the drama, the narrative figure. The self as author, the I, imaginatively constructs a story in which the Me functions as the protagonist and in which other figures that are part of Mine function as antagonists (e.g., "my wife," "my friend," "my father," "my mother," "my enemy"). Valuations are typically units of meaning that the I as author relates about the Me as actor involved in the interactions with others.

One fundamental assumption is that each valuation has an affective connotation (i.e., emotional value). This assumption agrees with James (1890), who assumed the existence of "self-feelings" and described the relation of feelings to the situation in the following way: "The words 'me' . . . and 'self,' so far as they arouse feeling and connote emotional worth, are objective designations, meaning all the things which have the power to produce in a stream of consciousness excitement of a certain peculiar sort" (p. 319). More specifically, each valuation implies an affective modality, or pattern of affects, that is characteristic of the specific valuation. When we know what type of affect is implied by a particular valuation, we know something about the valuation itself.

In order to capture certain differences in the functioning of the affective component of the valuation system, the *latent–manifest* distinction was introduced into valuation theory (Hermans, Hermans-Jansen, & Van Gilst, 1985a; Hermans & Van Gilst, 1991). In accordance with the metaphor of the person as a motivated storyteller, it is assumed that a small set of basic motives is represented latently in the affective component of a valuation. When, for example, a person tells of a stimulating success about which he or she feels "great," it is assumed that the gratification of a self-enhancement motive is reflected in this feeling. Basic motives are assumed to be similar across individuals and to be continuously active within them. They are basic in the sense that they are considered to represent implicit or unconscious elements of human experience and to be universal across time and space. The valuations represent more conscious elements of human experience and are specific to particular individuals. At the manifest level, a great diversity of valuations vary phenomenologically not only between individuals but also within a single individual across time and space. It is assumed that basic motives at the latent level are able to generate a great diversity of valuations at the manifest level and to influence their organization (see Figure 2.1 for the relation between valuation, affect, and basic motives).

Two basic motives characterize the affective component of the valuation system: the striving for self-enhancement, or S motive (i.e., self-maintenance and self-expansion), and the longing for contact and union with the other, or O motive (i.e., contact with other people and the surrounding world). This distinction results from a review of a number of researchers' conceptions of the basic duality of human experience: Bakan (1966), who viewed agency and communion as fundamental dynamic principles; Angyal (1965), who distinguished between autonomy (self-determination) and homonomy (self-surrender); and Klages (1948), who considered Bindung (solidification) and Lösung (dissolution) as basic motives of human character.[2]

When a person values something, he or she always feels something about it and in these feelings basic motives are reflected. For example, when a valuation (e.g., "I won that game by hard training") represents a gratification of the S mo-

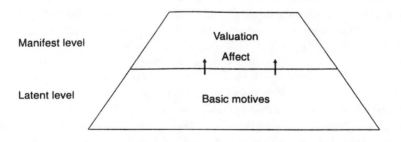

FIGURE 2.1. Relation between valuation, affect, and basic motives.

tive, the person experiences a feeling of strength and pride in connection with the valuation. In a similar way, a valuation (e.g., "I enjoy my son's playing the piano") can function as a gratification of the O motive. Feelings of tenderness and intimacy experienced in connection with the valuation are indicators of this motive. In other words, basic motives, assumed to function on the latent level, are expressed in the affective component of the valuations on the manifest level. Note that the latent–manifest distinction is a purely theoretical one. It is, however, a useful distinction, because it will help us, as we will see in the following chapters, assess the implicit or less conscious aspects of the valuation system. For the present, it is sufficient to recognize that the basic (latent) motives are hidden in the affective component of the valuations. Note also that the motives are not construed as drives or as impulses requiring tension reduction but as basic goals that are supposed to be important, in one way or another, in everyone's life.

Valuation theory emphasizes the role of social interactions in the development of one's self-narrative. Valuations not only are the result of numerous preceding social interactions with significant others (Chapter 7) but also play a central role in the contact between client and counselor, or psychotherapist (see Manual). The aim of valuation theory is not only to study the content and organization of valuations but also to stimulate the valuation process toward the direction of increased flexibility. This means that the aim is not only the telling but also the retelling of one's story in such a way that alternative narrative constructions become available as a result of a cooperative enterprise between psychologist and client. The self-confrontation method, presented in the next chapter, provides a concrete procedure that invites the two parties to cooperate in realizing a gradual transition between assessment and change.

THE CONSTRUCTIVE NATURE OF VALUATION: THE MANIFEST LEVEL

In order to better understand the term *valuation*, the relationship must be explained between events as elements of any narrative and the process of valuation that organizes them into personal units of meaning. A great variety of events can be organized in a valuation such as "My father used to compare me with my brother in an unfavorable way; this has made me very competitive." Such a valuation is combined with other valuations to form an organized self-narrative.

Events and Valuations

What is the difference between an event and a valuation? An event, or something that happens, typically refers to a change of situation (e.g., an accident, a visit, a prize). As long as nothing has been said about the personal meaning of such an event, it can never be a valuation. It only becomes a valuation when it can be seen as part of an interpreting self that is extended to the event in question. For example, receiving a prize becomes a valuation when the individual acknowledges the prize as supportive of certain capacities he or she wants to develop. Or, in a more complicated way, when a person is concerned about a misfortune that strikes the life of another, the valuation of such an event always implies an implicit or explicit imaginative reference to one's own self ("Suppose it were my children . . ."). It is the workings of the interpreting self that makes a given event highly significant for one person but meaningless to another.

There is, however, a less obvious difference between an event and a valuation. In a valuation a person typically relates and condenses a number of events into a single unit of meaning. For example, a woman may describe her mother's death by saying, "Mother's death made me feel deeply human, especially in sharing my sorrow with my father and sister." The details of the funeral, the discussions with specific people during the funeral, and so on, do not have much meaning in and of themselves; rather, as parts of an overarching unit of meaning, they each articulate some aspect of the experience.

A valuation may, therefore, include many concrete acts and events, although many of them may be forgotten or neglected when a person is formulating the common personal meaning. The condensing and grouping of events into a personal valuation may also be reflected in a general "if-then" statement, such as the following: "If I had an emotional problem, my husband would often only say a few words or nothing at all." In this case, the repetitive cycle of events indicating a major lack of communication is reflected in a single summarizing unit of meaning.

As a process of meaning making, valuation always implies the activity of relating events to one another. As Rychlak (1988) and others have argued, meanings, in a psychological sense, always reach beyond the specific and signify something beyond the obvious. A relation or relationship is being emphasized whenever we speak about the meaning of anything. A specific event never has a meaning in itself but reveals its meaning only when viewed in the light of something else. Something like an accident can only mean something to a person when the specific event is, for example, contrasted with a previous state in which things were normal or considered from the perspective of a serious reduction of possibilities in the future. The constructive process of "active relating," typical of an intentional self, brings specific events together into patterned totalities that function as units of meaning in an interpreting mind (as seen, for example, in the accident victim's comment "I cannot engage in my favorite sport anymore").

The Contextual Nature of Valuation

A valuation finds its most typical expression in a sentence where the I describes some aspect of the Me or Mine that is felt to be of particular relevance. Just as a sentence is typically embedded in some discourse and therefore derives some of its significance from the surrounding context, so too can a valuation be fully understood only in relation to other valuations that precede and follow it. Take, for example, the following sample of valuations from a single client.

1. "Father had a great deal of patience with other people, but I was just a source of irritation for him."
2. "I become uneasy when people indicate that I have not fulfilled their expectations."
3. "In order to avoid this happening, I play it safe and prepare things very well."
4. "My life has something compulsive to it."

In this case, a client understands his uncertainty (Valuation 2) as resulting from his relationship with his father (Valuation 1). However, this uneasiness is not only an observation for him but also a fact to be dealt with (Valuation 3). And the constant need to deal with this fact then creates an emotional problem for this client (Valuation 4). Thus, the solution to one problem results in another problem, a phenomenon this client only becomes aware of when he reviews the entire story of his compulsion.

In other words, self-relevant traits or dispositions (e.g., being compulsive, hardworking, sometimes cheerful, artistic, politically active) can be historically deconstructed. A trait can be traced back to a series of successive valuations, which are in some sense its historical forerunners in a self-narrative. A self-relevant trait has the character of an "end valuation" that is construed as the final result of preceding ones. We often see that such an end valuation increasingly lives a life of its own; the person is often unaware of its roots because it has been stripped of any historically relevant specific valuations (e.g., a person might say, "I am an obstinate person; that's just the way I am"). It loses its dynamic character and ends as a static and more or less isolated self-description.

Values and Valuations

To understand the process of valuation, it is essential to recognize that individuals also participate in the value system of their society or group. When we use the term *value*, we mean any institutionalized principle that the members of a community or group collectively find important for the organization of their behavior and experience. Whereas a valuation is a personal meaning expressed by an individual voice, a value is a collective meaning tacitly agreed upon and expressed by a collective voice. Like valuations, some values may be more important to the group than others, and this hierarchy organizes the collective meanings into a system. What then is the relation between values and valuations, or between a system of values and a system of valuations?

All kinds of institutions (e.g., family, church, professional organizations, political systems, military service) are based on value systems and play a role in the life of the individual, even before the individual becomes aware of their existence. This means that the individual's socialization requires at the same time a participation in these often conflicting value systems and a response to them in order to develop an autonomous and integrated self. During the process of socialization, therefore, some parts of an institutionalized value system may be welcomed by the individual while others may be criticized or even rejected. This can be seen in the following example of two conflicting valuations of religion in the self-narrative of an individual:

"The church: If you behave according to the rules and don't deviate, then it's okay.
God: A higher power, with whom I can discuss things that I can't resolve myself, to whom I can talk and pray."

As this example suggests, valuation is not simply an internalization of societal values; rather, a valuation is a personal interpretation, even a personal reconstruction of the values of a particular group or society in which the individual participates from the beginning. The self does not blindly accept general values, in part because these values, certainly in an individualized society, do not supply individuals with information that is precise and adequate enough for them to use in a diversity of situations. Officials representing institutions may tell about values, but the individual person retells them as part of a personal history and future.

Value systems are indispensable as global interpretive schemas that give order to our daily existence and direction to behavior. One cannot, for example, imagine two individuals communicating about their personal valuations without some basic set of shared meanings. However, value systems can also have a stifling effect on the individual in the form of strict role prescriptions, which often evoke a more personal reaction. In the following remark a daughter understands and supports the general value that parents have to take care of their children and that their children, in turn, should respect them for this. At the same time, however, she registers some dissatisfaction with the social restrictions placed on her interactions with her father: "I would like to share things with papa on a friendly and equal basis, but we both block it; we both stay in our roles of parent and child."

Collective values organize, restrict, and evoke personal valuations. However, at times a personal valuation can initiate or change a group value (e.g., when the hobby of an individual is accepted by the other members of the family as a common activity). As Deal and Kennedy (1982) have observed, shared values in an organization are often symbolized as slogans. Originally a personal belief of the founder, such a slogan becomes accepted as the guiding principle for the organization as a whole (e.g., William Procter's principle "Do what is right"). A similar relation between values and valuations can be observed in families when one member introduces a new opinion, custom, or interest and thereby changes to some extent the values of the family as a group (e.g., "We learned how fantastic it is to bike from our son").

To summarize, each common value of each group is interpreted, more or less consciously, by each individual as part of his or her own personal narrative (i.e., valuation system). Conversely, a common value sometimes grows out of an influential personal valuation. Valuation is a process of participating in the values expressed in the collective tales of a community and at the same time reworking them and even adding to them. Such a cyclic relation not only prevents group values from becoming too rigid but also prevents an individualistic or purely private conception of valuation. This suggests that a valuation should not be understood as an inner representation of something in the world but as a reconstruction of socially defined reality by the individual.

PSYCHOLOGICAL MOTIVATION: THE LATENT LEVEL

Individuals are confronted with many different events and situations and therefore develop a large range of valuations. They have to select and organize these experiences into a set of workable meanings. This organization is not arbitrary, however, because a small number of basic psychological motives (the striving for self-enhancement, or the S motive, and the longing for contact and union with the other, or O motive) can be assumed to operate at the latent level of self-functioning. In the context of valuation theory, these motives are assumed to influence the system of personal valuations that is constantly being organized and reorganized in correspondence with the current situation.

Let us summarize several historical forerunners of the S and O motives, which have been selected as basic to the latent level of self-functioning. A historical outline not only emphasizes the basic character of the motives but also contributes to an understanding of their specific nature.

The Greek Philosopher Empedocles: "Strife" and "Love"

The search for basic forces operating in nature and organisms is not recent. Empedocles, the Greek philosopher who lived on Sicily from 490 B.C. to 430 B.C., was a self-styled god who brought about his own death by flinging himself into the volcanic crater atop Mt. Etna in order to convince his followers of his divinity. His philosophy was that all matter was composed of four essential ingredients—earth, water, fire, and air—and, in anticipation of the modern conservation of energy law, that things are merely transformed from one substance to another rather than destroyed or spontaneously brought into being. (Empedocles believed that when he jumped into the volcano he was not destroyed but only transformed.)

Like Heraclitus, Empedocles believed that two forces, Strife and Love, separate and bring together the four substances. Strife makes each of these elements withdraw from the others, Love makes them mingle together. In the beginning, moreover, Love was dominant and all four substances were intermingled. During the formation of the cosmos, however, Strife separated earth, water, fire, and air from each other. Subsequently, the four elements were again partially combined through Love as reflected, for example, by the occurrence of springs and volcanoes, which indicate the presence of both water and fire in the earth. Further, according to Empedocles, life originated in the growth of trees out of the earth. In plants and in lower animals the species and sexes were at first indistinguishable and only became separate when Strife again gained ground. Finally, Empedocles believed that the elements are most thoroughly mixed in the blood and that humans therefore think chiefly with their blood.

Empedocles' philosophy suggests that motivation is twofold: There is a striving toward an independent existence and at the same time a tendency to want to participate in something greater. Moreover, his view suggests that these two orientations are complementary.

Bakan's "Agency" and "Communion"

In his 1966 book, *The Duality of Human Existence*, Bakan distinguished between two basic life orientations and adopted the terms *agency* and *communion* to characterize these two fundamental modalities in the existence of living forms. Agency refers to the existence of an organism as an individual, and communion refers to the participation of the organism in some larger entity of which it is a part. Agency manifests itself in self-protection, self-assertion, and self-expansion whereas communion is expressed in the sense of being one with other organisms. One of the fundamental points made by Bakan, however, is that there may be a split between agency and communion, with, for example, agency becoming dominant and repressing communion.

This split between agency and communion is illustrated by Bakan's discussion of Weber's famous thesis regarding the Protestant ethic and the rise of capitalism. Weber observed in Protestantism a preoccupation with predestination, personal salvation, a vocational calling, and the ascetic ideal. Bakan suggested that this preoccupation is reflected in the agentic personality that has been dominant in Western culture. The pursuit of a career, profit seeking, a propensity for saving, regularity, self-control, personal reliability, the eschewing of sociability (*Gemütlichkeit*), the eschewing of magic and mystery, a high degree of impersonality, distrust in interpersonal relations, and loneliness— all are modern-day characteristics of the agentic personality. Weber, in his thesis, suggested that the pervasiveness of the Protestant ethic can be related to the rise of capitalism. Bakan went on to suggest that, indeed, the Protestant ethic involves both the exaggeration of the agentic features of the psyche and repression of the communal component; he noted that this exaggeration can lead to a form of "unmitigated agency," where agency unmitigated by communion may degenerate into aggression and destruction.

Two points in Bakan's analysis are specially relevant to our thesis: the idea that human motivation can be conceived of as a duality and the notion that under certain cultural conditions one of these motives can predominate over the other. In other words, when a distinction is made between striving for self-enhancement (S motive) and longing for contact and union with the other (O motive), it may be expected that societal or cultural values may contribute to a predominance of one motive over the other, that is, may disrupt the balance of the motives within the individual.

Angyal's "Autonomy" and "Homonomy"

A similar view was expressed by Angyal (1965), who characterized personality as "part-Gestalt" in that the individual is a whole in itself and at the same time a part of a superordinate whole that transcends the individual. For this reason, Angyal referred to two opposite directional trends in human motivation: autonomy and homonomy. The trend toward autonomy consists of expansion through assimilation and mastery of the environment. It is expressed by the desire for superiority, acquisition, exploration, and achievement. The trend toward homonomy consists of people's motivation to fit into the environment and participate in something that is larger than themselves, namely, a union with a social group, nature, or a supernatural omnipotent power. Homonomy expresses itself through such specific motives as the desires for love, interpersonal contact, aesthetic pleasure, contact with nature, and religious experience. According to Angyal, "the whole concept of homonomy could be equated with love" (p. 16).

Angyal characterized a well-functioning personality as one that is able to flexibly move between autonomy and homonomy. In the case of malfunctioning, there is an extreme emphasis on one of the two and a concomitant rigidity of personality. The person with an excessive emphasis on autonomy is often compensating for real or felt lacks, tends to show an overreaction to threat, and is afraid of and unable to show a need for homonomy. In contrast, people with a fixation on homonomy do not have the strength to stand on their own feet, are often extreme conformists, and react to the environment as if they were straws in the wind. In Angyal's view, only one of the two basic trends has been developed in the neurotic personality, or perhaps neither; the healthy personality, however, has the capacity to flexibly combine autonomy and homonomy.

Angyal's emphasis on the notion of flexibility will have important implications for our discussion of dysfunctional valuations (Chapter 6), where it will be demonstrated that some clients are not able to move flexibly from one motive to another and from one type of valuation to another.

Klages's "Bindung" and "Lösung"

In the European psychological tradition we also find the same basic duality used to characterize personality functioning. Klages (1948) distinguished between two dynamic forces: *Bindung* (solidification) and *Lösung* (dissolution). *Bindung* refers to the striving for self-maintenance; just as rings give a barrel a solid internal coherence, *Bindung* maintains a strong and independent individual. This motive can be characterized by the urge for action, the enterprising spirit, the desire to possess, the pleasure of attack, or the need for revenge, but it may also be characterized by the need to comprehend things in the world or criticize them. In contrast, *Lösung* motivates people to decenter so as to be able to open themselves to the external world. This motive is reflected in such things as *Mitleid* (compassion), *Mitfreude* (shared gladness), a love of nature, a need for admiration, and a need to love. On a more spiritual level, *Lösung* is evidenced by a general love of beauty, intellectual passion, and utopian desires.

Klages criticized Nietsche's *Wille zur Macht* (will to power) as being overly biased toward the force *Bindung* and as being so one-sided as to result in an *Übermensch* (superman) caricature of the nature of human beings. Klages claimed that the two basic trends—solidification of the individual and merging with the environment—are equally important, dynamic principles of personality.

One could go on and on with a review of the literature in which thinkers from divergent backgrounds espouse similar views on the fundamental duality of human motivation. There are, for example, Adler's (1922) distinction between the striving for perfection and the desire to be part of a community; Grünbaum's (1925) *Hersschen und Lieben* (mastery and love); Binswanger's (1963) "dual mode," represented by two people in love, and "plural mode," the world of formal relations, competitions, and struggles; Nuttin's (1965) distinction between *le besoin de se maintenir* (the need for self-maintenance) and *le besoin de contact* (the need for contact); Koestler's (1967) "self-assertive" and "integrative" tendencies; Deikman's (1971) "action mode" and "receptive" mode of consciousness; Fowler's (1981) description of the rapprochement of the "rational" and the "ecstatic" as the highest stage of human faith; Gutmann's (1980) observation of the blending of masculinity and femininity after mid-life; McAdams's (1985) distinction between power and intimacy needs; and Markus and Kitayama's (1991) emphasis on the importance of independence and interdependence for the self from a cultural point of view. All these thinkers have espoused the view that a person is in one respect an autonomous individual and in another a participant in a larger whole.

Beyond Self-Esteem

Taken together, the two basic motives of human nature provide a perspective on the self that transcends the Western cultural bias toward self-esteem. The literature on the self over the past several decades has, from a motivational point of view, been heavily dominated by a concern with the self-esteem motive (see Allport, 1960; Beane & Lipka, 1980; Rosenberg, 1979; Sampson, 1985; Shavelson, Hubner, & Stanton, 1976). Self-esteem belongs more to the realm of what we have summarized as the S motive than to the realm of the O motive. This emphasis on self-esteem in psychological assessment and research has been disadvantageous in that it has neglected the importance of flexible movement between the two motives. It is precisely in the flexible movement between the S and O motive that a more extended and flexible functioning of the self is developed.

Let us now proceed with a clarification of the general relation between latent motives and the manifest level of specific valuations.

AFFECT: THE BRIDGE BETWEEN MOTIVATION AND VALUATION

Recall James's (1890) definition of the self as "the sum total of all he can call his, not only his body and his psychic powers, but his clothes and his house, his wife and children, his ancestors and friends, his reputation and works, his lands and horses, and yacht and bank-account" (p. 291). Having said this, James immediately went on to say, "All these things give him the same emotions. If they wax and prosper, he feels triumphant; if they dwindle and die away, he feels cast down, not necessarily in the same degree for each thing, but in much the same way for all" (pp. 291–292). In other words, James conceives of the self as extended to a variety of things and reacting to each with the same set of emotions. Similarly, we conceive of valuations as the phenomenological variety of concerns relevant to an individual that are associated with a particular set of affective states (e.g., one may experience anxiety and anger in relation to both one's father and one's superior).

In valuation theory it is assumed that the basic motives are reflected in the affective component of a valuation. Let us explain this with two different valuations:

1. "At home I often get my way by pushing just a little bit."
2. "I feel great when I take a good picture."

Assume that feelings of strength and pride are general indicators of the self-enhancement motive (S motive). The presence of these feelings in both of the valuations is evidence that they are expressions of the same underlying motive. Put differently, the valuations pertain to quite different aspects of the self (they differ on the manifest level), although they are rooted in the same basic motive (they are similar on the latent level). In this construction the affective component provides the bridge between motivation and valuation. The affect associated with a valuation can be considered an expression of the basic motives from the *latent* level.

Let us look now to some valuations representing the longing for contact and union with the other (O motive):

3. "During the stormy weather, when we were on the North Sea, I felt a real bond with my brother; I felt lost in the elements and still kept my balance without having to struggle to be strong."
4. "Singing in a group is mostly the way I express my feelings."

Both these valuations from the same client—although they are clearly different manifestations of the self—imply strong feelings of love and intimacy. If we assume feelings of love and intimacy to be indicators of the O motive, then the two valuations can again be seen to differ on the manifest level but not on the latent level.

The aforementioned valuations lead to a concept that plays a major role in valuation theory and the methodology to be presented in the following chapters, namely, the concept of *generalization*. This term refers to the highly dynamic nature of the valuation system. Put briefly, the more a particular valuation generalizes as part of the system, the more it determines the general feeling of the person under consideration. When one asks a person how he or she feels in general, it is highly probable that particular experiences are coloring this general feeling more than others. For example, if the person is living in a period of conflict with his or her parents, there is a good chance that the feelings associated with this conflict are more likely to determine the person's general feelings in this period than, for example, the good contact this person experiences with his or her friends. In other words, the more generalizing power a valuation has, the more influential the affective component of this valuation is in coloring the way the person generally feels in a certain period of life.

In order to explain the concept of generalization more precisely, let us return to the example of the four valuations mentioned previously, all of which came, in fact, from the same woman. In this case we have four valuations and four feelings: strength and pride as indicators of the S motive and love and intimacy as indicators of the O motive. In our example, strength and pride are to a greater degree associated with Valuations 1 and 2 whereas love and intimacy are associated to a higher degree with Valuations 3 and 4. Suppose we ask the client how she has been feeling lately in general, without explicitly referring to any specific valuation. We ask her to give her answer in terms of the four aforementioned feelings. If she indicates that her general mood is more associated with feelings of pride and strength than with feelings of love and intimacy, it would suggest that self-enhancing valuations (Valuations 1 and 2) are more influential in coloring her general feeling than are contact and union valuations (Valuations 3 and 4). We would conclude then that Valuations 1 and 2 have, for this person in this period of life, a higher degree of generalizing power than Valuations 3 and 4. This is a very simplified example, however. In practice we have more valuations, more feelings, and more complicated affective patterns (see Chapters 3 and 4). For our present purposes, suffice it to say that the notion of generalization reflects the fact that in the organized valuation system not all valuations are of equal importance and that the organization of the system is of a highly dynamic nature. Depending on the flow of experiences over time and space, valuations that are strongly generalizing in a particular period may lose their generalizing potential in the next period even when they continue to be part of the system. Psychotherapy also plays a role in influencing the generalization of the valuations and their implied time perspective. We know that clients may change their time perspective in the course of psychotherapy or as a result of it. Initially, they may be strongly preoccupied with certain negative events in the past, but later this preoccupation may give way to a more positive future orientation. In terms of valuation theory this means that in the course of time valuations referring to the past lose their generalizing influence whereas valuations referring to the future increase their generalizing potential in the system as a whole.

In close correspondence with the concept of S and O feelings, our construct, *well-being*, or the difference between positive and negative feelings (see Chapter 3 for further explanation), plays a central role in valuation theory. On the path to fulfilling basic motives, people meet obstacles. The world is never in full agreement with our strivings and longings. We are purposefully oriented to the world, but obstacles often prevent the achievement of our goals, an outcome that results in negative feelings. On the other hand, when we achieve something or succeed in overcoming obstacles, we are rewarded with positive feelings. It is supposed that each valuation is associated with a pattern of positive and negative feelings so that the difference between both types of affect may give information about the extent to which the basic motives are gratified.

TELLING AND RETELLING ONE'S SELF-NARRATIVE

So far, we have described how two components of the guiding metaphor of the motivated storyteller, namely, story and motivation, are expressed in valuation theory. As a story or narrative, the self is considered an organized process of valuation, representing the *manifest* level of self-functioning. The notion of motivation is elaborated in terms of two basic motives (self-enhancement and contact and union with the other), representing the *latent* level of functioning, with affect as the theoretical bridge between the two levels. Now we arrive at the third component of the metaphor, the notion of "telling."

The act of telling always presupposes a dialogical relationship between a teller and a listener, who may change roles in a mutually supported process of exchange. This process is of pervasive influence throughout an individual's lifetime, as Fogel (1993) has so vividly demonstrated in his book *Developing through Relationships*. In the context of the present chapter, we argue that the client's self-narrative results from the contributions of both the client and the psychologist and, indeed, that there exists no such thing as a ready-made self-narrative or valuation system when the client approaches a psychologist. Instead, the valuation system emerges as the result of a collaborative enterprise to which both psychologist and client contribute as mutually complementary agencies, each from their specific expertise. The client is the prime expert on the manifest level, and the psychologist is the prime expert on the latent level of self-functioning. The *local* knowledge the client has about his or her particular historical situation and the *global* knowledge the psychologist has about clients in general are combined in such a way that they lead to the construction and reconstruction of the client's valuation system.

At the moment that psychologists and clients meet, clients have certainly collected a vast amount of raw material about themselves throughout their life course. They have gone through a history of contacts with other people and have experienced themselves in a variety of situations. For example, they remember a positive remark made by a teacher 20 years ago, cannot forget their first falling in love, know that they have always dreamed of becoming a movie star, are presently struggling with a problem with a colleague, or have definite plans for a trip to Switzerland somewhere in the near future. The psychologist knows nothing of this before meeting the client. For clients, however, these experiences function as important meaning units that may become part of the self-narratives that are constructed in cooperation with the psychologist. In other words, clients have a large data bank available about their own local situation, that is, a particular history and life situation, that has been emerged from a plethora of previous interactions with others. This data bank includes the basic material that the client organizes into meaning units in collaboration with the psychologist. Clients are meaning experts of their own lives—or, at least, potential meaning experts—and the knowledge they bring can never be replaced by any psychologist or professional owing to the fact that each person emerges from a history of particular interactions.

The psychologist, on the other hand, has had experience with a great variety of individuals and knows about general structures and processes in self-narratives, knows, for example, the differences between functional and dysfunctional characteristics of the self (see Chapter 6). Knowledge of general theories of the self, of basic processes of human motivation, of the methodology to investigate and procedures to influence the process of valuation—these constitute the specific expertise of the psychologist. Psychologists use their experience and specific expertise, their global knowledge, to structure and restructure the self-narrative of each particular client.[3] In fact, valuation theory implies a combination of narrative thinking and propositional thinking. As Maloney (1992) holds, most skilled counselors and therapists assert that even when they are intensely engrossed in helping clients create new life stories, they retain a metatheory and conceptual dynamics in the background of their mind.

However, the specific expertise of psychologist and client functions only as a starting point for the dialogical process. In the course of time, psychologist and client are involved in an ongoing process of interchange that has its implications for both parties. The psychologist becomes interested in the particular story of the client and in the way the client selects events and combines them into a structured self-narrative. In dealing with this story, the psychologist in turn is invited and even challenged to investigate to what extent his or her general knowledge is applicable to the individual case and in what respects the individual client represents a corroboration of or exception to the psychologist's general knowledge (Hermans, 1992c). During a process of intensified communication with the psychologist, the client learns how to construct a coherent story on the basis of recollections of the past, reflections about the present, and hopes and anxieties about the future. The psychologist as a careful listener invites the client to structure his or her experiences into a comprehensible narrative. Moreover, the client learns to detect in his or her story significant affective patterns that are reflections of basic motives. An important result of this communicative self-exploration is that central themes become visible in the self-narrative that pose suggestions to the client of how to proceed.

When the communication between psychologist and client has arrived at the stage where possible emphases, biases, or even holes in the valuation system become visible, clients are invited to reformulate their valuation system. This transformation of the client's story requires a retelling of the self-narrative in terms of changing valuations. In this retelling a peculiar implication of the approach presented in this book becomes visible, namely, the gradual transition between assessment and change. As we will see in the next chapter, the self-confrontation method not only provides a concrete procedure for investigating the content and structure of the client's self-narrative but represents a systematic strategy for changing the content and structure of the self-narrative in the direction of a more flexible valuation system.

In sum, valuation theory provides the conceptual basis for a process of interchange. This means that the theoretical components (the manifest and latent levels) are distributed as two positions in a dialogical relationship. The client is approached as a meaning expert on the manifest level, and the psychologist functions as a scientist who is an expert in the perspective of the latent level. The client's knowledge is primarily of local significance whereas the psychologist's knowledge is of a more global or general nature. The two contributions are mutually complementary. The client may use the extended and rich experience of the psychologist for the structuring and restructuring of his or her own self-narrative. The psychologist may profit inasmuch as the client's local knowledge may enhance the seminal character of general psychological theory.

NOTES

1. In this book we present many different aspects of how valuation theory works, and some readers may get a better sense of the theoretical issues discussed in this chapter after having read about how clients make valuations and how these are fine-tuned to fit the parameters of what a successful valuation is. These issues are discussed in Chapter 3, on methodology.

2. Motives other than the ones mentioned here are not excluded from valuation theory in characterizing the affective component. The present formulation of valuation theory is more an invitation to devise new or additional concepts, methods, and practices than a closed conceptual system.

3. For the distinction between global knowledge and local knowledge, see Hintikka (1968) and Fischoff (1978).

CHAPTER 3

The Self-Confrontation Method: Constructing and Reconstructing One's Self-Narrative

The method of self-confrontation has been developed in order to contribute to the construction and reconstruction of the self as an organized process of valuation. It is an idiographic instrument in which subjects are invited to give their own view on their past, present, and future world in their own terms. The method was devised to increase the client's and the psychologist's insight into the specific content and organization of the client's valuation system and to stimulate its further development. For the client, the method is a self-investigation comprising a strong element of self-confrontation. Through this self-confrontation the client condenses a variety of valuations into a structured whole, a "psychological mirror," which then serves to evoke the question of how to further develop this set of valuations. For the psychologist, the method functions not only as a means of arriving at a survey of the client's valuation system and the relation between its various parts but also as a means of checking and correcting, when necessary, the presuppositions he or she has built up about the self of the client. The contact between psychologist and client during the self-confrontation procedure can best be characterized as a dialogical relationship in which both parties exchange their specific knowledge, ideas, and insights.

This chapter will make the distinction between *phases*, *subphases*, and *functions* of the self-confrontation method (see Table 3.1). There are three phases: (1) the first self-investigation, in which clients tell their self-narratives in the form of a valuation system; (2) a validation/invalidation process in which cli-

TABLE 3.1. Phases, Subphases, and Functions of the
Self-Confrontation Method

Phases	Subphases	Functions
Investigation 1 (telling)	Valuation construction Affective exploration Discussion with client	Assessment
Validation/invalidation (action)	Attending Creating Anchoring	Process promotion
Investigation 2 (retelling)	Valuation reconstruction Affective exploration Discussion with client	Evaluation

ents act in such a way that the valuation system or relevant parts of it are changed (invalidated); and (3) a second self-investigation, in which clients retell their self-narratives in the form of a reorganized system of valuation. Together these phases form a cycle in which the second investigation may be the beginning of a new round of investigation (I), validation/invalidation (V), and investigation (I). In this way the IVI cycle represents an alternation of self-reflection (investigation) and action (validation/invalidation). The basic idea is "reflection in action"; that is, reflection is embedded in action, and action in reflection.

The three phases correspond with the three functions of the self-confrontation method. The *assessment* function refers to the investigation of the content and organization of the valuation system as a whole. The *process-promotion* function corresponds with the validation/invalidation process. The *evaluation* function is used for the investigation of the content and organization of the valuation system as it is reorganized as a result of the invalidation process. (The three functions will be discussed at the end of this chapter, preceded by an actual case that shows how the method works in practice.)

Before we start, we would like to emphasize that the self-confrontation method has been devised in keeping with valuation theory, although it is by no means the only way in which this theoretical framework could be elaborated. Rather, it must be seen as one among a number of possible methodological constructions (for suggestions, see Manual). At the same time, it must be stressed that the method should not be viewed merely as a technique in isolation from its theoretical background. If alternative methodological constructions are considered, the basic metaphor (Chapter 1) and valuation theory (Chapter 2) should guide their development.

The present chapter explains the several parts of the method in full detail before presenting an illustrative case study. Some readers may prefer to reverse this sequence in order to get an impression of how the method works in practice before studying the methodology.

THE FIRST SELF-INVESTIGATION: CONTENT AND STRUCTURE OF THE VALUATION SYSTEM

The aim of the first self-investigation is to construct a valuation system in such a way that it leads to a well-directed process of change. The investigation includes several phases: formulation of the valuations, exploration of associated affect, and discussion with the client. Before starting with these phases, let us first characterize the spirit of the method.

Spirit of the Method

The spirit in which the individual approaches a self-investigation is a major factor in developing a favorable attitude for administering the method. In general, two expectations must be considered unfavorable. If an individual takes the attitude "Go ahead; show me what's wrong with me," he or she does not appreciate the basic intention of the method. Clients with this attitude expect to be made the object of an examination by someone else, with the resulting information being fed back to them so that they can know a little more about themselves. In other words, they expect to receive, on the strength of "test findings," results or advice formulated by the psychologist, who in turn bears exclusive responsibility for the examination. Another attitude, also to be regarded as inauspicious, can be summed up as follows: "I've come to you for help because things have become too much for me; I expect you to put me back on my feet again." The problem here is that the client simply unloads his or her responsibility on the psychologist. The onus of initiative then rests squarely on the helper, and the client can maintain a wary distance. Of course, such unfavorable attitudes can be corrected, but they should be discussed before starting the self-investigation.

The psychologist may also cloud the intention behind the self-confrontation method. For example, he or she may introduce it in the following manner: "I propose to administer a method in order to investigate your self-concept." This introduction is clearly based on a misperception of the method as a mere assessment tool in the hands of the psychologist. This manner of presentation suggests that the psychologist is the examiner and the client's self the object of study. But this misses a fundamental tenet of valuation theory: The client must function as the I who studies the Me in collaboration with the psychologist. Another misunderstanding can arise if the psychologist takes this stance: "I provide you the means for confronting you with yourself, so that things may change that otherwise are not changeable." This attitude misses the idea that the self-confrontation procedure is a collaborative procedure that does not isolate the client from the productive dialogical relationship with the psychologist.

In order to establish the atmosphere for a productive self-investigation, psychologist and client must work together to create three important attitudes: commitment, cooperation, and shared responsibility. Before clients start a self-investigation, they must be aware of the possibility of coming face to face with themselves. It requires a certain amount of courage to go beyond superficial talk or to even confront the need to change one's personal situation in a decisive way. Moreover, the commitment must be intrinsic; that is, the client must be interested in the advancement of self-knowledge and self-organization as a goal in itself. A purely extrinsic commitment (e.g., attempting to investigate the self for payment, for credit points, or out of a desire to conform to the wish of a significant other) often works against the possibility of deep self-exploration. In addition to an attitude of commitment, the self-confrontation method requires cooperation, the trusting involvement of two people in a process of dialogue. In this respect the method differs from the impersonality of traditional standardized tests and questionnaires. The self-confrontation method is a collaborative undertaking where insights, initiatives, and plans emerge from the interaction. Finally, both psychologist and client are responsible for the investigation. Clients are primarily responsible for the selection, formulation, and interpretation of significant meanings in the self-investigation. Morever, only the client can decide, with the professional help of the psychologist, what to do with the results of this investigation.

Instruction

The mutual expectations of psychologist and client are discussed in a preliminary interview in which the points of commitment, cooperation, and shared responsibility are made explicit. Instructions are then given orally, immediately preceding the self-investigation.

To begin with, the psychologist explains what the successive parts of the procedure will be like so that the client understands the function of each stage. Next, the psychologist points out that this investigation should be followed after some time (typically a few months) by another investigation so that the client and psychologist can compare the valuation system on two occasions and reflect on the observed constancies and changes. It is emphasized that a single self-investigation never produces a fixed picture; rather, each investigation yields a survey of a given period in the client's experiential history. To provide for an optimally favorable attitude toward the self-investigation, the psychologist emphasizes that, in principle, anything may be brought up that the individual regards as significant, that, as far as the psychologist is concerned, there are no restrictions on the content of the valuations to be discussed. The degree to which a client succeeds in being open and sensitive to the different aspects of the self is closely bound up with the manner in which the investigation, including the relationship with the psychologist, develops. Finally, psychologists should be aware of the following points: Subjects must set their own pace, allowing themselves the time needed to complete each part of the investigation. They should also be made to realize that the method is intended not only to produce results but also to provide practice in the art of self-reflection.

Formulation of Valuations

The valuations are formulated in response to sets of open-ended questions pertaining to either the past, the present, or the future (see Table 3.2). The questions have a broad scope, permitting clients to select topics out of their history and formulate them in their own way.

In order to facilitate the feeling of cooperation, the psychologist and client are seated side by side or at right angles to each other. The psychologist

---

TABLE 3.2. Questions of the Self-Confrontation Method

Set 1: *The Past*
These questions are intended to guide you in reviewing one or more aspects of your past life that may have been of great importance to you.
- Has there been anything of major significance in your past life that still continues to exert a strong influence on you?
- Was there in the past any person, experience, or circumstance that greatly influenced your life and that appreciably affects your present existence?

Set 2: *The Present*
This set consists of two questions referring to your present life that will lead you, after a certain amount of reflection, to formulate a response.
- Is there anything in your present existence that is of major importance to you or exerts a significant influence on you?
- Is there in your present existence any person or circumstance that exerts a significant influence on you?

Set 3: *The Future*
The following questions referring to your future should again guide you to a response. You are free to look as far ahead as you wish.
- Do you foresee anything that will be of great importance for or exert a major influence on your future life?
- Do you feel that a certain person or circumstance will exert a significant influence on your future life?
- Is there any future goal or object that you expect will play an important role in your life?

---

reads the questions from one of the sets aloud, and the client reads along. Each set, printed on a separate card, is composed of two or three questions relating to the same point in time. When one set of questions has been read, the client may respond in various ways. He or she may tell a story as a reaction to all of the questions or may come up with a single answer based on one question. All of this is possible and permissable because each question need not be responded to specifically but serves, in combination with the others, to invite clients to reflect on their life situation. Since the questions are not to be used as questionnaire items but only as stimuli for self-reflection, clients are permitted to diverge from them as much as necessary. (One answer may even be followed by yet another answer).

The client, together with the psychologist, peruses the first set of questions and thinks for a while. Certain story fragments occur, varying from clear recollections of events or circumstances to blurred chaotic memories. If the silent reflections are protracted and apparently inconclusive, the psychologist will invite the client to think aloud. As the client verbalizes the mental processes stimulated by the questions, the psychologist jots down notes on the matters raised. When the client's flow of experiences stops, the psychologist temporarily takes the initiative and proceeds to reformulate succintly the various points that have arisen. Clients thus get an abridged playback of their own associations, which will aid them in ordering their experiences. When listening to the helper's recapitulations, the client will very likely embark on a fresh round of storytelling, because he or she senses something more fundamental than what has just been told. This process, interspersed with the psychologist's recapitulations, may continue for quite a while. When this process has come to an end, the client (and not the psychologist, although the latter may provide help) must formulate a final response that can be set down on a file card. These cards should be relatively small in order to encourage a concise formulation of the significant experience (for other reasons, see Manual). When the interaction process between client and psychologist approaches the point of definitive formulation, the client should be instructed that the finalized response is to be a sentence, or in cases where this is difficult or impossible, a single word or phrase. The ideal expression is the sentence as it provides a clearly delineated and condensed valuation.

Below is an example of how a valuation can arise in response to the set of questions of Table 3.2. The client is Linda, the 28-year-old, who is the woman described in the case study later in this chapter.

Linda: (*thinks a while*) My parents . . . Mother was always ready for us, for my brother and sisters. . . . They always treated us as equals. . . . They always tried to keep me stimulated, for example, with clubs and piano lessons.
[The psychologist reviews the foregoing and then tries to recapitulate. The

client does not come up with a definite formulation and continues with her memories.]

Linda: When my mother was sick, she did not let anybody know it. . . . Her back was operated on when I was 16. . . . That was a difficult time, but that was just temporary. . . . I could always talk well with my parents.

[The psychologist reviews the preceding account, sums it up again, and then asks the client if she can now express, in a sentence, what she has in mind.]

Linda: (*suggests the following formulation*) "My parents have always treated us as equals; they always tried to keep me stimulated; I could always talk very well with my parents."

[The psychologist inquires whether this formulation covers adequately what the client has in mind and asks if this is indeed the major point she wants to make. The client confirms this, whereupon the psychologist asks if the same set of questions give rise to other significant experiences (see Table 3.5 for additional valuations from the same client).]

In this way, the same set of questions referring to the past may elicit a number of valuations. When the client and psychologist have selected and formulated those valuations that are felt to be most relevant from the past, they then proceed to the set of questions referring to the present and then to those concerning the future. Following reflection on the three sets of questions, a client typically has a minimum of 15 valuations. (For an extended set of questions that may increase the total number of valuations, see Appendix 1.)

There are several points the psychologist should keep in mind when eliciting the valuations:

1. The sentence should overtly concern the self. If the valuation "Walking in the woods is wonderful" is offered, the client should be encouraged to phrase it as "I find walking in the woods wonderful" or, even better, "I find walking in the woods wonderful, especially at dawn," the latter formulation being more personal and detailed (see Manual).

2. The sentence should be a close approximation of the client's intended meaning. The interaction between psychologist and client has the character of an "approximation process," in which the final formulation is gradually brought into close agreement with the client's intention. This approximation process gives the client and the psychologist the feeling of having gotten to the point. Note that the intended meaning is not fixed from the beginning but may be deepened or even changed in the course of telling.

3. Each sentence should be a single meaning unit. If client and psychologist have the feeling that two meanings are intermingled within the same formulation, it is advisable to separate the two meanings into two different sen-

tences. The psychologist may ask the client, "Do you have the feeling that this formulation is a single unit, or is it complex, with different meanings?"

4. As an utterance told to another person, the sentence should be communicative and intelligible. Not only the client but also the psychologist should be able to understand what has been said. When clients make use of strange words, slang, or neologisms, these should be clarified.

5. The sentence should be a final sentence, which means that those aspects of the intended meaning that are felt by the client to be most crucial should be included in the statement. Note that formulating a final response forces the person to include the most relevant meaning elements as part of the sentence (for the term *relevance*, see Hermans & Kempen, 1993, pp. 22–23).

In such a way, client and psychologist proceed together to articulate a self-narrative in terms of a limited number of I–Me sentences, which when taken together constitute a valuation system. However, an additional investigation of the affect associated with the valuations is needed in order to understand their organization because the organization of the self-narrative derives not only from specific valuations but also from the thematic influence of the basic motives.

Affective Exploration: From the Perspective of Basic Motives

Now we have arrived at the second stage in the self-confrontation method, the connection of the valuations with a standard list of affect terms. As explained in the previous chapter, affect is an intrinsic aspect of valuation; in order to understand a valuation, we must know its affective properties. At the same time, the affective properties reveal the workings of the basic motives. Whereas the valuations represent the main contribution from the client, the affect terms and affective patterns represent a significant contribution from the psychologist's knowledge of basic motives.

For the study of the affective component of the valuations, we use a standard set of affect terms, applicable to the various valuations generated by a single individual and to the valuation systems of different individuals. In the course of developing this method several lists of affect terms have been used. The list, presented in Table 3.3, is selected on the grounds that it contains a minimum number of affect terms that in combination permit a maximum of information to be gained about the motivational aspects of the valuation system. The affect terms can be divided into four groups: affect referring to self-enhancement (S), affect referring to contact and union with the other (O), affect referring to positive (pleasant) experiences (P), and affect referring to negative (unpleasant) experiences (N). The rationale behind this classification is that by making explicit the affective component of a valuation we get information on the deeper motivational level of the process of valuation. A simple example is "I passed a difficult exam." When this valuation is associated with more self-enhancement affect

TABLE 3.3. Affect Terms Used in the Self-Confrontation Method

1. Joy (P)	9. Unhappiness (N)
2. Self-esteem (S)	10. Tenderness (O)
3. Happiness (P)	11. Self-confidence (S)
4. Worry (N)	12. Intimacy (O)
5. Strength (S)	13. Despondency (N)
6. Enjoyment (P)	14. Pride (S)
7. Caring (O)	15. Disappointment (N)
8. Love (O)	16. Inner calm (P)

Note. S, affect reflects self-enhancement; O, affect reflects desire for contact with others; P, positive affect; N, negative affect.

than affect referring to contact and union and with more positive than negative affect, we know that this valuation is a gratification of the self-enhancement motive. Other valuations with more complex affective patterns and with more complex relationships between the formulation of the valuation and the affective pattern will be discussed throughout the book. (Note also that for clinical purposes we recommend a more differentiated list of affect terms. For this list, see Appendix 2; for reasons, see Manual.)

Indicators of Self-Enhancement

Several affect terms were chosen because they refer to the experience of self-enhancement: self-esteem, strength, self-confidence, and pride. Such terms indicate that the self is experienced as an autonomous entity strong enough to cope with the situation at hand. By using these terms, valuations that have this type of experience can be distinguished from those that do not.

Indicators of Contact and Union with the Other

The following affect terms were selected because they reflect the experience of contact and union with the other: caring, love, tenderness, and intimacy. More generally, these four terms are assumed to indicate the experience of participating with someone or feeling close to someone or something (e.g., a group of people, a particular place, an animal, a gift that functions as a symbol).

Indicators of Positive Affect

When the basic motives are gratified, one may expect positive affect as a result. The following terms refer to generally pleasant feelings resulting from gratification of the self-enhancement motive or the contact motive: joy, happiness, enjoyment, and inner calm.

Indicators of Negative Affect

When the basic motives meet insurmountable obstacles or are not at all gratified, we may expect negative affect. The following terms were chosen as general indicators of this feeling: worry, unhappiness, despondency, and disappointment. With the use of the positive and negative affect terms we can study which valuations represent a gratification of the basic motives (more positive than negative affect) and which valuations represent a blockage of the basic motives (more negative than positive affect).

Origin of the Affect Terms

How did we select the aforementioned affect terms? Why these and not other terms? We started in the early '70s with a list that included a broad variety of positive and negative affect terms and made selections based on the fundamental character of the positive–negative distinction in psychology and psychotherapy. In the course of time we discovered that two affects included in the list—self-esteem and love—proved to be of particular importance in the daily life of many people. In close correspondence with a review of the literature (e.g., Angyal, 1965; Bakan, 1966), we became aware that these affects represent basic psychological motives, which we later labeled as the S and O motives. We added more affect terms for each motive to our list to provide a certain variety within each group. We then checked the internal homogeneity of the terms within each group with reliability coefficients (alpha) and the differentiation between the two groups by computing correlations between them (see Note 4). For positive and negative affect we chose some terms that are generally interpreted as pleasant and unpleasant, respectively, and checked their psychometric qualities in the same way as described in the preceding sentence (see Note 4). In this way we acquired a series of terms to study the affective properties of valuations. The degree of S and O affect reflects the extent of gratification of the basic motives whereas the degree of positive and negative affect reflect the extent to which these motives meet superable or insuperable obstacles. (For an extension of the affective realm with, for example, stress, see Manual).

Matrix and Indices

The affective rating process results in a matrix in which each cell represents the extent to which, for a given individual, a specific affect is characteristic of a specific valuation. An example of such a matrix is presented in Table 3.4, as filled in by our client Linda. In this matrix the rows represent the valuations

TABLE 3.4. Matrix of Valuation × Affect: Raw Ratings from Linda and Indices

Valuation[a]	Affects[b]																Sum scores				Gen.[c]	Id.
	1 (P)	2 (S)	3 (P)	4 (N)	5 (S)	6 (P)	7 (O)	8 (O)	9 (N)	10 (O)	11 (S)	12 (O)	13 (N)	14 (S)	15 (N)	16 (P)	S	O	P	N		
1	4	2	3	1	3	3	3	4	1	2	2	1	1	4	1	1	11	10	11	4	-.45	.50
2	0	3	0	3	1	0	1	0	4	0	1	0	2	1	1	0	6	1	0	10	.58	-.73
3	0	1	0	3	0	0	1	0	5	0	0	0	2	0	4	0	1	1	0	14	.81	-.86
4	0	1	0	4	1	0	0	0	5	0	1	0	4	0	5	0	3	0	0	18	.84	-.93
5	3	2	2	2	2	3	3	2	2	0	2	2	0	2	1	1	8	7	9	5	-.19	.32
6	0	2	0	2	0	0	2	0	4	0	0	0	5	0	1	2	2	2	2	12	.56	-.70
7	4	3	2	3	2	3	1	0	0	0	1	0	1	1	2	0	7	1	9	6	-.03	-.15
General feeling	1	1	1	5	1	1	2	3	4	1	1	2	4	1	4	0	4	8	3	17	—	.79
Ideal feeling	4	3	5	1	4	5	4	5	1	5	4	5	0	3	0	5	14	19	19	2	-.79	—
Mean	1.6	2.0	1.0	2.6	1.3	1.3	1.6	0.9	3.0	0.3	0.3	0.4	2.1	1.1	2.1	0.6	5.4	3.1	4.4	9.9		

[a]The rows labeled 1 through 7 correspond to the valuations listed in Table 3.3.

[b]The columns labeled 1 through 16 correspond to the affects listed in Table 3.5. The numbers in the body of the table are the raw scores (0, not at all; 1, a little bit; 2, to some extent; 3, rather much; 4, much; 5, very much) assigned by the client to each affect with respect to each valuation.

[c]Gen., Generalization index: the correlation of the general feeling with each of the valuations; Id, Idealization index: the correlation of the ideal feeling with each of the valuations.

and the columns the affect terms. (Note that the numbers heading the columns in Table 3.4 correspond to the numbers preceding the affect terms in Table 3.3 and that the rows in the matrix correspond with Linda's valuations in Table 3.5 later in this chapter.)

The client, working alone now, concentrates on the first valuation and indicates on a 0–5 scale to what extent he or she experiences each affect in relation to that valuation (0, *not at all*; 1, *a little bit*; 2, *to some extent*; 3, *rather much*; 4, *much*; and 5, *very much*).[1] These scores form the first row of the matrix. After the first valuation the client concentrates on the second valuation and characterizes it using the same list of affect terms (the scores for which constitute the second row in the matrix). In this way, all valuations are successively characterized with the same list of affect terms and each valuation can be associated with a particular affective profile.[2]

With this matrix various computations are possible. The main indices are as follows:

1. Index S is the sum score of the four affect terms expressing self-enhancement (Numbers 2, 5, 11, and 14 of Table 3.3).

2. Index O is the sum score of the four affect terms expressing contact and union with the other (Numbers 7, 8, 10, and 12). For each valuation, the S–O difference can be determined. When the experience of self-enhancement is stronger than the experience of contact, S > O; when it is weaker, O > S. When both kinds of experience coexist, S = O.

3. Index P is the sum score of the four general positive affects (Numbers 1, 3, 6, and 16).

4. Index N is the sum score of the four general negative affects (Numbers 4, 9, 13, and 15). For each valuation, the P–N difference can be studied. This indicates the well-being that the person experiences in relation to the specific valuation. Well-being is positive when P > N, negative when N > P, and ambivalent when P = N. (Note that the scores for each of the four indices—S, O, P, and N—range from 0 to 20. See Appendix 2 for a more extended list of affect terms that can be used to study valuations in more detail.)

5. Clients are asked to characterize their *general feeling* by responding to the question "How do you generally feel these days?" This question does not require the formulation of an additional sentence but is answered directly by an affective rating on the 16 affect terms. This pattern of scores is added as an additional row to the affect matrix (see Table 3.4). The general feeling can then be studied with the same indices (S, O, P, and N) that are also used for the specific valuations. The P–N difference of the general feeling functions as a simple index for well-being.

6. Clients characterize their *ideal feeling* on the basis of their response to the question "How would you like to feel?" This question is also answered by an affective rating on the 16 affect terms and is included as a final row in

the affect matrix (see Table 3.4). The discrepancy between general feeling and ideal feeling can be used as a more complex measure for well-being. The stronger the discrepancy in the expected direction (on S, O, P, and N), the lower the sense of well-being is. In the case of negative well-being, it is expected that the ideal feeling has clearly lower N and higher S, O, and P than the general feeling.

7. Index r represents the extent of correspondence between the affective modality of two valuations; that is, it is the correlation between the profiles for any two rows of the matrix. This correlation indicates any similarity between the patterning of the affective profiles for two valuations. In a *modality analysis* a valuation that is of particular interest is selected as pivotal and then correlated consecutively with each of the other valuations in the system. When, for example, in the life of a particular client the mother functions as prototypical for the contact with many other people, it is expected that the valuation referring to the mother shows high positive correlations with valuations referring to other people (if people are experienced as similar to the mother) or shows high negative correlations with the valuation referring to others (if people are experienced as very different from, or even as opposites of, the mother).

8. The generalization index is the correlation between the affective pattern associated with the general feeling and any other valuation. This correlation gives an indication of the extent to which a particular valuation colors the affective modality associated with the general feeling. For example, in a person who is constantly thinking of the past as a lost paradise, those valuations referring to the past may show higher correlations with the general feeling than the other valuations referring to the present or the future. In a later investigation, after a period of psychotherapy, the generalization index of valuations referring to the past may decrease whereas the generalization index of valuations referring to the present and future may increase.

9. The idealization index is the correlation between the ideal feeling and any valuation. This correlation indicates to what extent a particular valuation is experienced as ideal. The idealization index shows that certain valuations fit more with the individual's ideal self than do others. Moreover, in the case of clients seeking psychotherapeutic help the valuations that color the general feeling are often different from those that approximate the ideal feeling. Under such circumstances the general feeling typically has an affective modality that is in contrast to the affective modality of the ideal feeling (i.e., the general feeling and the ideal feeling bear a negative correlation.)

10. The affect means can be computed within each column of the matrix. These means show what specific affect is most typical for the valuations as a whole (highest mean) and what affect is least typical for the valuations as a whole (lowest mean). That is, the relative degree of S and O affect within the system is indicated.[3]

To summarize and preview the use of these indices in the remainder of this book, let us consider a client at the beginning stages of psychotherapy. This client may have a general feeling with a low sum score for S affect, a low score for O affect, a low score for P affect, and a high score for N affect, a pattern that suggests that this person generally feels both basic motives to be largely unfulfilled. In contrast, the ideal feeling may show high scores for S, O, and P and a low score for N, indicating that the client would like to see the motives fulfilled to a greater degree.[4]

Discussion of the Results with the Client

After the first two parts of the self-investigation are completed, most clients are tired, or even confused, and would like to have a chance to digest the many impressions, associations, and thoughts that have been brought to light. During this period the psychologist should take time to perform the aforementioned qualitative and quantitative analyses. The discussion of the results with the client usually occurs after about a week's time.

The discussion between psychologist and client should be based on the overall picture provided by the system of valuations referring to the past, present, and future. The client may have forgotten some things or may be dissatisfied, after some reflection, with his or her formulation of some of the valuations. These are signs that the client is involved in the process, and it is therefore advisable that the psychologist start the discussion by asking, "What have you thought, done, or felt these days as a result of the self-investigation?" The answer then gives the psychologist an impression of the extent to which the client is involved in the process of self-exploration. This question also brings the self-knowledge of the client into contact with the psychologist's knowledge of the present system.

The discussion has the quality of an intensive self-reflection on the part of the client and a profound dialogue with the psychologist. It is based on the overall picture provided by the system, a picture in which valuations referring to past, present, and future are brought together so that new relations, hitherto hidden, can become visible. By bringing these together, we are touching upon a very specific characteristic of the self-confrontation procedure, which, unlike short talks and interviews that often have a momentary quality, allows psychologist and client to base their discussion on an overview of the relevant meaning units and the interrelationships and overall structure of these units. Psychologist and client have the opportunity to investigate and discuss which valuations are most important, both from the perspective of the content of the story and from the perspective of the affective organization of the system. It may be revealing for clients to discover, contrary to their expectations, that a particular valuation is more important than others; such a valuation may, for example, show the highest amount of negative feelings or the highest degree of generalization in the system as a whole. It may also be quite revealing when a particular valuation that functions for the client as an isolated meaning shows a specific affective modality that is also present in another valuation. For example, two valuations may refer to quite different content aspects of the self-narrative (e.g., a memory of a depreciatory remark by a teacher and present problems in one's work situation) but may be associated with highly similar affective patterns, suggesting that they have similar affective meanings. When confronted with such a similarity, the client is challenged to explore the valuations in their dynamic relationship so that they can become freed from their isolated positions.

The discussion invites the client to focus on the fundamentals of the valuation system. Valuations that have a great variety on the manifest level may show clear similarities from the perspective of the latent level, thus suggesting that they have a common motivational base. The client may detect that a great many valuations show a relative dominance of affect referring to self-enhancement over affect referring to contact and union. Seeing that this is a structural characteristic of the valuation system as a whole may motivate the client to address this imbalance and to look, with the assistance of the psychologist, for ways to strengthen the contact and union part of the system.

In order to understand how the self-confrontation method realizes a gradual transition between assessment and change, we shall discuss the concept of theme in self-narratives. As we have argued in Chapter 1, it is the theme that organizes the plot of a narrative and orders specific events as elements of a comprehensible tale. A self-narrative, in the form of a valuation system, is also organized on the basis of one or more themes. Identification and formulation of these themes is a necessary part of the self-confrontation procedure because insight into the thematic organization of the system makes the client aware of the difference between essentials and inessentials. The identification of the organizing themes is essential inasmuch as this makes the client aware that the guiding theme is determining to a large degree which events are selected as relevant to the plot structure. A plot has, as an organized structure, considerable continuity over time and space whereas specific events, and even specific valuations, may fluctuate in significance and are often replaceable by other events or valuations. For example, a person may discontinue an exhausting sports training program and decide to follow a meditation course; if after a while he or she becomes psychotic, the reason may be that in both the sport and the meditation this person wants to be the best and, as a consequence, becomes extremely involved in the activity. The theme in this case is "always trying to be the best," and this theme manifests itself in a diversity of events and valuations that vary according to changes over time and space. How then can we detect the main theme in a valuation system?

As discussed in Chapter 1, self-enhancement and contact and union with the other may be considered both as basic themes in collective stories (hero and love stories) and as basic motives in the self. These motives, however, are highly general orientations that do not say much about the particular ways people live their lives in order to realize these motives. The question, therefore, is how can the general motives be translated into the particulars of the client's personal history? There are two ways in which this can be realized. First, the affective indices (S, O, P, and N) associated with the particular valuations indicate the way in which the basic motives are expressed in the personal situation of the client. Second, by computing the correlations among the affective profiles of different valuations within the system one can explore which valuations have a common affective basis. This commonality then may be considered as a guiding theme in a person's self-narrative and may represent one of the basic motives or some combination of them in terms of the particulars of a person's life.

In fact, the identification of one or more guiding themes in the valuation system is one of the main activities of psychologist and client in the discussion of the results of the self-investigation. The theme must be derived from the client's own valuation system and formulated in his or her own terms. In this way the client is well aware of which valuations the theme is based on. Suppose the theme sounds like this: "I always want to be the best, even in situations where it is better not to be so." This conclusion, in fact, marks the end of the discussion with the client; at the same time, it is the beginning of the action phase. How does this transition between discussion and action take place?

At the end of the discussion the psychologist invites the client to simply pay attention to the theme he or she has formulated. That is, the client, who is not yet stimulated to change the theme or its implications, is instead asked to simply be aware of what happens. The client goes home with the aim of directing his or her attention to those situations in which he or she is again "trying to be the best." This emphasis on awareness as the initial phase of change has several advantages. First, self-reflection is not limited to the session with the psychologist but is also practiced in daily life. Second, the client has in the form of a self-formulated theme a device available that is highly suitable for helping him or her recognize the many instances where the given behavior happens again; thus, his or her power of observation is sharpened. The client discriminates between situations in which the theme is determining his or her actions and the situations in which it is not. Third, many clients are exceptionally sensitive to pressure from other people, including the psychologist, or from themselves. In fact, many clients have previously made desperate attempts to change their own feelings, thinking, or behavior and in doing this have often put themselves under considerable strain, however unproductive. The invitation in the beginning of the change process to simply attend to what happens frees such clients of this unreasonable pressure to overcome their emotional obstacles.

THE VALIDATION/INVALIDATION PROCESS

Each person has a story to tell about his or her own life. When a person has constructed a story in which life events are ordered, he or she simultaneously develops a tendency to consolidate the story and a concomitant resistance to change it. The construction of a story is a way of organizing one's interaction with the world, and once this organization has been achieved, a person finds his or her identity in the particular story. Of course, there may be events that are incompatible with one's self-narrative. In that case there are at least two ways to protect one's story against events that could undermine it. First, it is possible to simply avoid particular events so that they cannot have a correcting influence on the story. A valuation like "I am entirely incapable of having a relationship because no woman in the world exists that could get along with me" might be based on a man's anxiety about intimate contact. Such a valuation will not be modified as long as he avoids all those situations that could diminish his anxiety. Second, a person being confronted with an event that is incompatible with his or her self-narrative is always capable of interpreting or reinterpreting the event in such a way that it fits into the existing story and further corroborates it. For example, people who see themselves as unattractive may not believe other people who express their appreciation of their appearance, however honest these compliments may be. In fact, the "unattractive" person may uphold this valuation by believing, for example, that the other person has extended the compliment for some ulterior motive or as a means of offering consolation. By avoiding events that may threaten a given valuation and by interpreting events in such a way that they fit into existing valuations, people give their self-narrative, which is a structure for ordering their experiences, a certain degree of stability over time and space.

Once having told their stories, people are, in fact, more concerned with validating than invalidating their view of themselves and the world. The self-confrontation method, therefore, was developed not only to assess one's self-narrative but also to change it. Of course, it is taken into account that the tendency to validate one's story is certainly not of an absolute nature. The fact that clients make contact with a psychotherapist or counselor in order to work on their problems is a clear indication that they are open, to a certain degree, to the idea of exploring alternative possibilities for their behavior or experience. Every therapist, however, is acquainted with the problem of resistance to change, a phenomenon that plays a role even in the case of so-called motivated clients. Therefore, a systematic strategy is needed for realizing a transition from assessment to change in such a way that the client is motivated to explore alternative stories or parts of stories in order to promote the valuation process as a whole. This implies an invalidation of existing parts of the valuation system and a validation of those parts that are modified or even new. We speak of a validation/invalidation process to indicate a way of organizing and reorganizing the valuation system in order to develop a workable self-narrative. This process is actually part of the daily lives of all people. In the context of psychotherapy and counseling, however, it requires special attention in a systematic procedure to change the valuation system.

The essence of the validation/invalidation process is what we have described as the plot structure of one's self-narrative. In the dialectical relationship between plot and events, new events may or may not change the plot. When new events are systematically avoided or made to fit into the existing system by reinterpretation, the events, no matter how new or deviant they may be, do not have any changing influence at all. New events only have a stimulating or changing influence on the system when they are recognized as potential sources of increased self-knowledge and self-development.

The validation/invalidation process goes through three phases that can be labeled as "attending," "creating," and "anchoring" (ACA). That is, clients first give their full attention to the ongoing events. Then they initiate new actions and experiment with new ways of behavior; that is, new events are created. Finally, the new events, organized as units of meaning, are anchored in the valuation system by practicing. These phases can be repeated more than once after each self-investigation, in which case the three phases work as a cycle. Let us describe the three phases in more detail.

Attending

In the attending phase, clients are stimulated to involve themselves in a learning process in which they are focused on observing, remembering, and telling the ongoing events of their lives as relevant to the valuation system and its further development. Clients learn to develop an increased attention and sensitivity to the vast field of their daily life and to explore the relationship between their existing self-narrative and the ongoing stream of events. In this phase it is crucial that clients become aware of the fact that events do not have meaning in themselves, fixed or otherwise. Rather, even within the constraints of cultural values events allow for an array of possible interpretations that make them suitable for inclusion in alternative meaning units. Only when events are recognized as the basic material for possible meanings can the necessary condition be met for stimulating the dialectical relationship between plot and event in such a way that existing units of meaning are modified or new ones developed.

As Sluzki (1992) has so forcefully argued, learning to see exceptions in one's story is of crucial significance for its further development. When, for example, a client says, "Everything that I have tried in the past has failed," not much room is left in this valuation for events that are incompatible with this view. As long as the client holds on to the all-inclusive "everything," he or she is blind to deviations from this view and makes himself or herself insensitive to alternative possibilities in the present and future. In other words, this strongly generalizing statement invites the client closer to validation than to invalidation. In order to change such a valuation, it is important that psychologist and client start a process of exploration in which the client is stimulated to search for possible exceptions to the general statement both in the past and in the present. The psychologist might ask the following questions: "What was your first failure?" "What happened before?" "What made it a failure?" "Was there any event, later or before, that looked like a success?" "Did this happen only once?" "Do you expect that your future will be the same?" Such questions focus on the time aspect of one's narrative. The spatial aspect underlies questions such as the following: "Who defined this as a failure, you or another person?" "With whom do you compare yourself?" "When do you define another person's action as a failure?" "What does he or she consider a failure?" With these and other questions, the psychologist directs the client's attention to events as movements in time and space and emphasizes their contextual nature. Clients are invited to carefully examine their present situation not only in the session but also between successive sessions and to report what happens in the form of concrete observations, not abstract conceptions. The psychologist, guided by an attitude of openness, empathy, and curiosity, invites the client to tell which events fit and which do not fit with the existing valuations. This systematic attempt to discriminate between events that fit and those that do not contributes to opening a valuation system that may otherwise remain closed owing to conservative valuations that blind the client to alternative narrative constructions.

In the attending phase, clients also learn to understand the nature of the S and O motives and to actively apply them to daily events, an exercise that helps them differentiate between events that are relevant with respect to one or the other motive. The client not only tells the psychologist about the ongoing events but also indicates which S and O feelings are aroused by these events. In this way clients learn both to differentiate between S and O affect in their own situation and to become sensitive to the affective nuances that exist between various affects within the two affect categories (e.g., the difference between caring and intimacy).

In order to check the progress a client has made in the attending phase, the psychologist may open a session by inviting the client to tell what happened since the last session or what he or she noticed. When the client responds with "Nothing has happened" or "I've noticed nothing special," this may be a sign that he or she has not made much progress in observing, remembering, and telling recent events that are significant from the perspective of the valuation system. In this case the psychologist invites the client to inspect in more detail recent situations in which the client was involved, with the aim of increasing the client's sensitivity to concrete events and directing his or her attention to events that are deviant from existing valuations.

The strategy of sharpening the client's awareness of concrete and significant events may be very helpful at the start of the change process. The success of these attempts is, however, highly dependent on the clients' capacity to direct their attention to these events and on their openness to admit that these events are relevant to their self-exploration. Often "new" events are kept below a critical level of awareness so that they are not consciously observed and remembered. It is here that we arrive at another characteristic that is highly typical of the self-confrontation procedure: the placing of events and valuations in the context of the valuation system as a whole. The quintessence is that this placing broadens the array of possible meanings of a particular event or valuation. For example, the valuation "Everything I have tried in the past has failed" may receive additional or new meanings by taking into account that this valuation shows an affective commonality with such other valuations as "I have had too many disappointments in my life." As a result of seeing this relationship the client may discover that he or she keeps the failure valuation intact in order to protect himself or herself against further disappointment. Being aware of this, the client may, in the validation/invalidation period, become more open and sensitive to deviating events that may contribute to a modification of the original valuation. In other words, events are typically considered as contextual data; they are part of valuations as broader meaning units, and these valuations are in turn part of a broader valuation system. The contextualization of events broadens the possible meanings of events. In the example, the client not only focuses on failures but also on ways of preventing disappointments; focusing on the latter may increase awareness that the client is preventing himself or herself off from having experiences of a more positive kind. The contextualization of events increases the number of perspectives from which specific events may be viewed, thus creating a multiplicity of angles that works against the habitual or emotionally based tendency to lock up the event into one and the same meaning unit.

Creating

Whereas the first phase in the validation/invalidation process centers around learning to attend to what happens, the second phase aims to stimulate the client to create new ways of behaving and to order the results of this behavior into new valuations or modifications of existing valuations. The supposition is that events are not simply things that happen to a person involved in a particular situation. People are able to influence the life situation in which they live to a certain degree. This implies that they may take initiatives to create new events in an attempt to alter existing situations, add to them, or transform them into something different. Events typically happen in the person–situation interaction, and this implies that the person has an influence on the events and their interpretation.

After the client has achieved a heightened self-awareness in the phase of attending to current events, he or she takes the first steps toward deviating from existing event structures and predominant valuations. The client who is struggling with the theme of failure and is accustomed to defining his or her own actions as invariably inadequate may be invited to try out new actions that are critical from the perspective of this theme. For example, a man who is used to letting his wife organize his birthday party (about which he is never satisfied) may take the initiative to do it himself. Or a client who is extremely afraid to say no when someone asks for a favor may come to the point where he or she makes the first attempt to express this word without too much panic. Or people who are used to avoiding situations in which they expect shame to be aroused to an excessive degree may take the initiative and now explore such a situation in order to see what happens and to observe their own reaction as well as that of other people. All such initiatives are discussed with the psychologist, who at the same time serves as a safe or stimulating background for these explorations. The psychologist has an important role to play not only in the sessions but between the sessions as well. The client's awareness of the fact that what he or she is doing will be discussed with the psychologist often functions as a responsive background, even when the psychologist is not physically present. That is, the imaginal presence and support of the psychologist, an often underestimated aspect of therapy and counseling, give the client's actions a relational flavor. Actions can always be told, receiving a great deal of their meaning from the act of telling.

Central to the second phase of the validation/invalidation process is the "principle of feasible steps." That is, psychologist and client are aware that in the beginning of the process of change it is important that new actions not exceed a certain level of difficulty or risk. If the first initiatives were to systematically fail, they would contribute to the further generalization of negative valuations in the system rather than lead to their transformation or to a limitation of their influence. Therefore, psychologist and client carefully plan new actions in such a way that the chances of a positive outcome are optimal (e.g., the psychologist helps the client with sharp and concrete formulation of action plans; actively relates the new events to the system; and urges the client to make notes in a logbook). Only when the first tryouts are successful can actions of a more difficult or risky nature be undertaken with some assurance that the result will be an increase in the level of S affect.

Note that planning action with steps gradually increasing in difficulty does not ignore the fact that the taking of initiatives is often a highly spontaneous phenomenon (as is increased awareness in the first phase). Clients are often motivated to try out something new by the self-investigation alone. After they become aware of their valuations and their mutual relationships, they often begin trying new behaviors even before any planned changes are discussed with the psychologist. Some clients also take the principle of feasible steps into account in a spontaneous way. For example, a woman who reported always feeling forced to act in the service of others started to invalidate this valuation by not offering her guests sugar with their coffee and giving them the opportunity to take it themselves. Such a change might seem like a small detail, but at this point in this client's change process it was a breathtaking enterprise that was loaded with meaning because it symbolized for her another way of positioning herself with regard to other people. Moreover, these small changes can have far-reaching consequences for the person because they may be followed by more conspicuous actions that may be more impressive in the long run.

In order to check if the process of change is going in the intended direction, it is recommended that the meaning of the new initiatives be examined. Usually the meaning of the changes is evaluated in the second self-investigation. When, however, psychologist and client do not want to perform a complete self-investigation or when they want to have a quick check between two full self-investigations, they can opt for a short "standstill" in a so-called evaluation session. Such a session takes place when, after a period of trying out new actions, psychologist and client want to evaluate the personal meaning of the first changes. The psychologist assists the client in formulating the meaning of the changes in terms of one or more valuations. The client then characterizes the affective significance of these valuations with the familiar list of affect terms. On the basis of the affective indices, it can be assessed to what extent the new valuations contribute to the client's self-enhancement and contact with the other. Moreover, the new valuations can be assessed as positive, negative, or ambivalent. If the new valuations represent successful attempts to change the person–situation interaction, a significant amount of self-enhancement affect together with a high degree of positive affect is expected. In this mini-investigation one can check if the general feeling has been changed since the first self-investigation and determine to what extent the new valuations have a generalizing power. The latter analysis gives additional information inasmuch as one may find that new valuations are very positive but do not have generalizing quality because they are not yet anchored in the valuation system.

The short evaluation has several advantages in the total process of change. First, psychologist and client pause to look back and evaluate what has been achieved so far. Second, because psychologist and client may have divergent impressions or opinions about the nature and intensity of the change, it is revealing for both to evaluate the process so that assumptions may be checked. Third, the progress that has been made can be considered from the perspective of the basic motives. This may be profitable, especially in those cases in which one or both motives were weakly represented in the initial valuation system. By considering the new valuations from the perspective of the basic motives, evidence can be found with regard to the motivational significance of the new valuations.

Anchoring

The third phase of the validation/invalidation process involves the anchoring of the valuations. Whereas in the second phase the client has experimented with alternative narrative elements by creating new events and valuations, in the third phase these changes must be established as parts of the valuation system. Even in those cases in which new actions are welcomed by psychologist and client as significant changes in a process, the client may fall back to earlier modes of experience and action because the new actions are not yet incorporated as stabilized parts of the valuation system. Therefore, the main activity in the third phase is practice: repeating actions, and inventing new ones as variations on the theme, long enough to transform them into new habits.

A problem met in the third phase is the possibility of relapsing to previous forms of action. The risk of relapse becomes particularly high when there are significant others in the life of the client who evoke the familiar behaviors they expect of the client. There are two ways to deal with this problem. First, the client may continue practicing after learning why the inadequate old forms of behavior have returned. This requires that the client gain insight into the conditions (when, where, how, and why did it happen?) that led to giving up a recently acquired behavior pattern. Second, it may be useful to invite significant others to perform a self-investigation so that they too become involved in the process of change, as may happen in the case of marital or family therapy (see Chapter 4 and Manual). In such cases the validation/invalidation process may profit from the active participation of significant others as coconstructors of meaning.

The third phase of the validation/invalidation process may end with a second self-investigation after the client has practiced long enough to develop stabilized valuations that enhance coping efforts in his or her current situation. For the process of anchoring, clients must have the opportunity to validate their new valuations in a variety of situations in order to avoid becoming "super-specialized" in validating experiences (e.g., coping with shame in contact with only one other person and in one activity only). Moreover, it is important that clients practice in situations that vary in level of difficulty. If they are prepared for new behavior in easy situations only, there is a considerable risk that they will fail in situations of a more challenging nature.

It is possible that the second self-investigation will reveal that the new valuations are not anchored well enough in the valuation system. It may be found, for example, that the new valuations have no generalizing potential or that they have had no influence on the rest of the system and instead occupy a rather isolated position in it. When no integration has been achieved, more practice is needed or additional self-exploration is required. A third self-investigation, after an additional period of practice, will then be conclusive in determining whether the validation/invalidation process has resulted in valuations that are sufficiently stabilized as parts of an otherwise developing valuation system.

THE SECOND SELF-INVESTIGATION

The second self-investigation, which shows the development of the system as a whole, is in most cases performed some months or half a year after the initial investigation. Usually it takes place when psychologist and client feel that significant parts of the system have been changed. The second investigation follows roughly the same procedure as the first one. The initial valuation-construction phase is slightly modified, but the remainder of the investigation is the same as in the first investigation. In the second investigation clients are confronted with the valuations formulated in the first one rather than asked to construct an entirely new set of valuations. That is, following each of the questions used to elicit the original valuations, the psychologist now produces the statement provided by the client in the first investigation. For each statement, clients are instructed to consider whether they still accept its content, that is, whether they would still come up with the same answer to the same question. The psychologist then explains that when this is not the case, the client has the following options:

1. An old valuation may be reformulated (*modification*).
2. An old valuation may be replaced with a new one (*substitution*).
3. An old valuation may be discarded altogether (*elimination*).
4. An additional valuation may be created (*supplementation*).

In this way the client indirectly points to the constant and changing parts of the system. As we shall see, clients typically change only part of their system, even when they are in a period of massive life reorganization. This holds for the affective associations as well. In a previous study (Hermans, 1986) we compared three self-investigations from a client that were spread over a period of 1½ years. When test–retest correlations were computed, a high degree of stability was found in the affective profiles of identically formulated valuations, with a median correlation approaching .90 and with some showing almost perfect stability ($r = .99$). The test–retest correlations for valuations that had in some way changed were generally lower and in one case had even dropped to a negative coefficient of $-.64$. These results have at least two implications. First, the low test–retest correlation in the case of modified valuations should not be taken as an indication of unreliability but, rather, as a sign of meaningful change. Second, the occurrence of very high and very low test–retest correlations within the system of a single individual suggests that constancy and change are not mutually exclusive but are two simultaneous manifestations of human development (Thomae, 1988). Moreover, this simultaneity may be of particular significance for the development of the self in psychotherapy: Clients' resistance to change is often reduced when they can hold on to some constants that provide a necessary degree of self-continuity. Without this base, clients may simply seek self-maintenance in an overly compulsive way and may thereby preclude the possibility of change.

It is, of course, possible to perform a second, or even third, investigation after some years, even when there has been no systematic action program. Such an investigation is performed in order to follow a person's development.

CASE EXAMPLE

In order to illustrate the procedure, we present some valuations from our client Linda, a 28-year-old woman who had serious problems with relationships, particularly in her work situation. She was referred to us by the industrial psychologist from her company and decided to do a self-investigation in order to arrive at a better view of her personal situation. In Table 3.5, a sample of seven of her valuations is presented, along with some indices already described in this chapter, including the general and ideal feeling measures (for her raw ratings see Table 3.4). Let us first have a look at some conspicuous aspects of Linda's valuation system.

- An examination of seven valuations indicates that the level of S and O affect is rather low, with the exception of a valuation that refers to contact with her parents as a positive experience (P > N).
- Linda expresses in Valuations 3 and 4 a fatalistic view of her ability to take control of her life: S and O affects are reduced to a minimum, and both valuations are felt to be very negative.
- Although Linda expresses a rather optimistic and enterprising attitude toward the future in Valuation 7, there is only a modest level of S affect and a slight predominance of P affect over N affect.
- Comparing the different valuations, we see that Valuations 3 and 4 show the highest correlation with the general feeling, suggesting that these two valuations are particularly generalizing in the system. At the same time, they contrast strongly with the affective ratings associated with the ideal feeling. This large difference in the generalization and idealization of these valuations creates a great deal of tension in the system.

A relevant question in the application of the self-confrontation method is: Which valuation represents the relevant starting point for a discussion? Which valuation can feed the dialogue between psychologist and client? In this case, Valuation 3 was chosen by the psychologist and the client as the central topic for

TABLE 3.5. Valuations of Linda's First Self-Investigation, Their Scores on S, O, P, and N Indices,[a] and Their Extent of Generalization and Idealization

Valuation	S	O	P	N	Gen.	Id.	Correlations with Valuation 3
1. My parents have always treated us as equals. They always tried to keep me stimulated. I could always talk very well with my parents.	11	10	11	4	-.45	.50	-.59
2. After high school I never managed to build up a group of friends; I felt left out and stuck between two worlds.	6	1	0	10	.58	-.73	.76
3. I tried to be what I was supposed to be at my work and lost all my self-confidence.	1	1	0	14	.81	-.86	—
4. Everything that I've tried has failed, due to either circumstances or myself.	3	0	0	18	.84	-.93	.94
5. Wendy is a good friend.	8	7	9	5	-.19	.32	-.18
6. Bodily complaints: Every time I find that I have a problem, my body signals it in one way or another.	2	2	2	12	.56	-.70	.67
7. I want to do something myself that I enjoy, something that is useful.	7	1	9	6	-.03	-.15	.00
General feeling	4	8	3	17	—	-.79	.81
Ideal feeling	14	19	19	2	-.79	—	-.86

[a]S, sum score of the four affect terms expressing self-enhancement (numbers 2, 5, 11, and 14 of Table 3.3); O, sum score of the four affect terms expressing contact and union (numbers 7, 8, 10, and 12); P, sum score of the four positive affects (numbers 1, 3, 6, and 16); N, sum score of the four negative affects (numbers 4, 9, 13, and 15).

discussion. They felt that its content had important repercussions for the system as a whole and noticed that in comparison with the other valuations it ranked quite high in the extent of generalization and also in negative affect.

As usual, a modality analysis, was performed, in this case with Valuation 3 as the pivotal valuation correlated (see the correlations with Valuation 3 in Table 3.5.) The highest correlating valuation (with Valuation 4; $r = .94$) was then selected out, and the client was invited to concentrate on the common meaning between the two valuations. Let us take a closer look at this example. The two valuations are as follows:

Valuation 3: "I tried to be what I was supposed to be at my work and lost all my self-confidence."
Valuation 4: "Everything that I've tried has failed, due to either circumstances or myself."

Linda provided an interpretation that included elements of both valuations: "I became very tense and tried to maintain an image of myself.... Therefore, many things that I attempted to do failed.... I listened to no one.... The goal was still more important."

The psychologist then proceeded to the valuation with the second-highest correlation (Valuation 2) and asked Linda to compare this with the pivotal valuation ($r = .76$):

Valuation 3: "I tried to be what I was supposed to be at my work and lost all my self-confidence."
Valuation 2: "After high school I never managed to build up a group of friends; I felt left out and stuck between two worlds."

Linda again followed the instruction to look at what is common to both valuations and gave this interpretation: "I was also very tense in high school from trying to maintain a certain image.... I therefore couldn't build up a real group of friends."

The valuation with the third-highest correlation (Valuation 6) was then compared to the pivotal valuation ($r = .67$):

Valuation 3: "I tried to be what I was supposed to be at my work and lost all my self-confidence."
Valuation 6: "Bodily complaints: Every time I find that I have a problem, my body signals it in one way or another."

Linda's interpretation: "I can feel this tension in my body.... Sometimes my muscles are so tense that I can't do anything.... Through being so goal oriented, I lose contact with myself."

The psychologist and client can continue with this as long as they feel it is fruitful and as long as there are high correlations (a correlation of .60 can be used as a minimum, but this choice is, of course, arbitrary). They may also select a different valuation as pivotal and penetrate the system from another side. When the process of comparing a pivotal valuation with the other valuations is finished, the psychologist briefly reviews or repeats each of the interpretations for the client. Next, the psychologist asks the client which element or common theme in all of the comparisons appears to be the most essential. Linda's response was, "I have not listened enough to myself." After some pause for reflection on this highly condensed and highly significant piece of self-insight, the psychologist proposed that Linda carefully observe when she listens to herself and when she does not. The psychologist also proposed that Linda make notes on her own observations in order to discuss them in the next session.

The insight achieved through the modality analysis and formulated as a summary of interpretations may be reached within a single session, although several sessions are more likely to be necessary to arrive at this point. It is essential in the application of the self-confrontation method that the client and the psychologist move toward a summary in which a central theme in the story of the person is made explicit. The client can then go home with this theme in mind and try to become more sensitive to the patterns of experiences and interactions in daily life that are closely related to this theme. That is, the modality analysis takes us to the heart of the self-confrontation method because it is the most direct road to a theme that plays a major role in the ordering of the client's life in a particular period.

The modality analysis also illustrates how the assessment process itself can lead to change. The client, moving from one set of valuations and their interpretation to the next, gradually articulates some common themes and establishes some order in his or her experiences. As the contours of the central theme become clearer, the change process gains direction, and eventually the client and psychologist arrive at a point where they can translate the guiding theme into concrete behavioral steps to be incorporated into the client's daily life.

In Linda's case a validation/invalidation period of 6 months followed the first self-investigation. That is, Linda discussed her daily experiences with the psychologist in biweekly sessions. In these sessions Linda's experiences were discussed in light of the valuation system, with attention paid to experiences that were in agreement with the valuation system, as well as to those that were not. In the following paragraphs we give some examples of what the three phases of the validation/invalidation process looked like in Linda's case.

During the first phase Linda was primarily focused on the fact that she used to react to problems with bodily complaints. For example, if she received a telephone call at a moment when she was busy with something, she found it extremely difficult to tell the caller that she had no time to talk, nor could she even propose to contact the other person at another time. Instead, she reacted with a headache. More generally, Linda reacted with headaches and other psychosomatic complaints when she suppressed her own wishes, particularly in situations in which she had the feeling that she had to please the other person.

In the second phase Linda tried out some new actions, beginning with actions that involved low risk and later progressing to more difficult tasks. For example, she discovered that she used to consolidate her feelings of failure by systematically not doing anything. After a while she took the initiative to make contact with the company doctor to ask for advice concerning a problem she wanted to discuss with him. What is significant here is the fact that it was she who decided to go to the doctor; usually it was the doctor who made contact with Linda. The risk of this action was rather low as she knew the doctor and felt she had a good relationship with him. Sometime later, Linda requested permission from her company to do part-time volunteer work with children, a request that was conceded. This was a choice of her own that contributed greatly to her self-confidence, for she was then able to realize an old desire she had given up earlier. Linda was no longer afraid that her own wishes would conflict with the expectations others had of her.

The second phase of the validation process gradually merged into the third phase. Increasingly, Linda felt she was on the right track. She became more and more convinced that she herself could solve her problems by listening to her own feelings rather than trying to conform to the expectations of others. Moreover, she felt that she was able to make decisions and attend to her own life, mainly by first listening to her feelings and then acting accordingly.

Six months after the first self-investigation, Linda and her psychologist had the impression that there were important changes in her valuation system, and therefore they decided to do a second investigation. Table 3.6 shows how the original valuations developed over time and gives an indication of the constancies and changes in the system. The following observations can be made:

- There are valuations from the second investigation that are identical to those from the first investigation (Valuation 2), practically identical (Valuation 5), slightly modified (Valuations 3 and 7), and fundamentally changed (Valuations 1, 4, and 6).
- There are now some valuations with a high level of S affect in combination with high P (Valuations 4, 6, and 8), indicating that Linda felt some degree of self-enhancement in certain areas where she did not experience it before.
- A valuation expressing a high degree of self-enhancement (Valuation 4) has the highest correlation with both the general feeling and the ideal feeling. Note that this valuation is particularly relevant from the perspective of the validation/invalidation process. We can conclude that the change process

Table 3.6. Valuations of Linda's Second Self-Investigation, Their Scores on S, O, P, and N Indices, and Their Extent of Generalization and Idealization

Valuation	S	O	P	N	Gen.	Id.
1. I want to build up something new with my parents: more equal love.	15	5	3	9	.24	.02
2. After high school I never managed to build up a group of friends; I felt left out and stuck between two worlds.	4	0	0	9	-.61	-.68
3. I was completely molded by others at my work and therefore lost myself.	8	0	0	13	-.32	-.47
4. Through my own efforts, things are working out now; I consciously chose, for example, to do volunteer work and to go to the company doctor for advice.	14	6	15	3	.68	.68
5. Wendy is still a good friend.	9	5	7	1	.38	.50
6. I am more aware of myself now and listen better to my body. I listen better to my feelings, and as a result I live differently.	12	5	10	3	.54	.59
7. John [husband] and I want children in the future; moreover, I want to pursue a combination of studying and volunteer work.	13	16	15	1	.57	.64
8. I've learned to make decisions differently: I give myself the time to choose, I see the consequences better, and I listen to myself better. I also permit myself to have doubts.	12	3	9	5	.55	.45
General feeling	14	11	13	6	—	.87
Ideal feeling	17	11	19	1	.87	—

resulted not only in increased self-enhancement but that this change also had a strong generalizing potential.

• Linda's relationship with her parents (Valuation 1) received a new basis: She wanted to diminish a nostalgic dependence and become more independent, a desire that appealed more to her S motive than to her O motive. This, however, cost her some pain (N > P).

• Linda's outlook on the future (Valuation 7) became broader, more articulated, and more concrete. This valuation increased on the S, O, and P indices and has a stronger correlation with Linda's general feeling. And the pattern of scores for Valuation 7 at the second investigation equals the pattern of Valuation 1 at the first investigation: Linda's ideal modality (i.e., affective pattern) moved from the past to the future.

• Valuation 8 expresses the main thing Linda learned. Such a valuation is called a "key valuation," and when the client does not spontaneously include it (as Linda did), the psychologist may ask for it in order to evaluate the role of significant learning experiences in the process of change. Note also the comparative aspect of this valuation, which explicitly denotes a movement from past to present (see also Valuation 6).

• Interestingly enough, the affective status of Valuation 3, which was chosen as the pivotal valuation at Time 1, did not change in a positive direction at the second investigation. We see in this case, instead, that in the second investigation the client attributed at least part of her problem to her work situation. Apparently, Valuation 3 at the first investigation represented a mingling of internal and external attributions. At the second investigation, however, Linda was able to make a clear distinction between an externally caused situation (Valuation 3) and her own motives and abilities (as reflected in Valuation 4 and 6).

As demonstrated by Linda's case, the central themes in a self-narrative can be investigated in close cooperation with the client and the examination of these themes in the context of daily life can, in turn, lead to further development of the self-narrative. This case also shows that the method of self-confrontation is a combination of openness and structure. It is open to the world of the clients, who are approached as experienced and knowledgeable subjects with regard to their own situation. At the same time, the procedure, as a systematic way of organizing and reorganizing the client's self-narrative, is structured.

In sum, the self-confrontation procedure follows a cycle of investigation (I), validation/invalidation (V), and another investigation (I). In this IVI cycle the second investigation is the end of the first cycle but may at the same time function as the beginning of a second cycle. More cycles may be needed in those cases in which the change process is extended over a longer period in time. The IVI cycle reflects the dynamic character of the method: It begins with a thorough investigation of the thematic structure of a self-narrative (I), which develops into a thematic restructuring in the validation/invalidation phase (V), the nature of which is then evaluated in a second investigation (I). In all three phases the person is considered and approached as a motivated storyteller.

ASSESSMENT, PROCESS PROMOTION, EVALUATION

The self-confrontation method serves three purposes: It is an assessment instrument, it contributes to the process of valuation, and it can be used as an evaluation method.

Assessment

As an assessment technique the self-confrontation method assumes an I that actively investigates the Me in its different manifestations. For example, if the I is depicted as the center of a circle (as suggested by James, 1890, p. 297), one can imagine what happens when the I moves upward and reflects down on its own landscape. In this way a self-investigation, performed as a coconstruction with the psychologist, provides a bird's-eye view of the valuation system, condensed into a more or less ordered system of divergent experiences. This view is not, however, the perception or judgment of a detached observer. It is, rather, an exciting, communicative view, to some extent unfamiliar and sometimes quite frightening. From this perhaps peculiar perspective, people can see things in a different light; recognize that they themselves are to a certain degree the creators of the landscape they see; and, as a consequence, feel some responsibility for it. Having seen things from a different perspective, moreover, clients may also realize that the existing system has its lacunae and perhaps its contradictions and that it is not the only system they can adhere to. There may be a growing awareness that it is possible to construct a system formulated in another way. Some individuals become seriously discontented with their formulations and immediately realize that what they have said is not right. Sometimes within a few days after the investigation they may say, "Some of my valuations have already changed" or "If I were to do the investigation again, I would put some things differently." These remarks are not to be taken as an indication of dishonesty but, rather, as an indication of the client's growing awareness of what is not, in fact, the case. The psychologist may stimulate this process of reflection by explaining to clients that this is an investigation in which not only the results but also the truths they learn about themselves in the course of the investigation count. Clients must understand that the self-investigation is not a test where they wait for the results but an ongoing dialogue that demands close attention to the self. Clients are viewed as meaning experts who know most accurately which experiences in their life are relevant to themselves.

They have a large data bank about their life available and are uniquely able to communicate what they feel to be meaningful. Psychologists are professional experts and are knowledgeable about the details of the methodology, its theoretical background, and its possibilities. They also have experience with other clients and may be able to apply this experience for the elucidation of the individual case.

One may object here that the self-confrontation procedure asks people to do things that they are simply not in a position to do. Many clients, for example, are not very self-aware or cannot enter into a productive dialogue and are therefore seeking therapeutic assistance. One might even raise the point that dialogical relationships are characterized not only by intersubjective exchange but also by relative dominance of the parties involved (Hermans & Kempen, 1993; Linell, 1990) and that in this case the psychologist can be considered to dominate the relationship with the client, who is often in a dependent position and not acquainted with the assessment situation. The answer to this objection is straightforward: The procedure presupposes what it wants to make true. That is, in performing a self-investigation, the client is led in an exercise of self-reflection with as much aid from the psychologist as needed. Here the spirit of the method, as described in the beginning of this chapter, is quintessential. The psychologist offers the client the possibility of a thorough investigation based on commitment, cooperation, and shared responsibility, and the client draws from this relation strength and inspiration to move forward. Moreover, the good psychologist follows the client, and is sensitive enough to make the right interventions at the right moment.

Individuals with a particularly dysfunctional self (see Chapter 6) may also profit from such a dialogue. When a client feels unable to move in a desirable direction, the psychologist may be able to take the role of the client by concentrating on the structure of the valuation system and helping him or her gradually move to a point where self-motivated change is possible.

Promoting the Process of Change

Assessment and process promotion are closely related aspects of the self-confrontation method. Additionally, the modality analysis is an example of how one can gradually move from assessment to change. It is a technique that links the client's individual and spontaneous valuations to those themes that play a central role in the development of the self. As we have seen, the theme that results from the modality analysis functions as a guiding principle for the activities and initiatives in the validation/invalidation process. Clients run through three phases that mark the gradual transition from assessment to change. As we saw in Linda's example, the client's own formulations are the basic material of this process.

The fact that the client's own valuations are at the center of the valuation process does not exclude the possibility that the psychologist may formulate alternative statements and offer them to the client as supplemental valuations to be incorporated into the system. It should be understood that such valuations cannot be completely created for a client because the psychologist never knows for certain what the client will see as a relevant or meaningful piece of information. Thus, offered valuations are possible valuations from the client's point of view, and their transformation into personal valuations has to be explicitly examined (e.g., by relating them to spontaneous valuations and studying their affective profile). In the following paragraphs we summarize several types of provided valuations we have explored in our research.

Supplemental Proverbs

Thomas Carlyle once said that there may be more spiritual power in a single proverb than in a total philosophical school. Or, as Joseph Roux put it, "A short bang on the target, that must a proverb be." With these striking characterizations two main similarities between a proverb and a supplemental valuation can be sketched. Both represent a contraction of a story, and both are expressions of particularly meaningful experiences, with the difference being that proverbs have become part of the collective stories of a culture whereas valuations remain a part of the personal story.

The following question may then, of course, be raised: What happens when personal and collective meanings meet? Or, more specifically, in what way can a valuation system be affected by a proverb? Once again, however, this question cannot be directly answered because one never knows the extent to which a proverb has meaning for a particular individual. In other words, one must have some guarantee that the proverb has an affective appeal to the subject.

With this idea in mind, we presented a heterogeneous set of 35 proverbs from various philosophers, artists, and writers to a group of clients at the end of the valuation construction phase (Hermans & Hermans-Jansen, 1978). We then asked the clients to select a proverb that particularly appealed to them and one that they particularly disliked. The clients were then invited to include both or one of the statements in their self-investigation. One client chose the following statements:

- "Art of living: Being satisfied with a minimum, treating it as the maximum" (appreciated proverb).
- "Keeping up appearances is the most expensive affair in the world" (disliked proverb).

In his second self-investigation, 2½ months later, this client added a new valuation to his system: "I try to keep up appearances but don't feel at all good about it." Moreover, this client was found to have modified some of his remaining valuations in the direction of the proverb. For example, at Time 1 he said, "I rebel against the people who are closest to me and confront me" whereas at Time 2 he admitted, "I fight with myself because I see myself as insincere." Observe that the disliked proverb was incorporated into the valuation system at Time 2, even though a content analysis of the system at Time 1 showed no evidence of spontaneous valuations relevant to the theme of keeping up appearances. The client transformed the third-person formulation of the proverb at Time 1 into a first-person formulation of the valuation at Time 2 presumably because he strongly related to the proverb provided. In other words, the proverb provided a central theme that had a reordering influence on the system as a whole. Admittedly, the influence of a single proverb was rather exceptional in this case, but we can nevertheless learn from it. External formulations have the power to supplement the system and in some cases lead to a major reorganization around a theme that was previously not explicit.

Nonverbal material or symbols also have an important role to play in supplementing the valuation system and giving it a new impulse. Hermans and Van Loon (1991) have experimented with the symbol of the tree, which has the capacity to evoke a variety of different and even contradictory valuations and therefore can function as a suitable means to study opposite aspects of human valuation. A woman performed two self-investigations, one before and another after a weekend workshop organized around the symbol of the tree. As part of the procedure, participants were invited to articulate their personal association to the symbol of the tree in both investigations. In the first investigation the woman offered the following (Valuation 1): "A bare tree is a symbol of nakedness, receptivity, and fertility." This valuation had the highest correlation with a valuation (Valuation 2) she offered that referred to people to whom she felt attracted: "I feel attracted to people who have a certain calmness and intensity." After the workshop, in which members of the training group discussed and exchanged their interpretations with the other participants, the woman formulated a new, more idiosyncratic, valuation (Valuation 3) of the tree as a means to face an incident of rape earlier in her life: "Letting mud go through me until there is only pure food (task of a birch)." This valuation, in which she strongly identified with the tree, had the highest correlation with a new valuation (Valuation 4) that was not included in the first investigation: "I was raped and I didn't know it for a long time; I now feel able to face it." In this case we can see how the tree, taken up in the valuation system and discussed in the training group, functioned as a concrete tool for facing an unresolved experience in the past. Whereas in Valuation 1 the woman talked about the tree in a rather impersonal way, the tree in Valuation 3 was merged with her own body and played a part in a process of purification. As we have argued (Hermans & Van Loon, 1991), symbols (e.g., tree, way, cave) have the capacity to give form to divergent and even opposite experiences in the self and to contribute to their integration. Valuations evoked by symbols represent the embodied nature of human existence and function as routes toward new meaning structures.[5]

Valuations Constructed and Supplied by the Psychologist

Whereas a proverb, or any part of a collective story, typically has an impersonal tone, a valuation supplied to a client by the psychologist may be of a more personal nature. In a previous study (Hermans, 1981), a client consulted a psychotherapist (Els Hermans-Jansen) with regard to some problems he was having with his wife. After some sessions the psychotherapist had the growing conviction that it would be good for the client to talk with his wife about the problems. The client, however, would not agree to do this and explained that his wife did not even know that he was in psychotherapy. After some discussion of this point the psychotherapist and client agreed to include in the self-investigation a valuation formulated by the psychologist (and pertaining to the problem at hand). Valuation 1 was phrased in this way: "The psychotherapist does not feel at ease about the fact that my wife does not know that I come here." The client was then invited to phrase his own statement (Valuation 2) regarding the significance of the supplied statement. "I am not able to discuss this problem with my wife without conflict." This statement was then scored on the standardized set of affect terms, like all the other spontaneous valuations, and the highest correlation was found to be with the following two statements (Valuations 3 and 4, respectively): "I feel so limited in what I can do with my wife that I can't do the things I would like to do; this has accumulated over a long period of time so that I suddenly discharge myself" and "I always panicked when my mother started grumbling; I still try to avoid this."

In these uttterances we can see that the problem in the psychologist–client interaction, once it was made explicit, exemplified a problem in the interaction between the client and his partner and that this problem, in turn, had a historical relation to the mother–child interaction. With a modality analysis these sentences revealed a common theme, which could be taken up as a guide in the following therapy sessions.

This example reflects what one could call the "dramatization of human experience": The contraction of a part of an individual's history into a limited number of meaningful statements constitutes a self-story, and this story reveals a central theme. Six weeks later, the client in this example formulated a new valuation (Valuation 5) in a second investigation: "When my wife grumbles and it is her problem, I let her try and solve it and just try to stay out of things." The conspicuous thing here is that Valuation 5 is not simply a modification of Valuation 3 or 4; instead, the client, having recognized the common meanings in the valuations, phrased a new valuation in terms of both Valuation 3 and Valuation 4.

When the question of the most productive way of phrasing things for a client is debated, we would probably find that psychologists working in different ways and in different settings have their own ideas. The essential point to be made here, however, is that a valuation offered by the psychologist, if chosen carefully, may have a pervasive impact on the valuation system of a client and may thereby contribute to the process of change aimed at in a self-confrontation.

Evaluation

The evaluative function of the self-confrontation method depends in part on the results of the qualitative and quantitative analyses of the second and any successive self-investigations. These analyses provide a review of the constancies and changes in the client's valuation system. We saw that in Linda's case, the second self-investigation included several elements referring to the validation/invalidation process that were evaluated as contributing to the system as a whole.

The meaning of self-confrontation and the therapeutic contact can also be evaluated specifically through the introduction of supplemental standardized valuations into the system. In order to demonstrate this procedure, we will give one example in which the attempt to promote change was succcessful and one in which it was not. In the successful case a relatively high number of valuations in the system changed, resulting in a reversal from the first to the second investigation of the P–N difference for the general feeling. In the unsuccessful case there was little change and no reversal of the P–N difference.

Evaluation of a Successful Promotion of Change: An Example

For evaluation purposes the psychologist can phrase a limited number of the relevant aspects of the therapeutic situation and introduce these into the client's valuation system. In our research we have worked with two comparative aspects phrased in a standardized way.

	S	O	P	N
Valuation 1. "My self-confrontation"	13	7	13	7
Valuation 2. "The sessions with the psychologist [or insert the psychologist's name]"	16	14	15	6

These phrases were offered to the client in the second self-investigation as provided valuations. They were then scored with the same standard set of affect terms used with the spontaneous valuations.

In the analyses the valuation concerning the individual's self-confrontation (Valuation 1) was selected as the pivotal valuation in the modality analysis; it correlated with all of the other valuations in the system. The highest correlation ($r = .79$) was found with the following spontaneous valuation:

	S	O	P	N
Valuation 3. "I don't let myself get carried away by my internal sense of duty."	13	5	14	2

The valuation concerning the sessions with the psychologist (Valuation 2) was then correlated with all of the other valuations. The spontaneous valuation correlating highest ($r = .84$) with the pivotal valuation was found to be the following:

	S	O	P	N
Valuation 4. "I feel connected to people who strive for real love."	14	16	16	7

Several things can be observed in connection with this example. First, the offered self-confrontation valuation, with S > O, appeals specifically to the S motive whereas the valuation offered about the sessions with the psychologist (with both S and O high) appears to appeal to both motives. That is, there are two complementary aspects to the therapeutic situation from a motivational point of view: the relation with oneself (Valuation 3) and the relation with the other (Valuation 4). In addition, the highest correlations with the provided valuations in both cases involved dynamically formulated valuations (3 and 4). This is an indication that the method of self-confrontation and the associated sessions with the therapist indeed have a dynamic character and that the client indeed experiences the process aspect of the method.

Evaluation of an Unsuccessful Promotion of Change: An Example

In the unsuccessful case both psychologist and client wondered after 4 months of working together if there had been any change in the client's valuation system and decided to evaluate the progress. The standardized statements were found to have the following scores:

	S	O	P	N
Valuation 1. "My self-confrontation"	12	4	6	13
Valuation 2. "The sessions with the therapist"	11	4	6	16

The highest correlation ($r = .79$) with "My self-confrontation" was the following spontaneous valuation:

	S	O	P	N
Valuation 3. "I think a lot about myself, and I don't find that healthy."	15	4	4	12

The spontaneous valuation with the highest correlation ($r = .86$) with "The sessions with the therapist" was the following:

	S	O	P	N
Valuation 4. "I have the feeling that I don't belong to the world; I am standing on the outside asking the questions."	11	4	4	13

As can be seen from the indices for both the offered and the spontaneous valuation in the first correlation (Valuations 1 and 3), the client is involved in a self-confrontation that has the same affective mode as the valuation "Thinking about myself is unhealthy." This means that the client both wants and does not want a self-confrontation and thereby blocks the entire process. The picture is similar for the sessions with the therapist: The high correspondence in the affective patterns of the offered and spontaneous valuations ($r = .86$) suggests that the client feels alone, and this is the reason for needing contact with the therapist.

In all of the aforementioned valuations (1, 2, 3, and 4) we see a particular pattern of scores (which will be discussed in depth in the following chapter), namely, the combination of S > O and N > P. This pattern is characteristic of valuations associated with some degree of opposition or conflict and, therefore, with an aggressive feeling or tone. In the content of Valuations 3 and 4, this opposition or protest is rather implicit and may play an important role in the client–therapist interaction without the client actually being aware of this. Such an organization, therefore, creates a paradoxical situation: The client asks for psychotherapeutic assistance in the expectation of self-enhancement and then tries to arrive at self-enhancement by resisting that assistance (note the high S scores). However, we can only understand this paradox if we consider the meaning of the therapy for the client, who may have a low level of self-awareness and is therefore not conscious of this aspect of the self-confrontation. Concretely, the affective pattern of responses points to information (implicit in the valuations) that is blocking the intended process of change. By making this information explicit, we obtained information other than that in the content of the valuations and thereby fostered a more complete self-narrative and, hopefully, the opportunity for change.

These cases of a successful and an unsuccessful promotion of change center around what can be metaphorically viewed as a process of finding an entrance into the valuation system. It is assumed that possible meanings that are sent from the situation of self-confrontation to the individual and that arouse some affective response have somehow entered into the valuation system. However, the door of this entrance is not always open. In the psychotherapeutic situation, finding such an open door is of vital importance, but this is not always easy because the resistance from the client may be beyond awareness and control. A timely evaluation procedure may, therefore, provide the psychologist and client with the information needed to catalyze the change process or at least to reduce the level of resistance.

It is assumed in valuation theory that the therapist is not necessarily a significant other but is certainly a representative of one or more significant others. And some of these significant others, in self-confrontation terms, may represent possible entrances into the valuation system of a particular individual. Contact with the psychologist may evoke memories of previous contacts with significant others and may thereby open one entrance to the client's valuation system. As psychoanalysis has extensively shown, the meaning of a particular significant other may be reactualized by the current situation and, as a consequence, gives rise to the phenomenon of transference. Valuation theory assumes that the concept of a significant other is a broad one that includes parents, siblings, uncles, aunts, teachers, friends, colleagues, and even groups of people. (In our "unsuccessful" example of promotion of change the therapist was representative of "the entire world" from which the client felt separated.) In the present framework, transference can be methodologically translated into the similarity of the affective modalities associated with the therapist and a significant other (whether this be a partner, a friend, a colleague, or even a pet). Note, however, that this connection is not necessarily fixed. Various significant others may be represented by the same therapist; that is, as stories about the past unfold, and as various significant others are confronted, the psychotherapist is given yet another face.

In sum, the assessment, process-promoting, and evaluation functions of the self-confrontation method correspond with the three main phases of the IVI cycle (investigation, validation/invalidation, investigation), as summarized in Table 3.1 in the beginning of this chapter. As we have seen in the case study, the self-confrontation method combines two types of analyses, qualitative and quantitative ones. The qualitative analysis refers to the content of the valuations in the individual's self-narrative, which represent the manifest level of functioning. The quantitative analysis is used to get a clearer view of the affective organization of the valuation system from the perspective of the latent level.[6]

NOTES

1. A distinction can be made between intensity and frequency in the level of affect (for more on this distinction, see Diener, 1984). Discussions with clients reveal that some prefer to rate their affect on the basis of frequency, others on the basis of inten-

sity. The problem becomes even more complex when one and the same client prefers frequency for one valuation and intensity for another. There are even indications that within one and the same valuation, one affect invites scoring on frequency and another invites scoring on intensity. We have concluded that it is quite difficult to solve this problem without making the methodology highly complex. Moreover, the theoretical importance of this distinction for valuation research and practice is not self-evident. In the combination of valuation and affect, the focus is not so much on frequency or intensity but on the experiential relevance of a particular affect for a particular valuation. For that reason we have used broad indications (not at all, to some extent, etc.) that allow frequency as well as intensity scoring or some mixture of both.

2. Filling in the matrix can be done by paper and pencil or by working on a computer. In the computer program CONFRON (Van Gilst & Hermans, 1988) valuations formulated in the preceding part of the therapy session are entered and stored. The program then successively presents each affect term in combination with each valuation and upon completion of the matrix computes all of the indices to be used in later analyses.

In a previous study (Hermans, Hermans-Jansen, & Van Gilst, 1985b) a special computer program was written that assisted the client in formulating the valuations themselves. These formulations were compared with valuations from the same clients made in interaction with a psychologist. Although the number of clients was small ($N = 5$), the valuations were found to differ dramatically. The valuations made in collaboration with the psychologist were generally clearer, more differentiated, and more communicable, whereas the valuations made with the computer program were less structured and sometimes less socially acceptable. It was concluded that the two methods cannot be used interchangeably.

3. Since the affect terms are compared across the valuations, the general feeling and ideal feeling are excluded from the calculation of the means. With reference to the general and ideal feeling there is another point that deserves special attention. As we have explained, the discrepancy between general and ideal feeling is an indication for well-being. In order to get a more complete picture, however, this indication must be supplemented by the relation between positive and negative affect as typical of the system as a whole, that is, by the means of index P as compared with index N. Note that these means are based on the affective component of *all* valuations, whereas the affective modalities of the general and ideal feeling represent the two final rows of the matrix. The indications of well-being as discussed here give different information about well-being and therefore may deviate from one another in some cases. For example, a person who has felt bad for a while (general feeling is negative) may nevertheless have a relatively large number of positive valuations in the system as a whole (mean P > mean N). In such a case, one specific valuation (a negative one) has a temporarily strong generalization in the system whereas the generalization of the other (positive) valuations is temporarily reduced. Most typically, the general feeling, as sensitive to the immediate life situation, gives a short-term picture of well-being, whereas the means of P and N provides a more long-term structure.

4. The indices described were psychometrically analyzed with a group of 43 students (20 men, 23 women) and a group of 40 clients (20 men, 20 women). In the student group the reliabilities (coefficient alpha) of the S, O, P, and N indices were .83, .86, .85, and .88, respectively. The correlation between S and O was .27, and the correlation

between P and N was −.79. In the client group the reliabilities of the S, O, P, and N indices were .83, .89, .93, and .91, respectively. The correlation between S and O was .64, and the correlation between P and N was −.70. When the groups were compared, clients showed lower S scores ($p < .001$), lower O scores ($p < .05$), lower P scores ($p < .001$), and higher N scores ($p < .001$). No differences were found between men and women. (For an analysis of the validity of index r, see Hermans, 1987b, pp. 169–171.) The validity of the S and O affect terms was checked by presenting 127 valuations from different clients to five judges who read the content of the valuations with no information on the affective properties as indicated by the clients. The judges then rated the valuations for the extent the content reflected self-enhancement or contact and union with the other. The interrater reliability of the five judges was .86 (coefficient alpha). When the ratings of the judges were compared with the affective ratings of the clients, it was found that valuations that were rated by the judges as expressing self-enhancement had clearly higher S affect than O affect. In contrast, valuations that were judged as expressing contact and union had higher O than S affect (Hermans, Hermans-Jansen, & Van Gilst, 1985a). The validity of P and N affect terms can be checked simply by comparing them on the so-called ideal feeling. It is expected and repeatedly found that all affect terms labeled as positive have higher scores on the ideal feeling than the affect terms labeled as negative. Note that all these findings are on the group level. On the individual level there exist deviant findings that can be detected and further explored for their psychological significance.

    5. Van Loon (1992) studied the symbol of "the way," which plays such an important role in Tao philosophy (Tao is "the way of nature," the ordering principle in the universe). Symbols of this kind (e.g., way, tree, cave) can be considered as elements of pictorial valuations as opposed to conceptual valuations. (See also the dream investigations in Chapter 5.)

    6. The IVI cycle is not only applicable to the psychotherapeutic process but also to the scientific process. Scientist-practitioners work on the basis of reflection-in-action, that is, reflecting on their practice in an investigation (I), changing their practice through action (V), and returning to a reflective investigation (I) again. The attending-creating-anchoring (ACA) cycle also is applicable to the scientific process. Scientists-practitioners develop an unusual concentration on or attention to the problem at hand (A), discover something relevant as part of a creative act (C), and then need time to anchor the discovery in their own mind and in the collective mind of the scientific or professional institution (A). In essence, both cycles are the same for psychologist and client and express the basic similarity between scientists and laypersons as reflective investigators of reality.

    The basic metaphor of the person as scientist also underlies Kelly's (1955) personal construct psychology. The difference in our approaches is that Kelly conceived this metaphor primarily in terms of hypothesis testing and prediction whereas we consider this metaphor as embedded in a psychology of storytelling. The potentials of a narrative approach did not, however, fully escape Kelly's visionary attention. As Mair (1989) has argued, there are narrative elements in Kelly's basic position, and his later essays in particular (Maher, 1969) are of a narrative kind.

CHAPTER 4

The Nature of Valuation:
Structure and Process

I am always inwardly strengthened in my course and steeled against the
loss of my actual social self by the thought of other and better possible
social judges than those whose verdict goes against me now.
                                                            —William James

In the foregoing chapters it was argued that the rich phenomenological variation of valuations is rooted in a limited set of basic motives on a more latent level. And in the application of the self-confrontation method we see that these basic motives are typically expressed in the affective component of a valuation. In the present chapter we describe some general types of valuation, which reflect the organizational structure of the person's valuation system, and possible changes of valuation from one type to another. In describing these types we elucidate the social and imaginative nature of human valuation. Special attention is devoted to the "imaginal figure," which represents the imaginative quality of narrative particularly well. Finally, some implications for mental health are discussed.

The types of valuation to be discussed in this chapter are summarized in Figure 4.1. They can be conceived of as major themes (though not the only ones) in the personal stories people tell about themselves. The same classification will appear later in this book when types of collective stories are presented (Chapter 5) and types of dysfunctions of the self are discussed (Chapter 6).

THE AUTONOMOUS QUALITY
OF SELF-ENHANCEMENT

We have designated the form of valuation that typically represents a high degree of autonomy and productive coping with the environment as +S. Valua-

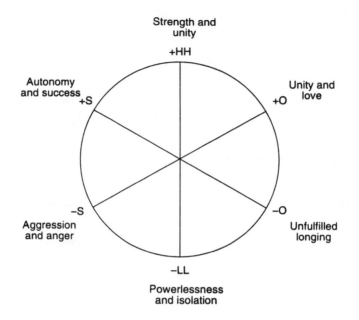

FIGURE 4.1. Types of valuation (+S, positive self-enhancement; –S, negative self-enhancement; +O, positive contact with others; –O, negative contact with others; +HH, positive combination of high self-enhancement and high contact with others; and –LL, negative combination of low self-enhancement and low contact with others).

tions of this type are associated with more self-enhancement affect than affect referring to contact and union with another, and at the same time these valuations are associated with more positive than negative affect. (The indication +S means that the emphasis is on S rather than O and on positive rather than negative affect.) There are as many phenomenological variations of this type as there are individuals. Sometimes these valuations can be as simple as the following:

	S	O	P	N
"I enjoy making things or repairing things."	20	1	17	3
"I hope to achieve a better position through my evening courses."	17	4	12	4

Sometimes people find a more complicated and less transparent route to self-enhancement:

	S	O	P	N
"During vacation I took over the responsibilities from my parents because I knew the language, and I made contact with other people through my sisters."	13	1	17	5

Although these valuations are from three different clients, they all have one thing in common: These clients see themselves as the autonomous source of self-enhancement. They have the conviction that they can influence the situation, produce a favorable outcome, and enjoy a certain degree of self-esteem under these circumstances. It would be a serious oversimplification, however, to view self-enhancement as merely the experiencing of the positive outcome of one's own efforts and initiatives. The phenomenon of self-enhancement can only properly be understood when we take seriously the principle of reflection (Rosenberg, 1979), which states that people view themselves the way they think others view them. Thus, even when people have the expectation that they are capable of something, they are still more or less dependent on how they perceive others to respond to their achievements. Some people mention this explicitly in their valuations:

	S	O	P	N
"My work is challenging because it involves solving problems, achieving, and being recognized. A strong positive appreciation must be present."	14	5	15	4

In some instances, this dependence on the judgment of others predominates in the self to such a degree that a valuation with a high degree of self-enhancement can become extremely negative, indicating anxious worrying about the reactions and expectations of others:

	S	O	P	N
"After a reading, I received a positive reaction and applause from the school principals: 'The smartest we've ever had.' Oh, if I can only live up to this! When will they discover the reality?"[1]	16	0	4	17

In this valuation a brief moment of self-confidence is quickly associated with anxiety, in part because the individual realizes that the present recognition of his achievement implies greater expectations for the future. As long as people dwell on the opinion of the other, a strong belief in their own capacities may not evolve. As this example shows, the content (i.e., the formulation) of the valuation must be taken into account when interpreting the significance of the affective index. The simple presence of self-enhancement affect does not mean much if one does not examine the content—or, even better, the valuation system as a whole, as we will see later. Put differently, valuations showing the same degree of self-enhancement may differ in the degree of autonomy associated with them. It is often the content of the valuation that informs us about the nature of the valuation. Consider, for example, the content of the following valuation, from which we see that some people are more capable of resisting, relativizing, or postponing the other's applause:

	S	O	P	N
"I learned a lot during a period of nonsuccess, from the fact that there were people who did not value my behavior and ambition. I am aware that I don't always fit into social value-systems."	17	8	13	10

Apparently, experiences of self-enhancement may differ in the degree to which they get internalized: A high degree of internalization represents an inner strength that allows a person to be less dependent on support from the immediate situation. People with a low degree of internalization are highly dependent on feedback from others and typically need to be told continuously that they are doing well or are good; conversely, any form of negative feedback is threatening to their self-esteem.

According to Becker (1971), we are constantly running an "inner newsreel" containing all of the symbols of self-esteem. In a scenario in which the most minor events are recorded and in which the most subtle gradations in the things that make us feel good about ourselves take on immense proportions, we are constantly testing and rehearsing who we are. Becker refers to the movie *Requiem for a Heavyweight,* in which Anthony Quinn plays a man who in order to maintain his self-esteem is constantly reminding himself and others that he was once the "fifth-ranking contender for the heavyweight crown." This made him feel important, gave him continual nourishment, and allowed him to hold his head up under the shabbiest of circumstances. In a sense, this character's life was a constant attempt to internalize one particularly relevant, particularly positive extension of the self.

When valuations express an overreliance on others and on external reflections of the self, such as in the following valuations (all made by the same client), it is important to try to move the valuation system in the direction of greater internalization.

	S	O	P	N
"I really enjoy having achieved something, knowing that it's good, and knowing that others also think this."	11	4	17	10
"I spend a lot of time worrying about what others think of me."	13	8	11	10
"I *have* to achieve something in order not to disappoint family and friends."	5	6	5	11

Psychologist and client worked on this overreliance on external evaluations, and 3 months later the following temporally structured valuation was created:

	S	O	P	N
"At first things caught me by surprise, and I made decisions on the spot. Now I am planning, and I finish things. When there are interrupting tasks, I do them, provided that they don't interfere with what I plan. I am not merely adapting to others."	17	9	8	4

This valuation illustrates a clear transition from an external to a more internal locus of self-enhancement. The individual came to realize that self-enhancement and conformity to others' expectations are not identical.

It is assumed that the more internalized a valuation is, the more flexible it is with regard to the extensions of the self. This makes for the difference in, for example, the reactions of two people who have both lost their job: One reacts with finality ("This is the end of my career") whereas the other has courage and confidence ("Now I will have to use my abilities in some other way"). Whereas the externalized self-enhancement shows a fixed reliance on specific extensions and, moreover, is in constant need of confirmation, the internalized self-enhancement has a more autonomous quality and a broader range of available extensions.[2]

Valuations of the +S type are of special importance for the notion of change because they indicate the ability to form a "naked self-enhancement" valuation (i.e., not—or not yet—mitigated by the longing for contact and union). It is this type of valuation that clients typically lack at the onset of counseling or therapy, a valuation they need to find their own way in life. In the practice of the self-confrontation method a typical finding is that clients include in the second self-investigation, in the case of a successful validation/invalidation process, a greater amount of +S valuations than before. Experiences of contact and union may, of course, play a crucial role in facilitating the process of change, but the first manifestations of this change in the developing valuation system are more in terms of increased S than O affect.

OPPOSITION: ANGER AND HATE AS DEFENSIVE FORMS OF SELF-ENHANCEMENT

Valuations of the −S type have more self-enhancement affect than affect associated with contact and union with the other (S > O), and at the same time they are more negative than positive (N > P). As already noted, this affective pattern can indicate an anxiety-based overreliance on the opinions of others, or, more generally, it can reflect negative implications of self-enhancement (e.g., being punished for acting in a strong way). In the majority of the cases, however, it indicates some kind of opposition in which individuals feel opposed to somebody or something that is threatening their self-esteem and are therefore, with stress, trying to defend their position (e.g., they make themselves strong in situations where their self-esteem is threatened).

At first sight it may seem strange to observe that a high level of S affect (which is usually experienced in a positive way) coexists with a high level of N affect. Indeed, what is found here is that S affect (such as self-esteem, strength, etc.) emerges in a negative context. The easiest way to understand this is to imagine a situation in which a person is furious or outraged. In such a state a person may feel an enormous strength and clench both fists, but at the same time there is a very negative feeling of anger, disappointment, or even powerlessness. A high S and high N go together here in forming the specific quality of the −S experience.

The self-enhancement motive was originally defined as the need for self-maintenance and self-expansion. In support of this definition we have found in the practice of self-investigation the existence of +S valuations. These valuations are mainly expressions of self-expansion (i.e., pride in the realization of particular plans and goals) in which any resistance from the environment is seen as a challenge rather than as a major block (the reason these valuations are typically positive). In contrast, −S valuations typically reflect the need for self-maintenance, self-defense, or self-expansion in situations where there is a serious blockage of the person's attempts at self-enhancement. It is characteristic of −S valuations that the attempts at self-enhancement are not stopped but instead continue or are even reinforced by blockages or frustrations. (For extensive discussion of –S affect, see Hermans, 1992b.)

The most frequent versions of type –S valuations suggest, in one way or another, that the person is against others (either an individual or a group) who are felt to be dominating opponents.[3]

	S	O	P	N
"I am opposed to those people who want to decide for me what I must do."	15	0	3	16
"I don't want my parents to meddle with affairs that concern me."	10	0	2	12

The experience of aggression is also usually found in –S valuations, suggesting that anger and feeling aggressive can be understood as expressions of the (sometimes implicit) attempt to restore a threatened self-enhancement:

	S	O	P	N
"I experience terrible aggression and powerlessness when I expect to have a grip on a situation and the power of others prevails."	17	0	3	16

After discovering that anger and feeling aggressive are typical of –S valuations, we wondered whether the emotion of hate could also be found in this type of valuation. We were particularly interested in this emotion for two reasons. First, since hate is generally seen in our culture as an unacceptable emotion, we wondered whether people would even be willing to include it in a self-investigation. Second, although hate is phenomenologically related to anger and feeling aggressive, it may also differ from these emotions. A person who is angry or aggressive may be strongly antagonistic toward someone and may even want to harm or attack that person; such feelings are also inherent in hate. The difference, however, is that in anger or in feeling aggressive the possibility of restoration of disturbed contact is not entirely excluded. Hate, however, implies (certainly at the moments one is entirely in the grip of this passion) the complete and definite negation or even destruction of the other. In this sense, hate is the end of a dialogue.

Starting from these considerations, we selected out all those valuations from various clients that included the term *hate* and then examined the affective profiles associated with these valuations. Here is a valuation from a man who felt his whole being was violated by his father:

	S	O	P	N
"I felt anxiety . . . opposition . . . hate when I was 16 years old. I was acknowledged only as part of my father's ego ('Those are *my* children') . . . hate."	13	3	2	11

Although this client explicitly mentioned his hatred of his father, the experience of hate has generally a culturally unacceptable quality. Although our cultural heritage includes a prohibition against hating our fellow humans, from a motivational perspective wishing another dead can maintain a certain degree of self-esteem. The conflict between feeling hatred toward someone or something and knowing that this is not allowed is, in psychoanalytic terms, a typical id–superego conflict. This conflict can be resolved or avoided simply by excluding the hateful valuation from the system. This line of reasoning led us to suspect that many people really do at times hate others but do not dare to include this in their personal stories. We therefore asked several clients who did not make any spontaneous reference to a hateful attitude in their self-investigation whether they could describe a personal situation that might give rise to the experience of hate. They were then asked to score this valuation on the standardized set of affect terms. We followed this procedure with ten clients and found that eight of them were able to refer to an experience of hate in their own life and give a short description of the situation leading up to this emotion. For example:

	S	O	P	N
"My best friend went out with my girlfriend."	8	1	2	18

The client was then asked to rate, more specifically, the experience of hate:

	S	O	P	N
"I felt hate."	18	1	3	12

We found the experience of hate tended to belong to −S valuations and, like anger, to represent a defensive form of self-maintenance, although hate is an experience of a more extreme kind.

In one case a client reported strikingly low S scores, suggesting a weak hate experience:

	S	O	P	N
Valuation 1. "A friend who owed me a lot accused me of doing things I had actually never done."	4	3	4	14
Valuation 2. "I felt hate."	5	0	2	18

Why was the level of S affect so low in this case? Was it because the client actually felt no fierce hate, or was she simply using a strong word for a weak emotion that lacked a venomous character? We asked her to imagine someone who had experienced hate, and she then provided the following affect pattern:

	S	O	P	N
Valuation 3. "That person feels hate."	14	0	0	8

This pattern of findings suggests that the client was able to imagine a powerful degree of hate (as indicated by the high level of S in Valuation 3), even though she did not report it to that degree for her own experience (low level of S in Valuations 1 and 2). This suggests that she is familiar with the affective characteristics of hate but at the same time mitigates or even suppresses this experience when it pertains to herself.

This finding brings us to a phenomenon that plays a significant role in the practice of self-investigation: the discrepancy between text and affect, or a particular affect pattern that is not in agreement with the formulation of a valuation. Such a discrepancy, which can be found in all types of valuations, frequently occurs in −S valuations. In the following valuation one would not expect such a high level of S affect:

	S	O	P	N
"Laura [a colleague] accuses me of not being involved enough, of not fighting as much for my personnel as for myself."	12	1	3	13

One would expect an accusation to lead perhaps to a reduced level of self-esteem. If we take the affective pattern here seriously, however, it must be indicative of some implicit (defensive) need for self-maintenance. In order to check this, we went on to perform a modality analysis with this valuation as the pivot. The highest correlation ($r = .87$) was found with the following valuation:

	S	O	P	N
"I oppose the managers; I find them stupid and hypocritical. Moreover, they don't listen to me."	8	1	0	16

In this valuation there is an explicit reference to a feeling of opposition. Indeed, the high correlation between the two valuations suggests that the affective pattern associated with the pivot valuation also contains a large element of opposition. Thus, one can use modality analyses (and content analyses of the system as a whole) to study the occurrence of implicit meanings.

For a particular individual, −S valuations (explicit or implicit) may even come to play a central role in the valuation system as a whole. This is indicated by a high proportion of −S valuations in the system and their high correlations with the general feeling. There are primarily two main reasons for such a predominance of −S valuations. First, the person may be in a particularly stressful situation, requiring that he or she be on the defense against threatening forces. In this case it can be expected that when the situation becomes more relaxed, −S valuations will make room for other types of valuations. Second, −S valuations may have a rigid character; that is, they have become a permanent part of the system. This means that even when the source of threat has disappeared, the valuation system does not correspondingly change. In fact, people may sometimes even seek or create oppositional situations, in part because this is the only way they can gain some degree of self-enhancement. Thus, we might guess that a person with a predominance of −S valuations at one time may be very unsure of the outcome of other attempts at self-enhancement. This phenomenon can often be observed in adolescents as part of a transient developmental stage, but we may also find it in a more rigid form in adults who experience struggle as the central part of their existence (see Other-Directed Hostility, Chapter 6).

When the pattern of −S valuations is in essence indicative of a defensive and negatively felt striving for self-maintenance, one can expect the individual to move toward a more positive form of self-enhancement after going through a well-guided validation/invalidation period. Starting from this assumption, we followed in three successive self-investigations over a period of 1½ years (more extensively reported in Hermans, 1987a) the valuation system of a woman with serious identity problems. The following is a valuation offered early in her therapy:

	S	O	P	N
"Because I expressed my opinion and was therefore seen as impudent, my father hit me."	13	1	0	16

The client came to realize in the following sessions that she herself created an oppositional attitude not only in relation to her father but in relation to other people as well. She then tried, with the help of the psychologist, to express her opinion *in the right situation and at the right moment.* A year later the original valuation was modified as follows:

	S	O	P	N
"When I feel that there is understanding and an opportunity for discussion, I can express my opinion."	16	2	13	0

This change from a −S to a +S valuation suggests that a certain level of self-esteem, originally attainable in only a negative way, can be obtained in a more positive manner. However, as long as people see no alternative route to self-enhancement, they may cling to oppositional and aggressively tuned interactions at the expense of their own well-being, and they may continue this for some time because they do not know whether a more positive approach can maintain or enhance their self-esteem to the same degree.

UNITY AND LOVE: BEYOND SELF-ESTEEM

Valuations of the +O type have more affect referring to contact and union with another than affect referring to self-enhancement (O > S) and more positive than negative affect (P > N). At first sight it may seem strange that valuations with a strongly reduced degree of self-esteem (i.e., low S), may be experienced as positive. However, the existence of positive affect does not depend completely on fulfillment of the self-enhancement motive; positive feelings can also arise from realizing the O motive. More concretely, the existence of +O valuations indicates that a diminished degree of self-enhancement can be positive when it opens the gate to increased contact and union with something else (a person, group, animal, object, or the surrounding world in general). The positive feelings then result from greater fulfillment of the O motive than from decreasing fulfillment of the S motive.

In the category of +O valuations we can find, for example, esthetic experiences:

	S	O	P	N
"I enjoy singing with a group of people, being together without any pressure."	4	13	19	0

The need for contact and union with another can also be satisfied by intense contact with the environment:

	S	O	P	N
"I enjoy elder-blossoms, the smell of hay, and the silence."	7	17	15	1

Valuations pertaining to a religious belief or a particular philosophical view of the world are also often related to the positive fulfillment of the need for contact and union with the other.

	S	O	P	N
"With religious beliefs I try to provide a basis for my life: Zen meditation and the book of Etty Hillesum [a Dutch mystic writer]."	4	13	18	2

There is, of course, also fulfillment of the need for contact and union with the other through the experience of comfort or consolation. Such experiences often give relief not only from the strain of individual mastery and control but also from extreme grief. In the following example, a woman in a long, childless marriage felt guilty about an abortion. Just before his death, her husband, who knew about the abortion but had never directly discussed it with her, made a statement that she later remembered and rehearsed internally for comfort.

	S	O	P	N
"I was happy that Peter, before he died, said, 'It's unfortunate that we decided to do it this way.'"	5	20	14	3

This statement allowed the woman to feel that she was not solely responsible for the abortion.

Valuations of the +O type typically have a receptive quality to them. That is, a certain degree of openness is required for intensified contact to occur. A receptive attitude, moreover, may develop into a giving or caring attitude when a person who has been sensitive to the worth of another is motivated to protect or increase the well-being of the other. For example:

	S	O	P	N
"I want to give my child warmth and a home."	9	18	14	5

Similarly, a subtle balance between giving and receiving is often part of the fulfillment of the need for contact and union with the other:

	S	O	P	N
"I will wait patiently until my wife feels the need to approach me physically."	4	13	12	6

Sexual experiences, particularly those with a receptive attitude, also often belong to the +O category:

	S	O	P	N
"I really enjoy being completely passive when in bed with my girlfriend, to be spoiled by her and not have to worry about being active."	0	15	19	1

Note, however, that this sexual experience is of quite a different motivational nature than sexual contact enjoyed as a self-enhancing activity:

	S	O	P	N
"I feel like a complete woman if I can determine when a man has his orgasm."	14	8	20	1

Sexuality, in general, does not exclusively belong to one of the motivational types discussed in this chapter. Rather, there may be as many variants of sexual experience as there are types of valuations, and a variety of forms may occur together within the same individual.

Valuations of the +O type are an important part of the experiential palette for at least two reasons. First of all, they show a form of well-being that is primarily derived from the contact motive, that is, a fulfillment of a need that may be less dependent on one's own individual performance. Second, this type of valuation is particularly important for a person's understanding and acceptance of events or circumstances that are beyond his or her control (e.g., as expressed in the experience of gratitude).

On the basis of these considerations, let us examine some of the valuations from a client who was highly action oriented and who felt the need to have everything in his life under control, including the incurable handicap of his daughter[4]:

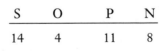

	S	O	P	N
Valuation 1. "My restlessness: Everything must happen quickly; I am hot-tempered; I say few words; I want everything fast and good."	14	4	11	8

	S	O	P	N
Valuation 2. "Examinations evoked so much stress in me that I began to have physical problems that I thought were serious (something with my heart or brain)."	9	3	5	12
Valuation 3. "In my work, I want to be successful and have a solid career."	16	2	15	5
Valuation 4. "Sometimes I rebel against the fact that Rita has a handicap; I find it difficult to accept."	8	10	2	7

The man's problem was not a lack of self-enhancement but, rather, a usurping degree of self-enhancement, which led to a generally stressful attitude (Valuation 1) and to nervous behavior in achievement situations (Valuation 2) as well as in nonachievement situations (Valuation 4). In order to deal with the tension that was so central in the first investigation, the client decided to go into physical therapy in order to learn to relax. One year later he performed a second self-investigation, in which Valuation 4 was modified as follows:

	S	O	P	N
Valuation 5. "I can better accept Rita's handicap and therefore Rita herself."	8	14	12	8

Although the increase in O affect was not large, the reformulation suggests that the client had learned to accept the existence of a situation that was beyond his control.

In more general terms, the Rogerian concept of acceptance can be translated in terms of +O valuations, that is, in terms of the experience of being accepted and accepting another person. The adoption of such an accepting attitude may also lead to expanded self-esteem because a feeling of strength often emerges from the experience of being accepted. This implies that self-esteem or inspired strength may not necessarily be the direct result of attempts at self-enhancement but the indirect result of entering into a mutually accepting climate.[5]

UNFULFILLED LONGING: *FUGIT AMOR*

Valuations of the −O type can be characterized as having a greater degree of affect referring to the need for contact and union with the other than of affect referring to self-enhancement (O > S). At the same time, there is a greater degree of negative than positive affect (N > P) associated with these valuations. This pattern of affect is in most cases an indication of a "*fugit amor*" theme, that is, the adoption or maintenance of a loving orientation toward another person or object that is, or is imagined to be, unreachable.

The metaphor of *fugit amor* has received moving expression in the statue of the French artist Rodin (see Figure 4.2). Rodin, inspired by Dante's *Divina Commedia*, was greatly affected by the sad love story concerning Paolo and Francesca, who fell in love with each other even though Francesca was married to Paolo's older brother (Schmoll, 1978). Meeting in secret, they were finally betrayed by a servant, who told the husband. The husband immediately went to the place where the lovers met, caught them in the act, and subsequently murdered both of them. Rodin's statue shows how the lovers, in Dante's story condemned to hell, are in close proximity but are not able to touch each other.

A typical manifestation of the *fugit amor* experience is the broken-off love affair. Reflecting back on a beautiful time with his girlfriend, one man came up with the following valuation:

	S	O	P	N
"I regret that it is over with Alice. I want to hold on to this feeling, and I will not allow the clichés to prevail; I find her too valuable."	6	16	2	13

FIGURE 4.2. *Fugit Amor* (1887), detail. Photographed reproduction of a sculpture by Auguste Rodin. Reproduced by permission of the Schuler Verlagsgesellschaft, Herrsching am Ammersee, Germany.

The *fugit amor* theme is related to the feelings associated with the death of a loved one. In particular, the feelings associated with the anticipated death of a significant other have been found to reflect this pattern of affect.

	S	O	P	N
"I am afraid of the time when my grandma will die."	5	14	1	11

In some cases an individual may even react to the experience of *fugit amor* by assuming the role of the dead person under certain circumstances:

	S	O	P	N
"It is as though I think I can preserve the intimacy I had with my father, and others, by doing things the way he did them: eating salmon on his birthday, trying to bring my mother and sister closer together."	3	11	4	16

One can conceive of the underlying structure of the *fugit amor* experience as consisting of two components: a loving orientation toward another person or object (the *amor* component, responsible for the O > S difference) and an obstacle or boundary making this person or object unreachable (the *fugit* component, responsible for the N > P difference). This structure is the latent base of a great variety of valuations. Depending on the individual history and life circumstances, the feeling of *fugit amor* may have different manifestations: an impossible or forbidden love affair, the death of a beloved friend, an anticipated farewell, the longing felt by an immigrant for his or her native country, a Faustian longing for youth, a feeling of intimacy toward another person coupled with an inability to express this tenderness.[6]

Although not necessarily a part of *fugit amor*, feelings of guilt are frequently found to be associated with the experience. For example, when one feels particularly responsible for the well-being of another, these feelings may be spontaneously expressed.[7]

	S	O	P	N
"I feel guilty with regard to the children because, as a result of the divorce, I've taken away some of the opportunities that they otherwise would have had."	1	16	5	17

The *fugit amor* character of a valuation may also be implicit but deducible from the discrepancy between text and affect. The following remark was made by a man during a period in which he felt seriously depressed:

	S	O	P	N
1. "I suddenly lost the staying power which, over the years, had seen me through the problems at home."	4	13	0	15

In comparing the affect scores with the text of the valuation, one can see that the low level of S (4) is reflected in the text ("lost the staying power"). However, no part of the text reflects the high level of O (13). A modality analysis was then performed with this valuation as the pivot, and the highest correlation ($r = .73$) was found to occur with the following statement:

	S	O	P	N
2. "Due to our preoccupation with our sick daughter, our son was rather neglected."	6	16	5	11

In this valuation, there is a clear congruity between the text and the affect pattern associated with it. The high correlation between the two valuations therefore suggests that a *fugit amor* concern is implicit in the first valuation and reflects a depressive state with a component of guilt.

When the psychologist senses an implicit *fugit amor* experience, he or she may invite the person to talk about it and thereby remove the discrepancy between text and affect. This may be done in the same investigation in which the incongruity is detected by asking the client to reformulate the valuation. Some clients will find it difficult to effect such a quick reformulation and will require more time to digest the matter. Take, for example, a woman who implied the feeling of *fugit amor* in one of her first valuations, and 8 months later modified the content of this valuation in such a way that it actually reflected this feeling. The initial valuation was as follows:

	S	O	P	N
"Mother is so inconsistent. She flits back and forth between the role of the lower-class housewife and that of the intellectual."	1	8	0	14

This formulation smacks more of censorship than of a desire for contact with a loved one, and in this sense resembles the psychoanalytic concept of reaction formation. The client seemed completely unaware of a *fugit amor* experience. However, when her attention was brought to the discrepancy between the caring feelings that she associated with her mother and the judgmental nature of this particular valuation, she decided to pay special attention to her contacts with her mother in the future. In the second investigation she explained that the old formulation no longer expressed the way in which she perceived her mother, and she modified the old statement to read as follows:

	S	O	P	N
"I wish my mother had been different. We could have shared so much."	0	5	0	11

At this point the woman has admitted a desire for an idealized mother, a statement that is more congruent with the *fugit amor* pattern of affect associated with the original critical valuation. At the same time, we can see that the S – O and P – N differences have become less pronounced. This may be a sign that the client, having confronted herself with the *fugit amor* aspect of her feelings toward her mother, has now started to put them in a different perspective. In any case, she has at least assimilated this valuation into her valuation system and is therefore in a position to deal with it.

When *fugit amor* valuations play a dominant role in the system, and particularly when they have a strongly generalizing influence, they result in an overall negative well-being (N > P for the general feeling). In such cases a change during therapy from a –O type valuation to +O type valuation is certainly one of the possibilities (although a change to a S type of valuation is even more probable, as we shall see later). Such a change then signifies a shift from a negative to a positive state of well-being, depending on the extent of generalization of the +O valuations.

Consider the following example of an adolescent girl who felt her relation to her mother to be particularly difficult and who therefore rebelled against the dependency she felt. The daughter ventilated her opposition to her mother in valuations with an implicit feeling of *fugit amor*.

	S	O	P	N
Valuation 1. "I found the ducks that my mother painted stupid because they were painted out of vanity."	3	18	2	15
Valuation 2. "When my mother reacted to me in a fierce and emotional way, she gave me the right to retreat into myself."	5	12	0	15

In a self-investigation performed 22 months after the first one, this girl eliminated Valuation 1 from her system as irrelevant and substituted Valuation 2 with two complementary valuations, each bearing a high level of positive affect.

	S	O	P	N
Valuation 3. "My mother is the most beautiful and sweetest in the world. I don't mind if she becomes old and ugly or neglects herself."	9	16	16	4
Valuation 4. "I have my own place, and I can see the developments of my mother and of myself independently."	17	16	17	0

Presumably, the daughter is now capable of a positive attitude toward her mother because she feels more independent, as indicated by the high S score for Valuation 4. Note that this allows the positive fulfillment of the O motive in both Valuation 3 and 4.[8]

POWERLESSNESS AND ISOLATION: BASIC ANXIETY

A category of valuations that is highly loaded with negative affect is the −LL type of valuation, a label used to indicate that there is a low level of self-enhancement affect and a low level of affect referring to contact and union. This category is composed of valuations stemming from a situation where both motives are unfulfilled at the same time. The person typically has the feeling that there is no way out, and for this reason one can describe the valuations in this category as expressing powerlessness and isolation. Typical examples are as follows:

	S	O	P	N
"I have the feeling that John can only be strong by keeping me weak."	0	0	0	20
"I have often been victimized, which has made me fearful of my environment."	0	1	0	15
"Violence and aggression have knocked me down."	3	0	0	18
"I was raped about 8 weeks ago by a man; because of this I feel humiliated and sad."	0	0	0	18

The typical affect associated with the –LL category of valuations is anxiety. The original Latin term *angusta* ("enclosed") describes the experience of anxiety: a person who feels closed in feels no way out. A characteristic feature of intense anxiety is the experience of being victimized; there is a reduced feeling of strength to master the situation, and there is no feeling that the experience is being shared with another.

Although the anxiety of the –LL type can be considered the closest approximation to the experience of being locked up, there are two other types of anxiety that frequently show up in the practice of self-confrontation: the –S type of anxiety and the –O type.

In the –S type of anxiety, people feel anxious about their own aggressive impulses. They may be afraid of losing self-control and doing harm to themselves or someone else, or, more generally, they may fear the negative consequences of their own attempts at self-enhancement.[9] And because this type of anxiety is generally in conflict with existing norms, it is often associated with feelings of shame and guilt.

Anxiety of the –O type shows a different picture: The person feels anxiety over the actual or anticipated loss of significant others (see Bowlby's [1980] discussion of separation anxiety). In other cases, anxiety does not result from an actual or anticipated loss or separation but from the threat of becoming too close to someone; that is, from the threat of having to surrender oneself or of becoming overly dependent. In this case, closeness is experienced as being at the expense of one's autonomy or self-control.

A special case of –O anxiety is the anxiety for intimacy that is aroused when getting very close to another person. Part of this anxiety is the threat of losing one's autonomy or, more generally, of giving up one's self-enhancement, implying a reduced shielding against the other. The situation of close proximity to someone or something often implies a heightened vulnerability that becomes particularly threatening when the person has the feeling that he or she is no longer able to control the situation.

When such valuations refer to a specific object or situation, this "objectified anxiety" may be described as fear (e.g., "I am afraid that I will fail that examination"). However, when the formulation of the valuation is phrased in general terms and has no specific object, there is reason to speak of anxiety ("I always feel anxious"). Anxiety can manifest itself in a broad variety of specific valuations, but these will typically be found to have been indiscriminately associated with this affective state. Moreover, in this case high levels of anxiety will be found to characterize a large majority of the valuations included in the system. It is also expected that anxiety has a stronger generalization in the system than fear.

Since –LL valuations are typically associated with anxiety and other forms of negative affect, people try to move away from this position. As already suggested, clients with a high proportion of –LL valuations in their system typically begin by changing their system in the direction of greater self-enhancement. The reason is clear: Such clients are primarily concerned with being able to stand on their own two feet again. This observation does not deny, of course, that clients will profit from a trusting relationship and from accepting contact with a therapist. It is simply meant to emphasize the fact that a basic level of autonomy and strength is needed in order to build or rebuild a self capable of coping with the environment.

An example is given below of the valuations of a client who felt "locked up" because she wasn't able to express her feelings:

	S	O	P	N
"I am closed. I don't dare let my deepest feelings be seen, and therefore others don't understand me."	1	0	1	15

Ten months later this valuation was reformulated as follows:

	S	O	P	N
"I must stimulate myself to react more directly when I feel something."	8	4	11	9

Although the content of the first valuation refers to contact with another, the modification in the later valuation is in the direction of more self-determination. Correspondingly, the self-enhancement affect increased somewhat more at the second investigation than did the affect referring to contact and union. Although the level of the S affect has increased, it is still not very high, and the P and N scores indicate an experience of ambivalence; nevertheless, the valuation is moving more in the S direction than in the O direction and is more positive than negative.

A low level of S and O affect is typically associated with a high level of N (and with a low level of P) affect. However, it is possible to have low levels of both S and O and nevertheless experience more P than N affect. That is, +LL valuations do exist, although they are rare and therefore are not included in Figure 4.1., they indicate that the absence of self-enhancement and contact and union *can* apparently be experienced in a positive way. But for what kind of valuation is this peculiar pattern of affect characteristic? The content of the valuations showed a striking similarity across people and can be described as passive enjoyment or empty satisfaction.

	S	O	P	N
"I can really enjoy a frivolous comedy that simply flows over you and doesn't call for any thought."	1	0	11	0

	S	O	P	N
"I can enjoy watching a building being built."	0	0	12	0
"No shoulds."	2	0	13	2

In some sense, however, one must question how positive these valuations are. Clients may include such valuations in their system precisely because they represent an escape from all the other tensions or negative feelings they are carrying around with them. That is, these clients may simply be trying to free themselves from internal normative pressures (i.e., pressures from themselves, other people, groups, or institutions). Fulfillment of the two basic S and O motives is simply not at issue. Rather than accept the challenge of obtaining fulfillment of these motives (so basic to the self), these clients simply accept a ready-made feeling of well-being instead. The commonality of the divergent but rare valuations in this category seems to be an attempt to be freed from motivational pressures.

We have sometimes found mystic experiences as also belonging to the +LL type of valuation. A woman who did not believe in God or the hereafter told of an experience she described as mystic:

	S	O	P	N
"Suddenly understanding everything, even the history of creation—a peak experience as a spiritual orgasm."	0	0	5	0

In rating her affect, the woman tried to characterize her affect during the experience, an attempt that resulted in a score of 5 for inner calm (index P = 5) and a score of zero for all other feelings. When the woman rated the same experience in retrospect, she gave a totally different affective response:

	S	O	P	N
"Suddenly understanding everything, even the history of creation—a peak experience as a spiritual orgasm."	20	15	20	0

Apparently, the affective experience was evaluated as highly rewarding and significantly enriching for the woman's life. As such, the mystic experience was highly rewarding with respect to both basic motives. Whereas both motives may be fulfilled after the mystic experience, the moment of the experience itself can be understood as a transient state of being empty of and temporarily transcending one's basic motives.

COMBINING HIGH LEVELS
OF SELF-ENHANCEMENT AND CONTACT

The final and most integrative form of valuation is represented by the +HH type of valuation, in which a high level of self-enhancement affect and a high level of affect referring to contact and union coexist and in which there is more positive than negative affect ($P > N$). In this valuation type the basic motives coincide (i.e., the fulfillment of one motive goes with fulfillment of the other), thus creating high levels of well-being. One can often observe more than one emphasis in a valuation of this type, that is, high levels of both S affect and O affect, as in the following examples:

	S	O	P	N
"I made a puppet—something from myself for my girlfriend."	16	14	17	0
"My creative ability in writing is to share something of myself with other people who recognize themselves in it; this was the basis of short but intense friendships with a number of people."	18	16	18	1
"I don't want my self-confidence to fade away; I want to be healthy enough that I choose only healthy relationships or no relationships at all."	15	17	18	2
"I feel that by having a job I support the movement that gets more women into all kinds of jobs."	17	16	17	4

In this category one can frequently find valuations that refer to positive contacts (or moments of contact) with significant others. But relations with significant others can be of many different types; furthermore, various types of valuations can refer to different facets of the same relationship at the same point in time. For example, in one and the same valuation system a person may refer to the moments of conflict in a relationship in terms of −S valuations, to the moments of utmost powerlessness and isolation in terms of −LL valuations, to the highlights in terms of +HH valuations, and to the beautiful but forever-lost aspects in terms of -O valuations. It is just such diversity that makes it so difficult to end a relation even when it seems necessary to do so. People who are in a period of serious conflict or alienation from their partners know that there are or were other elements in the relationship besides the ones that currently dominate it. Nevertheless, these other, more positive, kinds of experience are in the background, and the person simply cannot know if these aspects of the relationship can return or if they have disappeared for good.

In valuations of type +HH, one can frequently see that one emphasis explicitly refers to the one motive while the other refers only implicitly to the other motive. The following valuations are from the same client:

	S	O	P	N
"I really take pleasure in having played a good tennis match."	13	13	18	3
"I enjoy togetherness, coziness."	13	14	19	4

In the first valuation the client does not explicitly say that she enjoys the togetherness that is part of the game, and in the second valuation she does not explicitly mention the self-esteem derived from contact with other people. Such implicit elements in valuations may indicate that some parts of the valuation are, indeed, on a less conscious level. It can be observed that valuations referring to friendships typically belong to category +HH and often have an implicit S element. That is, when people feel close to a friend, they experience both mutual support and respect and thus experience not only contact but also positive self-esteem.[10]

Some caution should be taken in interpreting valuations of this sort, particularly when the system contains only valuations with +HH affect and none in which one of the motives predominates. A system consisting of only +HH and −LL type valuations is typically an indication that the client cannot differentiate between fulfillment of the S and O motives or has emotional reasons to avoid such a differentiation. There is differentiation, for example, when a person is able to call one motive into the foreground while leaving the other in the background. This flexibility resembles Angyal's (1965) plasticity–rigidity dimension. In a rigid system, Angyal observes, the person takes a fixed position and is relatively immovable; in a system with a high degree of plasticity, the person is more flexible and can move from one motive to the other within the system. This moving requires a certain differentiation between the two basic motives in the system. (Criteria for assessing differentiation are presented in the Manual.)

Finally, it can be asked whether +HH valuations represent the endpoint of the motivational scale, since as an integration of the basic motives valuations of this type are usually associated with a high level of well-being (P > N). This is, however, not always true because the relative dominance of a particular valuation type in the system will depend heavily on the immediate situation. For example, a person who comes into unavoidable conflict with other people will often need −S valuations as a strong motivation to fight against threatening forces. And when these valuations are already part of the system, they will receive a higher degree of generalization (as a defensive response against a perhaps otherwise overwhelming environmental influence). This means that an individual may temporarily move from a +HH type of generalization to a −S type of generalization. Thus, although +HH valuations may stay in the system as general orientation points, the organization of the system is never fixed as long as people are still sensitive to changes in the situation around them.

In sum, the relationship between the two basic motives is essentially one of mutual interdependence, although the potential for conflict is also always present. Conflict can arise when the situation requires that one of the two motives be temporarily dimmed, for example, in order to avoid interference with an adequate response to the prevailing situation. In a situation of threat or conflict an unmitigated self-maintaining response may be perfectly appropriate since conceding to feelings of union with the threatening force may only interfere with the effectiveness of one's response. Conversely, in order to experience a particular esthetic or religious phenomenon to its full, a person may temporarily set aside the self-enhancement motive in order to be as open as possible to the experience at hand. On the other hand, a valuation system is only complete when it is an expression of the two basic motives. This means that the person must have the capacity to respond with both S and O valuations.[11]

Two conclusions concerning the change process must be drawn. First, the direction of change depends heavily on the assessment phase and the emphases psychologist and client put on the validation/invalidation process. Second, despite this openness, there is one route that is often followed by clients who are confronted with a great deal of unresolvable problems and complaints, expressed in the form of a high frequency of strongly generalizing −LL valuations in the system: The movement is often toward −S valuations or directly to +S valuations and, if the process is continued, to +HH valuations. Even when the first investigation is dominated by −O valuations, movement is most typically in the direction of one of the types in which S affect is predominant. In other words, in the course of psychotherapy, development of the S motive gets priority over the O motive. It must be added, however, that there are important exceptions to this general finding. The approach presented in this book adheres strongly to idiographic methodology, and there is a theoretically founded appreciation for exceptional development.

TWO VALUATION SYSTEMS: THEIR DIALOGICAL CHANGE

The dialogical basis of valuation theory becomes particularly evident when we focus on the interaction between the valuation systems of two different people. The question is, How does one system get organized and reorganized in response to contact with another valuation system? When two people, A and B, have daily interactions with each other, what is the content and organization of A's valuations referring to B and, conversely, what is the nature of B's valuations in relationship to A? Put more dynamically, when one system changes, does the other system change correspondingly? Or put another way, when a valuation system is a coconstruction in which more than one person is involved, what role does the coconstructor play?

These questions were central in an investigation of a married couple. The partners completed self-investigations independently of each other (after they agreed to do so in a preliminary discussion with the psychologist). The investigations took place during a period of serious marital problems, with the goal of bringing more order and clarity into the nature of their relationship. The self-investigations, after being discussed with the partners separately, were later used as the basis for a series of joint sessions. In these sessions under the guidance of the psychologist who had assisted them in their self-investigations, the couple tried to improve their communication. In order to tap any developments in their valuation systems, both individuals completed a second self-investigation 6 months after the initial one.

The validation/invalidation process between Investigation 1 and 2 was essentially the same as described in the previous chapter. That is, when the self-confrontation method is used in marital therapy, the same three phases (attending, creating, and anchoring) apply. The main difference is that after the partners do their self-investigations separately, they focus on their mutual relationship as the main source of events. For the first phase this means that the partners attend to those events in their relationship that are relevant from the perspective of their valuation systems (they focus on those events that are covered by the valuations that refer to their relationship). In this phase it is very helpful when the partners have an opportunity to exchange parts of their valuation systems (this, however, requires great care and prudence on the part of the psychologist, especially when the partners are in a situation of conflict). In the second phase the partners start to experiment with initiatives and new forms of behavior, which are evaluated in order to check if they can be included in new valuations moving in the desired direction. In the third phase the partners continue practicing in their daily situation in such a way that newly acquired behavior becomes a more stabilized part of their interaction.

The valuations of a woman, Jennifer, at Investigation 1 and 2 constitute Table 4.1 and the valuations of her partner, John, at Investigation 1 and 2 constitute Table 4.2. Only those valuations that refer to their mutual relationship and to relevant events from their individual pasts are presented. What stands out from a comparison of these tables is summarized as follows:

- Jennifer's perception of her contact with John shows a striking similarity to the problems characterizing her past, both in content and affective patterning (compare, for example, Valuations 2 and 4 in Table 4.1).

- Jennifer has an oppositional attitude toward John, which becomes stronger from Investigation 1 to Investigation 2 (see the increase in S affect in Valuation 5 in Table 4.1). At the same time, however, Jennifer has picked up on John's new attempts to listen to her, as reflected in the valuation with the highest level of generalization at Investigation 2 (see Valuation 4 in Table 4.1). The continuation or strengthening of Jennifer's opposition, therefore, does not exclude a growing openness (see the increasing level of O affect for Valuation 4 in Table 4.1). Note that just by becoming more able to resist John, Jennifer is able to create more openness to him. Considering all the changes together, however, we observe that Jennifer is strengthening the S side of her valuation system more than the O side.
- Although Jennifer somewhat modifies the formulations referring to the past, she also consistently increases their level of S affect and decreases the N affect to almost zero in doing so (see Valuations 1–3 in Table 4.1). The specific pattern (high S, low O, low P, low N) is an indication of "armoring," of becoming hard and strong and simultaneously insensitive to positive and negative stimuli. Apparently, Jennifer tells the same story about her past at Investigation 1 and 2, but at Investigation 2 feels capable of shielding herself against the negative emotional impact of the past.

In sum, we can clearly see in Jennifer's case that a change in the social relationship with her partner coincides with a change in her attitude toward her past. The changes manifest themselves simultaneously in two parts of the system that are dynamically related.

The following observations can be made from a study of John's valuations:

- Although it contains valuations that are different from those of Jennifer, John's system also shows change: He expresses at Investigation 2 his intention to listen more attentively to his wife (Valuation 5 in Table 4.2), and this valuation shows up with an increased level of S and O affect (compare this to Jennifer's Valuation 4 in Table 4.1). This means that the respective valuations are both moving in the direction of the +HH type.
- Although John's problems in the relationship with his wife have not disappeared at Investigation 2, the level of negative feelings have diminished (see Valuations 2–4).

There is, however, an important difference between the partners: While Jennifer changed her (negative) attitude toward her past, John did not change his (positive) attitude toward his past. On the contrary, the fact that his Valuations 1 and 5 at Investigation 2 show similar patterns of affect and show the highest degree of generalization suggests that the two valuations are mutually supportive. From a developmental point of view, there is a significant similarity be-

TABLE 4.1. Jennifer's Valuations Referring to Her Past (Valuations 1–3) and to Her Partner (Valuations 4–5) and Their Scores on Several Indices at Investigations 1 and 2

Valuations at Investigation 1	S	O	P	N	Generalization index	Idealization index
1. My parents lived only for themselves; I didn't have much love.	2	4	3	11	.78	−.51
2. As a girl, I didn't count at home; whenever I wanted to say something, I was told, "keep your mouth shut. What do you know about it?"	2	0	0	13	.69	−.68
3. I had to work when I was 16; I feel like I missed the boat (learning a profession).	0	4	3	16	.74	−.64
4. I can't talk with John. It always turns into a fight. He doesn't listen; he always has his answer ready, always an opinion.	1	1	1	14	.85	−.72
5. I resist John.	6	0	1	15	.55	−.73
General feeling	2	5	4	11	—	−.39
Ideal feeling	11	16	20	1	−.39	—

Note. S, affect referring to self-enhancement; O, affect referring to contact with the other; P, positive affect; N, negative affect.

tween the cases of Jennifer and John. We see both constancy and change: Some valuations change in content and affective patterning while others remain strikingly constant. This observation, which is a very typical one in valuation research, suggests that people do not change without having some element of stability—even when the stable valuations are associated with negative affect (e.g., Valuation 5 in Table 4.1). Some degree of constancy can be viewed as strategic self-reorganization.

In the case study just described, it can be observed that valuations referring to the present relation with the partner are significantly related to valuations referring to the individual's past. Moreover, a change in the relation to the partner instigated a change in the client's attitude toward the past. This observation is in agreement with Verstraeten's (1978) study of couples with communication problems, a study in which she found an interdependence between the systems of the individuals on the one hand and, on the other, a perception of the current

Valuations at Investigation 2	S	O	P	N	Generalization index	Idealization index
[Same formulation as at Investigation 1.]	11	0	0	1	.25	.22
[Same formulation as at Investigation 1.]	12	0	0	3	.15	.10
[Same formulation as at Investigation 1.]	13	0	0	1	.13	.28
John really tries to listen to me when I ask him to.	12	8	15	0	.53	.79
[Same formulation as at Investigation 1.]	12	1	1	11	.02	−.38
General feeling	11	10	13	8	—	−.42
Ideal feeling	20	19	20	0	.42	—

marital problems as a repetition of situations located in one or the other partner's past. That is, the between-system organization was clearly found to be related to the within-system organization. (See also Gergen & Gergen's [1988] plea for a social psychology that is both relational and diachronic).

THE ROLE OF IMAGINAL FIGURES IN VALUATION

The process of valuation can only be described adequately if attention is also given to its imaginative storylike character. The story a person tells about his or her own life is not only a description of a series of events but also a motley mixture of fact and fiction. This story includes not only social selves in factual interactions but also social selves that play a role in imaginal interactions.

TABLE 4.2. John's Valuations Referring to His Past (Valuation 1) and to His Partner (Valuations 2–5) and Their Scores on Several Indices at Investigations 1 and 2

Valuations at Investigation 1	S	O	P	N	Generalization index	Idealization index
1. I had a pleasant childhood.	15	20	20	0	.20	.84
2. It starts as soon as I get out of bed: "This is not right, that's not right," etc. When I come home in the evening, it's exactly the same. It's as if I'm a child and as if I can't do anything on my own.	0	1	1	18	−.27	−.84
3. I miss some warmth, a bit of sincere love from my wife.	2	5	1	17	−.19	−.64
4. Jennifer is always hard on me. She says that I don't understand her and that I can't talk with her.	4	8	1	16	−.19	−.55
5. I'm always the one who has to make up, but then I get criticized for forgetting things so quickly.	3	6	1	14	−.23	−.69
General feeling	13	7	11	8	—	.17
Ideal feeling	13	16	16	2	.17	—

Note. S, affect referring to self-enhancement; O, affect referring to contact with the other; P, positive affect; N, negative affect.

As we briefly mentioned in Chapter 1, Caughey (1984) describes how we phase in and out of actual worlds and imaginal realms. When we attend to virtually any form of the media, we leave our objective social situation and are transported into vicarious, sometimes artificial, social situations. Through processes like identification, we experience pseudosocial roles and interact in our imaginations with media figures. Likewise, in the daily stream of consciousness—in memories, anticipations, and fantasies—we typically become entangled in social interactions with imaginal replicas of our actual friends and acquaintances. And, of course, in dreams we enter imaginal worlds in which we are almost never alone; we take on varied identities, assume roles, and play out social interactions with dream beings. Caughey emphasizes that within these realms we are engaging not in private but in social experiences. Therefore, he

Valuations at Investigation 2	S	O	P	N	Generalization index	Idealization index
[Same formulation as at Investigation 1.]	17	18	19	0	.73	.94
Jennifer always wants to have the upper hand; what she wants, she gets.	3	3	0	11	−.33	−.62
[Same formulation as at Investigation 1.]	0	6	0	10	−.29	−.51
[Same formulation as at Investigation 1.]	2	4	0	13	−.56	−.80
I want to listen to Jennifer and immerse myself in her.	12	16	17	1	.68	.94
General feeling	14	14	13	6	—	.73
Ideal feeling	13	15	18	0	.73	—

objects to the presupposition that social relationships are always actual social relations between real people. The social relations of the self may be far more inclusive than ordinarily conceived. The self in its relations with other selves may transcend the boundaries of social life as objectively defined.

Watkins (1986) also convincingly argues that a great deal of our experience is based on "imaginal dialogue." It is not only children who invite imaginal others to enter their worlds. She refers, for example, to Machiavelli, who had imaginal dinner conversations with historical personages, to Petrarch who wrote letters to the eminences of classical antiquity, to Landor who wrote volumes of imaginal dialogues between sages and stars of different countries, and to Pablo Casals who told his listeners, "Bach is my best friend." Indeed, Watkins concludes, art, drama, poetry, and music, as well as the spontaneous appearance of personifications, keep us in conversation with imaginal others. In Watkins's view, these imaginal others affect our interactions with actual others just as surely as the other way around.[12]

Over the years, we have observed many valuations referring to imaginal figures, that is, supposed beings, particular personages, animal-like figures, monsters, supreme beings, or other anthropomorphic figures, that cannot be experienced with the five senses but nevertheless have an aura of fact about them. And it should be noted that the people who identified such imaginal figures spoke about them with the attention and care they used to speak about their factual significant others. Over the course of time, we came to realize that more people have such a figure in mind but simply do not mention it. This is, of course, because the self-investigation is a relational procedure in a social situation and therefore also a form of self-presentation to another person (the psychologist). To a certain degree the psychologist is perceived as representing the values of our culture and as presenting certain constraints on the expression of experiences (e.g., strange images or fantasies are typically considered to be highly questionable, if not unacceptable, in our culture).

In order to pursue our suspicion, it was decided to ask more specific questions about the possible existence of an imaginal figure in the person's life and to present the individual with some stimulating examples.

"Is there, in your world, an *imaginal figure* that plays an important role in your life? What kind of role does this figure play? Is this figure, for example,

- Somebody whom you admire and who interacts in some way with you in your mind?
- Someone with whom you converse in your mind?
- Some kind of adviser?
- A guardian spirit?
- An enemy who threatens you?
- A monster that may swallow you?
- A human being that manifests itself in the form of an animal?
- Someone who speaks to you from the future?
- An imaginal lover?
- A picture or statue that comes to life?
- A dead person who is still present?"

At the end of the valuation construction phase this question was presented to a variety of clients and the "role of the imaginal figure" was then phrased as an additional valuation. In the following paragraphs we present examples illustrating various functions served by such imaginal figures.

An imaginal figure can compensate for a felt lack in someone's existence.

That is, if some significant other does not or cannot fulfill a person's needs, he or she may create an imaginal figure to fill this gap. Consider the following valuation:

	S	O	P	N
"I wish there was a woman with whom I could go to bed, but there isn't."	12	18	18	0

Although this man is well aware that such a person does not exist at this time for him, this valuation is an approximation of a +HH valuation, which suggests that the emphasis of the valuation is the wishful thinking in the first part of the sentence. Three months later the client modified the formulation slightly:

	S	O	P	N
"I wish there was a woman with whom I could go to bed, but there isn't; she is an unobtainable fantasy."	0	7	0	10

The emphasis has shifted now to the last part of the valuation, as indicated by the additional words "an unobtainable fantasy" and the drastic change of the affective associations into the more realistic −O type. In other words, as long as reality was unbearable to this client he remained addicted to his fantasy, but as soon as he was again able to confront the realities of his life he had the courage to abandon his compensating ideal.

Another function of the imaginal figure is to provide "transitional help" from one situation or state to another; that is, an imaginal figure may be conjured up in order to facilitate a transition. In the following example a woman conjures up an imaginal figure for the transition from wake to sleep:

	S	O	P	N
"Before going to sleep, there is a person who gives me peace by touching me."	8	12	12	3

Let us take a closer look at the verbalizations that preceded this valuation: "People I meet in daily life often appeal to me in one way or another. Then I fantasize about these people ... not in a sexual sense but in an affective and physical sense. In reality I would not dare to do this. But in my fantasy I can arrange that it happens as I want it ... the moments ... in the evening when I go to bed and cannot sleep; I call it up and then I don't even finish my fantasy ... I'm already asleep." In this case we can see that actual people are transformed in the client's fantasy into beings who know precisely how to help her fall asleep.

The use of imaginal figures in childhood was described by Winnicott (1971), who observed that children use transitional objects—a piece of a sheet, an old cloth, a teddy bear—to facilitate the transition from wake to sleep. Such objects are part of sleep rituals, and Winnicott interpreted them as "a defense against anxiety" (p. 4). These rituals are not limited to infancy: "Patterns set in infancy may persist into childhood, so that the original soft object continues to be absolutely necessary at bed-time or at a time of loneliness or when a depressed mood threatens" (p. 4). Similarly, in his study of rites of passage, Van Gennip (1909) emphasized the role of ritual in guiding the individual through the important life transitions of birth, puberty, marriage, old age, and death. Each transition is associated with certain ritual behaviors that provide a necessary degree of structure. In many primitive tribes imaginal figures such as ghosts, spirits, or masks play a central role in these rituals.

More generally, the phenomenon of transitional help points to the importance of continuity during the change process. Thus, during a period of transition, when continuity comes under pressure, individuals (sometimes with the support of society) can react by calling up imaginal figures to provide the necessary degree of structure or continuity.

When people are very emotional about something, they may need or want to give symbolic form to these emotions. As can be used from the following valuation, an imaginal figure can provide an important means for the metaphorical expression of emotion:

	S	O	P	N
"There is an animal, a sort of monster, a dragon, that is eating me up from inside."	2	0	0	15

In a modality analysis with this valuation, the highest correlation (.95) was with a valuation referring to an event in the past:

	S	O	P	N
"My sister forbade me to tell that I almost drowned."	2	0	0	14

This statement refers to a time when as a small boy the client was taken to the beach by his sister. While she was petting with her boyfriend, he wandered into the water and almost drowned. Later, fearful of their parents, the sister put the boy under pressure not to tell anyone. Comparison of these two valuations makes clear that the client's later use of an imaginal figure was a metaphorical means of expressing emotions that would otherwise have remained locked up.[13]

As may be expected, the conscience can be vividly personified as an imaginal figure. In the following example a woman tells of her imaginal contact with three deceased members of her family:

	S	O	P	N
"Grandma, mom, and dad are with me; sometimes I evaluate what I do against what they would think."	14	15	14	5

In this +HH valuation the interaction is positively experienced and the imaginal figures are freely consulted.

In other cases the imaginal interaction may be more rigid, indicative of a strongly internalized superego that is functioning more as an inner dictator. Let us take a closer look at one woman's inner voices:

	S	O	P	N
"God and my father [deceased] are watching me, and later I will have to justify myself to them."	6	5	3	10
"I view father as my protector, who sees things with me, lets me talk to him, shout at him; I involve him, make him a companion."	11	15	17	4

In the case of this client, two different functions have been fulfilled by the imaginal figure; the father is viewed both as a severe judge (in the first statement) and a conversational partner (in the second). Moreover, these two functions of the father are associated with contrasting patterns of affect. In conversations with the psychologist the same client noted that there was an inner voice that played an important but somewhat ambiguous role in her daily life. Psychologist and client decided to examine this inner voice in relation to the imaginal aspects of her father. This was done by considering the two roles of the father and the inner voice as three versions of the way the client believed she ought to feel. She was asked to respond to the following questions with the standardized series of affect terms:

	S	O	P	N
Question 1. How should I feel, according to my father and God who are watching me?	6	4	3	12
Question 2. How should I feel, according to my protective father?	19	17	18	0

	S	O	P	N
Question 3. How should I feel, according to my inner voice?	3	1	6	17

The correlation between Question 1 and 3 was .71, and the correlation between Question 2 and 3 was −.84. This indicates that the affective meaning of the client's inner voice was indeed similar to the observing father, suggesting that her inner voice was functioning as some sort of restrictive superego. This information, along with the negative correlation indicating a contrast between the protective-father role and the inner voice, was then used by the psychologist and client in an attempt to move the self-narrative more in the direction of an accepting and supportive self.[14]

An imaginal figure can also provide a sense of protection. This protective imaginal figure may be the product of a single individual's imagination or part of a collective story. A typical example of the latter is the figure of a guardian angel in the Roman-Catholic tradition. Such an imaginal protector, originally introduced to an individual in school and church, may later be incorporated into his or her personal valuation system. In the following valuations one person derives a certain degree of self-confidence from an angel whereas the other experiences the angel as a particularly accepting being:

	S	O	P	N
"I have a guardian angel who takes care that everything is turning out well. I assume this beforehand; I therefore take more risks."	9	2	11	1
"My guardian angel enables me to accept the course of things."	5	11	12	2

A person may create a place in his or her life for an imagined protector because of a felt lack of protection. When this is the case, the imaginal figure is clearly fulfilling a compensatory function. However, this is not necessarily always the case, as revealed by the modality analysis with the last-mentioned valuation as a pivot. The highest correlation of the guardian angel valuation was found to be with the following statement (.86).

	S	O	P	N
"Laura [client's wife] gives me a feeling of protectedness, of safety."	6	17	16	2

Why does this man need an imaginal protector when he in fact finds protection in his contact with his wife? And who is the primary protector? Does the imagination function as a facilitator for contact with the wife, or does his relationship with his wife strengthen his belief in a supernatural being? These are questions that cannot be answered by a simple modality analysis. It would require an extensive longitudinal study of this man to increase our understanding of the phenomenon under consideration. At the moment, the safest interpretation within the present theoretical framework is to consider angel and wife as different manifestations of the common theme of protection, with reality and imagination both contributing to its consolidation.

Gods, imagined as "ultimate rescuers" (to borrow a term from Yalom, 1980), radiate their meaning to the farthest reaches of human experience. A woman who attempted to drown herself, for example, later provided the following valuation, suggesting that some higher force was responsible for her survival of her suicide attempt.

	S	O	P	N
"I pray every day before going to sleep, also in the day, for myself and also for others. . . . The clearest hint I received when I was lying there at the border—it was as if somebody said to me, 'It is not yet your time'; it was as if I then returned to life."	12	12	15	7

In the case of this woman, God served a number of functions at once: companion, judge, and protector. As James (1890) put it: "Yet still the emotion that beckons me on is indubitably the pursuit of an ideal social self, of a self that is at least worthy of approving recognition by the highest possible judging companion, if such companion there be. This self is the true, the intimate, the ultimate, the permanent Me which I seek. This judge is God, the Absolute Mind, the 'Great Companion' (pp. 315–316). As James's statement suggests, a god may be a meaningful imaginal figure par excellence. Such a figure, in which multiple imaginal figures are concentrated, symbolizes the experience of ultimate value.

The Imaginal Other Has Its Own Valuation System[15]

An imaginal figure can be seen as another person who is dialogically related to the usual valuation system of the person. Such a construction is certainly possible inasmuch as an imaginal figure may be involved with the person in a question-and-answer process and may agree or disagree with the person. In other words, the imaginal figure may function as an antagonist belonging to a highly dynamic, multivoiced self (Hermans, Rijks, & Kempen, 1993). On the basis of this notion, we collected two valuation systems from two positions in the life of one and the same person, Kathy, one from her usual position and one from the position of an imaginal figure with whom she had contact from a young age. We will describe the content and structure of the two systems as dialogically related self-narratives.

Kathy was a divorced woman of 31 who had been brought up in a lower-class family. She had not completed high school, worked as a graphic designer, and had no psychiatric history. She participated in a self-investigation project on the "multivoicedness" of the self. She did so because she was interested in exploring the role of her imaginal figure in her life. She described this figure as "a guide who helps me to find my way in life" and said that she had been in touch with this figure since her early nursery school years.

Kathy performed the self-investigations according to the described procedure but from two perspectives: one from her familiar position (as Kathy) and one from her imaginal position (i.e., She formulated the valuations and performed the affect ratings as if she were the imaginal figure). We will present the two valuation systems from Time 1 and from Time 2, 6 months after the initial investigations, in order to assess the extent to which they changed. Kathy formulated 27 valuations from the usual I position and 27 valuations from the imaginal position. A representative sample of the two groups of valuations at Investigation 1 and at Investigation 2 is presented in Table 4.3. Note that in the interval between the two investigations there were no sessions with any psychologist; thus, all the developments were of a spontaneous nature.

The main properties of Kathy's valuation systems can be summarized as follows.

- The content of the valuations is markedly different between the two positions, indicating different self-narratives. We can see that not only Kathy's own valuations but those from her imaginal other show a clear temporal organization. The content of the valuations suggests that the imaginal figure had quite different meanings for Kathy in different time periods (compare, for example, Valuations 11 and 12).
- Whereas the valuations from Kathy's own position are mainly focused on her relation with the world (e.g., parents, studies), all the valuations from her imaginal other are focused on the relation with Kathy. The imaginal figure has a clear function for Kathy, serving primarily as her protector (Valuation 10) and as a figure who compensates for her lack of contact (Valuation 9).
- There is a considerable constancy in the valuations. In Kathy's usual position, five of the seven valuations receive the same formulation at Investigation 2 as at Investigation 1; moreover, the scores on the affective indices S, O, P, and N are remarkably stable. Further, in the case of Kathy's imaginal figure, five of the seven valuations receive the same formulation in both investigations.

- Nevertheless there are some significant changes from Investigation 1 to Investigation 2. Of particular interest is the improved cooperation that is experienced both from Kathy (Valuation 7) and from her imaginal figure (Valuation 14). Note that this improved cooperation is also expressed in the common movement toward clear +HH valuations (Valuations 7 and 14) from Investigation 1 to Investigation 2.

Summary

We dealt with the imaginal figure in some detail because this subject is rather neglected in psychological research but is nevertheless, as Caughey (1984), Watkins (1986), and others have suggested, an essential aspect of the self. It represents the specific human capacity to enlarge systems of meaning beyond the limits of the world that is defined as factual. The imaginative quality of the process of valuation derives not only from the social but also from the existential nature of the human being. When existentialists use the term *Geworfenheit* ("thrownness"), they mean that the human being, thrown into space and time, is confronted with a yawning gap that has to be filled but can never be filled completely. In trying to fill this existential gap, humans are forced to rely on an imaginal world of their own creation, and the self as a personal story in the context of the collective stories of a culture is in part a product of this imagination.

This existential perspective on human nature also elucidates the character of the basic motives, which can be described as existential goals characterized by continuously yielding horizons. That is, we are striving and longing for end points that can never be reached, and in this sense the stories we tell about our lives are also essentially unfinished stories. It was this human condition that the French philosopher Lacan (1966) had in mind when he distinguished between need and desire: The object of a need is fixed, whereas the object of a desire shifts. For example, a person has a need for oxygen, and oxygen can fulfill this need. One's desire, however, may shift—from one object or person to another (e.g., family member, friend, place of birth, a certain old building). This shifting character of the object of desire results from *le manque d'être* ("the deficiency of being"), which can never be completely removed. And because the basic motives can never be completely fulfilled, the number and variety of valuations fluctuate. We can conceive of valuations as continuously created units of meaning that arise at the manifest level under the influence of never quite completely fulfilled motives at the latent level.

IMPLICATIONS FOR PSYCHOLOGICAL HEALTH

In this chapter we have outlined a typology for different valuations in terms of the basic motives and have demonstrated some of the possible directions change

TABLE 4.3. Kathy's Own Valuations and the Valuations of Her Imaginal Figure and Their Scores on the Affective Indices at Investigations 1 and 2

	S	O	P	N	G
Kathy's own valuations at Investigation 1					
1. I always had to conform to the image my parents and the nuns had of me.	0	0	0	18	.06
2. When I was alone, I constructed a fantasy world where I made myself a very strong person.	16	12	16	2	.11
3. I've always searched for my own opinion, my own values.	16	0	2	7	.60
4. When I was 17, 1 ran away from home; I left a poem of which the last two lines were "I have to leave, I love you too much."	7	5	0	18	.30
5. I have a strong will to survive; they can't easily break me.	13	0	4	3	.41
6. I really want to finish my studies.	7	0	4	2	.66
7. I have a guide who helps me to find my way.	12	10	14	10	.04
General feeling	11	6	9	10	—
Ideal feeling	17	15	20	0	−.08
Valuations from Kathy's imaginal figure at Investigation 1					
8. I am the other one in Kathy. Sometimes she needs a good kick.	3	8	2	0	.06
9. As a child Kathy was quiet and reserved; I played with her in her own world.	3	8	16	0	.04
10. Sometimes I had to protect Kathy from her fantasies.	6	12	0	5	.37
11. I stimulated Kathy to opposition during her adolescence: "Let's *not* do that for change; you don't have to do everything they say."	15	1	7	5	.36
12. Between her 18th and 22nd year Kathy pushed me away; she didn't want to be bothered by me.	4	6	0	14	−.08
13. Kathy looks to her work through my eyes.	7	5	7	1	.42
14. I must be careful not to dominate Kathy; I must also listen to her.	9	6	0	11	.42
General feeling	15	11	10	9	—
Ideal feeling	18	14	19	0	.32

Note. S, affect referring to self-enhancement; O, affect referring to contact with the other; P, positive affect; N, negative affect; G, generalization index. From Hermans, Rijks, and Kempen (1993). Copyright 1993 by Duke University Press. Reprinted with permission.

	S	O	P	N	G
Kathy's own valuations at Investigation 2					
1. [Same formulation as at Investigation 1.]	0	0	0	18	−.83
2. [Same formulation as at Investigation 1.]	16	13	16	2	.80
3. [Same formulation as at Investigation 1.]	16	0	4	7	.11
4. [Same formulation as at Investigation 1.]	7	5	0	19	−.71
5. [Same formulation as at Investigation 1.]	13	0	10	1	.55
6. I really want to finish my studies; I want to be good in the field I've chosen.	10	0	8	4	.41
7. I have a guide who helps me to find my way; I've recognized and become more accepting of him; we have become better friends.	12	13	16	6	.77
General feeling	11	10	14	2	—
Ideal feeling	20	18	20	0	.84
Valuations from Kathy's imaginal figure at Investigation 2					
8. I am the other one in Kathy. Sometimes she needs a good kick, or she needs a hand to hold and take her along.	8	11	9	6	.56
9. [Same formulation as at Investigation 1.]	7	8	15	0	.45
10. [Same formulation as at Investigation 1.]	8	4	0	4	.00
11. [Same formulation as at Investigation 1.]	16	1	7	3	.26
12. [Same formulation as at Investigation 1.]	0	2	0	14	−.25
13. [Same formulation as at Investigation 1.]	11	8	10	2	.24
14. We are together; we have both accepted that.	13	15	14	4	.41
General feeling	9	11	12	9	—
Ideal feeling	20	19	20	0	.22

can take. What are the implications of this view for psychological health? Simply put, psychological health depends on a differentiated but nevertheless integrated valuation system that allows for the flexible movement between different types of valuations as the situation demands or allows.

When we refer to the *differentiation* of the system, we mean that the self is composed of an articulated set of valuation types that can be clearly distinguished from each other (Figure 4.1). A differentiated system includes a variety of types of valuation, a variety that enables the person to respond with a particular type of valuation to a particular situation and to temporarily dim the other types. The notion of differentiation does not necessarily mean that all the types shown in Figure 4.1 must be part of the explicitly formulated valuation system. In fact, those valuations that are included in the system are to a certain degree representative of the present life situation of the person. Markus and Wurf (1987) use the term "working self" to indicate that not all elements that are part of the self are accessible at any one time. The working self or "self of the moment" is best viewed as a continually active, shifting array of accessible self-knowledge. This means that the valuation system as formulated in a self-investigation is a "working self" that may shift according to changes in the person–situation interaction (e.g., other things may be remembered when the present life situation of a person changes in important respects). Although the different types of valuations represented in Figure 4.1 need not always be part of the explicitly formulated valuation system, they are part of a possible set of personal meanings.

The notion of differentiation can be further extended by inclusion of different positions. In this chapter we have given a first example of the "multi-voicedness" of the self (Hermans, Kempen, & Van Loon, 1992) by distinguishing between the usual position from which the person tells a narrative, and the position of an imaginal figure from which he or she tells another narrative. We have seen that the imaginal figure has its own story to tell in the form of a separate valuation system that is dialogically related to the valuation system that is commonly called upon. Although we will address this issue more fully in the following chapters, the point we are making here is that we approach the self as a complex phenomenon that is not only multifaceted (i.e., a multiplicity of valuations in one system) but also multivoiced (i.e., a multiplicity of I positions, each with its own system).

The *integration* aspect of psychological health refers to the valuations as parts of an organized whole. A certain level of integration is required in order to assimilate new experiences, relativize the various valuations according to their importance, see their connections, and discern their common themes. Whereas differentiation ensures a well-articulated self-narrative, integration guarantees a well-ordered story line, which contributes to the distinction between matters of primary and those of secondary importance and facilitates the transition from assessment to change. As we saw in the last chapter, the formulation of a guiding theme in one's self-narrative greatly helps to see the significance of one's present concerns. It also helps to make the client more sensitive to ongoing events and more open to the possibility of considering new behaviors in order to reconstrue the self in such a way that it functions better than before. Such a guiding theme may coincide with one of the valuation types discussed in this chapter. The overview of types of valuation in Figure 4.1 may serve as a guide for discerning alternative themes in the validation/invalidation process. When, for example, it is learned in the assessment phase that the guiding theme is centered around +O valuations (unity and love), with an apparent absence of +S valuations (autonomy and success), psychologist and client may decide after a discussion of the results of the self-investigation to focus on events that are relevant to the latter type of valuation. In this way the classification scheme in Figure 4.1 may be useful in discerning alternative possibilities for change. The range of possibilities can be widened even more by the construction of imaginal positions, which may suggest other themes. When, for example, the usual position of a client is organized around the theme of powerlessness, the construction of an imaginal position (e.g., a wise adviser or guide) may bring the client into direct contact with another theme that is central to the valuations of the imaginal position. In this way a different voice may bring about actions that are otherwise beyond the reach of the usual valuation system and may thereby enrich the validation/invalidation process.

Whereas the criteria of differentiation and integration refer primarily to the structural aspects of psychological health, the notion of *flexibility* has direct consequences for its dynamic aspect. There is flexibility when a person is not rigidly occupied by one type of valuation (or by one position) but has the capacity to move from one type of valuation to another (or from one position to another) in correspondence with ongoing events. The flexible person is not one who is constantly repeating the same story theme in spite of changes in his or her life situation but one who is capable of producing different themes when necessary. For example, when a person loses a significant other, a normal reaction is a −O valuation (i.e., an unfulfilled longing for contact with the unreachable other). During the period of mourning these valuations take a more or less central place in the organized valuation system. However, in the normal course of development these valuations gradually move into the background of the system (as indicated by a decreasing correlation between these −O valuations and the general feeling). In contrast, −O valuations become dysfunctional when they continue to predominate in the system (see Chapter 6).

When a particular type of valuation is called into the foreground (as indicated by emphasis in the formulation, degree of associated affect, and generalization), flexibility requires that the other types do not simply disappear. For example, a highly achieving person with a strong self-enhancing orientation is nevertheless not very flexible if he or she cannot temporarily put in the background the need for self-enhancement in order to experience some kind of contact and union (e.g., in art, nature, sex, religion, meditation, or love for work). Conversely, a person with a very caring and cooperative attitude lacks flexibility if he or she is not able to defend his or her own position when necessary. When the self-confrontation method is applied in a nonclinical population, one typically observes that a person has different types of valuations associated with different situations (e.g., at work, with family, with friends, during recreational activities, when alone, etc.), that is, with more emphasis on one than on another type. In a clinical population, however, the variety of types is often highly restricted as a result of an accumulation of unsolved problems; most typically, one of the negative valuation types dominates the system.

A dynamic point of view applies also to the positive and negative aspects of the self. Flexibility in a valuation system does not imply the presence of positive valuations to the exclusion of negative ones. That is, a flexible person does not exclude or suppress negative valuations but accepts them as unavoidable and even intrinsic aspects of human existence. It is often found that positive valuations refer to some persons and negative valuations to others. This, however, is a rather simplistic form of organization. A more complex valuation system exists when different types of valuation refer to one and the same individual. For example, a gratifying contact with a partner or friend (+O or +HH valuation) may also include some fear of conflict with that person. This fear may prevent the individual from entering into a situation of disagreement or opposition (−S) even when this is actually necessary. In fact, this avoidance of conflict makes the relationship rather inflexible as far as it is based on positive affect only and leaves no room for negative affect. The relationship becomes more flexible when the partners learn to include within their respective valuation systems not only positive but also negative valuations regarding their mutual interaction. In that case one can observe that the relationship with the significant other is expressed in terms of several valuations, each with its own specific type of affective modality and generalizing potential. Even valuations having the highest level of negative affect (the −LL type) may be functional under certain circumstances: They certainly let the person know what it feels like to be powerless and isolated. More generally, knowledge of and acquaintance with the rich variety of human experience not only enhances the flexibility of the system but also widens a person's ability to understand and empathize with the difficulties of others.

The notion of flexibility is not incompatible with the observation that people are generally striving toward positive rather than negative experiences. This implies that in order to reach a satisfactory level of well-being people will prefer a predominance of positive valuations (the upper three valuation types in the circle) over negative ones (the lower three types in the circle). This is in agreement with the general finding that in the process of change people try to move their general feeling into the direction of a closer approximation to their ideal feeling, which typically has an affective pattern of high S, high O, high P, and low N. In the theory proposed here, the notion of flexibility is considered to be more essential to psychological health than is a feeling of well-being (P > N). That is, a positive feeling of well-being is considered a relevant aspect of psychological health but is not identical to it; positive development can be fostered by negative experiences.[16]

As already noted, psychological health can only be understood as an individual story in the context of collective stories, which are the transmitters of general values. It can therefore be asked, To what extent are the values of a particular group differentiated, integrated, and flexibly organized? When a person lives or has lived in a group where some values are strongly emphasized (e.g., subordination of the individual to the group versus greater emphasis on the individual's goals than those of the group), the valuation system of the individual will clearly be influenced. And the question becomes whether or not the value system adhered to by the family, school, club, military system, employer, and so on, is heterogeneous enough to permit and provide for individual development. If, for example, a person is born the son of a criminal, is raised in a slum, and later spends a few years in prison, it is highly likely that the value systems to which he has been exposed will leave their mark on his personal valuation system.

The conception of psychological health proposed in this book involves recognizing the full meaning of Rogers's term "fully functioning." That is, the person who is capable of moving back and forth between different types of valuations, including the negative ones, and who, moreover, lives in a situation that provides the opportunity to do so is a fully functioning individual. An individual is fully functioning insofar as he or she is able to confront and to move flexibly between all of the different types of valuations (see Figure 4.1)—that is, not only valuations referring to self-enhancement (the left part of the circle), and those referring to contact and union with the other (the right part of the circle), but also positive (pleasant) and negative (unpleasant) valuations.[17]

NOTES

1. This complex valuation has two emphases: One is represented by the first part of the sentence ("the smartest we've ever had") and another by the second part ("when will they discover the reality?"). Different emphases may attract different kinds of affect. In this valuation the S affect is concentrated in the first emphasis and the N affect in the second. The number of emphases within a single valuation is an indication of the complexity of a valuation. (For discussion of the term *emphasis*, see Manual.)

2. A special case of external dependence is "derived self-enhancement." This exists when people gain self-esteem through association with someone who is perceived as particularly strong (e.g., "I admired Debby's way of life, her independence, her self-assurance, which she conveyed to me"). Adorno's classic study of the "authoritarian personality" (Adorno, Frenkel-Brunswik, Levinson, & Sanford, 1950), who feels the need to identify with a powerful hero in order to compensate for inner weaknesses, is also an

example of derived self-enhancement. The presence of derived self-enhancement should be sharply distinguished from the presence of an inspirational device, figure, or statement that has been incorporated into the individual's valuation system. A striking example is Martin Gray's story (filmed as *For All Those I Loved*): Interned in Treblinka, Gray lost his parents and siblings in the war and later lost his wife and children in a forest fire in France. Later, in a television interview, he recalled what his father always told him—"Martin, you must always go on"—and reported that this statement often gave him strength at difficult moments. In other words, this heavily internalized valuation was highly flexible and could be applied in a broad range of situations.

3. Note that the combination of S > O and N > P is not always an indication of opposition. In the foregoing section we noticed that this affective pattern can also refer to the anxiety that can result from increased expectations or overreliance on the opinions of others. With the use of a more refined list of affect terms (Appendix 2), it is possible to distinguish between the two forms of valuations under discussion. The negative consequence of self-enhancement is typically associated with a higher level of anxiety and a lower level of anger, in contrast to the affect pattern associated with opposition.

4. A bias toward the self-enhancement motive or the contact and union with the other motive can be detected by quantitatively comparing the mean S score of all spontaneously formulated valuations with the mean O score. We speak of a clear bias when one mean is twice as high as the other. This quantitative analyses, as already noted, should be followed up with a qualitative analysis in order to isolate the common themes in the formulations.

5. A high level of *secondary* S affect may emanate from the feeling of contact and union with the other. In this case the valuations in questions will have high levels of both S and O affect (representing strength *and* unity; see type +HH in Figure 4.1).

6. This pattern of affect is also basic to the oedipal relation in Freudian psychology: the child has a loving orientation toward the parent of the opposite sex, with the parent of the same sex acting as an obstacle. In Lacan's (1966) version of psychoanalysis, language (*la langue*) represents the fatherlike law, which is an obstacle to the wishes of the child and to which it has to submit.

7. For a more complete understanding of the *fugit amor* concept it should be noted that "a loving orientation toward another person or object that is, or is imagined to be, unreachable" also implies a loving orientation toward a person or object whose well-being or worth is perceived as unreachable. Parents, for example, may be worried about their child's future, thereby overlooking the child's present needs, wishes, and aspirations. In addition, some caution is required in interpreting the −O type of affective pattern. This does not always indicate a *fugit amor* theme. Sometimes it refers to the negative implications or consequences of an experience of contact and union (e.g., recalling a love that is regretted). The evidence for a *fugit amor* experience can be checked by performing modality analyses and examination of the system as a whole.

8. Note that all of the illustrations in this section refer to a loving orientation toward another person who has become unreachable. Although this is the prototypical version of the *fugit amor* experience, other forms do exist, for example, experiencing oneself as unreachable for another loved person or experiencing a loved aspect or "subself" in oneself as unreachable.

9. In her study of achievement motivation in women, Horner (1972) observed a phenomenon called "fear of success," which played a role in women in which high

achievement was perceived as conflicting with their social roles. Fear of success can be interpreted as the felt negative consequence of self-enhancement, that is, as fear resulting from a conflict between actual valuations and the norms of the group or culture.

10. Valuations of type +HH generally have the highest level of positive affect in comparison with all of the other types described. In rare cases, −HH types are found, where high levels of S and O are nevertheless associated with more negative than positive affect. The interpretation of such a valuation is quite difficult because of its complexity. Van Dassel (1985) found a high frequency of this type in the valuation systems of hospitalized widows with unresolved grief experiences. These valuations may, however, also be found in normal functioning, for example, in the person who is persistently looking for self-enhancement and contact with the other although the other has become unreachable.

11. The idea that the two motives receive their integrated form as +HH valuations is in support of Maslow's (1970) concept of "postambivalence": "whole hearted and unconflicted love, acceptance, and expressiveness" (p. 283).

12. Watkins (1986) refers to Corbin's (1972) distinction between the "imaginary" and the "imaginal." Corbin rejects the word *imaginary* because its usage is easily contrasted with the real. *Imaginary* is equated with the unreal, the nonexistent. Our high evaluation of the sensible world, the material and the concrete (what we take to be real), shines a pejorative light on the imaginary. By using the term *imaginal* Corbin hopes to undercut the real–unreal distinction and to propose instead that the imaginal not be assessed in terms of a narrowed conception of reality, but in terms of a broader one that gives credence to the reality of the imaginal.

13. In collective stories, metaphors are also used to express certain emotional experiences. For example, we speak of "the monster of war," "old man winter," and Mother Nature and compare spring to an innocent young girl.

14. Rosenberg (1979) distinguishes between three main aspects of the "ought self": conscience (or superego), role demands (e.g., the nurse should be kind), and idiosyncratic self-demands (e.g., "I must be a good husband"). In our research the affective profile derived from answers to the "ought questions" often correlates very highly with the affective profile referring to the ideal self. This suggests that people typically interpret the "ought question" in terms of Rosenberg's idiosyncratic self-demands.

15. The case study presented in this section is discussed in Hermans, Rijks, and Kempen (1993).

16. There is another reason to be cautious about defining well-being only in positive and negative terms. Gelderloos (1987) found in a longitudinal study of long-term meditators, for example, that the most experienced meditators (Sidhas) associated higher levels of both positive and negative affect with their valuations over time. This was interpreted as an increased capacity to integrate both types of experiences and to actually transcend a positive–negative dichotomy. (See also the Jungian notion of unification of opposites as a criterion for psychological health [Jung, 1959].)

17. The notion of "fully functioning" is particularly relevant to −S valuations in view of the fact that Rogers is often criticized for what others see as the neglect of aggression in his theory and therapeutic system (e.g., May, 1966).

CHAPTER 5

Dreams and Myths:
Routes to the Less Conscious
Areas of the Self

When Abraham (1909) argued that dreams are private myths and that myths are collective dreams, he meant that both dreams and myths are products of human imagination. Indeed, dreams and myths can be conceived of as stories. As told stories they not only reflect the ordering influence of the human psyche but also function as an important means of communication with others and with oneself. Dreams as personal stories and myths as collective stories often include similar symbols (e.g., fish, water, tree, bird, monster). These symbols represent subconscious levels of experience. Therefore, analysis of dreams and myths is particularly significant to any psychology of the self that takes seriously the intrinsic relatedness of conscious and subconscious meanings. The inclusion of dreams and myths in a psychology of valuation has the potential advantage of disclosing sources of meaning of personal and universal significance. The purpose of this chapter is to explore several ways in which dreams and myths may contribute to the understanding of the content and organization of the process of valuation.

DREAMS AS PERSONAL STORIES

In the previous chapters two procedures for examining the subconscious aspects of the valuation system were briefly described. The first one is the inspection of the valuation system for a discrepancy between text and affect, that is, for places where the conscious formulation of the text of a valuation presents information other than or in conflict with the less conscious affect pattern found to be associated with the valuation. Upon detection of the discrepancy, the person may be invited to reformulate the valuation in such a way that the text is more congruent with the affective information. In doing so, the client may extend the self-narrative to include some of the less conscious aspects of the self. The second procedure involves providing the client with possible supplemental valuations. When clients perceive such "external" statements (e.g., proverbs, passages from a novel, direct statements from the psychologist) as personally relevant, they may become more conscious of certain aspects of themselves.

There is also a third road to the less conscious layers of the self, a road that is considered in the psychological and psychoanalytic literature to be a "royal road": the dream. Dreams, or at least particular types of dreams, are interesting because they represent ordered stories in which, using Sarbin's (1986) terms, the person/author sees himself or herself as an actor relating to other actors. But to what extent is there really a similarity between stories and dreams?

For Foulkes (1978), who considered the dream to be a pictorial sentence (e.g., "I wanted to fly but couldn't move"), the achievements of dreaming are ordinary rather than exotic, linear rather than nonlinear, and generally expressible in words. He also suggested, based on this assumption, that it may be most profitable to focus on the many strong structural parallels between dreams and ordinary, serial, linguistically guided thought. To dwell on the features that dreams may share with poorly understood and highly specialized altered states of consciousness (e.g., Tart, 1969) may not be the most fruitful approach to studying dreams.

Continuity between Waking and Dreaming

An additional reason for studying dreams in close connection with other variants of human experience is that there is solid evidence for a continuity between the concerns and characteristics of dreams and waking life. For example, demographic variables, such as sex, age, race, marital status, and social class, are often reflected in the content of dreams. Winget, Kramer, and Whitman (1972) found all of these factors to be associated with dream content, with sex showing the most content differences. Whereas women reported more characters and emotions in their dreams, men had more aggression and achievement themes in theirs.

Whether or not sociocultural differences are reflected in dreams has also been examined by Levine (1966), who analyzed the dreams of three groups of Nigerian schoolboys. On the basis of his knowledge of the power systems of three culturally distinct groups, the Hansa, the Yoruba, and the Ibo, Levine predicted the frequency of achievement imagery in the recalled dreams of the individuals within each group. He was thereby able to order the groups accordingly. The more powerful groups had dreams with more achievement imagery.

Research by Breger (1969); Domino (1976); Foulkes (1967, 1971); Foulkes, Larson, Swanson, and Rardin (1969); and Hermans (1987b) has also pointed to the continuity between waking and dreaming. Foulkes, who studied the dreams of children at different age levels, offered two hypotheses: (1) Children's dreams are mostly realistic representations of their waking life, and (2) when waking life is disturbed by some personality dysfunction, dreams are also disturbed. The continuity between dreaming and waking has also been found in adults. In their review of the literature of various demographic and personality characteristics, Webb and Cartwright (1978) concluded that dream characteristics correctly reflect the emotional concerns of waking life. In other words, dreams are more continuous with waking life than has been suspected.

Although it is undoubtedly true that people dream a number of dreams each night, as rapid eye movement (REM) research has shown, some dreams are nevertheless felt to be more important than others. Moreover, these dreams are often reported to other people or reflected upon in some other way as intriguing or meaningful stories. Even when people are not aware of the precise meaning of such dreams, they are often still felt to be of particular importance, to imply some basic truth or relevant message. In Jung's (1967) terms, these dreams are considered "big dreams," in contrast to the many quickly forgotten "small dreams" that pass through our minds. Thus, even when one considers dreams as originating from unconscious personality domains, one must admit that at least some dreams have particular relevance to the self.

Actually, the difference between conscious and unconscious is not, in fact, a set dichotomy. Rather, the conscious/unconscious distinction is a theoretical one and is part of a broader analytic strategy. Freud, for example, took the unconscious as primary and moved from the unconscious to the conscious, as expressed in his famous statement "Wo es war, soll Ich werden [Where id was, ego shall be]." James (1890), however, was primarily interested in the "stream of consciousness," and moved from the conscious to the unconscious. In his comparison of James and Freud, Hart (1981) emphasized that although these thinkers had very different views of the unconscious, they were both nevertheless concerned with conscious *and* unconscious processes. Hart concluded that for James the unconscious was attainable from consciousness and was felt but unnamed whereas for Freud the unconscious was neither felt nor named but causative (i.e., underlying most behavior).

When the act of conscious self-reflection, conceived of as a dynamic relation between the I and the Me, is considered in this context, it can be seen that "gaps" in the consciousness (James, 1890, p. 259) represent aspects of the Me that are felt as relevant by the I but cannot yet be filled. The exploration of the unconscious from the perspective of the conscious has an important implication, moreover, which can be seen as an advantage: If an individual can feel certain gaps during the process of self-reflection, the relevance of these gaps can be taken as an index of the need to incorporate certain unconscious material into the working self.

On the basis of these considerations, the following were taken as starting points for our dream analyses:

1. Dreams can be described as "pictorial sentences" or "pictorial valuations" (e.g., "I climbed a high ladder"), whereas waking experiences have more the character of conceptual valuations (e.g., "I passed a difficult test"). If dreams are treated as part of the total valuation system, they can be studied, in keeping with the continuity hypothesis, as part of a system of meaning. As Kramer (1982) has observed, meaning does not exist in the dream itself but is attached to the dream by some external system of reference. In this case, the organized valuation system provides the context for an individual's interpretation of a dream and for the study of dreams.

2. Dreams, in so far as they are related in sentences, can be conceived of as manifest valuations whose variability in content may be nearly endless. This means that both dreams and speech represent Chomsky's problem of generativity, that is, the question of how humans can generate an infinite set of surface expressions from a finite base of experience. Both Freud (1900) and Chomsky (1968) have responded to this question, each in his own terminology. Freud distinguished two levels of personality functioning (i.e., the latent and manifest levels), and Chomsky distinguished between the deep and surface levels of syntactic structure. In both cases, however, the deeper or latent level is characterized by a relatively small set of operations. Freud's and Chomsky's views suggest that dreams, seen as another set of manifest valuations, should also be understood as based on a latent set of motives.

3. Although dream symbols may be very vivid and allow for extensive and detailed reporting, the meaning of these symbols is not always immediately clear. Dream symbols, in all their richness, are typically ambiguous and interpretable in many ways. Through their linguistic expression, which requires a certain degree of interpretation, the inherent ambiguity of the dream can be reduced, which often leads to an increased awareness of the dream's significance for the self.[1]

4. As part of an organized process of valuation, dreams are temporally and spatially structured. As Eigen (1983) has emphasized, dreams develop typically over time (e.g., involve a journey or a long climb up a ladder). Moreover, dreams typically develop in an imaginal space. In that space the dreamer sees himself or herself as an actor confronted with other actors (e.g., in a fight with an opponent or in a loving encounter with a special person). And in keeping with the continuity hypothesis, changes in the content and organization of the dream represent changes in the content and structure of the valuations (e.g., changing from the position of loser toward the position of winner).

Procedure for the Investigation of Dreams

In self-investigation research over the years, we have observed that clients sometimes spontaneously relate one or more dreams in response to the questions used to elicit valuations (Chapter 3). On the basis of this observation and in order to study dreams in a more systematic way, we added the following question to the valuation elicitation phase: "Have you had a dream that you consider important enough to include in your self-investigation?" Using this question with a variety of clients, we found that about 30% reported a dream.

When clients want to include a dream, they are asked to give a full report of the content of the dream to the psychologist. This report includes the chronological sequence of events and circumstances (as the client remembers them). Next, clients are invited to select those parts of the dream that they perceive to be most relevant. These parts are then phrased as one or more sentences, which are then treated as dream valuations; that is, they are rated by the client on the same list of affect terms. It is then possible to characterize the affective properties of dreams by using the indices previously described and comparing these to the affective properties of the other valuations in the client's system. In this comparison, index *r* plays a crucial role. When one wants to study a dream valuation in the context of the valuation system as a whole, the affective profile of this particular dream valuation can be correlated with the profiles of each of the other valuations (i.e., with each selected as the pivot in a modality analysis). The waking valuation showing the highest correlation (i.e., the valuation bearing an affective profile similar to that found to characterize the dream) is most relevant for the interpretation of the particular dream.[2]

In the case of several successive self-investigations with the same individual, changes in the dream valuations can be studied using the following questions as guides: In a subsequent investigation has a particular dream been eliminated as unimportant, modified in significant aspects, or replaced by another dream? If it is modified or replaced by another dream valuation, what is the affective profile of this valuation? How does it relate to the other valuations in the system? All of these analyses can contribute to the understanding of the personal meaning of the original dream and its significance for the self.

The Repetitious Traumatic Dream

Because dreams are continuous with waking life, they may constitute a useful device for identifying the important issues in a person's waking life. Moreover, in accordance with the continuity hypothesis, it is neceassary to study the content and ordering of the dream in relation to the content and ordering of the valuation system as a whole. Of particular relevance here is the so-called repetitious traumatic dream, where a highly negative event (or series of events) frequently occurs in a dream. The event is always the same, shows no significant change over time, and is generally associated with a high level of anxiety. The term "repetitious traumatic dream" is from Kramer (1982), who in his dream research distinguished between a "repetitious traumatic" pattern, in which no progress occurs and the problem is essentially restated in each occurrence of the dream, and a "sequential progressive" pattern, in which a problem is stated, worked on, and resolved.

One example of a repetitious traumatic dream comes from a client whose mother committed suicide during a fight with her husband. The client formulated her dream, which she labeled as "a frequently occurring nightmare" since childhood, as follows:

	S	O	P	N
Valuation 1. "I continually see how my mother mutilated herself."	0	3	0	13

The same client presented the following valuations from her waking life:

	S	O	P	N
Valuation 2. "Because we moved constantly, I now never feel at home."	0	3	0	15
Valuation 3. "I was often slapped, and therefore I am afraid of my environment."	0	1	0	15

These waking valuations correlated most highly (.97 and .93, respectively) with the dream valuation. Looking at the content of the valuations, we observe in Valuation 2 the word "never" and in Valuation 3 the word "often." These suggest that the theme of isolation and feeling unsafe is a frequently occurring one. Undoubtedly, her mother's suicide had a great impact on this client's life, but this is not enough to describe her present situation. Her situation is better understood if we see the dream as symbolizing her existence in time and space, as bearing the same pattern of affect as valuations, suggesting that she never feels safe or at home anywhere. In this sense, the repetitious nature of the dream reflects the static nature of the system as a whole.

The Sequential Progressive Dream

In dreams of a sequential progressive type the dream does not rigidly recur but shows some kind of progressive change (i.e., plot development). We suspect that this change is related to a similar sort of progression in the waking valuation system (or a subcomponent of it). In order to illustrate this possibility, we present an analysis of the dream of Karin, a client who remembered, before she entered therapy, that she had been sexually abused by her father (discussed by Hermans, 1987b). Karin's dream was analyzed in three successive self-investigations over a period of 14 months, during which time she was experiencing marital problems. In the first investigation she gave the following report of a dream she had had 8 weeks before :

"I was with Tim [her youngest son] in a fun fair with several cycle tracks. I was afraid to walk on those tracks. Tim led me by the hand, though. At a given moment we couldn't go on. We were standing on the roof of a bandstand, and he said, 'We can jump down here; then we are closer to the exit.' He jumped; I was still standing there. I did not have the courage to; then a tall, wide-shouldered man in a torn shirt appeared and said, 'Come and stand on my shoulders; then I'll help you get down.' At the exit, however, there was a tub with goldfish in it, and Charles [her husband] forced me to eat them. I did not want to, but he held my hands behind my back and forced me to eat them."

This dream report, with several shifts of scene and twists in the story, was ordered by Karin, with the help of the psychologist, into four sequential sentences. In each sentence she combined those elements of the dream that she considered to belong together (see the left side of Table 5.1). Each of these four dream valuations was then correlated with all of the other valuations in the system in order to isolate and compare those correlating the highest with the dream valuations (see the right side of Table 5.1).

Six months later, in the second self-investigation (Time 2), Karin included a new valuation in her system, which was apparently derived from the fourth element of her dream: "Now I am swallowing all those fish against my will." She was now using a symbol in the original dream to metaphorically characterize her present negative situation: Between the first and second investigations she separated from her husband, who was now preventing her from seeing her children. The relevance of this aspect of the original dream is also indicated by the most highly correlated valuation, which suggests a negatively experienced need to stand up to her husband.

We were able to follow the dream over time because Karin performed a third investigation, 8 months after the second one. In this investigation she reported that she had had the original dream again but with the last part modified. This was then phrased as a modified dream valuation (see Table 5.1). A most impressive change is revealed when the last dream part is followed over time. At Time 1 there was a complete lack of self-esteem, which did not change much when Karin provided the metaphorical transformation at Time 2. But at Time 3, the modified dream shows a strong S > O asymmetry, with a high correlation with a more positively experienced waking valuation, as we can see in Table 5.1.

TABLE 5.1. Comparison of Dream and Wake Valuations Presented by Karin

Valuations	S	O	P	N	r	Highest-correlating wake valuations	S	O	P	N
Investigation 1 (comparison of dream valuations, on left, with wake valuations that correlate most highly)										
Tim [son] took my hand and led me through the fair.	6	19	16	4	.76	I feel responsible for the atmosphere, wherever I am.	7	14	9	9
We were standing on the roof of a bandstand and he said, "We can jump down here; then we are closer to the exit."	0	8	3	17	.74	I often feel nervous and anxious.	0	8	0	20
Tim jumped. I did not have the courage to. Then a tall, wide-shouldered man in a torn shirt appeared and said, "Come and stand on my shoulders; I'll help you get down."	8	16	20	0	.79	I am beginning to accept my body as it is; I am satisfied with it.	17	18	18	0
Holding my hands behind my back, Charles [husband] forced me to eat the fish, although I did not want to.	0	0	0	20	.99	Mother accused us of seducing father.	0	0	0	19
Investigation 2 (comparison of a new wake valuation, on left, with the wake valuation that correlates most highly)										
Now I am swallowing all those fish against my will.	3	0	0	20	.86	I am taking a firm stand against Charles.	11	1	0	20
Investigation 3 (comparison of modified dream valuation, on left, with the wake valuation that correlates most highly)										
The fish have become transparent, and only a few of them are left. They look jellylike, while at first they were solid fish, and my hands are no longer held behind my back, either.	17	0	5	4	.88	I feel that I must show Charles that I am his match.	17	1	10	5

Note. S, affect reflects self-enhancement; O, affect reflects desire for contact with others; P, positive affect; N, negative affect; r, product–moment correlation between the two affective profiles. From Hermans (1987b). Copyright 1987 by *Journal of Personality and Social Psychology.* Reprinted with permission.

The last element in the original dream (Time 1), which played such a crucial role in Karin's later modifications of this dream, was highly related to past experiences of powerlessness with her parents. Karin still had bad memories of her father's incestuous behavior with her and her sister. When her mother discovered the incest, she blamed Karin and her sister for it, a reaction that led Karin to have an extremely negative valuation of her past. It seems that this past experience of powerlessness had been reactivated by Karin's current troubles with her husband, who in the dream symbolically forces her to eat something against her will. Later (Time 3) Karin had a dream that symbolized her increased strength in the struggle with her husband.

In sum, we observe in this case a change in a dream and a concomitant change in the valuation system. This suggests that the dream images give expression to corresponding developments in the valuation system as a whole. That is, the dream provides a powerful symbol (the fish), which is used by the client to give metaphorical expression to a relevant aspect of her waking life. (For other case studies involving the relation between dreams and metaphors for waking life, see Hermans, 1987b.[3])

Interpretation on the Subject Level or on the Object Level

From the perspective of self-narrative, there is a remarkable difference between waking and dreaming states. In the waking state one's coactors are in fact other people who have an existence separate from oneself. In the dream state the coactors may be other people, but as actors in one's own dream they are the product of one's imagination. This brings us to a distinction, originally made by Jung (1967), between the interpretation of dreams "on the object level" and "the subject level." When a dream is interpreted on the object level, the other people in the dream refer to characteristics of other people in the dreamer's actual social relations. When the interpretation is on the subject level, the other people refer to aspects of the dreamer's self. In other words, on the subject level, coactors are to be interpreted as characteristics of the dreamer.

Let us look at the following example from a 28-year-old client who reported a dream she had as a 7-year-old girl waking up after surgery. In this dream a significant other played a central role, which later appeared to be the client herself. The dream unfolds in three successive sentences.

	S	O	P	N
Valuation 1. "We went camping on an island with the whole family; the water rose and we had to creep closer and closer together."	0	1	0	3

	S	O	P	N
Valuation 2. "The water washed away the sand, and I disappeared into the sea."	0	0	4	1
Valuation 3. "Aunt Bea held out her hand to me."	2	0	4	1

The three dream elements all have very low levels on the indices, suggesting a low level of affective significance. On the basis of this observation alone, one would be inclined to think that the dream has little, if any, relevance to the present self. However, in the second investigation, 9 months later, the client decided to retain the dream in the valuation system. At this point the indices were much more extreme, with a significant addition to the third dream valuation (Valuation 6).

	S	O	P	N
Valuation 4. "We went camping on an island with the whole family; the water rose and we had to creep closer and closer together."	1	0	2	14
Valuation 5. "The water washed away the sand, and I disappeared into the sea."	2	0	0	17
Valuation 6. "Aunt Bea held out her hand to me. . . . I was Aunt Bea."	12	2	12	0

When Valuation 6 was selected for further study, it showed the highest correlation ($r = .94$) with a valuation in which the client assessed her sessions with the psychologist:

	S	O	P	N
Valuation 7. "The sessions with the psychologist gave me some security, the feeling that there was some place where I could unload my problems and have them taken seriously."	11	0	13	0

The high correlation between Valuations 6 and 7 suggests a relation between the meaning of the dream and of the therapeutic sessions: In the sessions the client has found stable ground where she can help herself. However, such an interpretation evokes an intriguing question. The saving hand in the childhood dream

could not have been from the psychologist or from the client herself in psychotherapy since the psychotherapeutic situation simply did not exist in her life situation at that time. If we conclude from this that the relation detected between
the dream and the therapeutic sessions is meaningless, how can we possibly hope
to understand the nearly perfect similarity between the affective profiles of the
two valuations? Our suggestion involves the symbolic nature of dreams and the
fact that a dream can have many meanings. The symbol of the saving hand (or,
in a more religious form, of the saviour) can have various interpretations, depending on the sociocultural situation and specific aspects of the individual's personal
situation. In other words, the saving hand is a rather general symbol, which leaves
room for interpretation in terms of the people who can function as saving figures
and the circumstances that may call for such a figure. Such a symbol is a signal
that the dreamer is highly sensitive to a protective or saviour figure. In this case,
the child needed protection and therefore thought of a beloved relative. Later,
the saving figure became herself; that is, the dream called for a subject-level
interpretation rather than an object-level one.

The Dream Filling a Gap in Consciousness

The dreams discussed so far in this chapter all relate to some aspect of the individual's present valuation system. In one way or another, they are already formulated in the waking valuations. But one may go one step further to ask whether
the waking valuations occur before or after the dream valuation. Dreams that
occur before are of particular importance because they draw attention to a particular aspect of the individual's life situation that is as yet not explicitly formulated in the waking system. When a dream succeeds in isolating experiences relevant to the self, a more complete self-narrative is the result. In the following
paragraph we briefly discuss a case in which information was formulated as a
dream valuation before it was formulated as a waking valuation.

This case concerns a client who recalled a dream he had after the death of
his father 12 years earlier, a dream he had never understood. The dream was
introduced in the first investigation as the following valuation:

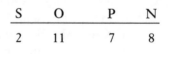

	S	O	P	N
Valuation 1. "After the death of my father I went home. Father lay upstairs in a coma, and we all knew that he would come out of it. He came out of the coma, and that was a strange experience."	2	11	7	8

In the second investigation this dream was eliminated from his system simply
because he no longer saw its relevance (he was then quite busy with his rela-

tion with his mother, who was still alive and attracted a great many of his valuations). In a third investigation, 15 months after the first one, the client referred
to the dream mentioned in the first investigation and explained that this dream
had in fact made him think about his relation to his father. He proposed two
new valuations in place of the original dream for inclusion in the third investigation:

	S	O	P	N
Valuation 2. "After his death, father was placed on a pedestal; no wrong could be said about him."	0	1	0	13
Valuation 3. "My father was a stranger to me."	3	2	1	12

Apparently, the position of his father "upstairs" in the dream made the client
conscious of the holy position occupied by his father, and this awareness later
manifested itself more explicitly as Valuation 2. Similarly, the "strange experience" in Valuation 1 led him to the perception of his father as a stranger in
Valuation 3.

The fact that certain valuations derive from a dream, however, is by no
means an argument that all dreams fill a gap in the conscious self. There are
several points that deserve attention when considering the possibility that
dreams are used to complement and extend the conscious self. First, it is a precondition that clients themselves select a dream that they see as particularly
relevant. Second, clients must then select those aspects of the dream they perceive as most relevant and formulate them as separate sentences. Third, the
affective involvement of the client in the dream must be assessed (see the discussion of the indices in Chapter 3). Fourth, there is a possibility that the dream
delivers valuations with a content that has not yet been addressed in the system as a whole. Finally, it must be shown that the waking valuations derived
from the dream influence to a significant degree the content and organization
of the valuation system as a whole (i.e., make the system feel more complete to
the client). In conclusion, the possibility that a dream is filling some gap in the
conscious self can only be evaluated following careful quantitative and qualitative analyses of the valuation system itself.

The Murderer as Antagonist: Opposing Forces in an Extended Self

The dreams discussed so far do not profit sufficiently from the dialogical nature of the self. In order to take an additional step, let us take the following
description of the dialogical self as a starting point:

We conceptualize the self in terms of a dynamic multiplicity of relatively autonomous *I* positions in an imaginal landscape. In its most concise form this conception
can be formulated as follows. The *I* has the possibility to move, as in a space, from
one position to the other in accordance with changes in situation and time. The *I*
fluctuates among different and even opposed positions. The *I* has the capacity to
imaginatively endow each position with a voice so that dialogical relations between
positions can be established. The voices function like interacting characters in a story.
Once a character is set in motion in a story, the character takes on a life of its own
and thus assumes a certain narrative necessity. Each character has a story to tell about
experiences from its own stance. As different voices these characters exchange information about their respective *Me*'s and their worlds, resulting in a complex, narratively structured self. (Hermans, Kempen, & Van Loon, 1992, pp. 28–29)

On the basis of this definition, we have explored dreams not only from the
perspective of the protagonist but also from that of the antagonist, inviting the
former as well as the latter to tell his or her own story in the form of a separate
system of valuations. The guiding question in these explorations is, To what extent is it possible to extend the self beyond the limits of existing self-boundaries
by including oppositional characters in the dream as parts of a broadened self-
narrative?

The following case is of a 50-year-old man, Paul, who wanted to perform a
self-investigation during a period of conflict with his partner, a woman who was
10 years his elder. His partner proposed that Paul do a self-investigation, which
she had already done in an earlier period, and he consented in the expectation
that it would help him to clarify his situation and the relationship with her in particular. Before we describe one of his dreams, in which a murderer played a central role, let us first have a look at some of the valuations of Paul's ordinary valuation system, in some of which he also refers to his partner (Valuations 4 and 5):

	S	O	P	N
Valuation 1. "After my mother lectured me about sex, she conveyed her anxiety to me."	2	0	0	13
Valuation 2. "I had a happy youth: a lot of freedom and a very good friend."	17	16	19	1
Valuation 3. "I have problems with other people when I feel that they give me less space than I need."	1	0	1	17
Valuation 4. "Kitty [his partner] challenges me, is very direct, goes her own way, is attractive and unconventional."	11	19	17	9

	S	O	P	N
Valuation 5. "Kitty has something superior; she always stresses this very much. I often feel weak, but her general attitude that we balance each other out corrects this."	11	18	15	7
Valuation 6. "I feel strongly opposed to hypocrites who present something as being in the general interest where it is, in fact, of personal interest."	9	0	0	10

In Valuation 5, Paul identifies his main problem in the relationship with his partner, but he seems to cover this problem with a highly positive appreciation of her attitude that they balance each other, which functioned as a commonly endorsed ideal in their discussions. The result is that Valuation 5 as a whole is very positive and of the same type (+HH) as the preceding valuation. At the end of the valuation construction phase, however, Paul told of a dream in which he saw himself acting as a priest who was confronted with a dangerous opponent who had the double identity of priest and murderer:

"I'm in a village that seems to be threatened by a murderer. Vaguely I remember two dead bodies, one in the neighborhood of the confessional and one in or near the church. I take care of the people coming to the church as well as possible, a consoling center of safety and trust. . . . Outside, high above the village, a murderer is climbing up to the spires of the tower. I'm close upon his heels. The only things with which we can pull ourselves up are small pointed projections with ornaments. At any moment they could crumble under my feet. This is madness, I decide. I stop. . . . Downstairs in the village, I find myself among the people again. Out of a group an older woman approaches me, and says, 'Thanks for what you have done for me.' I understand that she means a kind of priestlike help. I feel a vague sense of surprise. However, in the back of my head I think or, better, I observe, hesitatingly and not without compassion: 'Yes, but you will be the next victim.'"

Upon awakening, Paul was puzzled by this intriguing dream. In particular, he asked himself how he, in the role of pursuer, not being the murderer, could know that the woman (standing for his own partner, he suspected) would be the next victim. When only the murderer could know who would be the next victim, how could he himself, in the position of the pursuer, have this knowledge? This riddle was reason enough to include the dream as part of the self-investigation and to explore more thoroughly the role of the different actors involved. It was decided to investigate the dream from two positions, that of the protagonist (the pursuer) and that of the antagonist (the murderer). Paul was asked first to formulate a series of valuations from the perspective of the pursuer, and later, in a second round, to formulate another set of valuations from the perspective of the murderer. In the latter case, he was invited to proceed as if he were the murderer and to formulate not only the valuations but also the associated affect from this perspective. Finally, after Paul had taken the opportunity to digest the results, he was asked, 2 weeks later, to examine his ordinary valuation system and focus on what he had learned from his dream investigation. He then decided to add three new valuations that were not yet included in his original self-investigation. The results of the entire dream investigation are presented in Table 5.2.

As Table 5.2 shows, there is a clear difference between the valuations of the pursuer and the murderer, both in content and associated affect. The murderer vents his blind aggression directly and vehemently (Valuation 7), acts as an anonymous power (Valuation 8), and expresses an attitude of animosity and crude indifference (Valuation 11 and 13). The affect pattern of the valuations from the murderer are very clearly of type −S, representing opposition and anger (see Figure 4.1). Note the very high S level of most of the valuations of the murderer (Valuations 7–13) and the absolute absence of any O affect. This is in contrast with the more moderate valuations from the pursuer (Valuations 1–6), which are not very articulated in S − O differences and less extreme in P − N differences.

Concentrating on the valuations from the pursuer and the murderer, Paul became even more convinced than before that the murderer was part of himself. He noticed not only that he felt a great deal of aggression toward his partner (the older woman in the dream) but also that he was "murdering" himself by not defending himself. The dream fostered in Paul the insight that he was complying too much to the demands of his partner: "I'm my own murderer by demanding too much of myself and reaching too high."

With this insight Paul was asked to formulate some valuations expressing what he had learned from this dream. He then added three new valuations (Valuations 14–16 in Table 5.2). As indicated by the affective indices, these valuations were not of the −S type, as one might perhaps expect, but of the −LL type. What is the reason for including such negative and rather weak valuations? Why would Paul not include strong, aggressive valuations in his own (waking) system after he had admitted that the murderer was part of himself? When these questions were posed to Paul, he answered, "I keep this far from me; I see this as something bad and it is not in this way that I have organized my life." In other words, although Paul admitted that the murderer was in himself, he kept the aggression of the murderer at a distance by not including it in his own valuation system. Note that it is not true that Paul was completely wary of −S type valuations. A valuation of this type was already included in his or-

TABLE 5.2. Valuations from the Pursuer and the Murderer in Paul's Dream and Paul's Own Responses to the Dream

	S	O	P	N
Valuations from the pursuer in Paul's dream				
1. There is a village community threatened by a murderer.	6	7	1	14
2. I chase him to the pinnacles of the tower.	9	6	2	8
3. I stop; it is becoming too dangerous.	6	2	1	14
4. I am down again among the people.	4	6	5	5
5. An older woman comes to me and says, "Thanks for the help you gave me" (as a clergyman gives).	13	10	7	2
6. In the back of my head I notice: "You will be the next victim."	6	4	3	4
Valuations from the murderer in Paul's dream				
7. I hate them; I kill them all.	16	0	2	15
8. They don't yet know me; I'm simply going to join them.	13	0	8	8
9. What does he want, the guy who follows me?	10	0	0	11
10. I will not fall down.	18	0	8	11
11. I'm fed up with it (being spiritual); what is left of me?	9	0	0	20
12. It didn't work up to anything.	3	0	0	20
13. I don't care anymore.	13	0	3	14
Valuations expressing Paul's own response to his dream				
14. There are a lot of situations in which I have harmed myself by not defending myself.	2	2	1	13
15. I don't know very well where the limit is between accepting and not accepting.	2	0	1	11
16. The feelings that are associated with my experiences—I'm not very well aware of them.	1	0	2	12

dinary valuation system (see the last one of the six valuations presented earlier in this discussion). However, this valuation lacks a fierce character both in the affective patterning and in the formulation. This suggests that Paul kept his aggression at a certain distance, giving it a rather peripheral place in his self-space.

However, this distancing from hate and aggression does not mean that Paul had learned nothing from his dream investigation. Paul is explicit about what he has learned in the formulation of Valuations 14 to 16 in Table 5.2. He has become more aware of how he relates to himself (Valuation 14), he is questioning what to accept and what to reject (Valuation 15), and he realizes that he has more feelings than he formerly was willing to admit (Valuation 16). The fact that this extension of his self-knowledge takes the form of negative valuations with low S and O affect suggests that Paul has become aware, with a considerable degree of pain and anxiety, of things that have broken through his usual self-definition. The fact that he is willing to accept some new insights (Valuations 14–16) means that the corresponding experiences are not repressed but, rather, transformed into a type of valuation that does not undermine the moral nature of his self system too much. Whether Paul is able to transform these potentially fertile insights into productive outcomes will depend on his further development (we had no opportunity to follow up this client).

Self–Nonself Boundaries in a Multivoiced Self

Paul's case touches the broader theoretical issue of the boundaries of the self. As Gregg (1991) has argued, people generally make a distinction between self and nonself, often in close correspondence with a distinction between in-group, the group one identifies with, and out-group, the group one does not identify with. A sharp distinction may result in a splitting between phenomena that are defined by the person as belonging to the self and those that are classified as nonself. In psychoanalytic circles it is commonplace to observe clients splitting off impulses from the self that conflict with superego moral demands.

From a dialogical perspective of the self it is assumed that there are multiple possible positions in an imaginal space about which the I can move. In Paul's case we have discerned at least three positions, each with their specific system of valuations: (1) the position of Paul himself, as expressed in his ordinary valuation system; (2) the position of the pursuer, as expressed in a series of dream valuations; and (3) the position of the murderer, which is associated with yet another series of valuations. When Paul uses the word "I," this I is primarily located at the center of his ordinary (waking) valuation system, for which he feels fully responsible. The I positioned in the pursuer (the good guy) is already at some psychological distance from Paul's ordinary position. The position of the murderer is even further removed, although Paul admits that the murderer is somewhere in himself. Although Paul does not go so far as to split off the position and the valuations of the murderer from his ordinary self, he is reluctant to accept those valuations as belonging to the center of his self-definition and to feel equally responsible for them.

In fact, we find in Paul's case an example of what Gregg (1991) has described as "identity-in-difference." The intentions of the murderer are perceived by Paul both as identical to his self (they belong to it) and as different from his self (they do not belong to it). In that case the valuations of the murderer are, paradoxically, inside and outside of the self at the same time. This peculiar form of self-organization can be understood by taking the multivoiced nature of the dialogical self into account. When the self exists in a multiplicity of positions, one may observe that one position is more familiar and safe than the others. The familiar position is most directly expressed not only by the word "I" but also by the person's first name ("I am Paul"), and these words indicate the center of one's self-definition. However, when other positions, less familiar and perhaps more threatening, enter the realm of the self (e.g., the murderer in Paul's case), these unfamiliar positions may be suppressed or even split off from one's usual self-definition. In that case, sharp boundaries are drawn very close around one highly centralized position, and any dialogical interactions with other positions are precluded. When the person succeeds in extending the self by including the less familiar positions as part of a broader multivoiced self, the widening of the self–nonself boundaries allows for a multivoiced self of a more decentralized nature. Instead of one centralized position, there is a greater diversity of positions. Each position has its own center of organization (and own specific narrative), allowing for a decentralized multiplicity of voices, as Sampson (1985, 1993) would describe it. In this more articulated multifaceted self the several positions are not simply equivalent; rather, the individual identifies more with one position than with another, even if fluctuations in situation and time permit the I to fluctuate among diverse or even opposite positions. The identity-in-difference organization of the self typically applies to those positions that are included in the self but at the same time receive a rather peripheral place in the spatial organization of the self.

The conflicting positions, even if included, keep their aura of being "not really me" or "something for which I am not really responsible." It is this ambivalence in the self-organization that accounts for the identity-in-difference phenomenon. A similar experience can be found in actual social relationships when one person recognizes himself or herself in another person. In his book *The Stranger*, the French existentialist Albert Camus describes the main character, Meursault, as a suspect in a court case who sees a journalist sitting in front of him. At that moment Meursault has the definite feeling that he, Meursault, is gazing at himself. In this case the journalist is a different person but, at the same time, identical to Meursault. In daily life, moreover, one may meet another person in whom one recognizes oneself more or less, in a positive or negative sense. In both cases, the other is different yet identical at the same time, an experience that is quite difficult to understand on the basis of traditional Aristotelian logic.

For a multivoiced conception of the self, the "as if" concept provides a powerful tool for extending the self to positions that tend to be excluded from the self or suppressed under the weight of a highly centralized organization. In the good tradition of personal construct psychology, Gestalt therapy, psychodrama, and many other fields in psychology and psychotherapy, we proposed to Paul that he speak as if he were the murderer. This instruction resulted in a set of valuations that were not included in the dream report presented earlier in this chapter. This means that the usual dream report is told from a particular position, in Paul's case, the position of the protagonist. We have followed a procedure in which we attempted to widen the self-boundaries to such a degree that Paul spoke not only about the murderer but also as if he were the murderer. As we have seen, the valuations of the antagonist (the murderer) were different both in content and organization from those of the protagonist (the pursuer). When we invited Paul to give a response to the murderer from his usual position, he transformed the very aggressive −S valuations into the more anxious −LL valuations. This suggests that Paul, confronted with a dangerous guest entering through the opened doors of his self, gave a response that was insightful and anxious at the same time.

In sum, a dialogical conception of the self allows for a widening of the self–nonself boundaries in such a way that positions that are closed off from the self under usual circumstances are taken up as part of an extended, multivoiced self. In this active process of positioning the I fluctuates among diverse, opposed, and even conflicting positions, resulting in a more or less extended self. The narrative "as if" construction provides a productive strategy for opening the self to positions that are excluded from the usual self-definitions. This exclusion has assumed the nature of habit under the influence of socialization processes and cultural biases that foster a highly centralized, restricted self with sharp boundaries between self and nonself.

COLLECTIVE STORIES: THEMES IN GREEK MYTHOLOGY

The aim of this section is to draw some parallels between personal and collective stories by using various Greek myths to illustrate the occurrence of basic psychological motives. It must be emphasized that our intention is not just an analysis of Greek mythology. Rather, the illustrations are intended as an invitation to look at various products of collective imagination in greater detail. One could study in a similar way, for example, famous fairy tales, widely read novels, plays or movies that have been popular during a particular era, classic themes in the Bible, sculpture, pantomime, or perhaps even music. We have, for illustrative purposes, selected Greek mythology because Greek civilization has contributed to our Western culture in important ways and because certain themes in Greek mythology are easily recognized by people today. Special attention is devoted to the Narcissus myth, which serves as an example of how central themes in collective stories can be used for assessment purposes.

The choice of myth was based on the following two parallels observed between personal and collective stories:

1. A personal story can be typified by its most dominant theme (or type of valuation). A myth, as a collective story, can also be typified by its most dominant theme. For example, when one type of valuation dominates a person's system, let us say a +S valuation, we can conclude that this person feels, on the manifest level of functioning, that he or she is a strong person. Similarly, when we read the story of Odysseus and all his brave deeds, we can conclude that he was a hero; that is, we characterize him according to his most prominent deeds. In the same way, the Erinyes can be characterized as the goddesses of revenge and aggression (–S); the Muses as symbols of esthetic experience (+O); the story of Orpheus, who tried to bring back his lost Eurydice from the underworld, as a *fugit amor* experience (–O); Tantalus, who was severely punished, as representing isolation (–LL), and the powerful Aphrodite as the perfect combination of love and strength (+HH). (See Figure 5.1.)

2. Just as a personal story can be described as an organized process, so too can a myth be described as a composite of collective themes. A person with a predominance of +S valuations has not only this type of valuation in the system but also one or more other types (as we have seen in Chapter 4). Likewise, collective stories, particularly those with a strong dramatic quality, typically include more than one theme. In such stories the main theme gains in expressiveness and excitement through the tension resulting from the inclusion of a second or third theme in the same plot. In this context, the Odysseus epic can be reanalyzed to illustrate the use of contrasting themes to heighten the expressive quality of the story as a whole.[4]

Odysseus as a Hero (+S)

Odysseus is the hero of the *Odyssey*, Homer's epic poem, and one of the most frequently portrayed figures in Western literature.[5] According to Homer, Odysseus was the King of Ithaca, son of Laërtes and Anticlea, and father, with his wife Penelope, of Telemachus. Homer portrayed Odysseus as a man of outstanding courage, endurance, eloquence, resourcefulness, and wisdom. In the *Iliad*, Odysseus appeared to be the man best suited for coping with the crises or conflicts of the Greeks. His bravery and skill were repeatedly demonstrated in fighting.

Traits such as bravery, strength, diplomacy, and enterprising spirit can be historically deconstructed by isolating the outstanding achievements of Odysseus in the *Iliad* and the *Odyssey*. Odysseus became involved in the war against Troy when he was persuaded by Menelaus and Agamemnon to help rescue the kidnapped Helena. After many unsuccessful attempts to capture Troy, Odysseus devised the trick of the wooden horse, which was smuggled behind the city walls and later led to victory for the Greeks. During his 10-year return voyage to Ithaca, however, Odysseus encountered many barriers, dangerous situations, and challenges. For example, in the land of the Lotus-Eaters he managed, with great difficulty, to rescue a number of his com-

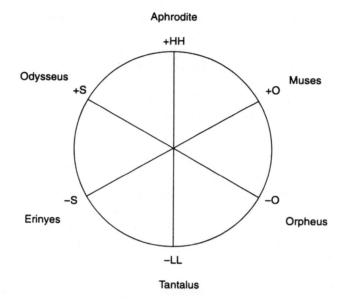

FIGURE 5.1. Types of stories in Greek mythology (+S, positive self-enhancement; –S, negative self-enhancement; +O, positive contact with the other; –O, negative contact with the other; +HH, positive combination of high self-enhancement and high contact with the other; –LL, negative combination of low self-enhancement and low contact with the other).

panions from their lotus-induced lethargy. Later he accidentally entered the cave of the one-eyed cyclops, Polyphemus. After the giant locked Odysseus and his companions in his cave and devoured several of his companions, Odysseus developed a tricky plan: He offered some strong wine to the giant, and when the cyclops fell into a deep sleep, Odysseus proceeded to blind his one eye with an arrow. After many other heroic deeds, Odysseus finally arrived in Ithaca, where his wife and son had been struggling to maintain their authority over the many suitors who wanted to marry Penelope. With the aid of Athena, Odysseus accomplished Penelope's test of stringing and shooting his old bow, and with the help of Telemachus and some loyal companions he slew all the suitors and was once again recognized as Penelope's long-lost husband.

Odysseus Reconsidered

It would be a gross simplification to reduce a multifaceted epic such as the *Odyssey* to a single theme. No matter how many brave deeds are told and how

impressive they may be, there are still other themes in the *Odyssey* that give
this epic its dramatic character. Throughout the entire epic the reader feels
Odysseus' continuous longing for his homeland Ithaca and for his wife Penelope
and son Telemachus. But this reunion is continually postponed by the obstacles
he and his companions encounter on their return voyage. For example, after
being the guest of Aeolus (the creator of the winds) for a month, Odysseus is
given a bag of winds to speed his return to Ithaca. However, as they approach
their homeland on the 10th day, the companions of Odysseus, expecting to find
gold and silver, open the bag while Odysseus sleeps. The turbulent winds escape and drive the ships back to the island of Aeolus once again. Aeolus now
refuses any further help because he thinks these strangers are targets of the gods'
vengeance.

The suffering of Odysseus increases when he arrives at the entrance of
the underworld and his mother, Anticlea, tells him that she died from grieving
for him. She also tells him about the grief of Penelope and about his father's
mourning for him. Thus, not only is Odysseus prevented from having a reunion
with his loved ones, but he is made painfully aware, from this moment on, of
the grief they are experiencing. Still later, after losing all his companions in a
tempest at sea and narrowly escaping death himself, Odysseus arrives at the
island of the nymph Calypso. Calypso wants Odysseus to be her husband and
promises him eternal youth and immortality for this. Alone on the beach with
the rising sun, however, Odysseus thinks of his wife, his son, and his home and
cries.

The dramatic power of the *Odyssey* derives at least in part from the contrast between Odysseus' need to continuously break through barriers and his
unfulfilled longing for reunion with his loved ones. In our framework this contrast is captured by an axis between +S valuations and −O valuations (the upper
left and lower right of Figure 5.1).

In a similar sort of contrast, the normally +S strength of Odysseus becomes
negative. A terrible vengeance on the suitors of Penelope (−S) is precipitated
by their treatment of Odysseus when, dressed as a beggar in his own palace, he
asks them for food. One of them, Antinous, throws a footstool at Odysseus instead, which inspires the others to also try to humiliate him. After succeeding
on Penelope's bow-test, Odysseus proceeds to kill Antinous, an act that begins
his mass murder of the suitors.

Odysseus' romantic contacts with several women (+O) are also part of a
recurrent theme, although even these affairs are often overshadowed by his deep
longing to return to Ithaca. One example is his contact with the evil enchant-
ress Circe, who initially turns some of his companions into swine. With the help
of Hermes, Odysseus is later able to undo this transformation, and only then
does he lie with Circe. Similarly, his 7-year stay with the nymph Calypso and
his relation with Nausicaa, who finds him on the beach after Poseidon destroys
his ship, are examples of transient moments of (more or less) intimate contact.

In fact, the contrast between vengeance and intimate love is captured by the axis between −S valuations and +O valuations (the lower left and upper right of Figure 5.1).

Odysseus also experiences powerlessness (−LL). For example, when he asks the cyclops Polyphemus for his hospitality, the giant answers by grasping two of his companions, shattering their heads against a wall, tearing them into pieces, and eating them for supper. And even though Odysseus manages to blind the cyclops, one nevertheless feels the constant threat of this antagonist who stands at the edge of the water (where he cannot reach his enemies) imploring his father, Poseidon, to take revenge on Odysseus. And, indeed, Odysseus does lose all of his companions in a heavy tempest at sea.

Finally, in a very moving passage, Odysseus is reunited with his grown-up son after landing in Ithaca, and together they formulate a plan against the suitors of Penelope. Clearly, this passage represents a combination of strength and union, indicated in our framework by +HH valuations.

To summarize, the fact that Odysseus is described as a prototypical hero, and thus the main theme of the story represents a +S type valuation, does not exclude the possibility that other important, and often strongly contrasting, themes can be found in this epic. It is this richness of themes, this great variation and yet artistic balance, this sublime alternation of the main theme with the subthemes, that makes this epic a masterpiece.

Let us now look, more briefly, at some other Greek myths whose main themes represent other valuation types (Figure 5.1).

Erinyes: Goddesses of Vengeance (−S)

The Erinyes are the goddesses of vengeance in Greek mythology (in Roman literature they are called the Furies). Most likely, they are intended to personify curses and may have originated in the popular imagination as the ghosts of the murdered. Some authors mention a single Erinys; Euripides was the first to set their number at three. In later writings they are named Alecto (Unceasing Anger), Tisiphone (Avenger of Murder), and Megaera (Jealousy).[6]

Rapp (in Roscher, 1965, vol. 1, pp. 1310–1336) draws a parallel between the Erinyes and turbulent thunderclouds. From the high-speed movement of the clouds arises the image of cloud women who move over land and sea in pursuit of criminals. Faster than ships, they finally swoop down and throw themselves at the victim.

The stories involving the Erinyes can be conceived of as variations on the −S theme: anger, revenge, jealousy, and cursing. They show that this theme is present not only in the self-narratives of many people but also in collective stories of Greek culture.

In apparent contrast with the threatening character of the Erinyes is their euphemistic designation as Eumenides (Kind Ones); this contrast can be seen as a secondary theme. According to Rapp (see Roscher, 1965), the terrifying goddesses, when worshiped, were transformed in the minds of the worshipers into beneficial figures.

Muses: Goddesses of Art (+O)

In Greek religion the Muses were a group of goddesses whose center was Mt. Helicon in Boeotia. At first the Muses were probably the patrons of the poets; later their interests extended to all of the arts and sciences. According to Bie (see Roscher, 1965, vol. 2, pp. 3238–3295), the Greek word *mousa* refers to the spiritual excitement of the epic singer, which provides the inspiration necessary for improvisation.

As early as the *Odyssey* there were nine Muses, although they were originally an undifferentiated group of deities. Differentiation began with Hesiod, who mentioned the names of Clio, Euterpe, Thalia, Melpomene, Terpsichore, Erato, Polymnia, Urania, and Calliope ("she of the beautiful voice"), who was the leader. The kind of music made by the Muses is best characterized by the Greek word *molpe*, which implies a combination of play, song, and dance. Sculptors gave each Muse a different attribute, such as a harp or a scroll. This practice probably inspired the distribution of the Muses among the arts and sciences (e.g., Erato as the Muse of love poems, Clio as the Muse of history, Urania as the Muse of astronomy).

As we have seen in Chapter 4, the theme represented by +O valuations includes personal experiences of an esthetic kind and often refers to the notion of beauty. The Muses are symbols of these aesthetic qualities par excellence.

Orpheus in the Underworld (–O)

Orpheus was a legendary figure in ancient Greece with a superhuman capacity for music and song. Traditionally considered the son of a Muse (probably Calliope), he joined the expedition of the Argonauts, where he used his bewitching music in a variety of ways; for example, he saved the Argonauts from the music of the Sirens by countering it with the even more beautiful music of his lyre.

In the most popular version of the myth, Orpheus is depicted in a love relation with his wife, Eurydice, and serves as a good example of the *fugit amor* theme. Eurydice (fleeing from Aristaeus, according to Virgil's *Georgics*) was bitten by a snake and died. In his grief Orpheus descended to the underworld and with his supernatural music tried to persuade the gods of Hades to release Eurydice. This part of the myth has greatly inspired poets in their description of the enchanting influence of music: Charmed by the lyrical voice of Orpheus, Cerberus, the three-headed dog guarding the entrance to the underworld, stood there with his mouths hanging open (Virgil); all shadows came near to listen

(Virgil); the Eumenides cried (Ovid); the fiery rolling wheel where Ixion was bound stood still (Ovid); Sisyphus took a seat on his stone (Seneca); and Tantalus stopped trying to drink the water (Ovid). The chief gods, Hades and Persephone, relented and permitted Orpheus to take Eurydice with him, provided he did not look back at her until they reached earth. Orpheus, however, could not control himself and looked back to convince himself of her presence. At that moment Eurydice disappeared to the underworld forever. After another effort to retrieve her from the underworld failed, Orpheus refused to eat. He was finally killed by the women of Thrace because he preferred to worship the rival of Dionysus, Apollo. In a Dionysian orgy he was torn to pieces.

The story of Orpheus, an example of the *fugit amor* theme, vividly portrays the experience of loss and subsequent longing and shows how contact (O) feelings can coexist with negative (N) feelings, so typical of valuations in this category.

Tantalus Tormented (–LL)

Tantalus was the son of Zeus and Pluto (daughter of Cronos). An exemplar of fullness and richness, he was a favorite of the chief gods and was therefore permitted to participate in their feasts and meetings. However, Tantalus was unable to bear all this happiness and good fortune and through his own deeds became separated from the world of the gods. Literature mentions several crimes committed by Tantalus. Some authors relate that his unbridled tongue divulged the secrets he had learned in heaven to humanity, others say he stole nectar and ambrosia to give to his human friends, and some accounts suggest that he offended the gods by killing his own son Pelops and serving him to the gods in order to test their power of observation.

There are alternative versions of how Tantalus was punished by the gods; in any case, he was severely punished for his lack of loyalty. One version relates that a large boulder was placed over his head threatening to smash him at any moment. A second version relates that Tantalus was left standing in water that rose to his neck but flowed away from him whenever he tried to drink it and that branches of fruit hanging over his head were swept out of reach by the wind whenever he tried to grasp one. Scheuer (see Roscher, 1965, vol. 5, pp. 75–86) concludes that the first version mentioned here is probably the original, although the relation of the second version to the word *tantalize* is more transparent.

The story of Tantalus tells us about an original situation of fullness and richness that is transformed into a situation of complete powerlessness. This transition corresponds to two polar opposites in valuation theory, +HH and –LL valuations. Actually, valuations of these types are present in the self-narratives of most people. They contrast strongly on the positive–negative dimension: +HH valuations have the highest levels of positive feelings and the lowest level of negative feelings whereas −LL valuations are associated with the lowest levels of positive feelings and the highest levels of negative feelings.

Aphrodite: Regina Caeli (+HH)

As the creative element in the world, Aphrodite was universally honored as Genetrix, and her bynames Urania (Heavenly Dweller) and Pandemos (Of All the People) indicate her great power to rule and unite people, a combination that enables her to exemplify the +HH type of valuation.

The myth of Aphrodite is characterized by Roscher and Furtwaengler (see Roscher, 1965, vol. 1, pp. 390–419) as a highly curious mixture of Semitic belief and Greek religion that can scarcely be distinguished. As far as is known, all Semitic groups, with the exception of the Hebrews, worshiped a goddess who represented the moon and fertility. These two elements were intimately related: The moon was thought to rule the sexual cycle of women and to be responsible for the dew so necessary for the soil in dry southern countries. Because the moon was thought to regulate women's fertility and, more generally, animal and vegetative fertility, Aphrodite was called Regina Caeli (queen of heaven) and was perceived as the most important of all the goddesses.

The notion of Aphrodite as promoter of human, animal, and vegetative fertility has been strongly developed. The Greek word *aphros* means "foam," and in one of the legends Aphrodite is born of the white foam produced by the severed genitals of Uranus (Heaven). Urania is therefore occasionally used as a byname for Aphrodite, and her power to rule the world is symbolized by the globe and compass she carries.

THE NARCISSUS MYTH AND THE CONCERNS OF CLIENTS: THE RELEVANCE OF THE MANIFEST–LATENT DISTINCTION

People love myths, fairy tales, novels, movies, and parables because the stories give expression and artistic form to their own experiences. The protagonist and the reader live in different places, under different circumstances, perhaps even in different eras. Despite such differences, the plot is usually familiar enough that the reader or listener may say, "It is as if I were doing this." This feeling of familiarity—despite phenomenological differences—provides further support for the latent–manifest distinction made in valuation research: The experiences of the reader and those related in the story may differ on the manifest level but bear certain critical similarities on the latent, motivational, level.

This two-level quality of recognition was clearly expressed by a client of ours who as a consequence of a divorce was losing contact with her oldest son. When she looked at a photograph of Rodin's sculpture of Paolo and Francesca, she commented, "That is what *I* am experiencing now." Although the sculpture depicts a man–woman relationship, the client was referring to her relationship with her son. However, the client was quite correct in grasping the commonality at the latent level: Both in Rodin's sculpture and in her relation with her son there is a *fugit amor* experience. That is, the feeling portrayed in the sculpture characterized the client's situation despite overwhelming manifest differences.

The latent–manifest distinction was more systematically explored in a recent study (Hermans & Van Gilst, 1991) of the relation between the thematic organization of the Narcissus myth and the themes present in the self-narratives of clients. The main question was whether the central passage in the Narcissus myth (Narcissus looking into the water) was a manifest expression of something that, on a deeper level, was also present in the narratives clients tell about themselves. Because the Narcissus study functions here as an example of an empirical study of the relation between individual and collective stories, we focus on the main parts of this study and refer to the original publication for details. (Note that the purpose of the Narcissus study was not to investigate the dysfunction of narcissism but, rather, to explore the meaning of the major theme in the story in relation to the daily lives of clients).

In brief, the study consisted of two parts. In the first part 10 judges read the story of Narcissus and then rated the experience of Narcissus gazing into the water with a list of affect terms in order to characterize the experience of Narcissus at that moment. This resulted in a so-called Narcissus profile. In the second part of the study the Narcissus profile was introduced into the valuation system of a number of clients who had not read the myth, and for each client the valuation with the highest correlation to the Narcissus profile was selected. These valuations are presented in Table 5.3.

In order to get a feel for the affective meaning of the central part of the myth, consider the following summary by Goldin (1967) of Ovid's famous narrative (*Metamorphoses III*, 338–510):

> The tale begins with a prophecy of Tiresias, who tells Liriope that her son will live a long time provided that he never knows himself—*si se non noverit* (348). Sixteen years later, Narcissus's beauty has aroused the desire of many youths and maidens but conceals a pride so hard that none may touch him. Hunting one day, he is seen by Echo, who immediately loves him. Because of Juno's curse upon her, Echo is unable to speak on her own initiative but can only repeat the last sounds uttered by another's voice; and here, by returning Narcissus's words, she reveals her love and asks for his own. She is cruelly repulsed, like everyone else. She is left with nothing but the desire that consumes her, wasting away her body until she is reduced to a mere voice.
>
> Another victim of Narcissus's hard-heartedness prays to heaven to make Narcissus suffer what he has caused others to suffer: to love and be unable to possess his beloved. This prayer is granted by Nemesis. One day, fatigued and

thirsty from hunting, Narcissus kneels down to drink from a spring. Then, as Ovid says, "another thirst increases within him" (415). He sees a beautiful youth in the water, whom he immediately desires. He does not know that that "youth" is his own reflection, that he himself is both lover and beloved. He begs the youth to come forward, for they are equally beautiful and nothing but the surface of the water separates them. After many passionate complaints, he suddenly realizes the truth: "*I* am that youth!—*Iste ego sum!*" (463). Yet he cannot stop loving what he now knows is his own reflection; he regrets that he cannot separate himself from his body. Now he already feels grief taking away his life. He loses his color, succumbs for the fire that is consuming him. Nothing remains of the beauty that Echo loved.

In his last moments she returns, and despite her anger she pities him. When he strikes his breast in grief, she returns the sound of the blows. As he dies, she repeats his last *vale*. But even after he enters the infernal regions, he gazes upon himself in the waters of the Styx. In the place where he suffered his torment on earth grows the flower that bears his name. (Goldin, 1967, pp. 20–21)

The Narcissus story from Ovid's *Metamorphoses* (III, 339–510; Dutch translation by De Laet, 1979) was presented to a group of 10 college students (5 men and 5 women). After reading the story the subjects were instructed to take the position of Narcissus as he continuously gazed at himself in the water and to ask themselves what he was feeling. The subjects then answered this question by providing ratings for a list of affect terms that included the 16 terms used in this book. The result was an affective profile for each subject in response to the Narcissus myth.

In order to study the affective meaning of the central part of the myth, the S, O, P, and N indices were calculated for each of the 10 subjects and then the mean score for each index was calculated. The index means were as follows: S, 7.50; O, 15.10; P, 6.40; N, 15.30. This affective structure (low S, high O, low P, high N), is characteristic of –O valuations: a longing for contact and union with someone or something else (O > S) that is not fulfilled (N > P).

In the second part of the study the valuation systems of 100 clients (homogeneous with respect to identity problems and problems in social relations but heterogeneous with respect to sex, age, and socioeconomic level) were studied in order to select those clients who had at least one valuation demonstrating a high positive correlation ($r > .50$) with the myth profile and at least one valuation with a high negative correlation ($r < -.50$). This procedure enabled us to compare two groups of valuations: one with an affective pattern similar to the Narcissus profile and one with an affective pattern that contrasted with the Narcissus profile. More specifically, the valuations demonstrating an affective profile similar or in contrast to that of the Narcissus myth were isolated by introducing the myth profile (i.e., the mean scores from the 10 judges in Part 1 for the 16 S, O, P, and N items) as an extra row in the valuation matrices from each of the 100 clients. (See Table 3.4 for the example of a matrix.)

TABLE 5.3. Valuations with Highest Positive Correlation and Highest Negative Correlation with the Affective Pattern Derived from the Narcissus Myth

Valuation with highest positive correlation	S	O	P	N	r
1. I think it's too bad that I couldn't remove some of my mother's loneliness when she was still alive with my cheerfulness.	3	11	1	11	.90
2. I have guilt feelings when thinking about my father: he did his best for me, and I failed.	1	18	0	19	.89
3. About 4 years ago, I encountered Irma covered with (what I thought was) blood; I was confused and felt terribly stupid for having done that to her.	2	15	0	19	.88
4. All the attention, involvement, and hugging were drowning me; I wasn't allowed to see anyone else and I couldn't.	4	17	1	20	.87
5. Dick's suicide: failing to do anything for him; not being able to stop him; that I didn't see through it all.	3	16	1	14	.82
6. Death, retirement, nursing homes; the waning of good health.	3	17	5	20	.80
7. First, I meant everything to him; now he means everything to me; the roles are now reversed.	1	10	3	15	.79
8. I think it's terrible that my sister and I can't communicate sensitively.	3	13	2	14	.78
9. I think it's sad that it's over with Jane [girl-friend]. I want to hold on to that feeling and not let the clichés get the upper hand; I think she's too valuable.	6	16	0	14	.76
10. I would like to share things in an equal, friendly way with my father but we both avoid it; we both hang on to our roles as father and child.	1	12	0	20	.75
11. I'm gradually feeling just as confined as in my first relationship; that history is repeating itself even up to the bitter end and that I have to carry this all with me; once again, I've "used" a partner.	4	15	1	14	.73
12. The burned-out, disappointed feeling since our first contact: trying to live up to my wife's expectations.	2	6	0	17	.72
13. Thinking about the broken relationship.	7	12	3	15	.71
14. There are still a lot of things that bother me; I'm standing before a wall, which I have to get through.	6	15	7	14	.68

Note. r, product–moment correlation between the affective patterns of the valuation and the Narcissus myth. From Hermans and Van Gilst (1991). Copyright 1991 by Canadian Psychological Association. Reprinted with permission.

Valuation with highest negative correlation	S	O	P	N	r
People who listen to me and don't immediately pass judgment.	13	2	10	0	−.84
I want to start studying; I think it's very important that I build something up for myself, that I have something fun for myself.	19	0	16	0	−.86
I enjoy my work: it gives me fulfillment, and I find it relaxing.	12	8	14	2	−.75
I dare to stand my own ground now.	11	1	11	0	−.87
If I don't like someone, I now dare to vote against them.	15	9	12	6	−.67
I'm a good teacher and I'm comfortable doing it.	17	6	14	8	−.51
I was only my achievements; they were valued.	18	5	15	0	−.64
I search for clarity and try to put that in words.	18	7	17	4	−.78
I set myself goals, I strive to achieve them, and live from peak to peak.	16	7	15	5	−.52
The complete exploitation of my abilities fulfills me if I take my limitations into consideration.	19	9	20	0	−.75
I enjoy tranquillity.	15	14	17	1	−.57
After the job change, I found that I could fulfill my job well, alone and independent; I could shape my work.	15	9	16	5	−.75
I know the work context, I fall back on my knowledge and intelligence; I am less concerned about acceptance by others.	12	0	6	1	−.66
My "Israel experience" gave me the feeling that I am somebody.	12	8	12	5	−.75

From the resulting correlations, 14 clients were found with one or more similar valuations and one or more contrasting valuations.[7]

The valuations of the 14 clients that show the highest correlation with the Narcissus profile are presented in Table 5.3. The positively correlated valuations show the following affective structure: low S, high O, low P, high N. This formulation typically expresses the theme of unfulfilled love (–O). On the other hand, the negatively correlating valuations have the following affective structure: high S, low O, high P, low N. This formulation is an expression of successful self-enhancement (+S). The latter type of valuation typically reflects high self-esteem and successful coping with the environment. In other words, unfullfilled longing, rather than successful self-enhancement, is typical of the part of the myth that was selected as central. In the lives of clients, a similar experience has been found. This means that however different the myth and the self-narrative may be on the manifest level, they have a common meaning on a latent level.

This study serves as an example of a relationship between two forms of narrative that are often studied and discussed as separate texts. Not only are the results significant for the exploration of the thematic organization of clients' self-narratives, but they may also have implications for the interpretation of myths as they are read and understood by people today. The empirical results of our study resist a naive interpretation of the Narcissus myth in terms of self-love. Such a term would be too crude and even misleading. As the story relates, Narcissus' suffering is clearly the result of some punishment (just as Paolo and Francesca were punished for their forbidden love in Dante's *Divina Commedia*), not just self-love. Narcissus is initially self-sufficient and in fact despises Echo and other lovers. When the unhappy lovers, in their turn, ask a goddess for revenge, she lets Narcissus suffer unrequited love. This element of suffering is also present in the content of the clients' valuations. Valuation 1 in Table 5.3, for example, which shows the highest correlation ($r = .90$) with the central part of the myth, is highly representative of its affective meaning. This valuation relates the regret a daughter feels when she realizes that it was impossible (and will always be impossible) to remove the loneliness her mother felt during her life. This preclusion of fulfillment brought about by death is also present in some of the other valuations (e.g., Valuations 2 and 5). On the basis of these considerations it may be concluded that the quintessence of the Narcissus myth is not love but lack. This lack receives spatial expression in Narcissus' continually stretching out his hand to an unreachable image. This form is strikingly similar to Rodin's sculpture of *fugit amor* in which Paolo stretches out his hands to Francesca in a futile attempt to reach her.

From a broader existential perspective, the stretching hands that will never reach their goal symbolize an existential experience that was phased by Lacan (1966) as "the deficiency of being." Along these lines the Narcissus story, like the *fugit amor* motif, can be considered an expression of basic existential desire.

As we have already suggested, the basic motives can be only temporarily satisfied, resulting in positive valuations. There is, however, no final reachable goal in human existence, only longing for such fulfillment. Narcissus functions as a symbol of the existential unfulfillment with respect to the longing for contact and union. Narcissus is unable to unite with the other and with himself, and this human condition symbolizes his existential suffering.

SUMMARY

The explorations described in this chapter were guided by several notions that are central in the book as a whole: the latent–manifest distinction, the notion of position, the spatial nature of narratives, and the boundary between self and nonself. Let us summarize these issues.

When one recalls an intriguing dream, it is intriguing in its context. That is, it is the latent significance of a dream that places it in the broader context of life. For example, Karin's dream of being forced to eat fish could be interpreted as feeling suppressed by her husband if one assumes a latent level underlying both the dream symbol and the valuation of her husband. Whereas a dream, as a product of personal imagination, can be thought of as being continuous with waking life, a myth, as an expression of collective imagination, can be considered continuous with daily life. Myths (and other collective stories) symbolize the common experiences and fundamental concerns of a particular people or culture. That is, myths do not represent extraordinary experiences that differ essentially from people's ordinary daily experiences. For example, the Erinyes as a mythical symbolization of revenge may be related to the daily life perception of turbulent thunderclouds (Rapp, in Roscher, 1965, vol. 1, pp. 1310–1336). From the perspective of the latent level, there is no single theme in the epic of Odysseus that is absent from the lives of ordinary people. Though the *Odyssey* vividly pictures heroic deeds and achievements scarcely realizable by ordinary people, the difference between myth and reality is only on the manifest level. On the latent level the impressive deeds of Odysseus and the small heroic deeds of ordinary people are essentially identical. It is precisely this thematic similarity that accounts for the fact that people recognize themselves in the achievements of the protagonists in great literary works.

Dreams and myths are populated by characters that can function as I positions and thus allow for the "multivoicedness" of the self. A dreaming person proceeds like an author writing a script in which he or she acts as one of the characters in interaction with other characters. As in a novel, a dream includes not only the protagonist but also the antagonist, both of which are possible positions for the self to take. These positions may enter into a dialogical relation with one another, linked in a process of question and answer or agreement and disagreement. Such a dialogical relation was inferred in Paul's case when he answered (as Paul) the murderer in his dream by adding three new valuations to his own system. Similarly, myth is also populated by positions. For instance, the readers of the *Odyssey* may place themselves in the position of not only Odysseus but also of Telemachus, Penelope, and even the suitors. Dialogical relations of all kinds may develop among the different positions that together represent the dynamic quality and complexity of literary works.

Myths, like dreams, are not only temporally but also spatially structured. They give "spatial form" (Frank, 1945/1991) to human experience. One could argue that in each person an artist is living who gives expression, often with a great sense of dramatic form, to positive and negative valuations in a diversity of situations. A dream always takes place in an imaginal space in which concrete forms (e.g., tree, fish, hand) function as symbols that may only be understood if the latent–manifest distinction is taken into account. Myths also are explicitly spatial. As in a dream, the story line in a myth is very perceptible. One can see what happens, while at the same time the thing that is seen functions as a symbol in the broader context of the story and the situation in which the story is conveyed.

The opening of the self toward possible positions and associated valuations takes us to the last and most problematic issue: the boundaries of the self. Characters in dreams, myths, and other kinds of stories can only influence the ongoing self if the boundaries are not so restricted and sharp as to create a split between self and story. When people are not sensitive to the speaking images of their dreams or to the pictorial language of myths, they may conclude that they do not say anything to them; they may even react with irritation or aversion. In fact, we use the term *boundary* in order to understand the phenomenon of self–nonself differentiation. However, the term is far from adequate in explaining the phenomenon under consideration. As we have seen in Paul's case, there is an intermediate area in the imaginal space of the self, where the notion of "identity-in-difference" applies. That is, there are characters that are defined by the person as belonging and not belonging to the self at the same time. The murderer in Paul's dream represented a position that was located in this intermediate area. As we have demonstrated, the murderer was accepted as part of Paul's self-definition yet kept "outside" at the same time. As long as one uses the term *boundary* in relation to the self, one is forced to locate a particular position as "inside" or "outside." However, the identity-in-difference phenomenon that applies so well to the experience of recognition in dreams, myths, movies, and in many social contacts suggests that a particular character is both inside and outside the self at the same time. This problem requires, as Gregg (1991), Hermans and Kempen (1993), and Marková (1987) have argued, a reconsideration of traditional Aristotelian logic, which is not very well equipped to deal with dynamic processes like the process of extending and shrinking of the self. The self, conceived of as multivoiced, is highly dynamic, because dialogical relationships are assumed between different positions. In the self as an imaginal space, the I is capable of moving back and force between different and even new positions in such a way that the valuations associated with these positions are changing to some degree in the process of moving. Dreams, myths, and other stories may function as invitations to conceptualize an open and dynamic self that gets extended in such a way that new routes of change may be explored.

NOTES

1. Dream symbols, like much other nonverbal material, may have a variety of connotations (see also Eliade et al., 1987). The symbol of the tree, for example, may include divergent and often contrasting meanings: light, darkness (its roots), strength, birth, growth, fertility, good, and evil (forbidden fruit). Dream symbols are different from denotative symbols, which have the character of a sign (e.g., a traffic light, an algebraic symbol, a well-defined word) and therefore are particularly suitable for explicit and efficient communication. Dream interpretation, therefore, can be considered the process of associating often ambiguous dream symbols with language and thereby selecting the relevant meaning from a broad range of possible meanings.

2. In a detailed analysis one examines not only the valuation bearing the highest correlation but also the valuations bearing the second- and third-highest correlations, provided they meet the criteria outlined in Chapter 3. Negative correlations may be used when one wants to explore valuations that contrast with the dream valuations.

3. In this section a dream was discussed in which the theme changed over time (from a −LL valuation in the direction of a +S valuation). Another possibility is that the same theme returns with different actors and different scenery; in that case the progression is dependent more on accidental variations in players and scenery than on the development of the theme.

4. The interaction of contrasting story themes, influencing one another, have their parallels in the nature of consciousness itself: "Into the awareness of the thunder itself the awareness of the previous silence creeps and continues; for what we hear when the thunder crashes is not thunder *pure*, but thunder-breaking-upon-silence-and-contrasting-with-it" (James, 1890, p. 240).

5. We have based our discussion on Roscher's (1965) *Ausführliches Lexikon der griechischen und römischen Mythologie* [Comprehensive Lexicon of Greek and Roman Mythology] and on the *Encyclopaedia Britannica*.

6. Jealousy can briefly be defined as an S reaction to an O frustration, most typically, in a competing lover. The difference between jealousy and envy is that the latter involves the S motive only (frustrated self-enhancement) whereas the former involves both the S and the O motive.

7. The 16 means of this extra row are the following (corresponding to the 16 affect terms, respectively, in Table 3.3): 1.4, 2.1, 2.1, 2.7, 2.0, 2.4, 2.9, 4.7, 4.1, 4.3, 1.7, 3.2, 4.3, 1.7, 4.2, 0.5. This extra row can be correlated with all the valuations of any personal valuation system. It is expected that the highest correlating valuations have a content similar to the content of the valuations of Table 5.3.

CHAPTER 6

Dissociations and Dysfunctions

In order to use an organized narrative system to understand the self, a person must be able to move flexibly from one type of valuation to another in accordance with changes in the immediate situation. When certain types of valuations are not represented, however, the flexibility of a person's valuation system may be seriously limited, and the result may be a dysfunctional self. In this chapter dysfunctions of the self are conceived of as a blocked process of valuation. Typically, the valuation process is blocked when the system has become rigidly organized around one type of valuation and movement to other types of valuations is prohibited. Although several dysfunctions will be covered in this chapter, depression will be given primary focus because of its high prevalence in the population (Davison & Neale, 1990; Schuyler & Katz, 1973; Seligman, 1973). But before describing the dysfunctions of the self, let us first consider a closely related phenomenon: dissociation.

DISSOCIATION: A PRECURSOR
TO DYSFUNCTION

Dissociation—or, in psychoanalytic terms, the use of defenses—often accompanies or even precedes dysfunction. Dissociation is the opposite of association. Experiences are associated when they have a chance to come together as parts in an articulated valuation system; experiences are dissociated when they are kept separate or given a marginal position in the system because of an overemphasis on other experiences. Dissociation refers to a forced organization of the system where experiences with a high degree of personal relevance are not well integrated into the system. It should be emphasized that dissociations belong to the self-organization of all people in their daily existence. However, when excessively used, they may result in a dysfunction of the self by keeping personally relevant experiences from self-awareness.

Dissociations occur under the influence of the basic motives (self-enhancement or longing for the other): People organize their valuation systems in certain ways in order to protect themselves as autonomous individuals or maintain contact and union with others. For example, sometimes people systematically omit experiences of closeness to another from their self-narratives; the reason may be that they perceive closeness as reducing their autonomy. In such cases, the type of valuation described as +O will not have an optimal chance of being integrated into the system, and as a result the flexibility of the valuation process in general will be reduced.

Whereas the term *dissociation* refers to a way of organizing the valuation system, the term *dysfunction* refers to a maladaptive functioning of the person–situation interaction. The more a valuation system is subject to dissociative operations, the greater the chance that the flexibility of the system will be reduced and that the individual will be unable to function adequately in conjunction with a changing situation. It should be added, however, that it is not our assumption that dysfunctions simply result from dissociations. For example, people may become the victim of severe violence or threat and this may have a long-lasting influence on the self quite apart from the nature of their dissociations. Dissociations can perhaps contribute to isolating these experiences or diminishing their emotional impact. However, dissociations are not the primary cause of the problems in such instances. It is safe, therefore, to start our analysis with the supposition that dissociations play an important role in the organization and reorganization of the valuation system but are not the only cause of dysfunction.

It should further be noted that this chapter does not deal with severe forms of abnormality or disorder. Rather, the phenomena to be described here can be typically observed in the area of transition between a healthy, flexibly functioning self and a less healthy, or more rigidly functioning, self. By looking not only at dysfunction but also at dissociative aspects of the valuation system, we are indicating our belief that psychologists can learn to sharpen their diagnostic eye and clients can become aware of their own self-limitations and take these limitations into account in their ongoing process of valuation.

Forms of Dissociation

Four forms of dissociation will be described: omission, fragmentation, subduing, and distortion.

Omission

When people avoid including in their valuation system an experience that nevertheless plays an important role in their personal world, we have a form of dissociation called omission. There are, of course, many events and circumstances in one's life that are not taken up as an explicit part of the self-narrative, nor should they be. Psychologists must therefore listen carefully to the stories people tell about their lives, for they are highly dependent on the information provided by the client and often lack explicit criteria for determining when a significant event or experience has been omitted from a self-narrative. On the other hand, there may be clear clues to lacunae in the client's story. For example, when the psychologist explicitly raises a particular topic in order to check its personal relevance and the client reacts in an emotional way, the psychologist may feel that he or she is on the right track and invite the client to explore the topic in greater depth.

This detection of a lacuna was explored in a more systematic way in a previous study (Hermans & Hermans-Jansen, 1976) in which a 27-year-old client, Charlotte, performed seven self-investigations within 1 year. At Time 1 she formulated only 16 valuations, with no reference to her parents and a generally low level on the affective indices. At Time 2, 3 months later, she referred to her father only passingly. It was only after some tears and with some pressure and encouragement from the therapist that Charlotte included the valuation, "The authoritarian nature of my father." This valuation had a level of negative affect (N) that exceeded all other valuations, suggesting that its inclusion was experienced as highly threatening to the idealized image Charlotte had about her father. At Time 3 she eliminated any reference to her father from the valuation system. Only in the sixth self-investigation, 5 months after the first one, did she include a more articulated valuation referring to her father: "I am opposed to the emotional, condemning, authoritarian nature of my father." Moreover, the level of negative affect (N) was now slightly above the mean. An analysis of this case led to the conclusion that at Time 1 the client's father was a relevant (highly emotional) part of her personal history but was omitted because the client felt she should become independent of her father (though she was unable to do so). Only later, when her valuation system was more integrated, did she feel strong enough to include valuations that expressed opposition to her father but were not exceedingly emotional.

Further evidence for the existence of omission in personal functioning was found by Zimeth (1982), who invited five adolescent school dropouts to perform a self-investigation. The results showed that these subjects, although socioeconomically disadvantaged, typically reported a high level of well-being (P > N for most of the valuations and for the general feeling). The content of their valuations often expressed physical comfort and enjoyment in the present (e.g., they referred to the activities of sleeping, drinking, eating) whereas past failures and concerns about the future were strikingly absent or marginally present. This picture suggests that the subjects organized their lives in such a way that they confined themselves to short-term considerations while simultaneously omitting from consciousness any troubling past or future concerns. At the same time, because this organization confirmed the status quo, there was no need for the subjects to change their situation.

The problems associated with detection of omission warn against the naive use of quantitative indices such as well-being or general feeling or the correlation between general and ideal feeling (Chapter 3). For example, research based on Rogerian theory, where self–ideal self discrepancies are used as a measure of adjustment, has provided contradictory findings. Turner and Vanderlippe (1958) found that college students who had a high congruence between ratings of self and ideal self, in contrast to students with a low congruence, participated in more extracurricular activities, had a higher scholastic average, were more popular with fellow students, and received higher adjustment ratings on personality tests. Other studies, however, have found a relationship between defensiveness and a high congruence between actual self and ideal self. Havener and Izard (1962), for example, found a relationship between high congruence and unrealistically high self-esteem in paranoid schizophrenics who were, in Rogers' terms, defending themselves against a complete loss of positive self-regard. Taken together, these and other studies suggest that a quantitative difference between self and ideal self alone is far too complicated to be an altogether satisfactory measure of adjustment (Higgins, 1987; Pervin, 1993; Wylie, 1974). Given this complexity, it seems necessary to study quantitative indices in light of the content and organization of the valuation system as a whole. Moreover, when there are indications of serious omissions, the existence of lacunae can be probed by providing target valuations (as discussed in Chapter 3). In this way psychologist and client can check how the valuation system reacts to these offered elements and can observe whether the system should incorporate such a valuation or not.

Fragmentation

Whereas omission results in an incomplete story, fragmentation leads to a scattered story. A person may include a variety of valuations in the system, but they are not integrated. However, fragmentation is more than simply a failure on the client's part to see the relation between valuations; there are often clear motivational reasons to avoid the perception of such a relation. Since in such cases the person would feel uncomfortable or even threatened by the connection, a "solution" is found by breaking the self-narrative (or part of it) into unrelated pieces. In doing so, the person tries to protect himself or herself against the loss of self-esteem or tries to keep idealized relationships of contact and union intact.

Fragmentation can be simply illustrated with the following three highly condensed valuations a client formulated about his experience in the military:

Valuation 1. "My situation in military service requires me to obey my superiors."
Valuation 2. "Fred and Jenny have been my friends for a long time."
Valuation 3. "I am opposed to people who abuse other people."

During military service this client was confronted with superiors whose ideas he strongly opposed. In the same period he discovered that there was growing contact between his girlfriend, Jenny, and his best friend, Fred. When he formulated Valuation 3, he was quite aware of its relation to Valuation 1: He knew that he felt abused by his superiors in the military. However, he was *not* aware of the relation between Valuations 2 and 3, although the correlation between them was even higher than the correlation between Valuations 1 and 3. He even resisted talking about the relation between Valuations 2 and 3, a resistance that was absent for the relation between Valuations 1 and 3.

The same three valuations were discussed with this client 1½ years later. He then explained that he really felt abused by Fred and Jenny (who had married in the meantime). However, he could not at the earlier time admit to himself that he felt abused by them because he had set them both on a pedestal and wanted to continue his friendship with each of them. Now he was at peace with the situation, could accept their marriage, and could therefore recognize that he had previously felt abused by his two friends.

The valuation system can also become fragmented as a result of *impulsivity*. People who are impulsive tend to react on the basis of one valuation while neglecting the relation of this valuation to all other valuations. In a deed of impulsivity a particular valuation is separated from others and even receives an absolute quality so that its integration into the system is greatly reduced. Most commonly, a valuation of immediate concern is separated from valuations referring to the future or the past. It is only after the impulsive deed, when the system needs reintegration, that the person may say, "I regret my behavior."

Subduing

"Subduing" is a form of dissociation that refers to the relation between the text of a valuation and its affective component. When a person formulates a valuation but strongly diminishes the associated affect, one can metaphorically say that such a person is speaking with a subdued voice. The phenomenon of subduing can best be observed when someone is relating a very emotional personally relevant experience but is doing so in such a toneless voice that the listener is surprised by the discrepancy between the serious character of the events and the seeming lack of emotion.

Let us, from this perspective, take a look at the following valuations offered by a client:

	S	O	P	N
Valuation 1. "I hate my uncle, aunt, and cousins; they lied about everything, they humiliated me in front of the neighborhood, and they hit me."	0	0	0	0
Valuation 2. "I hate my parents because they have given my uncle permission to hit me."	0	0	0	0
Valuation 3. "I feel misused by my family."	8	0	0	20

Strikingly, in Valuations 1 and 2 the client reports no affect at all, as indicated by the indices. In marked contrast, Valuation 3 shows a clear affect pattern, where the negative affect even reaches the maximum level of 20. Apparently, the client feels safe enough to report emotional experiences in the content of Valuations 1 and 2, but when she arrives at the point of relating her affect to these valuations, she reports zero levels for all affect terms. This suggests that vivid recall of her emotions is too much of a burden in this stage of self-confrontation. When the valuation is described in an abstract manner, however, as is done in Valuation 3, she can take a more distant stance, and consequently the associated emotions can be acknowledged and expressed. This example suggests that emotions are subdued as a form of self-protection when the arousal exceeds a particular level.

Distortion

Just as a newspaper can provide a distorted view of certain affairs, so too can a valuation be presented in a biased or colored light. Like the other forms of dissociation, distortion is also in the service of the basic motives. When people feel that a realistic account of events or circumstances would reduce their self-esteem or endanger a valued relationship, they may give a distorted account of the events instead. Distortion is a form of self-deception where one or more realistic elements of a self-narrative are modified in the service of maintaining one's self-esteem or contact and union with the other. This can be illustrated by attribution research (e.g., Bowerman, 1978) suggesting that the experience of success is typically attributed to internal factors (e.g., one's own aptitude) whereas failures are more often attributed to external factors (e.g., bad luck, the influence of specific circumstances). Sarbin (1986) has emphasized the need for maintaining one's self-esteem as a motivating force of self-deception: "In self-narratives that assign truth value to the contrafactual, the narrator constructs the text so that the self as narrative figure is protected, defended, or enhanced. The narrative smoothing . . . is carried out in the service of maintaining an acceptable identity" (pp. 16–17). Similarly, one can find examples where individuals are reluctant to accept increasing alienation in their relation with a significant other and therefore only remember the good moments while systematically distorting the bad ones.

Note that distortion need not lead to a positive bias in a description of one's self. It can also result in unrealistically negative views of the self. For example, when people are uncertain about how other people view them, they may prefer a clearly negative statement (e.g., "Nobody loves me") over a more painful and uncertain statement of reality (e.g., "I wonder if someone will ever love me"). Such a negatively biased distortion may reduce at least some of the uncertainty and is in this way a form of self-protection.

By following valuations over time, we can see how distortions get corrected and under what conditions this is accomplished. Let us, therefore, look at a valuation from a woman who had stopped working because she felt "useless" in her job:

	S	O	P	N
Valuation 1. "I have the feeling that I am useless because there has been so much automatization."	1	0	0	13

At Time 2, 7 months later, she modified this valuation and added a new one:

	S	O	P	N
Valuation 2. "I am worried about the automatization in society and the lack of employment."	3	5	3	8
Valuation 3. "I try to make the best of it (by applying for other jobs) and do not sit around in despair."	13	4	11	1

Apparently, at Time 1 this client was avoiding responsibility for her reduced self-enhancement and therefore attributing her problem to an external source. At Time 2, however, she was able to perceive automatization as a societal problem and not exclusively as the cause of her personal problem. She could do so because she now felt strong enough to pursue new initiatives (Valuation 3) and had dealt with her own problem (at least in part). In giving this more differentiated picture she not only took more responsibility for her own actions but was more capable of distinguishing a personal problem from a societal problem.

Becoming Conscious of Dissociations

As already noted, dissociations are the product of certain basic motives, and the person may therefore be totally unaware of a dissociation. This unconscious aspect may be a serious challenge to the notion of self-investigation. In the foregoing description of four forms of dissociation, dissociations were detected by a meta-analysis performed by the psychologist, not the client. Is it possible for a client, starting from a conscious level, to also detect a dissociation and incorporate it as part of a more extended self-narrative? The answer to this question is affirmative when clients in the process of self-exploration arrive at a point where they, as part of a dialogue with the psychologist, become aware of the lacunae, contradictions, or biases in their self-narratives.

Within the theoretical framework of self-investigation, a psychologist can only bring a supposed dissociation to the attention of a client in accordance with the client's speed of development, the supportive power of the valuation system as a whole, and the client's idiosyncratic terminology. Often it is premature to expect clients in a first self-investigation to be able to recognize and accept the dissociational aspects of their system. The following valuation, for example, was only included in the third self-investigation of a client with serious psychosomatic complaints 1 year after the initial self-investigation.

	S	O	P	N
"Sometimes I wonder if the things that touch me, and that I cannot remember a moment later, have to do with my bad memory or with my pushing away of emotions."	0	0	0	16

As can be seen, the client is finally recognizing the role of her emotional dissociations in the valuation system.

From a psychotherapeutic perspective, the advantage of including a dissociation (omission in this case) as a valuation in the system is that clients acknowledge and take responsibility for the fact that they are dissociating. Moreover, it may be expected that there is a growing sensitivity to those experiences that hitherto were beyond the reach of self-reflection. It is, however, not self-evident that clients will incorporate such valuations into the system. As just demonstrated, dissociation-related valuations are most often of type −LL, which indicates a *low* level of affect referring to self-enhancement, a *low* level of affect referring to contact and union, and a high degree of negative affect. Inclusion may put extra stress on the system, and therefore it is expected that dissociation-related valuations will be taken up into the system only when it is strong enough to support such negative affect. The supportive structure of the system, which is closely related to its flexibility, can be strengthened by including positive valuations, type +S in particular (see Chapters 3 and 4), before negative ones.

Dissociations and Psychoanalytic Defenses

Dissociations can be readily discussed in terms of defenses in the psychoanalytic tradition. There is, for example, a resemblance between omission and denial, subduing and isolation, and perhaps distortion and rationalization. Why then shouldn't we talk about defenses instead of dissociations? There are three main reasons for not referring to dissociations as defenses in the present conceptual framework. (For pedagogical purposes, we will use the Freudian definition of defenses.) First, Freudian defense mechanisms are assumed to be mainly a reaction to anxiety: We unconsciously develop ways of excluding certain experiences from awareness in order not to feel anxious. Thus, the defenses are working as intrapsychic mechanisms to help us avoid being overwhelmed by anxiety. Although anxiety is a most important emotion, it is not, in our view, the most essential source of dissociation. People dissociate on a motivational basis; that is, they organize their self-narratives in order to protect or enhance their self-esteem and maintain or improve the quality of their relationships. From this perspective dissociation is not primarily a reaction to the tension of anxiety or any other emotion but a means of organizing the self in the service of these basic motives (although this organization may be quite maladaptive). A second, closely related difference between defenses and dissociations is that defenses are intrapsychic while dissociations are more interactive. More specifically, dissociations may be understood as resulting from culturally guided interactions with significant others. Thus, in the discussion of fragmentation we saw a client who had great difficulty admitting that he felt betrayed by his girlfriend and best friend (who became intimate during his absence) in part because of the thought, consistent with cultural values, "My best friend should not have an intimate relationship with my girlfriend." Similarly, the client discussed in the section on omission felt strong emotions when she tried to acknowledge to herself the authoritarian style of her father. Her personal valuation may have been influenced by such cultural values underlying interactions in our society as "Children should love their parents" and "Parents should give their children enough freedom to develop their own personality." The importance of such values may vary from society to society and from group to group. Finally, dissociations are resolved not only by insight but also by action. In Chapter 3 we discussed the attending-creating-anchoring (ACA) cycle. When a self-investigation reveals the working of unproductive dissociations, the client is stimulated to enter the validation/invalidation period in such a way that dissociations are first explored in systematic self-reflection. This exploration is followed by the client's taking new initiatives in order to resolve a particular dissociation (e.g., exploring situations or experiences that were hitherto omitted in the self-narrative). Finally, the person continues by practicing in such a way that the habit of dissociation is replaced by the habit of association.

DYSFUNCTIONAL VALUATION SYSTEMS

One of the goals of this chapter is to explore the transition between a functional and a dysfunctional valuation system. In the foregoing discussion we saw how dissociations can work against a fully developed and well-integrated self-narrative. Mild forms of dissociation, as well as moderate use of them, belong to the normal process of valuation associated with everyday life. For example, people who are intensely involved in a project for a prolonged period of time may need to dissociate for some time with certain experiences that would otherwise interfere with their concentration. However, when people systematically avoid dealing with experiences of direct personal relevance, the capacity to give such experiences a place in the valuation system may be seriously impoverished. For example, a person who has not learned to deal with situations of failure may take self-deception as the solution, and delusions of grandeur may be the result. Quite simply, dissociations involving major life events may play a central role in the development of a dysfunctional valuation system (see also Chapter 7).

Before describing some forms of dysfunction, we should explain what a dysfunction is in the context of the present conceptual framework. This explanation will then serve as the starting point for distinguishing between three types of depression. A dysfunction can be defined as significantly reduced flexibility in the valuation system, which should include different types of valuation. In Chapter 4 it was explained that a healthy person has the possibility of moving from one type of valuation to another, depending on the nature of the immediate situation. It was also explained that such movements are only possible when the system includes a certain variety of such types, which serve as reference points for the various experiences of an individual. When certain life experiences are dissociated from the valuation system, the system may no longer be a well-balanced, integrated whole precisely because certain valuation types are missing. When such impoverishment occurs—or when an individual's personal history never provided the opportunity to develop a differentiated and integrated system—there will be a severe limitation in the person's ability to respond to different situations. Moreover, the dysfunctional character of a system may be disguised as long as the person is in a position to select situations in line with the type of valuation dominating the system. This way of organizing one's life has its limitations, however. For example, a person who wants to be admired by others may only select admirers as friends. However, other people may tire of such egocentrism, leaving the person with no one to continue feeding his or her ego. The final result, then, may be self-deception in a desperate attempt to gratify the S motive (e.g., "No one understands my genius").

A dysfunction can be described as a self-narrative restricted to a single theme in which the theme is identical to a type of valuation (see Chapter 4). It is as if the person can only create variations on a single theme irrespective of changes in the life situation. Thus, a depressive client only tells sad stories or has only stereotyped complaints, which represent an inflexible response to situations that may even contain a promising event or positive message. Whereas thematic variation may characterize the normally functioning valuation system, only variations on a single persistent theme can be observed in the person with a dysfunctional valuation system. Typically, there is only a single latent motive at work, giving rise to only a limited variety of valuations on the manifest level. For example, a person who is always in opposition to other people will consistently find himself or herself in conflict and can therefore be described as fixed to valuations of the −S type. In this sense one can say that a dysfunction is a persistent form of valuation that has become generalized over time and situations. Consequently, people with dysfunctional valuations (the depressive types in particular) are more predictable than people with a flexible system; one can often foresee their reactions, no matter what the situation. In contrast, people with a more flexible valuation system have different types of valuations available, and their reactions are generally less predictable.

Yet another aspect of a dysfunction is its cultural relativity. Becker (1971) suggests that the greatest discrepancy may be found between the definition of normal behavior in modern Western culture and in a society where there is a belief in a dual universe. People in the latter society tend to value experiences in the invisible world and have a talent for interpreting such experiences. As Becker observes, auditory hallucinations may be normal in a culture where one expects to hear the voice of God periodically. Visual hallucinations may also be normal in a society (such as the Plains Indians of America) in which one's guardian spirit is assumed to regularly manifest itself in a vision; similarly, among Catholics in southern Italy the "appearance" of the Virgin Mary is a blessed event. Still other societies give their highest rewards to the shaman, whose social function is to travel to the invisible world to deal with various spirits. In other words, one can only speak of dysfunction in light of shared cultural meanings and stories, which set the norms used to differentiate between normal and abnormal. When someone claims to be in touch with Beethoven, we assume he has a delusion because we consider the real Beethoven to be dead. However, if the notion of spiritism were to win favor in our culture and take its place in our collective beliefs, the same statement would be perceived as quite normal. In Bruner's (1986) and others' terms, different versions of reality or "possible worlds" exist, and a statement that is true in one world need not be true in another.

To summarize: (1) *Dissociations* are forced operations that in combination with important life experiences can lead to dysfunction. (2) *Dysfunction* is a reduced flexibility of the valuation system and/or a lack of thematic variation in the self-narrative, reflecting an impairment of the person–situation interaction. (3) The notion of dysfunction is nevertheless culturally relative, implying that the status of valuations as dysfunctional depends on the collective values of a community.

A schema representing the different types of dysfunction can be found in Figure 6.1. This figure corresponds to Figure 4.1, which represents a flexible valuation system in which a variety of valuation types (themes) are represented; the person with such a valuation system can move freely from one type to another as the situation requires. Figure 6.1 represents inflexible forms of organization; one type of valuation dominates the system, and the possibility of freely moving from one type to another is therefore strongly reduced or even absent.

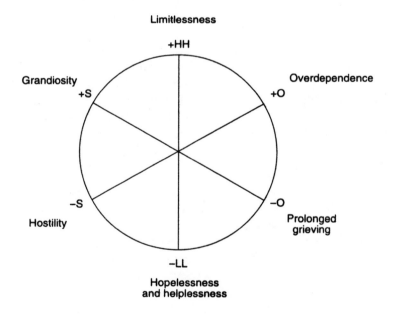

FIGURE 6.1. Dysfunctional valuations (+S, positive self-enhancement; –S, negative self-enhancement; +O, positive contact with the other; –O, negative contact with the other; +HH, positive combination of high self-enhancement and high contact with the other; –LL, negative combination of low self-enhancement and low contact with the other).

The two figures are comparable in that each valuation type in one figure has a corresponding type in the other, suggesting that each type in the healthy functioning system can at some time become dysfunctional. This also means that a person with a well-functioning valuation system can have some notion of what it means to be abnormal by imagining the persistent predominance of one type of valuation in the system over time and circumstances.

In the following paragraphs, clients illustrating various types of dysfunctions are described. Not all of their valuations are presented; the discussion revolves around those valuations that appear to dominate the system. The purpose of this discussion is to point to some phenomena in the organization of the self that are dysfunctional.

Three Forms of Depression

Unitary, dualistic, and pluralistic systems of classification have been developed in various attempts to classify depressive disorders (Corsini, 1987). Unitary approaches assume there is only one type of depression, which simply varies in severity. This view enjoys only limited popularity. Dualistic approaches assume two types of depression. The names assigned to these types include, among other dualities, reactive versus autonomous depression and neurotic versus psychotic depression. The most well-known dualistic conception of depression is unipolar versus bipolar. Unipolar depression is diagnosed when one or more episodes of depression occur whereas bipolar depression is diagnosed when episodes of depression alternate with episodes of mania. Pluralistic approaches assume there are many types of depressive disorders. The successive versions of the American Psychiatric Association's *Diagnostic and Statistical Manual* (DSM) lists more than a dozen different types of depressive disorders, including various schizoaffective disorders, psychotic-depressive disorders, and depressive personality types.

In exploring the transition area between normality and abnormality, we describe a limited number of depression types: (1) depression characterized by prolonged grieving, (2) depression characterized by self-directed hostility, and (3) depression characterized by helplessness and hopelessness. These types correspond to the three lower positions on the circle in Figure 6.1, −O, −S, and −LL, respectively.

Depressive Grieving

The following valuations show some features of a depression heavily colored by prolonged grieving. The valuations come from a 29-year-old client whose mother had been admitted to a psychiatric hospital when the client was 5 years old and who died a few years later. Her father died about 5 years prior to the self-investigation:

	S	O	P	N
Valuation 1. "My mother: We needed to keep each other at a distance because we saw each other so rarely."	1	10	0	16
Valuation 2. "Because of my desire not to become just like mother, I talked for hours with my older sisters, comparing my situation with that of mother."	7	0	7	18
Valuation 3. "I am saddled with guilt feelings about my father; he did his best and I have failed."	1	18	3	19
Valuation 4. "When I am at home all alone, I listen to organ music by Handel, let my emotions come, and then talk to my father: 'I am completely depressed now, but you have always done your best. I will not be like mother. I need other people now, but I will fight my way out of this.'"[1]	0	13	2	14
Valuation 5. "John [husband] wants to go into business for himself. I have the feeling that I should no longer hold him back; I am afraid for this."	2	13	1	9
Valuation 6. "Having children: My immediate environment influences me. A studying or working mother is a bad mother."	7	12	4	9
Valuation 7. "Dream: I am called by the hospital. In a room that has been closed off for many years a woman, who appears to be my mother, has been found. I look. When I open the door, everything looks quite normal. We both start to cry, and she asks, 'Where is your bow?'"	1	15	5	17

These valuations have, in their content and organization, some conspicuous features that make them approach the dysfunctional. A particular affective pattern (low S, high O, low P, and high N) is characteristic of many valuations from this client. As we have seen in Chapter 4, this pattern most often indicates a *fugit amor* experience. In the same chapter it was argued that a *fugit amor* valuation, like other types of valuation, belongs to the potential of the healthy individual. However, in the present example, there is a clear indication that the *fugit amor* experience is dysfunctional; that is, this experience has been generalized to a large degree over time and situations. Although her mother died long ago, the client is still mourning her death (Valuation 1) and even dreams that her mother has been found and is still alive (Valuation 7). The *fugit amor* pattern, moreover, characterizes her relation not only to her mother but also to her father (Valuations 3 and 4), her husband (Valuation 5), and her future children (Valuation 6).

There are several other observations that corroborate the dysfunctional quality of this client's depression: (1) There is some distortion in Valuation 1, indicated by the discrepancy between the text of the valuation ("We kept each other at a distance") and the high level of O affect, which is not reflected in the text. (2) The grieving is combined (in Valuation 3) with self-blame (see Beck, 1967, for the relation between depression and self-blame). (3) The formulations do not always reflect a strong concern for the other but, rather, sometimes take the form of a self-complaint (Valuation 3) and have an egocentric flavor (e.g., Valuations 2 and 5).[2]

It is important to note that not all these valuations have a *fugit amor* affective pattern. Valuation 2, although related to the lost mother, is an attempt by the client to defend herself against becoming like her mother and represents a movement to another valuation type (-S). Here we see that there is some attempt to maintain some degree of self-esteem, which may be helpful in trying to change her fairly biased manner of valuation.

Note also that the role of collective values in the system can be observed in Valuation 6 ("A working mother is a bad mother"), although in this case it is taken on and used to reinforce an already depressive form of valuation. That is, the collective value may be used as an escape from her own choices and responsibilities and may present a distorted picture of her own desires.

Depression with Self-Directed Hostility

Let us now look at some valuations representing a type of depression in which self-directed hostility plays an implicit or explicit role. These valuations come from a highly gifted student who nevertheless had the feeling that he was never respected by his parents:

	S	O	P	N
Valuation 1. "When I thought that I deserved punishment, I demanded punishment from my parents. If I didn't get it, then I went ahead and did it myself. I tormented myself . . . expiation."	8	3	5	14

	S	O	P	N
Valuation 2. "I have been under-estimated by my parents, especially with respect to my academic abilities. I stayed at college: It was my decision and was intended to thwart everyone."	12	2	9	11
Valuation 3. "I must adhere to certain rules (etiquette/social norms) and by doing so come into conflict with my own feelings. I then experience a blind rage and direct it at myself."	6	3	7	16
Valuation 4. "Sometimes I think that there is no feeling in me, and then I notice that I have my own feelings when the lightning of rage flashes through me."	10	2	10	13
Valuation 5. "I try to tune out my mind so that others cannot get a hold of me; I do that through making up stories, in incomprehensible language, and playing hide-and-seek with myself."	10	3	6	17
Valuation 6. "I can study only under extreme pressure."	12	6	8	19

In these valuations the affective pattern of –S (or some approximation thereof) is coloring a broad array of situations: the relation with parents (Valuation 1), past school achievements (Valuation 2), normative situations (Valuation 3), interactions with people in general (Valuation 5), and present study behavior (Valuation 6). This picture suggests a considerable generalization of hostility over time and situations, with a corresponding reduction in the flexibility of the valuation system.

Not all of the valuations reflect purely inwardly directed hostility: Valuation 2 refers to opposition in the external situation, and Valuation 5 implies a mixture of inward and outward hostility. It is expected that as the hostility becomes more self-directed, the depression will be more serious.

Note that in the case of self-directed hostility, the person–situation interaction is disturbed. That is, just as depressed mourners are wrapped up in themselves (Abraham, 1942), so too are depressed people with self-directed hostility primarily concerned with themselves. This means that the capacity to respond adequately to situational challenges and changes is severely diminished, just as it is in depressed mourners.

We prefer the term *hostility* over *aggression*, for aggression is usually considered part of the healthy person's system (Chapter 4). Hostility, however, persists over time and situations, which gives it a more persistent character and in turn produces a more distorted narrative than aggression does (see also Lester, 1972, p. 216).

Depressive Helplessness and Hopelessness

The depression in which positive feelings are generally most suppressed is type –LL, which is characterized by a low level or even an absence of both self-enhancement and contact and union with the other. As discussed earlier, this kind of valuation may also be part of a normal and healthy valuation system provided the system is still open to other types of valuation. We commonly say in this case that someone feels "down" and observe that he or she soon snaps out of it. When the openness of the valuation system is strongly reduced or absent, however, people can only respond with an excessive emphasis on valuations of type –LL, which implies that their downheartedness or apathy is persisting. This is illustrated by the following valuations, which are from a 45-year-old man who was in a period of divorce and had a tendency to evaluate everything from the perspective of his religious education:

	S	O	P	N
Valuation 1. "I have a norm awareness —'It ought to be so'—that has been forced on me by my mother and the Catholic church. It still plays a role in my life."	1	0	0	5
Valuation 2. "I was especially scared when I was in third grade: Someone threatened to put me in the basement and chain me up; I got stomachaches from this."	0	0	0	3
Valuation 3. "I cannot talk things through with Gwyn [wife]: She says that discussion is of little use."	1	0	0	14
Valuation 4. "I let her persuade me to have children."	1	0	2	7
Valuation 5. "The threat that hangs over the whole world: Any number of things can happen, and you can't do anything about them."[3]	0	0	0	16
Valuation 6. "Thinking about myself: I find that I think too much about myself."	2	0	0	14

	S	O	P	N
Valuation 7. "I have received a great deal of support from my friends in this situation."	9	12	14	1
Valuation 8. "I don't think about the future; I just want to stop."	0	0	0	13
Valuation 9. "I feel hopeless and have no outlook."	0	0	0	9

There are several indications of helplessness in this case: The client feels suppressed by institutional norms (Valuation 1) and overruled by significant others (Valuation 4) and shows an overdependence on the influence of others (Valuations 3 and 4). However, not all valuations are of this kind. The client is aware of the support of his friends, which is positively experienced and gives him not only a feeling of contact with the other but also some strength (Valuation 7). Nevertheless, this valuation does not reflect confidence in his own abilities but, rather, a form of secondary self-enhancement (see Chapter 4). There are also indications of hopelessness. This is clearly expressed in connection with the future in Valuation 8 and repeated again, in highly generalized terms, in Valuation 9. Note that persons with such overgeneralizing valuations in their system are unlikely to be open to good news, which can too easily be overshadowed by dark expectations or simply reinterpreted to fit in with preexisting negative valuations.[4]

From a theoretical perspective there is an important difference between helplessness and hopelessness: Helplessness refers to lack of fulfillment of the contact motive whereas hopelessness refers to lack of fulfillment of the self-esteem motive. Helplessness and hopelessness are the dysfunctional correlates (Figure 6.1) of isolation and powerlessness in the healthy valuation system (Figure 4.1). The latter two terms presuppose a differentiated and integrated valuation system that permits a person to move from one type of valuation to the other. A person who persistently feels isolated becomes helpless, and someone who persistently feels powerless will eventually feel hopeless.

Comparison of the Three Types of Depression

A comparison of the foregoing three types of depression indicates that depression involving helplessness and hopelessness is the most severe from a treatment point of view. In the other two types of depression (grieving and self-directed hostility) at least one of the two basic motives is involved. In a grieving depression the person is more or less oriented toward another person who has been lost or injured (−O). In self-hostile depression, people are primarily concerned with their self-esteem, although in a punishing way (−S). In both cases, at least one of the motives is involved, which keeps the individual in a state of active realization and thereby prevents him or her from falling into the deeper abyss of helplessness and hopelessness. A valuation system based on type −LL, in contrast, represents almost no involvement and therefore a deeper depressive state.

We speak intentionally of a *deeper* level of depression rather than the *deepest* level because the latter (e.g., a psychotic depression) falls beyond the scope of this discussion. Although we assume that depressions can vary in depth and severity, it may nevertheless be relevant to examine some of the indicators of this variation in valuation research. Let us, therefore, once again examine the valuations of the last client, particularly Valuation 9: "I feel hopeless and have no outlook." One may at first be surprised that such a pessimistic-sounding statement is associated with only a score of 9 for negative affect. One would expect a higher score inasmuch as other valuations from the same client that are equally general and pessimistic (e.g., Valuation 5) are associated with a much higher level of negative affect. What could be the reason for this relatively low N level? A hint can be found in Seligman's (1974) observation that although anxiety is the initial response to a stressful situation, anxiety is replaced by depression (passivity and apathy) when the person comes to believe that control is unattainable. In other words, it can be expected that a valuation expressing helplessness or hopelessness may show a decreasing level of negative affect when there is a diminishing expectation of self-enhancement or contact with other people. In the extreme case of apathy, it is expected that valuations will be characterized by low S, low O, low P, and low N. This pattern of affect is a result of severe and probably quite global dissociation. As already discussed earlier in this chapter, people may subdue the affect associated with a particular part of the self-narrative in order to diminish an unbearable level of emotion. Apathy, therefore, may be the result of persistent subduing.[5]

Anger may also be an indicator of the severity of a depression. As may be expected, the depression resulting from self-directed hostility has a high level of anger (assessed with the affect list in Appendix 2). Perhaps unexpected is the frequent observation that the valuation systems of clients who feel hopeless or helpless also often show quite high levels of anger. The difference between the two forms of depression is that in self-directed hostility (−S) a high level of anger is associated with a high level of S affect while in the case of helplessness or hopelessness (−LL) a high level of anger coexists with a low level of S affect. From this observation, a distinction can be made between anger with strength and anger without strength. Clinical experience to date suggests that anger that is felt as strong is more easily expressed in words, by intonation, or as "angry behavior" while anger that is not felt as strong is often "swallowed" and therefore unexpressed (see Perls, 1969.) In the practice of self-confrontation, clients who have swallowed their anger may indicate a high level of anger in connection with particular valuations and may know they are very angry even though they have great difficulty in expressing and communicating this emotion. It may be concluded that knowing the nature of one's anger is relevant not only for understanding a feeling of depression but also for moving from a depressive to a nondepressive state (i.e., from anger without strength toward anger with strength).

Finally, it should be observed that the three types of depression are not necessarily mutually exclusive. Despite the persistent character of depressive states, there may be a change from one type to another. For example, a person can experience a deeper level of depression when grieving or when self-directed hostility changes into helplessness or hopelessness. Conversely, improvement can be assumed at times when there is an increasing element of aggression that can be ventilated against the outside world.

Scenario for Coming Out of a Depressive State

When clients come to better understand the nature of their depressed state by doing a self-investigation, can they also learn how to get out of one? There are at least two points that deserve special attention here. First, for people in a depressive state the communicative function of the self-confrontation method and the quality of the contact with the psychologist are of utmost importance. A self-investigation and a modality analysis are not sufficient to change the client's situation. Certainly, a self-investigation may be the beginning of the process of invalidation if the condition is met that the psychologist helps the client express and communicate his or her experiences in a safe and supportive climate. A self-confrontation with a valuation system that is filled with negative valuations may be an extra burden when the quality of the communication is bad but a release when it is good. Second, in the case of depression it is expected that the validation/invalidation process will take a longer time than in the case of, for example, identity problems. Generally, it is our experience that the transition between the first and second phases of the validation/invalidation process ("attending" and "creating," respectively; see Chapter 3) requires more effort and takes a longer time in the case of depression than in the case of identity problems. The reason is that depressive people, particularly when they are in a state of hopelessness and helplessness, are quite stable in their clinging to negative valuations of their past, present, and future. Attending, therefore, means to them attending to the negative valuations that are already dominating their self-narratives. A redirection of such clients' attention to existing positive aspects of their life situation or an exploration and discussion of new behavior may therefore be required. This implies that in an early stage of the validation/ invalidation process new valuations, of a more positive kind, should be introduced as a first step toward counterbalancing the dominant negative valuations.

In order to give an impresson of the kind of invalidation clients may learn as a response to their depression, a short follow-up self-investigation was done with the client we presented earlier with depressive helplessness and hopelessness. For four years this client was almost continuously in psychotherapy, which ended when he remarried. One year later a final self-investigation was performed with the following question added: "Do you sometimes have depressive feelings, and if so, how do you get out of them?" With the help of the psychologist the client formulated six successive sentences in which he described in detail how he now proceeded in the case of depressive feelings:

	S	O	P	N
Valuation 1. "Sometimes I awake from a dream in which I felt I was being watched by my mother."	10	3	1	10
Valuation 2. "I then think that I am worrying about negative things in my current life (for example, unpleasant experiences at school)."	6	0	2	14
Valuation 3. "I then try to localize the cause of the unpleasant feelings."	9	6	7	8
Valuation 4. "If the unpleasant feelings don't go away after a while, then I get up and go drink some water; I drink the water slowly, sip by sip."	12	9	7	6
Valuation 5. "I then go back to bed and try to relax as much as possible."	11	12	10	5
Valuation 6. "Falling asleep for me means the disappearence of the negative feelings."	16	13	17	0

Notice, first of all, that the client was really the inventor of this procedure. Although he had learned from psychotherapy to carefully attend to his emotional reactions, to look for specific causal events, and then to spell out an appropriate response, the procedure was a creation of his own, one based on his own experiences. Second, although the psychologist asked for a situation in which the client had depressive feelings, the affective pattern of Valuation 1 was quite different from the affective pattern of the valuations present at the beginning of therapy. At that time they were, as we have seen, predominantly of the −LL type whereas now we see type −S (Valuation 1). In other words, the current affective pattern associated with a depressive state suggests the existence of (external) opposition. Apparently, the client now feels the power to stand up to his mother, an oppositional attitude that was completely absent at the outset of therapy. Note also that this corroborates the finding that clients first develop their system in the direction of self-maintenance and then work on their contacts with others. Finally, the client was not fixated on opposition; he had developed a means for returning to a relaxed state of mind (falling asleep again), as expressed in Valuation 6, which was associated with very positive type (+HH) affect.

The six aforementioned valuations can be conceived of as a scenario for coming out of a depression. The client has created a new subsystem of valuations that allow him to move flexibly from negative to positive feelings. Of course, different people may come up with different scenarios, and the scenarios themselves may differ in the degree of flexibility they provide. It is expected that the best scenario is the one that contains different types of valuations and is applicable across a wide variety of situations.

Three Types of Suicide

Although suicidal thoughts are not uncommon in normal people and a significant number of people who are not known to be depressed have at times attempted suicide, it is generally accepted that there is a relation between depression and suicide (e.g., Davison & Neale, 1990). For this reason, we will now discuss three forms of suicide that closely correspond to the three types of depression we have just described.

Mintz (1968), who isolated the various suicidal motives in the psychological literature, included in a review the following, among others: the desire to rejoin a dead one, aggression turned inward, and the desire to escape from pain or isolation (see also Stone, 1960.) These particular forms of suicide also correspond to and may stem from the forms of depression discussed earlier, that is, depressive grieving, depression with self-directed hostility, and depressive helplessness and hopelessness, respectively. Let us focus now on the difference between helplessness and hopelessness.

A depression of the −LL type is characterized by both hopelessness and helplessness at the same time (Shneidman, 1987, also recognizes the common emotion in suicide as hopelessness-helplessness). Depending on previous life history, however, one of the two states may predominate. In men, and particularly those whose valuation system is built on the S motive, depression usually entails a feeling of hopelessness. Depressive women, and particularly those whose valuation system is based on the O motive, are more in a state of helplessness and consequently are more likely than men to attempt suicide as "a cry for help" (Farberow & Shneidman, 1961).

In his theoretical analysis, *Suicide and Hope,* Farber (1967) argues that hope is characterized by a "sense of competence": the basic feeling that one can find the resources within oneself to cope with the demands of life. When this sense of competence drops to such a low level that even everyday life becomes too big or too intolerable, people may attempt to commit suicide. This situation is characterized by Farber (1967) as a "no-exit situation," with self-induced death as the only perceived exit. For example, a person who is incurably sick knows that the suffering will only increase and therefore may see suicide as the only alternative to the suffering.

Whereas hopelessness refers to the absence of self-enhancement, helplessness refers to the absence or impossibility of contact with others. This distinction is also directly reflected in the difference between an actual suicide and a suicide attempt. A state characterized by extreme helplessness implies an orientation toward other people (i.e., help from others is desired but unobtainable) whereas this orientation is less obvious in the case of extreme hopelessness. It is therefore believed that a suicide attempt is more probable in a state of helplessness and that an actual suicide is more probable in a state of hopelessness. Some empirical evidence in support of this conclusion can be found in Davison and Neale's (1990) review, in which they conclude that three times as many men succeed in killing themselves as women (although the ratio is approaching twice as many men as women, since women are becoming a higher-risk group). Conversely, three times as many women as men attempt to kill themselves but do not succeed. Since some degree of truth characterizes the claim that traditional role prescriptions lead to an emphasis on other-oriented valuations for women, their suicide attempts can be understood as resulting from helplessness rather than from hopelessness. In contrast, traditional role considerations may force some men to be more concerned with their own self-esteem. Given a state of hopelessness (and their use of more violent means), men are therefore more likely to actually kill themselves.

The literature on male and female tolerance of depression points in the same direction. Warren (1983) reviewed a number of studies on depression and help-seeking behavior and concluded that for many men depression is a very private experience; such men do not share their feelings with others and probably believe that depression should be hidden and should be alleviated without external help. This literature supports the view that hopelessness is more typical of men than it is of women.

OTHER FORMS OF DYSFUNCTION

Although the main emphasis in this chapter is on depression, other forms of dysfunction can also be described in terms of the types of valuations presented in Figure 6.1. We will now briefly discuss other forms of dysfunction in the light of common clinical observations and alternative theoretical conceptions.

Other-Directed Hostility

Hostility can be directed inward, as we have seen in our discussion of depression, but it can also be directed toward the outside world. In a study of the concerns of 38 delinquent boys between 18 and 22 years of age, Van Assen (1985) found a high frequency of valuations with a high degree of both negative affect and affect referring to the exertion of power (e.g., strength, self-confidence, self-determination, autonomy—all −S valuations). He concluded that these boys, having experienced a relative lack of control in their lives, were trying to obtain some self-esteem or power by "going into opposition"; that is, opposition was the *only* way they could achieve some mastery of their environment.

Van Assen's observations correspond to other findings regarding aggressive young delinquents. Staub (1986) found that delinquents persistently interpret the behavior of others as threatening and, as a result, react with "pre-retaliation." Toch (1969) has also found that some delinquents invariably use violence to defend themselves against belittlement. Indeed, the potential loss of or injury to one's self-esteem can cause anger (Alschuler & Alschuler, 1984; Mathes, Adams, & Davies, 1985).

In the psychological literature the concepts of self-esteem and well-being (happiness) are often seen as closely related and are even sometimes considered conceptually identical (e.g., Baruch & Barnett,1986; Buehler, Hogan, & Robinson, 1985). In studies that support this understanding it is supposed that a high level of self-esteem correlates with a high level of well-being. In marked contrast to this association, Hermans (1992b) focused on experiences in which a high level of self-esteem coexists with a low level of well-being, a condition he labeled "unhappy self-esteem" (in fact, a −S type of valuation). The self-statements of 15 clients showing unhappy self-esteem were compared, and it was found that the phenomenon clearly refers to anger and opposition. It was concluded that the phenomenon of unhappy self-esteem has a close conceptual relationship to anger and should be understood as a restorative reaction to an anticipated or actual loss of self-esteem.

Murray (1962) has also directed considerable attention to a type of personality organization characterized by persistent, outwardly directed hostility. In his description of people with a so-called satanic personality, he mentioned the following features: (1) a secret feeling of having been harshly, treacherously, unjustly, or ignominiously deprived of what are felt to be well-earned benefits, rewards, and glory; (2) a basic state of alienation, resentment, and distrust; (3) a hidden envy coupled with overt contempt for the achievements of others; (4) repression of any guilt feelings; and (5) the adoption of one or another strategy—slyness, evasiveness, subversion, or destructiveness—for venting a self-consuming hatred. A characteristic by which such people are most easily identified is the absence of any capacity to experience or express authentic selfless love, gratitude, admiration, or compassion (Murray, 1962, p. 49). Murray's satanic personality (or, in our terms, the hostile person) is largely fixed to the −S position in Figure 6.1 and is unable to move to the opposite +O position. The valuation system of such a person is, in our terms, basically unbalanced.

Murray provided this personality description as part of a treatise on the relationship between Satan and God, a treatise in which he argued that the relation cannot be conceived of in terms of two essentially different figures opposed to each other; rather, the figure of Satan should be understood as God's original companion and therefore as derived from God's nature. Murray's analysis provides an interesting metaphor for thinking about human nature and human motivation in particular. When we recognize hostility, revenge, envy, and hate as the bad side of human nature, the question of whether or not we also have bad motives arises. Many religious orientations suggest that there are both good and bad motives, that people may be inspired by God or by the devil. A typical humanistic-psychological answer, however, is represented by Rogers's statement that "human nature is basically good" and that human motivation must therefore also be basically positive, reflecting a tendency toward self-actualization (Rogers, 1951; see also Maddi, 1972). This point of view implies that bad behavior is the result of environmental forces blocking the expression of our true nature.

In contrast to humanistic theories (e.g., Rogers's view of human nature as basically good), valuation theory assumes that human motivation, as a central part of human nature, can be both good and bad. This view implies that the same self-enhancement motive can be expressed in a constructive way (e.g., through one's work) or in a destructive way (e.g., through deeds of revenge, hate, hostility, envy). Bakan (1966) also expressed in his concept of "unmitigated agency" the notion that the need for agency can become exaggerated while communion is simultaneously suppressed and that this need can thereby itself become a source of evil human activity. Correspondingly, we see hostility as a negative manifestation of morally ambiguous human motives.

Grandiosity as a Dead End

Grandiosity can be seen as a dysfunctional exaggeration of success and autonomy. In psychology this exaggeration is most typically represented by the more excessive expressions of the achievement motive, probably the most well-known and best investigated motive in the history of our field. The achievement motive was initially put forward by Murray (1938) and was later, through his Thematic Apperception Test (TAT), incorporated into the work of McClelland (McClelland, Atkinson, Clark, & Lowell, 1953; McClelland, Koestner, & Weinberger, 1989). Although diverse intellectual sources stimulated Murray's thinking, his conception of the achievement motive comes very close to the traditional work ethic in which one is exhorted: "to do things as rapidly and/or as well as possible; . . . to master, manipulate, and organize physical objects, human beings or ideas; . . . to overcome obstacles and attain a high standard; . . . to excel one's self; and to rival and surpass others" (Murray, 1938, p. 164). McClelland (1961) observed this parallel between motivation and the work ethic and began to talk of the "achieving society." Spence (1985), reflecting on the studies of McClelland and coworkers, analyzed the achievement motive from the perspective of Bakan's distinction between "agency" and "communion." She argued that the achievement motive is indeed typical of Western societies and that, moreover, in these societies the agentic takes precedence over the communal. This is in contrast to many Eastern societies, where the balance shifts more toward the communal.

On the basis of her analysis of Western societies, with their high degree of individualism and emphasis on the work ethic, Spence (1985) argued that a strong commitment to one's work, even noble work, is nevertheless often accomplished at the expense of others, that working hard, striving to perform well, and always needing to succeed can have socially deleterious effects if they are not embedded in some kind of commitment to a larger community. Moreover, highly competitive achievement strivings can often be self-defeating and destructive to the individual. For example, interpersonally competitive individuals are less likely to achieve than their less competitive peers (Spence & Helmreich, 1983). Additionally, as is well known, hard-driving Type A individuals often succeed in the short term, but in the long term their success is at the expense of their physical health (Jenkins, Rosenman, & Zyzanski, 1974).

Taking Spence's considerations into account, we would expect at least two kinds of valuation problems in our achieving societies: (1) People who are more interested in contact and union with the other than in self-enhancement will not be highly valued from the perspective of the dominant group, and (2) people who are excessively oriented toward self-enhancement will characteristically have only a small range of possible valuations. The latter will tend to answer indiscriminately with personal achievements and illustrations of their competence even in situations that do not invite them to do so.

Let us now look at some valuations with a rather subdued affective component from a man in mid-life who was working very hard at a full-time job and at the same time involved in a dissertation project:

	S	O	P	N
Valuation 1. "In my previous job I actually felt threatened by both the pupils and by the principal at different times."	0	0	0	4
Valuation 2. "The dissertation is the last chance for me to prove myself."	9	0	6	0
Valuation 3. "I would like to have more influence in the section where I now work, both in what is done and the management of it."	7	0	3	0

	S	O	P	N
Valuation 4. "I am longing for the moment that I can lay aside the burden of 'proving myself.'"	9	0	5	0
Valuation 5. "I don't perceive myself as being in unity with someone else."	6	0	1	0
Valuation 6. "I am who I am, and when another has problems with that, he can come to me."	9	0	3	0

Together these valuations present a picture of a person with a strong bias toward self-enhancement (Valuations 2, 3, 6), which he nevertheless experiences as a tremendous burden (Valuation 4). Note that even the possibility of being able to "lay aside the burden" is experienced as a form of self-enhancement, as indicated by the affective pattern associated with this valuation. Paradoxically, this suggests that trying to escape from self-enhancement can itself be a form of self-enhancement.

An essential feature of this case is the total absence in this client of a longing for contact with another individual, group, or imaginary figure; of esthetic experiences; of religious concerns; and even of love for his work. He simply responds to social situations by emphasizing his autonomy (Valuation 6), influence (Valuation 3) and achievement (Valuation 2). This organization implies that at least three types of valuation have systematically been omitted from his self-narrative: +HH, +O, and −O. As a result, it will be very difficult for this man to lay down his burden, by, for example, sharing his problems with another person or with an imaginal figure. Moreover, if this man meets with failure in his work, he will most certainly end up in a depression.

The general subduing of affect is also characteristic of a persistent emphasis on self-enhancement. This persistence may result in an overly rationalized and structured way of living, where feelings are perceived as useless or as something that interferes with efficient performance. When such individuals become aware of this affective indifference, they may say, "I feel like an automaton." When a person works, not persistently but at times, on the basis of an exaggerated self-enhancement motive alone, there are always some feelings of self-esteem, strength, self-confidence, and pride, often in combination with a variety of positive feelings. However, when the motivation is almost fully automatic, as in this case, the array of feelings may be severely limited, resulting in a drastic reduction in the flexibility of the valuation system.

Dependency and a Lack of Self-Reliance

Dependency can be defined as the seeking of support, companionship, security and/or permission from another person, social unit, or outside entity.

Dependency may also include a particular belief system to which the individual is highly devoted (Corsini, 1987). Phrased in this way, dependency is a normal phenomenon that belongs to the daily life of healthy people. However, when dependency is associated with a lack of self-reliance, it reflects—at least within our culture—a dysfunctional organization of the self (see, for example, Milton's, 1981, list of diagnostic criteria for the assessment of a dependent personality disorder). Such a dysfunctional organization is illustrated by the valuations from an adolescent girl who was so dependent on the support of her mother and family that she was afraid to leave the house:

	S	O	P	N
Valuation 1. "I was screamed at by the girls; I went inside and never left the house again."	3	4	2	15
Valuation 2. "Mother: I can tell her everything that has happened to me."	7	14	13	2
Valuation 3. "I am not so scared at home. There I think that I can become something, later, that it will be okay, that I will be happy."	8	16	17	2
Valuation 4. "I would like to be of help, for example, by doing the shopping."	8	18	16	3
Valuation 5. "I would like to meet somebody who would teach me how to have a normal life."	5	10	14	3
Valuation 6. "When I feel happy, I don't dislike anybody."	8	17	17	1
Valuation 7. "I will only fit in when I dare more."	8	16	16	3
Valuation 8. "Sometimes I am mad at myself, and then I hit myself because things are not going the way I want them to."	0	0	0	20

One can see that there has been little "separation individuation," to use a term from Mahler, Pine, and Bergman (1975), by this client; she keeps in close physical proximity to her mother (Valuations 1 and 3) and requests her mother's help (Valuation 2) before trying to solve a problem herself (see Aries & Olver, 1985). Valuations referring to her ideal self (Valuations 4 and 5) also assume some sort of dependency relation. Moreover, she is afraid of her own aggression (Valuation 6), and instead of giving a −S valuation here, she draws a veil over her own anger and phrases the valuation in such a way that it also assumes a +O pattern. The same is true for Valuation 7: While daring something could lead to positive fulfillment of the self-esteem motive, it is nevertheless subordinated to the contact motive. Finally, observe that where there is aggression, it is self-directed (Valuation 8) and must therefore be considered a failed attempt to master her situation.

Dependency on others can be a healthy phenomenon when the situation calls for their help (e.g., when an accident occurs, when one is sick, or when one needs the know-how of another). No matter how dependent one may be in a certain situation, the healthy individual usually maintains some degree of self-reliance to fall back on as the situation may demand. Dependency becomes dysfunctional when it stems from a lack of self-reliance. That is, dysfunctional dependency is an organizational problem. Overly dependent people not only rely on others but also try to avoid or escape situations that may call for self-reliance. This avoidance of challenging situations related to the S motive has the unfortunate consequence of narrowing the individual's other-related contacts and thus reinforces an overreliance on a single individual. For maintaining or increasing one's autonomy, it may be necessary at times to reduce one's contact and union with the other, but overly dependent persons find this extremely difficult. Because they systematically avoid conflict, possible manifestations or hints of the S motive (e.g., trying something themselves, expressing their aggression, presenting their opinion) are omitted from the self-narrative.

Limitlessness: Unrealistic Aspirations and Overinvolvement in Contact

The concept of "limitlessness" refers to an inability or unwillingness to perceive or accept realistic limitations on both the self-enhancement and the contact and union motive. In this case of dysfunction the two motives have become intermingled and fused and produce a lack of differentiation within the valuation system. Limitlessness will often manifest itself as a tendency to extend the self to its utmost.

The fact that the subject is unable or unwilling to accept limitations on either motive makes limitlessness different from grandiosity and overdependence. In the striving for grandiosity the person is unlimited only in terms of searching for self-enhancement; experiences referring to contact and union with the other are omitted from the self-narrative or are simply transformed to fit into a more grandiose conception of the self (e.g., arrogance, using love for self-enhancing purposes). In overdependence a person is preoccupied with contact and union with the other; experiences of autonomy are either omitted or de-emphasized in the service of maintaining a harmonious relationship with the other (e.g., trying to achieve something only to please another person). In the phenomenon of limitlessness, the two motives are indiscriminately active, the underlying drive being to achieve the highest possible level of both self-enhancement and union with the other. It is as if the two motives, entangled with one another, are forcing each other to reach beyond all limits.

Let us now look at some valuations from a 35-year-old woman who had been very involved with her work in a children's home that was suddenly closed down:

	S	O	P	N
Valuation 1. "At home we were not permitted to associate with certain people, and yet we had to see all people as people; this contradiction confused me."	13	13	14	6
Valuation 2. "The children's home became my whole life; with regard to the outside world we felt like one big family, and this was strengthened by the results we had with the children."	18	19	19	7
Valuation 3. "When I disagreed with the principal I thought, 'He knows more than I do' instead of 'You [principal] can say what you want!'"	16	17	16	10

Valuation 3 indicates that this woman found it difficult to enter into conflict even when she felt her opinion was justified. As can be seen, the S motive in this case is fulfilled to a high degree, although the client indicates that she did not express her own opinion. She certainly has some awareness of going too far in giving of herself. This awareness, however, does not prevent her from keeping the S and O levels very high, as can also be seen in most of the following valuations:

	S	O	P	N
Valuation 4. "When the threat that school would close came, I realized how far I had gone in the giving of myself."	10	16	6	19
Valuation 5. "Very difficult things (e.g., leading a new group) are a challenge for me because I have an excessive need to prove to myself that I can manage even that."	18	17	17	7
Valuation 6. "Sometimes I think I have gone much too far in my relationship with Rose [lesbian girlfriend]."	14	18	13	8
Valuation 7. "I can enjoy being very deeply involved, in love, in philosophy, et cetera."	16	13	18	11

	S	O	P	N
Valuation 8. "I hate those people who think of themselves as God."	16	4	5	17

Ironically, in Valuation 8 she is objecting to the existence of limitlessness in others while not really recognizing it in herself. Although we saw some awareness of her limitlessness in earlier valuations, here she is projecting her problem onto others in a rather aggressive way.

Taken together, the most striking feature of the valuations is their "superlative striving" nature: to become greater and greater (Valuation 5), to unite more and more (Valuation 6), and to go deeper and deeper (Valuation 7). The two motives are not clearly differentiated and in fact are highly fused, as indicated by the recurrence of +HH valuations. That is, it is often unclear which part of the formulation represents the S feelings and which the O feelings. Because of the drastic change in her work situation, this client is becoming to some extent aware of the lack of limitations of herself (e.g., Valuation 6).[6]

Psychosomatic Complaints and Body Language

One can tell a story not only with spoken or written language but also with body language, as in pantomime or ballet. Moreover, with body language one can express a number of feelings (e.g., pride, anger, tenderness, grief). Just as people are motivated storytellers in their use of spoken language, so too are they motivated storytellers in their use of body language.

The body would be insufficiently understood if it were considered only a part of the Me or the Mine. The body is also the I. This is what Merleau-Ponty (1945) had in mind with his concept of *le corps-sujet* (the body subject): The person not only has a body as a felt object, but the body is also a subject and one's symbolic relation with the surrounding world can only be understood in the context of a body subject that is moving through time and space in an intentional way. From this viewpoint someone who is walking with a bowed head may be expressing in a symbolic way some meaningful aspect of his or her relation to the world. Similarly, when people wrinkle up their foreheads, they express symbolically a problematic situation or surprise.

In our language we have a number of expressions that use bodily experiences to convey information about our feelings: for example, "I was fed up with it," "It makes me sick," "He did it at nauseam," "I felt oppressed," "I was throttled," "It kills me when he . . ." Sometimes the body's relation with the environment is explicitly stated: "I was in a tight corner."

When bodily symbolizations of mental experience come and go as a function of a changing situation, they belong to the normal reactions of the healthy individual. However, when, for example, someone feels throttled to such a degree that the capacity to move to another state of mind-body is greatly reduced, then we enter the realm of dysfunction. Thus, as with other realms of valuation, body language becomes dysfunctional when a particular response is given in a rigid and indiscriminate way, indicating that the reaction has been highly generalized over time and situations. From this perspective, psychosomatic complaints, particularly if they are persistent, can also be considered dysfunctional forms of body language.

The translation of body language into verbal language enables us to incorporate body language, and more specifically psychosomatic complaints, into our analysis of the self-narrative. This may lead to performing a self-investigation on the relationship between a psychosomatic complaint and the rest of the self-narrative. A typical observation is that many clients do not understand the relation between a psychosomatic complaint and the other parts of their valuation system. Even when they are aware of the link between the complaint and something of a more psychological nature, they often do not know which problem is involved. In other words, the valuation system is fragmented with respect to the complaint, its underlying valuation, and the other valuations of the system.

Let us review a case that shows how a psychosomatic complaint becomes included in a valuation system and changes over time. It concerns a client who at Time 1 was in an interpersonal conflict with his superiors: They accused him of illegal behavior whereas he considered himself not guilty. During the period in which the self-investigation was performed, the client suffered from blurred vision and saw only black at times, although his eyesight was considered to be perfect and a physical neurological examination did not reveal any organic basis for this disturbance. On the assumption that the problem was of a psychosomatic character, it was included in the valuation system:[7]

	S	O	P	N
Valuation 1. "There are moments when I cannot see anything; I see double, have blurred vision."	0	4	0	17

In order to investigate the significance of this problem in the context of this client's valuation system, Valuation 1 was selected as a pivot valuation in a modality analysis; the highest correlation ($r = .90$) was found with the following statement:

	S	O	P	N
Valuation 2. "I am worried about how my social situation will look in the future (finances, work)."	3	7	0	17

The personal meaning of the psychosomatic problem was discussed on the basis of this correlation (and others), and the psychologist and client concluded that the problem was not one of not seeing but of not seeing a way out, given the client's powerless position.

With this insight the client and psychologist decided to concentrate on clarifying and structuring the client's perspective by taking specific steps in preparation for events related to his work situation. These initiatives were evaluated and discussed on a biweekly basis. In a second self-investigation 6 months later the client formulated the main developments associated with the disappearance of his psychosomatic symptoms in the following two valuations:

	S	O	P	N
Valuation 3. "I am now dealing more concretely with the *real* cause (also with my lawyer)."	12	3	12	0
Valuation 4. "Previously I confused things; now I am more aware of myself, at times even before I begin a conversation, at other times in thinking about it afterwards."	11	6	9	3

The vision problem was reformulated in the following way:

	S	O	P	N
Valuation 5. "The blurred vision I had while driving and watching TV has diminished."	10	2	16	3

During this change process the client gained the following insight: His blurred vision and his worries about his work could be considered two manifestations of the same theme ("not seeing a way out"). This insight in turn allowed the fragmented valuation system of this client to become more of an integrated whole. At the same time, this insight was the catalyst for new behaviors, indicated by the evolution of the negative (−LL) valuations (Valuations 1 and 2) into the positive (+S) valuations (Valuations 3, 4, and 5). Note that the diminishing of the psychosomatic problem, indicated in Valuation 5, was associated not only with a change of P and N affect but also with a strong increase of S affect, suggesting that the client felt he was gaining control over the situation.

The concept of psychosomatic problems in terms of dysfunctional body language easily gives rise to the distinction between the process of communication and the process of expression. Often these functions coexist, as in the person who is extremely expressive while speaking. Nevertheless, the two functions can be kept separate: Logical reasoning can be communicative whereas an expressionist painting is not necessarily communicative to the same degree. It should be noted that a psychosomatic complaint is more expressive than communicative. As Freud showed in his early investigations of hysteric patients, certain experiences may be symptomatically expressed in such an indirect way that no observer (and often not even the patient) could possibly understand the meaning of the symptom in question. It is therefore concluded that the inclusion of a psychosomatic problem in the predominantly verbal valuation system of a client not only helps the client communicate the underlying problem to another person (i.e., the psychologist) but also facilitates the reintegration of a fragmented valuation system.

Splitting of the Self: The Case of the Witch

Until now we have dealt with forms of dysfunctional valuation and with the supposition that a person has only one valuation system. As indicated earlier, the self has a dialogical nature, which implies that it is multivoiced (Hermans, Kempen, & Van Loon, 1992), that it consists of a multitude of I positions. From each position the I can tell a particular story in the form of a valuation system, these systems being different for each position. Moreover, the I, moving back and forth among positions, can relate the several positions, and the corresponding valuations, in a dialogical fashion. We have explored in two ways the dialogical self as part of a normal, healthy functioning: One way is to ask people to mention a person or figure that plays an important role in their imagination (see Chapter 4 and Hermans, Rijks, & Kempen, 1993); they are then invited to construe two valuation systems, one from the usual I position and one from the perspective of the imaginal figure (e.g., a wise adviser, a deceased parent who returns in their imagination). Another way is to ask people to mention two contrasting sides of their personality and to consider these as I positions, each able to produce a self-narrative (Hermans & Kempen, 1993). For example, a person may say, "I have an open side and a closed side." In this case we invite the person to consider "open" versus "closed" not as something they have but as something they are. These traits then tell, as if they are persons, about their valuations, whose content differs for each position.

The notion of multiple personality is particularly relevant here because it implies a serious reduction of the integration of the self (in fact, a fragmentation of the self). As Watkins (1986) has argued, the main difference between imaginal dialogues and multiple personality is that in the latter there is a sequential monologue, rather than a simultaneous dialogue. In dialogical relationships there is a simultaneity of positions among which the I is moving back and forth so that question and answer, agreement and disagreement, between the several positions becomes possible. In the dysfunctional case, there are also several positions (e.g., Eve White and Eve Black in the famous case of Thigpen & Cleckley, 1954). However, a dialogical interaction between these positions is almost impossible. The client with a multiple personality can often tell something about the person in the other position but does so in a rather objectifying way. An example is the frivolous Eve Black, who said of the decent Eve White: "When I go out and get drunk, she wakes up with the hangover" (Thigpen & Cleckley, 1954, p. 141). As the example suggests, there is no real cooperation and interaction between the two positions; the person does in one position things that are entirely beyond the control of the person in the other position.

In the following paragraphs we present the case of a client who was very close to a multiple personality dysfunction during the period of investigation. We present this case in some detail because we want to demonstrate that the notion of the dialogical self provides not only a conceptual framework for the assessment of a dysfunction but also a strategy for moving the self in the direction of more integrative functioning.

Mary, a 33-year-old woman, had bad memories of her father, who was an alcoholic. When Mary saw a man who was drunk or smelled of alcohol, she was overwhelmed by disgust and panic. In her adolescent years she joined the drug scene, which she also remembered with panic and disgust because she was sexually abused. She had great difficulty telling how she was forced to have sex, sometimes even under the threat of a weapon. As a reaction to these experiences, Mary "protected" herself by always wearing a tampon and bathing with great frequency. Her problems became acute when she married a man whom she loved very much. In strong contrast to her intimate feelings for her husband were the moments when she felt a strong disgust for him. Sometimes, often at unexpected moments, she felt a sudden fierce aggression toward him that was entirely beyond her control. When her husband was sleeping, she felt an almost uncontrollable urge to murder him. When he was sick and lying in bed, she felt hate and a complete lack of any compassion (it was, as she later realized, as if she were watching her father sleep off the effects of a binge). There were times when she felt like a witch, an alien experience that frightened her, particularly when the witch took almost total possession of her. She was scared to death and sometimes felt as if she were being strangled by a power stronger than herself.

After Mary described her situation, we discussed her case and decided to propose that she perform a self-investigation from the perspective of two different positions, that is, from her usual position as Mary and from the position of "the witch." The rationale behind this proposal was the expectation of a repair in the split between the two positions (Mary and the witch) and unification of the fragmented self provided (1) the two positions could be clearly distinguished with regard to their specific wishes, aims, and feelings and (2) a process of dialogical interchange could be established between the two positions so that the witch could have the opportunity to tell what she wanted. In this way, we believed, Mary could take the needs of the witch into account without losing control of her violent impulses.

Before we give the central valuations, let us first have a look at the very peculiar way the witch was moving in space. As we know from folk stories, fairy tales, and other collective stories, the imaginal space in which giants and witches live and the surroundings and attributes of ordinary beings are conceived as markedly different. Here are some of the valuations from the witch:

	S	O	P	N
Valuation 1. "When I smell the smoke and alcohol, I want to fly (make myself scarce)."	0	0	0	13
Valuation 2. "Sometimes I feel it is coming over me. From above it comes down—a plastic coat; my skin feels different, the blood streams are different, and there is an entirely different energy in me."	8	0	0	4
Valuation 3. "I feel a unity with the mask of my mother—that is, with the untouchable in her and her saying, 'Nobody touches me' (we are plotting together against men)."	9	0	3	3
Valuation 4. "When people come too close in my life space, I start to spit poison (in the train or in a school course)."	13	0	3	0

These valuations from the witch represent an experience and use of space that is sharply in contrast with the spatial experience of Mary herself. Mary often felt her experiential space occupied by intruders, by whom she felt strongly threatened. The witch, on the contrary, had several methods of defending herself. She could change her life space and body by her capacity to fly away (Valuation 1), by metamorphosing herself (Valuation 2), by masking herself (Valuation 3), and by spitting poison (Valuation 4); in other words, the witch was able to maintain and defend herself against undesirable intruders (see also the relatively high level of S affect for most of the valuations). Thus, the witch was better equipped than Mary to forcefully make a distinction between safety zones and danger zones. Interestingly enough, the ability to make this distinction was used by Straus (1958) to distinguish normal functioning from abnormal (hallucinatory) functioning. In a hallucination a voice is suddenly heard, often without warning, against the will of the person and intrudes into his or her total space. When we apply this distinction to Mary's case, it appears that the witch recognized, more forcefully than Mary herself could, a sharp distinction between safety and danger zones. In other words, the witch was able to do something Mary could not do when she felt threatened by intruders. Therefore, it would be too simple to conclude that the appearance of the witch was abnormal. On the contrary, the activities of the witch were, to a certain degree, functional; that is, they helped establish a situation of safety.

In order to explore and foster a dialogical relation between Mary and the witch, we decided to select a number of valuations from each valuation system—four from Mary and four from the witch (these valuations are presented on the left side of Table 6.1). Then Mary was invited to rate the affective meaning of her own valuations (Valuations 1–4 in Table 6.1) and the witch also was invited to give her affective experience of Mary's valuations (compare the affective indices on the left side of the table). For example, Mary liked Valuation 1 ($P = 17$, $N = 2$) whereas the witch disliked the same valuation ($P = 0$, $N = 8$). In other words, Mary and the witch strongly disagreed about the affective meaning of this valuation. The extent of agreement/disagreement is further expressed by the correlation between the two affective ratings (from Mary and the witch) for each valuation. The correlation of $-.45$ for Valuation 1 means that there is a rather strong disagreement between Mary and the witch. As the correlations for the other valuations show, there is often a disagreement between the two positions. This applies not only to Mary's valuations (upper left part of Table 6.1) but also to the valuations from the witch (lower left part of the table). Note that an important exception can be found for Valuation 4, which evoked a clear agreement between the two positions ($r = .74$). This valuation refers to Mary's work situation, not her intimate relationships. Indeed, since a certain hardness is welcome in the workplace, Mary could cooperate quite well with the witch in that area of her life. In the intimate relationship with her husband, however, this hardness was extremely dangerous. See, for example, Valuation 6, in which the witch admitted enjoying having "broken" Mary's husband (a +S valuation), whereas Mary experienced this in a very negative way (a –LL valuation).

The psychologist discussed with Mary two ideas that were based on our analysis of her twofold self-investigation. First, she was advised to exercise (e.g., sports, biking, or walking) in order to expand her imaginal space and to express the dammed-up energy of the witch. Second, we proposed that she keep a diary in which she could write her daily observations, thus sharpening her perception. In the beginning of the validation/invalidation process, Mary primarily attended to what was happening (see Chapter 3). In particular, she trained herself to make fine discriminations between her own impulses, reactions, and emotions and those of the witch. It was certainly important for her to see at an early stage which situations the witch entered and took control of. To Mary's surprise, the witch appeared in situations that at first looked quite innocent, which explains why Mary often found out too late that she had gone too far in an emotional reaction.

Later, Mary started trying out new actions (i.e., creating new events; see Chapter 3). We give here, in her own words, an example of the type of strategy she developed to cope with the witch:

"A few days ago Fred was sick, with 104 degrees temperature in bed; he even had blisters on his lips. I made breakfast for him and brought it upstairs. When I entered the room and saw him lying in bed, I loathed him, and I thought, "Don't think that I'm staying at home for you!" (I was planning to leave for an overnight visit with friends in Amsterdam). Standing in front of the bed, I was thinking about this (with increasing venom) and became aware that the witch was coming up again. I left the tray with Fred and left the house for a walk. During this walk I felt that I could discharge a great deal of the energy of the witch. At the same time, I had the time to quietly reflect on the situation as it was: 'He is sick, he needs me, and I want to care for him.' I decided to buy a newspaper for him. When I came home, I explained to him that I would stay the night at home and would go to Amsterdam the next morning. (So, I did not leave the decision up to him but proposed it myself). Fred accepted this, and the next morning I went out to visit my friends."

Note that in her self-investigation Mary not only made a clear perceptual distinction between her position and that of the witch but also developed a concrete strategy to deal with her opponent. With this strategy Mary did not split off from or suppress the witch but, rather, tried to be as alert as possible to her arrival. When the witch appeared, Mary decided to take a break; she walked first (moving was important for the witch) and then made a more balanced decision.

One year after the first investigation Mary performed a second one in order to evaluate the changes. In the meantime, there had been a limited number of sessions in which Mary discussed her daily experiences with the psychologist. The modified valuations are presented on the right side of Table 6.1. The main indication of change is that there is more agreement between Mary's affective responses and those of the witch, both for the valuations from Mary as well as for those from the witch (see the high to very high correlations among the affective profiles). This suggests that a more dialogical relationship had developed between the two positions and that Mary had developed a more integrative valuation system. In order to judge to what extent this conclusion is justified, let us look at the results in more detail.

Before Mary started her second self-investigation, she agreed to follow the same instructions as for the first investigation. That is, she first took her usual position as Mary and then the position of the witch. Indeed, although she seriously attempted to do this, she discovered that it was almost impossible for her to let the witch speak as she had done the year before. When she

TABLE 6.1. Valuations from Mary and Mary's Witch and Their Mutual Affective Responses at Investigations 1 and 2

		S	O	P	N	r
Valuations from Mary at Investigation 1						
1. More and more I am permitting myself to receive.	Mary	12	12	17	2	−.45
	witch	4	0	0	8	
2. I want to try to see what my mother gives me: There's only one of me.	Mary	12	9	12	6	−.14
	witch	10	2	3	12	
3. For the first time in my life I am engaged in making a home ("home" is also coming at home, entering into myself)	Mary	16	13	17	4	.41
	witch	12	2	11	8	
4. In my work I can be myself. I am planning from which angles I can enter. The trust that I receive gives me a foothold, more self-confidence.	Mary	14	7	18	2	.74
	witch	16	0	13	0	
General feeling	Mary	15	13	14	6	−.33
	witch	8	0	0	15	
Ideal feeling	Mary	20	17	19	2	.94
	witch	19	18	20	5	
Valuations from Mary's witch at Investigation 1						
5. With my bland, pussycat qualities I have vulnerable things in hand, from which I derive power at a later moment (somebody tells me things that I can use so that I get what I want).	witch	14	0	13	0	−.09
	Mary	6	1	3	10	
6. I enjoy when I have broken him [husband]: from a power position entering the battlefield.	witch	18	0	19	0	−.55
	Mary	0	0	0	16	
7. When Fred becomes vulnerable, it makes me even more hard.	witch	16	0	8	4	−.08
	Mary	5	1	0	20	
8. I am there, and I am gone again.	witch	10	2	6	9	.43
	Mary	5	2	7	13	
General feeling	witch	8	0	0	15	−.33
	Mary	15	13	14	6	
Ideal feeling	witch	19	18	20	5	.94
	Mary	20	17	19	2	

Note. S, affect referring to self-enhancement; O, affect referring to contact with the other; P, positive affect; N, negative affect; r, product moment correlations between the affective profile from Mary and the affective profile from the witch; M, Mary; w, witch.

		S	O	P	N	r
Valuations from Mary at Investigation 2						
1. I dare to take care of myself more and more: receiving and asking.	Mary	15	10	16	1	.96
	witch	13	9	14	0	
2. I have something solid under my feet and I take more responsibility for my feelings and attitudes. When my mother doesn't see me, that is an injury, but she is not the only determining factor.	Mary	12	10	14	2	.83
	witch	13	6	13	2	
3. It more often feels safe inside myself.	Mary	17	14	19	0	.95
	witch	14	11	15	2	
4. As soon as I can be loyal to myself in my work, I will start again.	Mary	14	4	12	2	.69
	witch	14	4	10	5	
General feeling	Mary	14	11	13	3	.87
	witch	12	7	10	3	
Ideal feeling	Mary	17	16	16	1	.95
	witch	16	13	16	2	
Valuations from Mary's witch at Investigation 2						
5. I [M+w] want to be clear, don't want to manage along the game of the sweet pussycat; sometimes, however, my [w] reactions are too fierce.	witch	12	9	12	3	.97
	Mary	12	8	12	3	
6. When I [M] feel that I [M] get in touch with my [w] power, I [M] use all my [M] energy to fight against this. I [M] don't want that power; it is too painful.	witch	13	8	12	6	.64
	Mary	10	6	9	7	
7. When Fred becomes vulnerable, and I [M] feel this harshness, then I [M] enter into a fight with myself [w] and I [M] want to be there for him.	witch	16	14	16	4	.81
	Mary	14	12	13	5	
8. When this hard side comes and I [M] recognize it, I [M] get in touch. I [M] can look at it and examine from which it is a signal. I [M] then make a good use of it.	witch	13	11	13	4	.93
	Mary	15	10	13	1	
General feeling	witch	12	7	10	3	.87
	Mary	14	11	13	3	
Ideal feeling	witch	16	13	16	2	.95
	Mary	17	16	16	1	

was confronted with the valuations from the witch from Time 1 (left side of
Table 6.1), she was able to modify these valuations in accordance with her
current experiences (right side of table). The person who was speaking, however, was not simply the witch but some combination of her two selves ("Mary-
witch") or even primarily Mary. In order to check this significant change more
systematically, we invited Mary to indicate for each of the valuations in the
lower right part of Table 6.1 when the words *I* or *my* referred to Mary and when
they referred to the witch (these designations are represented in the table by
the letters *M* or *w* in brackets). The result was that most *I* and *my* words were
indications of Mary. One of the exceptions was Valuation 5, in which the word
I was seen as a combination of Mary and the witch and the word *my* referred to
the witch. This result seems to be quite intruiging from a psychotherapeutic
point of view. The valuations that were originally formulated by the witch (with
strong disagreement from Mary) were developed in such a way that although
one can recognize at Time 2 the original (Time 1) formulations from the witch,
the modified valuations at Time 2 are primarily from Mary! This can only mean
that Mary had also taken the lead in situations that were originally under the
control of the witch.

However, the observation that Mary had taken the lead did not mean that
a perfect dialogical relationship had developed between Mary and the witch.
Apart from the fact that Mary's reactions were sometimes too fierce (Valuation 5), there were still at Time 2 indications of a continuation of the struggle
between the two positions. This is expressed most clearly in Valuation 7: "Then
I [M] enter into a fight with myself [w]." Although there were still moments of
struggle, there was at the same time a symmetrical relationship. This is made
explicit in Valuation 8, in which Mary does not simply suppress her hard side
but proceeds to get in touch with it and examines the nature of the signal.
Equally important is her next remark: "I then make good use of it." In other
words, Mary used the energy of the witch for her own purposes.

The case of Mary is also interesting from a theoretical perspective. The
concept of the dialogical self has two main defining features: intersubjective
exchange and dominance (Hermans & Kempen, 1993; Hermans, in press). This
implies that dialogue always has an element of dominance and that dialogical
relationships can vary considerably on the dimension of symmetry versus asymmetry, as Linell (1990) has proposed. In Mary's case, we see both forces at work.
First, a process of dialogical exchange is stimulated in the process of self-
investigation by inviting both Mary and the witch to tell their story, each from
her own position. In this way the I had the opportunity to move back and forth
between positions and to see the differences, contrasts, agreements, and dis-
agreements. Second, there was a dominance relationship between the two positions during the total period we followed this case. In the period of the first
investigation the witch was certainly at times strongly dominant in Mary's self-
organization. Later, the witch was forced to comply, as a positive force, with

the wishes and aims of Mary, although the witch retained some opportunity to ventilate her energy. It was in this field of tension between exchange and dominance that Mary attempted to find her way.

In sum, the dialogical self not only provides a theoretical framework for distinguishing different positions in the self but also offers a basis for a concrete strategy for making the transition between assessment and change. Instead of fostering neglect, suppression, or a splitting off of incompatible positions, this strategy enables positions to be taken up in a dialogical process. Attention is paid not only to their intersubjective exchange but also to their relative dominance. As part of this strategy, the incompatible position is not simply "cured" or treated as an undesirable symptom but is taken seriously as a partner with whom it is possible to be on speaking terms. Thus, the dialogical process, with dominance and struggle implied, is a road to the integration of the incompatible positions that are part of a multivoiced self.

DISCUSSION: THE RELATION BETWEEN DISSOCIATION AND DYSFUNCTION

This chapter covers two related phenomena: dissociations and dysfunctions. The relationship between them is based on the assumption that systematic dissociation, in combination with the occurrence of major life events, results in dysfunction. However, the question of whether all forms of dissociation are equally relevant to all forms of dysfunction, as discussed in this chapter, remains unanswered. To remedy this, a brief summary of specific dissociations related to the dysfunctions discussed in this chapter follows.

On the basis of clinical evidence to date, two forms of dissociation seem to be equally relevant to all dysfunctions: omission and distortion. People with dysfunctional systems (i.e., valuation systems with a reduced degree of flexibility) tend to systematically omit certain types of valuation. That is, they avoid situations corresponding to these types and/or exclude valuations that would conflict with their dominant type of valuation. These people may also simply distort potentially contradictory experiences in order to fit them into the prevailing system.

Two other forms of dissociation, fragmentation and subduing, seem to show (besides a general relevance to dysfunction) a *specific* relation to certain dysfunctions. Fragmentation plays a role in the valuation system involving hostility, particularly other-directed hostility. Many people who are "preretaliating" in order to defend themselves against an expected belittlement are quite impulsive in their behavior. This impulsivity may lead them to act on valuations that are not necessarily relevant to the current situation and thereby to neglect the relation with valuations referring to the future. By a fragmentation of valuations related to the present and future these people may end up being hostile without realizing that they are frustrating their good plans for the future. The phenomenon called limitlessness is also often characterized by capriciousness and impulsivity leading to fragmentation of the system. Finally, psychosomatic complaints often indicate a fragmented system.

The dissociation called subduing also has a specific connection to certain dysfunctions. Subduing plays an influential role in the helplessness/hopelessness dysfunction, particularly when these states are characterized by apathy or passivity. Subduing may also be influential in people exhausting themselves in their striving for grandiose achievements, particularly when aspirations are so high that feelings (O feelings in particular) are seen as unnecessary or even as undesirable. Furthermore, subduing is often paired with hostility, where an avenger plans and acts in cold blood.[8]

When the self-investigation is extended to include a multiplicity of positions, dissociations are equally relevant. As we have seen in the case of Mary, fragmentation is of prime importance if parts of the self become highly autonomous and threaten the dialogical nature of the self-system. When positions are fragmented, people act on the basis of separated valuation systems with the result that centrifugal forces in the self become strongly emphasized and at the cost of the more integrative centripetal forces.

A definition of health in terms of a flexible valuation system (i.e., flexible movement between different valuations within one system and flexible movement between different systems as associated with different positions) has an important consequence. It suggests that a dominance of positive valuations can indicate a dysfunctional system. This kind of system was described in terms of the need for grandiosity, overdependency, and limitlessness. These phenomena are, in spite of their often positive character, dysfunctional because of the inflexible organization of the valuation system involved. Clearly, a blocked process of valuation can have an impact on either negative or positive affect. The implication of this view is that flexibility is a more essential feature of psychological health than strictly affective well-being. Another implication is that it is always necessary in assessing dysfunctions to examine the quantitative affect indices in light of the person's own specific formulation of the valuations. When the self-investigation includes more than one position, the same argument applies. When a position is associated with many positive valuations, this is not a guarantee that the position is part of a healthy self. We observed in the case of Mary that the witch experienced a high level of positive feeling, when she could "break" Mary's husband (Valuation 6 in Table 6.1). At the same time, Mary herself experienced the same valuation as highly negative. As this example illustrates, well-being is highly dependent on the position one takes in viewing the world and oneself. Although well-being certainly is an important facet of healthy functioning, it cannot be its ultimate criterion.

Finally, on the basis of a careful analysis of the valuation system, a psychologist may obtain concrete indications of dissociations and/or dysfunction before the client is aware of these. It is perhaps the greatest challenge to the psychologist to respect and promote the client's responsibility for his or her own self while drawing the client's attention to possible dissociations or dysfunctions. It is this tension that makes self-investigation a relational enterprise par excellence.

NOTES

1. Note that the imaginal figure in this valuation (the dead father) is part of a dysfunctional valuation system and should be distinguished from the healthy interaction with an imaginal figure in a flexible system (Chapter 4).

2. Abraham (1942) compared "melancholic depression" with "normal grief" and observed that the normal mourner is interested in the object and occupied with thoughts about the other whereas depressed sufferers are thoroughly wrapped up in themselves and beset with self-reproaches that have little or nothing to do with the other. This observation shows that people can report love and at the same time be preoccupied with themselves, thus creating love with an egocentric flavor (as indicated by the content of many of the valuations in this case).

Anger is also frequently displayed during bereavement, particularly when the death is sudden or untimely or in some way "unjustified." The object of the anger may be the deceased, or the anger may be displaced onto others. As Averill (1968) has argued, anger is a secondary reaction in the service of self-maintenance, a reaction to the pain and frustration of grief and not one of its essential aspects.

3. This statement refers to an affective state that has generalized over time and situations, resulting in a *mood*. Anxiety that is persistent and ubiquitous assumes a mood-like character. *Feelings* and *emotions*, however, are more localized because they usually have a specific object (e.g., "I am afraid of dogs"). Feelings and emotions differ from one another in that the former contribute to the organization of the valuation system by giving it direction ("I feel attracted to . . ."; "I don't like . . .") whereas the latter represent a temporary disorganization of the valuation system (becoming upset; losing one's head). Finally, the term *affect* is used as a summary concept encompassing mood, emotion, and feeling.

4. In an inflexible system limited to only one type of valuation, the valuations can nevertheless be unlimited in scope. In contrast to Beck (1967), who describes such statements as overgeneralizations resulting from "logical errors," we see such highly generalizing statements as "overvaluations" that serve an important organizing function in the service of basic motives. Such highly generalized statements as "I am completely worthless" or "I am a totally isolated person" can be understood as an attempt to obtain some certainty about one's self. Paradoxically, such certainty can be achieved in expressing a total absence of feelings of self-esteem and contact.

5. People who undertake a self-investigation may also have negative feelings about being apathetic. The fact that in a state of apathy all feelings (including negative ones) are subdued does not imply that one does not worry about this state of mind during the process of self-reflection. There is always an I that is capable of "feeling feelings." The two levels of interpretation can be distinguished more sharply by asking "How do you feel when you are *in* that state?" versus "How do you feel *about* that state?"

6. In the case of dysfunctional valuation there may certainly be a change, but this change is not of a flexible nature. For example, a person may shift from limitlessness to hopelessness and helplessness in a way that is similar to the change from a manic to a depressive state. This change, however, is not of a flexible nature; flexibility presupposes a self-system with a workable degree of organization, one that it is able to function in accordance with the situation at hand. Changes from depression to mania and back, and psychotic states in general, reflect a disintegration of the valuation system as a whole. That is, parts of the system function in a fragmented way; that is, the system responds only to highly specific and even distorted elements of the situation.

7. From the perspective of the latent level of the self, there are three kinds of complaints: (1) complaints about the anticipated loss of a loved one (−O valuation), (2) complaints that are a form of other-directed or self-directed accusation (−S valuation), and (3) complaints that express helplessness or hopelessness (−LL valuation). Psychosomatic complaints can be any of these types.

8. Subduing features the S motive more than the O motive. In a series of within-subject analyses we correlated the indices S and O with P+N (an index of "affective involvement"). It was then found that the correlation between O and the involvement index was consistently higher than the correlation between S and the involvement index. This result could not be reduced to differences in the standard deviation of the several indices. It was also found that a high level of O affect (+O and −O valuations) was associated with higher levels of involvement than a high level of S affect (+S and −S valuations).

CHAPTER 7

Motivational Characteristics of the Self: Lifelong Development

While an organized process of valuation is indispensable to understanding the self, a developmental perspective is also necessary. Such a perspective can help us understand not only how and when particular human motives manifest themselves over a long period of time but also why some types of valuation remain undeveloped while others are strongly emphasized and even come to dominate a particular individual's valuation system.

In this chapter, development is conceived of as a cyclic process of valuation. With this phrase we refer, on the one hand, to the manifest level of valuation, where the vicissitudes of a person's self-narrative are told as successive periods in his or her history. The term *cyclic*, on the other hand, indicates that at the latent level a limited number of basic themes recur in different periods of the life cycle. In other words, a person goes through a variety of significant periods and situations that together make up his or her individual history. At the same time, the person is periodically confronted with the same basic themes, which not only recur in different periods of life but also are common to people within our culture in general.

The cyclic conception of development, as elaborated in this chapter, starts from the assumption that experiences relevant to the realization of the self-enhancement and contact motives are recurrently present in all life periods. Development is seen in terms of the differentiation and integration of the latent motives, two of the main preconditions for a full-fledged, flexible valuation system. Finally, we argue that certain valuation types may become strongly accentuated at particular points in development and others de-emphasized or even omitted, depending on important life events and collective biases.

According to Clarke-Stewart, Perlmutter, and Friedman (1988), who have written an extensive review of lifelong human development, the life cycle can be divided into six stages: infancy, early and middle childhood, adolescence, adulthood and late adulthood. Infancy is considered to be the period from birth to age 1 ½ or 2 years. Early childhood extends from 1 ½ or 2 to age 5 or 6. Middle childhood, the elementary school years, extends roughly from age 6 to 11. Adolescence begins with the physical changes of puberty and extends to the late teens or early 20s. Adulthood consists of early adulthood, which extends through the 30s, and middle adulthood, which extends roughly to the mid-60s. Late adulthood, the last stage of life, begins at the end of middle adulthood. As we will see, the developmental topics discussed are not sharply restricted to a single period. Rather, some phenomena cross the age boundaries, and, as implied by the notion of cyclic development, some will reoccur.

INFANCY: EARLY DIFFERENTIATION
OF SELF AND OTHER

One of the major assumptions in valuation theory is the complementary existence of the S and O motives. But in order for these to complement each other, there must be some degree of differentiation between the self and the other. All evidence suggests that some differentiation is present from birth on.

Self and Other

In his research on infant development, Stern (1983) found evidence that the self and the other are differentiated affectively, perceptually, and cognitively from birth onward. Objecting to the notion of an early postnatal symbiotic state put forth by Mahler et al. (1975), Stern argues that developmental research indicates that the child is "an avid learner from birth." The very young infant is mentally active in constructing visual schemata and is soon able to recognize the mother's face. The interaction that characterizes mother–child contacts is described by Stern as "state sharing." This includes such events as smiling, mutual gazing, vocalizing together, interactional synchrony, and playing little games (e.g., pat-a-cake).

Stern considers moments of state sharing as the first glimpses the child receives of intersubjectivity, moments when, in our terms, the two basic motives, S and O are foreshadowed. During moments of state sharing the infant is "engaged in the slow and momentous discovery that his experience, which he already senses is distinctly his own, is not unique and unparalled but is part of shared human experience. . . . He is establishing subjective intimacy" (p. 77).[1]

Young children have been found to vocalize and converse not only with their parents and siblings but also with imaginal interlocutors (Garvey, 1984). Because young children are not yet able to think silently in words, as most adults do, they may speak out loud in order to rework a prior conversation or rehearse a new one. Garvey collected a variety of vocalizations that emerged from 28-month-old Sarah's room during one nap period. Sarah's vocalizations ranged from quiet murmurs to grunts, squeals, and intoned babbles, from humming to snatches of songs, rhymes, and counting; they also included talking with a doll and a bit of a telephone conversation. These observations suggest that the young child is involved not only in real conversations but also in imaginal conversations that are partly rehearsals of contacts with significant others. We see here a first glimpse of the ability of the growing infant to take several positions in an imaginal space.

The Need for and Quality of Attachment

The early need for attachment and the later loosening of this attachment are two of the major milestones in childhood. The classic description of attachment comes from Bowlby (1969), who suggested that attachment is an inherited behavior characteristic of the human species. As we all know, a caring adult is essential to an infant's survival; through crying, sucking, clinging, vocalizing, and following their parents around, infants constantly want to draw their parents into close proximity with them. Ainsworth (1973) added an important element to Bowlby's theory of attachment when she observed that the infant's constant desire for closeness must be balanced against a second goal, namely, the infant's wish to explore his or her surroundings. This extension of attachment theory bears directly on valuation theory, in which a similar distinction is drawn to characterize some of the main lines along which adults organize their self-narratives. That is, attachment can be viewed as the longing for permanent contact and union with the other (in this case the mother or caregiver), and exploration can be viewed as an early form of self-expansion. Let us, therefore, now take a closer look at Ainsworth's "strange situation" research with quite young children.

The so-called strange situation test was devised to assess the quality of attachment in 1-to-1½-year-old babies. In this test a baby is brought by the mother into an unfamiliar but unthreatening playroom with a one-way window. The mother, who has been coached ahead of time, puts the baby down by some toys and then sits in a nearby chair. Next, a stranger comes into the room, remaining quiet for a while. The stranger then initiates a conversation with the mother and eventually goes over and tries to play with the baby. The mother then leaves the room for 3 minutes. She then returns, the stranger leaves, and the mother stays with her baby. The mother then leaves the room a second time, and the baby is left alone. The stranger then re-enters the room and tries again to play with or console the baby (as the case may be). Finally, the mother returns, talks to the baby, and picks the baby up again.

Research of Ainsworth, Blehar, Waters, and Wall (1978) showed that most babies do not protest when their mothers put them on the floor and that very few babies are distressed at this point. But when the mother leaves the baby with the stranger, about one-fifth of the babies start crying immediately and about half start crying later during the 3-minute separation. When the mother returns, over three-quarters of the babies smile at her, go toward her, reach for her, or talk to her. One-third of the babies greeted the mother with a cry. When the mother leaves the baby alone (having already left the room once before), most of the babies get upset and more babies cry than before. Half cry so hard that their mother has to return before the allotted 3 minutes are up.

On the basis of the reactions of the babies in the strange situation, Ainsworth et al. (1978) distinguished between a *secure attachment* and an *insecure attachment*. When their mothers return to the room after the brief separation, babies with a secure attachment act happy, greet her, and yet still continue to play. Babies with an insecure attachment either ignore their mother or actually turn away from her when she returns to the room after the separation (*avoidant attachment*). Other babies are not comforted when the mother returns and picks them up, and they wriggle to be put down (*ambivalent attachment*).

There is some evidence that mothers who are strong, self-confident, and affectionate in situations not involving their infants may be more sensitive to their infants and have more securely attached infants (Benn, 1985). In contrast, mothers of avoidant infants have reported themselves to be relatively tense, and mothers of ambivalently attached infants have reported themselves to be less adaptable to new situations (Weber, Levitt, & Clark, 1986). Mothers who recall their childhoods as painful are likely to have avoidant infants. Moreover, mothers who either reported being rejected by their own mothers or could not remember their own childhoods were more likely to reject their own infants. Mothers who did not feel rejected by their own mothers or could express their anger and resentment toward their own (rejecting) mothers were less likely to reject their own infants (Main & Goldwyn, 1984). Clarke-Stewart et al. (1988) concluded from these studies that parental personality characteristics have a significant effect on infant attachment behavior, although developmental psychologists by no means fully understand what specific behaviors foster secure infant attachment.

There are also indications that the quality of attachment has consequences for later development. Children who were ambivalent as infants are often described by their preschool teachers as impulsive and tense or helpless and fearful whereas those who were avoidant are often described as either overly hostile or socially isolated from other children (Arend, Gove, & Sroufe, 1979; Sroufe, 1983). In kindergarten and first grade, children who were securely attached to both parents are reported to be more trusting and open with an unfamiliar woman (Weston & Richardson, 1985) and, in general, to have fewer psychological problems (Lewis, Feiring, McGuffog, & Jaskir, 1984).

Recall that the flexibility of a valuation system depends on the capacity to move between various types of valuations and that dysfunctional valuation systems (e.g., those characterized by depression or hostility) are often found to contain only one particular type of valuation, which has been generalized across situations and time. The empirical studies just cited suggest that the quality of childhood attachment may be relevant for an understanding of the genesis of a particular dysfunctional valuation, and valuation theory in general may be helpful in looking at infant attachment and its relation to various aspects of parental valuation systems.

Personal Space and Stranger Anxiety

Whereas attachment can be viewed as an early manifestation of the contact motive, behaviors that reflect the phenomena of personal space and self-boundary structures can be considered as early manifestations of the child's need for self-protection and self-maintenance. There is growing evidence that the development of a self-boundary structure coexists with the onset of what has been called stranger anxiety during the second half of the first year of life. It is then that young children begin to realize that a stranger has the potential to intrude on their personal space; this realization makes them fearful of all strangers who approach them, particularly in the absence of a caretaker (for a review, see Horner, 1983).

In order to understand the concept of personal space, we must first explain how it differs from the concept of territory. An important feature of personal space is that it accompanies the individual's movements whereas territory is fixed to a particular place. Burgoon and Jones (1976) define personal space as "the invisible volume of space that surrounds an individual . . . an invisible, dynamic, and transportable space the site of which is governed by the individual . . . at any point in time" (p. 131). As Horner (1983) has argued, personal space is not marked by rigid boundaries. Rather, boundaries fluctuate according to various social, psychological, and organismic conditions and become semipermeable when a certain degree of familiarity exists. In other words, boundaries are not fixed but are to some degree flexible, depending on the nature of the person's relationship with others.

Another concept that is similar to the idea of personal space is the so-called self-boundary structure (Fisher & Cleveland, 1958), which relates to the notion that in the course of time people develop a "behavioral space" that separates them from what is "out there." The self-boundary structure functions as a screen, which individuals carry with them at all times and which they can interpose between themselves and the outer situation at any time. A well-developed self-boundary structure is important for a feeling of safety. As Straus

(1958) has proposed, a person's experienced space can be characterized in terms of safety and danger zones. In healthy functioning there is a clear differentiation between the two zones, and in the case of impending danger the person is able to retreat to the safety zone. In maladaptive functioning (e.g., in a state of all-pervasive anxiety), the distinction has disappeared and space is experienced as dangerous in an undifferentiated way.

As stated earlier, the development of personal space is related to the emergence of stranger anxiety. When the child is 4 to 6 months old, the anxiety may be clearly observed: When an unfamiliar person appears, the baby frowns, takes a deep breath, turns away, or may even cry (Bronson, 1972). As the infant's cognitive awareness increases between 6 and 12 months, the likelihood that the infant will be wary increases correspondingly (Decary, 1974). The intensity of infants' reactions (ranging from wariness to intense fear) depends on their interpretation of the stranger and the situation (e.g., on who else is present and on how the stranger acts). In accordance with the notion of semipermeability of personal space, the infant will not react with intense anxiety when parents or other familiar people are present (Bronson, 1978).

To summarize, there is some differentiation between self and other from birth onward, with the infant already perceiving itself in the first year of life as the center of some personal space.[2] The baby also seems to be aware that the self-boundary is not rigidly fixed but semipermeable, given a certain degree of familiarity with the other party. That is, the infant is already capable of differentiating between self-protection and contact and union with a familiar other. Moreover, the baby can flexibly move between the two motives as the context requires. In the strange situation test it was observed that children who are developing normally psychologically move freely from closeness to mother to exploration of the environment and from exploration to closeness. It was also observed that aspects of the current situation (the mother's initial disappearance) have a direct influence on the infant's balance of closeness and exploration (the infants exhibited more distress and less exploration when the mother left the room). In other words, these young children could recognize their psychological needs in keeping with situational factors even in the first year of life.

EARLY CHILDHOOD: GROWING SELF-INTEGRATION

As we have seen, there is an initial differentiation between the self and the other in early infancy that manifests itself as fixed boundaries with respect to a stranger and semipermeable boundaries with respect to an intimate. As maturation proceeds, the child's capacity to interact with the environment increases to an astonishing degree. Two developments that contribute to a further differentiation of the basic motives should be discussed: the nature of the actions children may initiate as a response to their environment and their growing capacity for role differentiation. The valuations of boys and girls gradually begin to show a differential emphasis on the S and O motives, which is, at least to some degree, induced by cultural prescriptions for gender roles and the collective stories to which children are exposed.

A World of Action: Prosocial Versus Antisocial

When asked to describe themselves, young children usually mention something they like to do. In a study of 3-, 4-, and 5-year-olds, Keller, Ford and Meacham (1978) used open-ended questions and incomplete sentences ("[Child's name] is a boy/girl who . . .") to get children to talk about themselves. When the answers were coded into several categories (actions, relationships, body image, possessions, personal labels, gender, age, evaluation, personal characteristics/ preferences), the greatest percentage of responses fell within the action category (e.g., helping with dinner, brushing teeth, playing games). This finding was consistent for the 3-, 4-, and 5-year-olds and also for both boys and girls. In addition to the action category, possessions (e.g., toys, pets) appeared to be an important dimension for 3-year-old boys and girls.

In the second year of life children also begin to spontaneously perform caring acts. Rheingold and Emery (1986) were able to elicit such behavior from all of the 1½- and 2½-year-old boys and girls in their study. Most of the children acted out a wide range of caring acts, such as putting a doll to bed, feeding it gently, disciplining it, grooming it, carrying it, and giving it straightforward affection (Clarke-Stewart et al., 1988).[3]

Children as young as 2 years are also empathic and will try to express their concern for other people through prosocial actions, although they lack the skills to be really helpful. In studies where 2-year-olds and 7-year-olds were compared (Zahn-Waxler & Radke-Yarrow, 1979; Zahn-Waxler, Radke-Yarrow, & Brady-Smith, 1977), 2-year-olds were observed trying to offer comfort to people who were either hurt or crying by snuggling up to them, patting them, hugging them, and even offering to feed them. And, of course, the children offered what they themselves found comforting—a bottle, a doll, a cracker, their own mother's hand. Clearly sympathetic and wishing to be helpful, these very young children did not yet know the practical steps normally taken in trying to help others. Their offers of comfort will later become more elaborate and thus more appropriate. By the age of 7, children lend direct help, offer suggestions, attempt rescues, make sympathetic comments, referee fights, and protect victims.

At the preschool age we see not only prosocial acts but also antisocial acts. Between the ages of 2 and 4, children become first more and then less aggressive (Blurton Jones, 1972; Hartup, 1974). Quarrels between 2- and 3-year-olds are most often over playthings and possessions that should be shared. The aggression is direct and physical, such as hitting and stamping. After the 3rd year, however, physical aggression decreases and verbal insults take over.

The occurrence of both caring acts and antisocial acts in the same age period suggests that both motives, self-enhancement and contact, are at work in such a way that children move from the one to the other motive and back depending on changes in the situation. Moreover, these data suggest that aggression is a characteristic of normal development (see Chapter 4).

Sex Differences and Gender Roles

Sex differences and gender roles come into play as early as the preschool years and help organize the child's self-concept. These differences can be easily observed in the different play styles of children, and they become more extreme with age. The behavior of a 3-year-old is quite different from that of a 2-year-old. At age 2, boys and girls play much the same way and are interested in similar sorts of things. But by the time they are 3, boys and girls often act differently, and these differences grow more marked during the remainder of the preschool period (Pitcher & Schultz, 1984). In nursery school most girls like to paint, draw, help the teacher, play with dolls, dress up, look at books, and listen to stories. Most boys like to hammer, ride tricycles, and play with cars and trucks. Both boys and girls engage in fantasy play, but girls play house and boys imitate superheroes. Girls' fantasies often are tied with everyday, domestic roles whereas boys' fantasies are often magical, bizarre, or in the realm of the supernatural: A banana becomes a little girl's telephone and a little boy's magic wand (Haney, 1984).

In their play, boys act out masculine roles—warriors, mailmen, fire fighters, plumbers, fathers—and they prefer grandiose themes (Clarke-Stewart et al., 1988). They are masters of the universe, Superman, monsters, and dinosaurs. Boys make up their own exciting masculine world and explore friendships by being brothers (or blood brothers); exchanging roles, for example, good guys and bad guys, Batman and Robin; and protecting one another from danger. In their play, preschool girls are more likely to act out masculine roles than boys are to act out feminine roles, although most girls express only a brief interest in the power fantasies that fascinate boys. Most girls like to role-play domestic routines—getting married, cooking meals, shopping. Girls do not like to play killers and destroyers, just as boys cannot tolerate for very long their roles in girls' domestic fantasies (Clarke-Stewart et al., 1988).

Gender role differences, as might be expected, are very important in valuation theory because they point to the relevance of collective stories in determining how males and females in a given culture behave. There is evidence, for example, that parents treat boys and girls differently from birth. Girls are seen as smaller, weaker, and prettier and boys as firmer, better coordinated, stronger, and more alert (Rubin, Provenzano, & Luria, 1974).

Later, parents encourage their young sons and daughters to act differently in many areas. Girls are expected to enjoy dancing, playing with dolls, and dressing up; boys are expected to enjoy climbing, building, and exploring. Parents also give different toys and educational materials to boys and girls. They give toys that happen to involve manipulation, inventiveness, and extensive feedback about the physical world to boys and toys that encourage imitation and guidance from the caretaker to girls. Such differential treatment is clearly based on a set of cultural expectations about how children of each sex act, expectations that are communicated in sentences like "Natalie, would you help me clear the table?" and "Tim, would you take the garbage out?" Once engaged in these activities, children quickly take them up as part of their valuation systems, with early and clear-cut gender differences in behavior being the result.

With reference to gender role differences, two reservations must be expressed. First, the impact of collective stories about how boys and girls should behave does not deny the existence of sex differences from birth onward. Besides the obvious physical differences, there are more subtle biological (biochemical, hormonal) differences as well. Gender roles, as socially prescribed ways of behaving, are so interwined with possible biological tendencies toward physical aggression in males and nurturance in females that their effects on children's behavior are difficult to unravel. Current thinking suggests that in a culture prepared to offer guns to boys and dolls to girls even the slightest inherited predisposition can be built into a major psychological difference. And in speech addressed to them (e.g., "Aren't you a lovely girl!"; "What a big boy you are!") children constantly hear gender labels and stereotypical adjectives and therefore soon begin to label themselves accordingly (Kuhn, Nash, & Brucken, 1978). A second reservation is based on the fact that group differences found in gender studies apply to averages only. Not every boy is more aggressive than every girl, and not every girl is more nurturant than every boy.[4] In valuation theory (as already stressed in Chapter 4) a more refined picture can be obtained by incorporating an idiographic approach in which the relative degree of independence and dependence as well as aggression and nurturance can be assessed as part of the organized whole of a particular individual.

In the preschool years, as well as in later periods, identification plays a major role in the development of gender role differences and in the concomitant emphasis on either the self-enhancement motive or the contact and union motive. Parents, other children, and protagonists in the various collective stories children are exposed to elicit identification. From the perspective of valuation theory two forms of identification can be distinguished: self-enhancing identification and unifying identification. Self-enhancing identification occurs when children imagine that they are the other person or figure and that they therefore have the same features, capacities, strength, power, influence, or excellence. Unifying identification, on the other hand, is characterized by the feeling that one is part of a relationship with another person. Autonomy and independence are not stressed; rather, the child feels he or she is on the same communicative plane as the other figure. Self-enhancing identification typically fosters the child's feelings of self-esteem and mastery (see Chapter 4); the child derives capacities from the other without necessarily feeling any real link to the other. By contrast, unifying identification fosters two sets of feelings: being like the other but also being with the other (i.e., feeling some bond or participation).

In summary, in early childhood different kinds of behaviors are differentially linked to gender roles inasmuch as certain actions (e.g., aggression and manipulation) receive greater emphasis with respect to boys and other actions (e.g., nurturance and caring) are considered more appropriate for girls. This suggests that the gender role expectations conveyed in traditional education and in many collective stories may play a major role in defining the self, which will become organized primarily along the lines of self-enhancement in boys and along the lines of contact and union with the other in girls.

MIDDLE CHILDHOOD: THE POWER OF PEERS

Middle childhood is a period when peers have a decisive influence on the development of both the self-enhancement and contact motives. Children make a transition from a vertically organized (i.e., hierarchical) group (the family) to a horizontally organized one (peers), and this has far-reaching consequences for the way in which the two basic motives can manifest themselves. This expansion of the child's world creates new possibilities but also new dangers for maintenance of self-esteem and feelings of contact and union with the other. Attention in this section of the chapter will be given to the topics of individual competence and friendship and the delicate balance between competition and cooperation.

Competence as a Standard of Evaluation

The crucial means for arriving at a clear and realistic picture of one's assets and liabilities seems to be peer interaction. Peers are one's equals in size and age whereas at home an age hierarchy of older and younger siblings probably exists. In other words, children expect to differ from their siblings in competence on the basis of age alone whereas with a peer group they must prove that they are at least equal to others. At home we must be love-worthy; within the peer group we must be respect-worthy, competitive, and competent (Burns, 1979). The penalties for failure are humiliation, rejection, and derogation from others—and perhaps eventually from one's self. The differences in expectations from the family and from a peer group are due, at least in part, to the fact that the former places a high premium on behavior while the latter emphasizes performance. In fact, behavior unacceptable to parents may well be ignored by the peer group—or even respected (e.g., when the child is a highly competent football player). A child at this age lives in two different worlds and correspondingly develops two I positions. At home the child may feel accepted and loved by parents and siblings, but at school he may feel denigrated; as a result of such conflict he or she may have trouble integrating the two experiences.

The expanding social environment, particularly in the upper primary school, also offers exciting new means for self-expression: school performance, complex group activities (games), and extracurricular activities. Opportunities to excel or prove one's competence are in many ways expanded, although abilities and talents are usually evaluated in terms of school standing, peer acceptance, athletic achievements, and popularity. Thus, at this stage of life the self is based on an expanded frame of reference, one of social relationships and comparative performance. Children have an increased sensitivity to approval from significant others, in particular, their parents, peers, and teachers. Encouragement to develop special interests (e.g., art, music, a hobby, a sport) provides children with more evaluative contexts in which to compare themselves with others and detect other's evaluations of them (Burns, 1979).

Note that a difference between early childhood and middle childhood is in the further development of the ability to take the perspective of the other. As we saw in the previous section, in early childhood the child's self is primarily defined in terms of his or her actions and possessions and not so much in terms of how others may perceive him or her. In middle childhood, however, this ability to take the perspective of the other is strongly developed, and the child is able to comprehend the notion of a standard of excellence, which is closely related to Mead's (1934) "generalized other." The child knows that his or her performance is typically evaluated on the basis of some general standard that enables a comparison to be made to the performances of others. Thus, while the first self-narratives of early childhood refer to doing things ("I play ball"), the self-narratives of middle childhood imply a generalized standard of evaluation ("I am a good soccer player"). The existence of this standard suggests that it is not only the activities one performs but also the quality of one's performance of those activities that is relevant to the self.

Friendships as Two-Way Relationships

To describe middle childhood only in terms of achievement and competence would give an incomplete picture of this age period. The development of friendships suggests that the contact motive is also at work. That is, there is a growing awareness that life consists of mutual relationships in which each party contributes to the nature and permanence of the relationship (Newcomb & Brady, 1982).

During the elementary school years friends become quite important to children. Friendship extends their social world and offers them the opportunity to learn such social skills as communication and cooperation. Friendship is also the precursor to later intimacy. Schoolchildren share, talk, do things together, and form strong bonds with each other. If a close friend moves away, schoolchildren may even mourn their absence (Clarke-Stewart et al., 1988).

During the preschool years, friendships are fleeting things. Friends are valued for their material possessions and for living close by. Selman (1981) calls this the period of "momentary playmateship." Friendships exist for accidental reasons. For example, one boy mentioned in an interview, "He is my friend because he has a giant Superman doll and a real swing set" and a little girl explained, "She's my friend—she lives on my street." By the end of the preschool period and the beginning of the school years, children begin to realize that friendship may be based on more than possessions and proximity. They understand that intentions and feelings, not just things, keep friends together. However, they still take only the satisfaction of their own needs into account. For example, one child explained, "She's not my friend anymore because she wouldn't go with me when I wanted her to," and another asserted, "You trust a friend if he does what you want." Selman (1981) termed the form of friendship characterized by this pattern of responses the "one-way-assistance" friendship (see also Selman & Selman, 1979).

The one-sided quality of preschoolers' friendships changes into a more cooperative, sympathetic, mutual exchange during middle childhood. Friendships become "two-way relationships" (Selman, 1981), and they become more enduring. Friendships last longer in higher grades than in the lower grades (Berndt & Hoyle, 1985). As children grow older, their understanding of friendship increases and the friendships themselves deepen; 6- and 7-year-olds are likely to say that friendship consists of having fun together or sharing objects and toys. For 9- to 15-year-olds friendship consists of sharing thoughts and feelings. They understand that friends feel affection and respect for each other, that friends can relieve loneliness and unhappiness. Children of this age think important qualities in friendships are sharing problems, emotional support, trust, and loyalty (Berndt, 1978; Selman & Selman, 1979). They can say, "We can help each other when we are needed."

Developments in the quality of friendship during middle childhood indicate further differentiation of the self-enhancement and contact motives. As long as a friendship has, in Selman's terms, the character of "one-way-assistance," contact with the other is easily fused with or subordinated to manifestations of self-enhancement ("I want that toy"). However, once the child is capable of a two-way relationship, the contact with the other becomes a shared experience that must obey the rules of friendships ("This is a secret; don't tell anybody else!"), and such a friendship can only blossom fully when the perspective of the other—and in particular the feelings of the other—are taken into account. This implies that self-enhancement must not be pursued at the cost of the friend and that the need for union with the friend must be allowed to manifest itself as well.

The Delicate Balance between Cooperation and Competition

In the elementary school years children find important new possibilities for cooperation: by displaying generosity, helping, sharing, and caring. Yet, as Clarke-Stewart et al. (1988) argue, certain social values in our society—competition, individualism, acquiring property, and winning—are highly valued and may conflict with these prosocial actions (see also Spence, 1985, and our discussion of grandiosity in Chapter 6).

Suggestive of the influence of cultural values is the observation that helping and showing concern for others in distress declines toward the end of middle childhood (under certain circumstances). In an experiment sixth graders who were left alone in a room and then heard a bookcase crash and a child cry for help from another room were less likely than younger children to run to the rescue (Staub, 1975). Fourth graders tried to help if they were alone in the room but not if they were with another child. These children may have been inhibited by a fear of what their peers would think (i.e., that it's not cool to show concern), or they may for some reason have thought that rushing to help was the responsibility of the other child who was present. In any case, children in first and second grade were more likely to act helpful when they were with another child than when they were alone; clearly, they saw the presence of the other child as a source of support and certainly considered helping to be a good thing.

While prosocial actions decline in middle childhood, competitiveness increases. In school and in play, children learn that winning is fun. Competitive games, from baseball to badminton, give them arenas in which to assert themselves. Similarly, by getting good marks in school they can gain approval. Even in circumstances where cooperation would be most beneficial, elementary schoolchildren tend to compete. This has been demonstrated in studies using specially designed board games (Madsen, 1971; Madsen & Shapira, 1970). In one such game (there are a number of variants), four children sit around a square paper-covered board. In each corner of the board is an eyelet threaded with a string. The strings are attached to a metal cylinder holding a pen in the center of the board, and the children must each draw a line from the center of the board through a circle in front of them. The experimenter gives the following instruction: "When the pen draws a line across one of the circles, only the child whose name is in the circle gets a prize." But the children have to cooperate to draw the lines; that is, any child can prevent another from drawing a line simply by pulling on the string. The most effective strategy, of course, is to take turns, to let one another "win." Preschool children in the United States cooperated in just this way. But 7- to 9-year-olds typically chose to compete,

trying to get their line drawn first, even though it meant that no one could earn
a prize. In contrast, children from cultures in which competition is not stressed
to such a degree as in the United States (e.g., children from Mexico or from
Israeli kibbutzim) were not as likely to act competitively (Kagan & Madsen,
1971; Shapiro & Madsen, 1969).

Boys are likely to be rewarded for competing in our culture and are therefore especially likely to acquire a competitive attitude. Since girls are likely to
be rewarded for cooperation, they may take a dimmer view of competition (for
a review of studies, see Clarke-Stewart et al., 1988).

As the aforementioned studies suggest, cultural values have a significant
impact on the early stages of an individual's development. They may influence the relative balance of competitive and cooperative impulses and, con-
comitantly, of self-enhancement and contact with the other. Depending on still
later influences, the two motives can be further strengthened or weakened.
When a particular attitude (e.g., a competitive one) is consistently and frequently emphasized in later development and counterbalancing experiences
(e.g., of cooperation) are systematically omitted, the valuation system of the
individual may assume an inflexible organization (such as a dysfunctional predominance of +S valuations; see Chapter 6).

ADOLESCENCE: INTEGRATING A COMPLEXITY
OF NEW EXPERIENCES

In adolescence the child is confronted with a broad variety of new experiences
brought about by physical, sexual, psychological, and social changes. Taken together, these changes create complex problems that make self-organization the
major task in this period. From the theoretical perspective of this book, there are
three developments that are of direct relevance to the maturation process in this
period: (1) the shift from an external to an internal locus of self-knowledge, (2)
the flourishing of imagination, and (3) the importance of morality.

From an External to an Internal Locus of Self-Knowledge

As we have shown in our discussion of middle childhood, elementary school
children are able to make use of various standards in evaluating the competence
of an individual and the quality of a friendship. Moreover, children at this age
are also experienced in taking the perspective of significant others who may be
evaluating them (e.g., "You made the best drawing in your class" or "You are a
good friend because you protected me"). However, the question of whether or
not the children themselves apply these same standards in their self-evaluations
still remains to be answered. This question refers directly to the "locus of self-
knowledge."

According to Rosenberg (1979), self-knowledge in children and adolescents stems from two sources: the opinion of children about themselves (internal locus) and the opinion of a significant other (external locus). Campbell's (1975) studies of perceptions of illness among children between 6 and 12 years of age involved an external locus of self-knowledge. The research question was simply, How do young children decide whether they are sick? Is this decision based on direct experience (i.e., on feeling hot, tired, nauseous, pained, or dizzy) or on some outside influence? Campbell concluded that young children define themselves as sick chiefly because a parent tells them they are. The child's definition stems from the parent's definition. The child relies not on internal symptoms but on the external authority of the parent.

But what about judgments of intelligence, morality, and aesthetic value? Where does the final authority on these matters rest? In order to tap children's thinking on this issue, Rosenberg (1979) asked elementary school children and adolescents the following type of question: "If I asked you and your mother how smart [good, good-looking, etc.] you were and you said one thing and she said another, who would be right—you or your mother?" Between 67 and 78% of the children in the 8-to-11-year-old group reported that in the event of a disagreement the parent would be right. In contrast, between 50 and 68% of respondents 15 and older said that they would be right. These results suggest that in older children self-knowledge is based to a greater degree on internal rather than external judgments.

But what about the really intimate and private aspects of one's self, the aspects one generally shares with only a few people (or no one at all), that is, one's aspirations, dreams, feelings, ideals, thoughts, and worries? In order to get at this aspect of children's self-knowledge, Rosenberg (1979) asked his subjects the following question: "Who do you feel really understands you best? I mean, who knows best what you really feel and think deep down inside?" Subjects were then asked whether their mothers, fathers, siblings, friends, or teachers knew what they were like deep down inside. The percentage of the younger children (8-to-11-year-olds) who believed that adults are aware of their deepest inner thoughts and feelings was astonishingly high, with 79% attributing such knowledge to their mothers, 63% to their fathers, and 47% to their teachers. Among the adolescent subjects (15 years and older), the corresponding figures were 53, 31, and 23%. When the three questions dealing with faith in mother's, father's, and teacher's knowledge of the child's own thoughts and feelings were combined, 71% of the younger children and 37% of the older children showed such confidence in adults' knowledge of them. Rosenberg's (1979) conclusion: To an adult the inner workings of a child's mind may be one of the great mysteries of the universe, but children consider themselves to be an open book.

More than in the preceding period, in adolescence the individual is able to reflect on an inner world of thought, feeling, and desire; that is, the adoles-

cent has the capacity to introspect. In order for introspection to occur, however, one essential precondition must be satisfied: Adolescents must become
aware of their own thought processes. This enables them to think of an idea
and dismiss it as stupid, have feelings of greed or lust and then feel ashamed,
argue with their own conclusions, and deplore their own impulsivity. In other
words, adolescents have thoughts and feelings about their own thoughts and
feelings to a much greater degree than do younger children.

Adolescents are able to view themselves not only from the position of significant others but also from their own position, which becomes increasingly
autonomous. This is a definite step beyond simply taking the position of a significant other on one's self, which is typical of the elementary school child's
self-evaluations. By adding their own perspective to that of the other, adolescents can move back and forth between these positions; that is, they deepen
their knowledge of themselves in interchanges with others (e.g., parents, peers,
teachers). It is in this developmental stage that the means of self-investigation,
as described in this book, can be applied, both for their assessment, process promotion, and evaluative functions (see Chapter 3).

The detection and exploration of the inner world of the self has a profound influence on the adolescent's existence as a whole. Let us briefly look at
one aspect of the adolescent's life, where the impact of this new ability to introspect about one's self can be clearly seen, namely, in the formation of friendships. In this period, friendship—for both boys and girls—is much more likely
to be based on self-disclosure, asking for understanding, and offering empathy
than in an earlier stage of development (Bigelow, 1977). Friendships formed at
this age involve a fuller appreciation than ever before of personal idiosyncrasies and possible differences of opinion and interests. Adolescents come to realize that friends may be both close and independent at the same time, that is,
that while friends may be intimate and highly supportive, they also act on their
own behalf as independent individuals. Whereas friendship in the elementary
school years is primarily based on the sharing of things and sometimes thoughts,
adolescent friendship is based on an awareness that friends have their own
thoughts, perspectives, and inner experiences. Not only are adolescent friends
supportive and loyal, but they also realize that they need to give each other
breathing space (Selman & Selman, 1979). They are also increasingly able to
look behind another's social facade: They may understand that someone who
seems snobbish is really just shy, an understanding of contradictions that
younger children lack (Clarke-Stewart et al., 1988).

In summary, adolescents increasingly refer to an internal locus of self-
knowledge, are becoming aware of their own introspective world, and are increasingly able to respect the idiosyncrasies and inner experiences of the other.
In the context of valuation theory, these developments are manifestations of the
growing differentiation between person and other. One of the outcomes of this
differentiation is that the basis of friendship changes. The inner world of the

adolescent and the inner world of the friend represent two relatively autonomous positions or voices in the self (see Chapter 4 and Hermans & Kempen,
1993).[5]

Romantic Love and Heroism

Romantic love and heroism reflect the adolescent's intense concern with the S
and O motives, respectively. Much of this concern occurs in the imagination,
which broadens and deepens the adolescent's inner world. It is not, however,
the first time that this capacity has played a role in the child's life.

Already in the preschool period the child creates imaginal figures—at
bedtime or when playing alone. The function of such imaginal figures in the
preschool period is reflected in Winnicott's (1971) term for them—"transitional
object." An inanimate object may be transformed into an animate, loved being
that can serve as a companion in the transition from one state to another (e.g.,
from waking to sleeping). In popular language the transitional object is often
called "the hugger." In a well-loved children's story by Majorie Williams, *The
Velveteen Rabbit*, a young boy is very emotionally attached to his dirty, torn stuffed
rabbit. In the story a malevolent physician one day decrees that all toys associated with scarlet fever must be thrown away. Under this edict, Velveteen Rabbit has to be discarded. At that point in the story, however, Velveteen Rabbit
sheds a real tear, and out of that tear emerges a magic fairy who then kisses the
discarded rabbit and thereby changes him into a real-live rabbit who lives hap-
pily ever after in the nearby forest (cf. Bergmann, 1984).

The imagination of young children is not always tied to a concrete object
transformed by their fantasy, however. As observed by Manosevitz, Prentice,
and Wilson (1973), preschoolers may also create imaginal playmates that provide company in times of isolation or stress—and are also sometimes used as a
handy scapegoat. By playing and conversing with these playmates, children
develop an increasing capacity to differentiate between several positions, each
with its own narratively structured experiences (Hermans & Kempen, 1993).

Probably the experience that excites the imagination the most in adolescence is falling in love. This experience is highly emotional for many adolescents and may, to a greater or lesser degree, disorganize the valuation system
for a period of time. Ortega and Gasset (1957) have given a quintessential char-
acterization of this romantic love: "an abnormal state of attention which occurs in normal man." The attention becomes focused to such a degree that the
beloved other becomes everything. Besides the disorganizing impact of such
exclusive concentration, the experience of falling in love can take on a mythic
status. The beloved is seen not simply as a person who plays a significant role
in one's thought but as an incarnation of a mythical figure. The beloved is adored
as a Muse representing almost absolute beauty, charm, or love. The adored boy
or girl may also be seen as representing both love and heroism and may be as-

sociated with godlike qualities. Given these observations, we should not be surprised to see that Plato characterized romantic love as *theia mania* (divine mania), a term that is not much different from our notion of "love sickness."[6]

As long as adolescents can fulfill their desires for contact with a beloved—through fantasies, daydreams, or reality—this may be a positive experience. However, the adolescent may be overwhelmed by this romantic desire. The object of an adolescent's first great love may be totally unaware of it, and internal and external barriers may prevent a fulfillment of contact (e.g., shyness, emotional confusion, lack of communication skills, lack of experience with the other sex, uncertainty about the reaction of parents, fear of ridicule by peers). Given such problems—not just in adolescents but in adults as well—falling in love may often turn into a *fugit amor* experience, where love is associated with unhappy feelings (see Chapter 4). However, this depiction does not sufficiently characterize the unfulfilled longing of many adolescents. Often, adolescent lovers more or less consciously create barriers for themselves. This "self-starvation" can be described by the term *tristanism* (Norton & Kille, 1983).

The story of Tristan and Isolde is a medieval German epic by Gottfried von Strassburg (13th century), among others, that tells of the unhappy love between a knight, Tristan, and Isolde, the fair wife of Tristan's Uncle Mark, King of Cornwall. One time when they were together, the two innocently drank a magical potion that resulted in their making love. From that time on they were hopelessly in love. They could not, however, really unite because the legitimate husband of Isolde stood between them. Norton and Kille (1983) argue in their analysis of this legend that the two lovers did not truly try to overcome the obstacle (although they had many chances to do so) because they used their separation instead to exalt their love. In this sense tristanism requires obstacles (e.g., a King Mark, physical distance, the law, or sometimes the scruples of the lovers themselves). In a treatise on the same legend, De Rougemont (1956) also concludes that the essence of the tale is the separation of the two lovers. He argues that it must be understood as a separation in the service of love. That is, the lovers stay separated at the cost of their happiness in order to heighten their feelings of love. In other words, suggests De Rougemont, the object of their love has become love itself, or the sensation of being in love, a sensation that could very well disappear if the obstacle were to be overcome and the pair reunited. Both lovers therefore continue to dream the same dream, although they nevertheless remain isolated and lonely. This attitude is what Angyal (1965), in talking about adolescence, has called "being in love with love." Love—even unhappy love—may be cultivated in the inner world of the adolescent in an egocentric way.[7]

Whereas romantic love can be conceived of as a longing, with mythic shadings, for contact and union, heroism is to be understood as a mythic form of self-enhancement. This form of playing with imaginal positions has its forerunner in the preschool years, when children in their fantasy play are Tarzan or Superman. However, in those years heroism is mainly imagined in terms of physical strength and physical skills. Adolescents, in contrast, see themselves (or another) as a great actor, the lead singer in a band, a brilliant speaker, the best chess player, or a successful politician. With these qualities they glitter before the world.

Apart from the specific experiences just described, there are more general manifestations of the imaginative quality of the adolescent world: a heightened sensitivity to art in its many different forms (e.g., music, painting, sculpture, theater, dance) or an increased sensitivity to religious experience (e.g., traditional church involvement, participation in rituals, membership in a religious group). The developing imaginative capacity in adolescence corresponds, on a theoretical level, to the central role of imagination in self-narratives (Chapter 4).

Moral Maturation

Morality generally refers to principles or standards of "good" behavior and may be closely related to the individual's social responsibility. On the assumption that morality is a developmental phenomenon and that people differ in their levels of morality, psychological theories have dealt with the question, What is moral maturity?

This will probably never receive a uniform answer because the answer depends so heavily on the particular theoretical perspective one subscribes to. Trait theory, cognitive science, psychoanalysis, and social learning theory give different views on the subject of morality. However, many theoretical views have in common the assumption that adolescence in particular brings with it a higher level of moral awareness.

If moral maturity is described in terms of "moral valuation," it has several implications. First, different individuals find different things important from a moral perspective, and this emphasis is highly dependent on their individual history. Some people, for example, stress always telling the truth while others do not mind some stretching of the truth and put greater emphasis on always being kind to others (which can imply not always telling the truth). The point is that people are not viewed from the perspective of inborn moral traits. Rather, moral behavior depends on previous social interactions and on what the person has been led to see as morally correct. Second, moral valuation presupposes the notion of narrative or story. Recently, Vitz (1990) has argued that morality cannot be satisfactorily characterized as dependent on moral reasoning (as in Kohlberg's moral dilemmas). Rather, stories are a central factor in a person's moral development and are better guides than rules or maxims. Whereas rules and maxims state generalizations about experience, stories, including self-narratives, illustrate what those generalizations mean for a particular person located in time and space. As Robinson and Hawpe (1986) have observed, the oldest form of moral literature is the parable, and the most common form of informal instruction is the anecdote. Third, our moral judgments are perhaps more bound to cultural values than we might at first think. For example, there was a time when slavery was not regarded as a crime; similarly, the problem of apartheid went largely unrecognized for years. Discussions in schools about human rights and the growing damage to the earth reflect collective voices that go beyond individual preferences. Moral valuation should be understood not only as an individual learning process but also as participation in collective stories.

When moral valuation is viewed as emerging from social interaction and functions as an individual and collective narrative, the notion of friendship can be considered an essential defining factor. In fact, this idea has been around since Aristotle; his treatise *Ethica Nicomachea* devoted two books (8 and 9) to the relevance of friendship to ethics. Aristotle was well aware of the fact that morality is rooted in people's social feelings and in themselves. He described the highest level of friendship as a relation in which the friend is regarded as "another I," meaning that we see our friend as similar to and different from ourselves at the same time (Book 10, Chapter 4).

Following Aristotle, we propose viewing moral development as an offspring of social-affective development in general and the development of friendship relations in particular. As we have seen, adolescents are increasingly able to experience friendship as a combination of independence and interdependence. Adolescents begin to realize that their friends have an inner world of thoughts, feelings, and fantasies just as they do and that they too need their own personal space. At the same time, adolescents realize that friends can offer support and may, at times, need support and that they and their friends can share feelings and inner experiences as well.

Attempts to establish a balance between independence and interdependence can be observed in adolescents, although such a balance has not, in all likelihood, reached the point of full maturity in this period. It is a difficult task that requires a differentiation of "my life" from "your life" and yet maintenance of a concern for the other, a caring attitude. Indeed, an attitude of caring for people beyond our immediate reach (from other places in the world, other cultures, future generations) is in many ways a moral challenge of the first order—and perhaps a matter of survival to us all.

Gilligan (1982), in her critical discussion of Kohlberg's (1969) theory of moral development, argues that the worldviews of people and their conceptions of morality are highly related. Gilligan maintains that boys and men, by and large, are highly attuned to personal achievement, to the independence of each individual, and therefore favor a morality of justice in which individual rights are respected and equitable solutions are found for the conflicting and competing claims of all. On the other hand, girls and women, are more attuned to relationships and the connections between people and therefore favor a morality of caring, which refers to how people are obligated to one another.

Extrapolating from Gilligan's distinction, we might conclude that true moral maturity would be reached if or when both forms of morality are found in the same person. That is, one is concerned with (1) one's own independence, (2) the independence of others (implying that one is able to discern the difference between one's own interests and those of others and therefore does not fuse them), and (3) one's interdependence with others. The latter point in particular suggests that the person is able to flexibly move between two relatively autonomous positions (the I and, in Aristotle's terms, the other person as another I). Whereas the notion of independence refers to the relative autonomy of the two positions, the notion of interdependence emphasizes the importance of a dialogical relationship between them (Chapters 4 and 5).

These thoughts about morality also apply at the collective level. As part of a group or society the individual should ideally relate to other groups, societies, cultures, and future generations as "friends," respecting their individual histories, customs, preferences, and values while at the same time caring for them as interdependent parts of a world community. However, such a collective approach represents a great challenge to people's motivation because, quite simply, the basic motives discussed in this book also have their practical limitations. From a moral point of view, a major limitation is that neither motive extends very far in everyday life. We are inherently more concerned with our own well-being and that of our loved ones than with people on the other side of the world. Our loyalty is primarily to those who are close to us (as in the case of a parent who may be more worried about a criminal son than about the terrible consequences of his deeds). Furthermore, we may define the ecological surrounding as something "outside" instead of as part of an embodied self. Moral education is, therefore, inherently difficult to extend beyond the limits of our own personal concerns.

In an attempt to extend our moral reach, however, one powerful human capacity has been often overlooked: imagination. An essential feature of imagination is that it goes beyond the present, implying that we are capable of feeling concern for people, situations, and problems that are not part of our immediate situation. As is well-known, when faced with an apparently insoluble problem, people can create an imaginal figure to function as a personal conscience and adviser. Religion may serve the same purpose for some. The role of some higher or more encompassing viewpoint (position) in making moral judgments and in an awareness of social responsibility represents a relatively unexplored area of research.

In summary, adolescence represents a stage in the life of the individual in which independence and interdependence coexist as achievements of a developing self. In combination with the increasing capacity of imagination, these mental acquisitions form the basis for a morality that takes into account the intrinsic relativity of individual and society.

Storm and Stress or Transition?

At first sight, adolescence looks like a turmoil of changes, including growth spurts, the appearance of secondary sexual characteristics, the first menstrual period, hormonal changes, sexual desires and experiences, homosexual thoughts, cognitive changes, self-consciousness, smoking, use of alcohol, and experimenting with drugs. These changes are not only diverse but also relatively sudden. Abrupt mood changes are also characteristic of this period (Larson, Csikszentmihalyi, & Graef, 1980). One minute teenagers are basking in the glow of a recalled kiss, and the next minute they are miserable because a teacher tells them to stop daydreaming. One day a teenager feels warm and friendly toward family members and the next day is irritated by their unending demands (Clarke-Stewart et al., 1988).

Adolescents are confronted with a number of identity questions: Should I go to college? If so, where? Should I have sexual intercourse? Should I become politically active? Whom should I date? In adolescence the "I" is confronted with a diversity of possible positions that lack a stable organization:

> Sometimes I look in the mirror and say to myself, "Okay, who are you *really*, Natalie?" I pull my hair back and put on makeup and look very sophisticated. That's one me. I let my hair fall loosely on my shoulders, put on a Shetland sweater, and that's another me. I write poetry and stay up late to watch the stars and planets through my telescope; that's another me. I get really involved in my chemistry homework and think I'll be a doctor, or I want to be a translator, or I want to be a foreign correspondent. There are almost too many possibilities—Natalie, age 17. (Clarke-Stewart et al., 1988, p. 413)

Although all these developmental changes, mood changes, and confusing possibilities of positions, when taken together, could constitute a crisis, there is little evidence that this is the case. For example, Dusek and Flaherty (1981) repeatedly interviewed a group of adolescents between the ages of 11 and 18 years and asked them about sexual feelings, boy–girl relations, career choices, ideals, self-esteem, and other issues. They found that, in general, even important environmental changes did not cause major changes in the adolescents' identities. The self continues to evolve slowly and steadily. Another longitudinal study (Savin-Williams & Demo, 1984) supported this conclusion. Burns (1979) also holds the same opinion; he criticizes Erikson (1968) for lending considerable weight to the conventional but erroneous view that adolescence is a period of storm and stress. Erikson, suggests Burns, inappropriately over-generalized his findings, which were based on clinical analyses, to the adolescent population as a whole.

Before going on, let us first describe the term *crisis* in theoretical terms. In valuation theory a crisis can be described as a major disorganization of the valuation system. Such a disorganization typically occurs when a so-called core valuation loses its function. For example, when a student has centered his whole life around a Ph.D. degree (i.e., place of living, campus entertainment, contact with colleagues, future aspirations, respect from parents), a failure to achieve this goal could cause a crisis because all of the other, more peripheral, valuations in the system will be shaken. May (1966) offers an example in the area of sex. He notes that sexual gratification is, of course, of value for most people. He adds, however, that physical gratification in itself is only a small part of this issue, since a person will be thrown into conflict and anxiety when rejected sexually by one partner but not by another. Obviously, other elements—tenderness, understanding, prestige—give the sexual experience with one partner a meaning that sex with another partner does not have. From a theoretical perspective this difference can be understood in terms of centrality of a valuation. The greater the number of elements in the valuation system dynamically related to sex with this particular partner, the more profound the influence on the valuation system as a whole when this valuation is forced to change.

Rather than a period of crisis, adolescence is more accurately described as a period of transition, the period bridging childhood and adulthood. Transition, of course, calls for reorganization. The main argument for characterizing adolescence in terms of reorganization and not disorganization lies in the fact that a great variety and number of new elements are being introduced into the valuation system at this time. Rather than the breakdown of a core valuation, adolescence represents the building up of a sufficiently stabilized and integrated valuation system. Of course, an adolescent may go through a crisis when, for example, a parent dies or parents divorce, but under conditions of less discontinuity adolescence may be better described as a transition than as a crisis.

With the continual introduction of so many new elements the valuation system in adolescence is a temporarily fragmented one (Chapter 6), rather than a completely disorganized one. The stability of the middle childhood years is gone. Adolescents are now confronted with the task of organizing their valuation system on the basis of the divergent and often conflicting aspirations, feelings, and thoughts they have. The problem for adolescents is that they do not know or have not yet decided what is really important now and what is important in the long run nor how all their intense experiences, both positive and negative, should be arranged to form a coherent and stabilized whole. Some adolescents can relate to a different self-narrative each day. The point, however, is that a self-narrative emerges during this process of telling and retelling that has more richness, depth, and poetry than the simple aspirations and dreams of the elementary school child to become a cowboy or a nurse.

EARLY AND MIDDLE ADULTHOOD

Most publications concerned with life span development (for a review, see Baltes, 1979, 1987) argue that the traditional concept of development needs to be expanded to apply to the various changes that occur throughout life. While useful in some contexts, the growth concept, borrowed from biology, is simply inappropriate or too restrictive in other contexts. In his discussion of developmental models Baltes (1979) observed that the concept of development is often equated with maturation. However, research on life span development in a variety of areas, and most notably in the area of cognitive and social development, has indicated that such a conception of development is unduly restrictive (Baltes & Willis, 1978).

Baltes and Willis (1978) have proposed a view of development that is more complex than the simple unidirectional and cumulative conceptions. Clearly, interindividual variability increases as the life span evolves, though traditional models cannot take into account this variability. A broadened conception of development is needed, one that makes room for the particular life history of each individual. Moreover, this variability suggests that life span changes differ in terms of onset, duration, and termination.

In contrast to most child development theorists, life span psychologists conceptualize personal changes as closely related to life events. Such a conceptualization does more justice to the historical nature of human experience without neglecting important biological changes. Brim and Ryff (1980), for example, distinguish between biological events, social events, and events that happen in the surrounding physical world. Biological events encompass not only such maturational changes as changes in body size and in the endocrine system, brain, and nervous system but also susceptibility to disease and organ failure. For instance, both the onset of puberty and diminished production of progesterone and estrogen at menopause are well-known illustrations of changes in hormonal activity. Customary events in a person's social development, which reflect the various roles that people may take on during the life span with regard to family, friends, work, and community, include marriage, the birth of children, gaining independence from parents, establishing a home, starting work, making a career change, caring for aging parents, and accepting retirement. Noncustomary social events include the committing of deviant acts (e.g., crimes); being cheated, lied to, or derogated; involvement in extramarital affairs; physical violence; and accidents. Environmental events include the steady state of the physical world, the diurnal cycle, the changing seasons, the weather, and pollution, all of which provide a context of physical change slowly occurring during one's life span. Some of these forces are so slow that they do not give rise to events in the usual sense of the word. In contrast, unpredictable events in the physical world—earthquake, fire, hurricane, accidental injury— do give rise to critical life events.

The conception of development in terms of specific life events (biological, social, and environmental) is highly compatible with valuation theory; both assume the importance of a context for the individual that is historical, social, and biological. Life events refer to the changing person–situation interaction, and the process of valuation refers to the narrative construction of that interaction. As argued in Chapter 2, valuation is a constructive act in which certain events are selected as more important than others and then organized according to their personal relevance (see also Cohler's, 1982, concept of personal narrative).

When the life cycle is conceived of as an organized self-narrative, a distinction is made between events that occur on schedule and those that do not. An event is on schedule when it falls within the range of cultural expectation (initially based on maturational considerations); it is off schedule when it falls outside that range. For example, a child's death is perceived as disruptive and unscheduled whereas an old person's death is perceived as natural (Glaser & Strauss, 1966, 1967; Neugarten, 1968a). With respect to the timing of life events, Neugarten (1968a, 1968b) has stressed the succession of socially delineated age statuses the individual passes through from birth to death. That is, a socially prescribed timetable for the ordering of major life events exists. Men and women are aware of the social clocks operating in their lives and often describe themselves as early, late, or on time with regard to graduation, marriage, first-time employment, parenthood, job promotion, grandparenthood, and so on. Moreover, the social clock may directly affect the way people evaluate such experiences. For example, the cultural perception that a child's death is generally worse than a parent's influences individual experience. In such a case it can be seen that the personal valuation system is to some degree influenced by cultural values, in other words, that self-organization relates to social organization.

Let us now look at two major life developments: career development in early adulthood and midlife transitions.

Career and Sex Role Differences

By early adulthood, people make an initial commitment to an occupation, although some people then follow a more orderly course than others (Super, 1957). The orderly career path may already be prepared in adolescence ("I have always wanted to be a doctor"). Adolescents explore many fields and try to match their career opportunities to their personal interests and skills. Although actual commitments are typically made in the early 20s, people may get further training, whether in school or on the job, and they may continue to shift jobs in search of the one that best suits them.[8]

Early career performance may reflect pure self-enhancement. It may also reflect cooperation and contact with a mentor, an older, established worker who then serves as a guide and adviser and smooths the new employee's way to advancement and promotion. Mentors may be important to people in trade and business, and in many other professions they may be essential. In a longitudinal study of Harvard graduates (Vaillant, 1977), for example, those whose careers were relatively unsuccessful had not had mentors during their 20s and 30s. Mentors and significant others may function as important I positions; by moving back and forth between the mentor's view and their own view, young adults may extend and enrich their own experience.

There is some evidence that women in early adulthood use other pathways than men in obtaining a certain degree of self-enhancement. Whereas Erikson (1963) portrays males as growing in independence from others (and thereby differing after a time from females), Gilligan (1982) emphasizes that females tend to locate their identity within their relationships to others. It is easier for men than for women to subordinate personal relationships to their aspirations and their work. When men face the task of intimacy (in Eriksonian terms) and feel a conflict between the demands of their work and those of a personal relationship, they generally feel that society demands that they resolve the conflict in favor of work. Women, however, generally feel pushed to resolve the same conflict in favor of compassion, dependence, and gentleness. They are expected from childhood to be caring and have therefore not learned to subordinate the needs of others to their own aspirations. Moreover, when they attempt to do this, they often feel in conflict with societal values or even punished for being independent.

There is further evidence that development in early adulthood is different for men and women. Women have been found to assert and defend themselves differently from men. This is suggested by a study by Falbo and Peplau (1980) of power differences between men and women in marriage and other intimate relationships. Men are likely to wield power directly and expect compliance. Women in a relatively egalitarian relationship are likely to make requests and bolster these with a comment about how important they feel the request to be. Women in less egalitarian relationships are likely to resort to indirect means of wielding power, including hinting, withdrawing into silence, exhibiting emotional coldness, or simply going ahead and doing as they wish.

Taken together, these studies suggest that career development provides a continuity between adolescence and early adulthood for men. Moreover, the values of our society stimulate men to pursue self-enhancement through development of a career and to fulfill the contact motive through the establishment of a family. For women, especially those who want to pursue a career, there is less continuity between adolescence and early adulthood. Their career development is often interrupted, and they must therefore pursue other roads to self-enhancement.

There appear to be two roads to self-enhancement that are primarily based on the contact and union motive: (1) People may derive self-enhancement from the accomplishments of some individual or group with whom they are affiliated ("I am proud of your accomplishments"), and (2) they may experience self-enhancement by accomplishing something that contributes to an already existing contact with the other ("I am pleased to do something *for* you" instead of "I am pleased when I get positive feedback *from* you"). These two forms of valuation, where self-enhancement and contact and union with the other coexist, may be part of the self-narratives of both men and women, though they are more likely to occur in women than in men.[9]

Midlife Transition

Midlife is not only the transition from the first half of life to the second (at around 40–55 years) but also a period for evaluating one's life and for comparing experiences from the past with expectations for the future. As people evaluate their life up to this point, they are likely to feel that it will never match their ideals. Moments of disillusion are likely when they ponder their achievements in the workplace or the state of their marriage or other relationships and question the assumptions that have guided them to the brink of middle age. At midlife many men change the organization of their life and try to find a better balance between their personal achievement goals and their relationships; some change more radically by leaving a marriage or a job or by moving to a new place. Many women at midlife have grown children, who no longer need the daily care of earlier days; this shift creates new opportunities for them to change the balance between caring for others and realizing their own personal aspirations.

Does midlife transition necessarily imply a midlife crisis? The research on this question has produced mixed results. One study (Levinson, Darrow, Klein, Levinson, & McKee, 1978) found evidence for a crisis among the 40 men interviewed (10 businessmen, 10 factory workers, 10 novelists, and 10 biologists). In contrast, Vaillant (1977), who collected longitudinal data on Harvard graduates, has suggested that although some men do divorce, change jobs, or suffer depression at midlife, the frequency of these events is essentially the same throughout adulthood. Experiencing an actual crisis at mid-life is the exception, not the rule. While Vaillant's subjects are far from a cross section of the general American public, the California Intergenerational Studies (Clausen, 1981; Haan, 1981) may be more relevant to this issue. These studies included middle-class men and women and found that most of the men felt satisfied with their work situation at midlife and that most of the women felt self-confident. In a study specifically designed to identify the midlife crisis, McCrae and Costa (1982) found that it appeared anywhere between the ages of 30 and 60 and in only a few men. Finally, Clarke-Stewart et al. (1988) concluded from their review that the midlife crisis does not seem to be a general phenomenon.

With respect to the notion of a mid-life crisis, Neugarten (1970b) argues that predictable (i.e., on-time) events are not unsettling when they arrive, that it is the unanticipated, not the anticipated, that is likely to create a crisis. Major stresses are caused by events that upset the sequence and rhythm of the expected life cycle, as when occupational achievement is delayed or one finds oneself with an empty nest, grandparenthood, retirement, a major illness, or widowhood earlier than expected.[10]

On the basis of these arguments, we prefer the term *midlife transition* over *midlife crisis* to represent this aspect of the general period of middle adulthood. A midlife transition can be conceived of as a period of reorganization whereas a midlife crisis implies a disorganization of the valuation system. Moreover, in a period of transition on-schedule events play a central role, whereas in a crisis it is the off-schedule event, perhaps in combination with expected events, that results in a heightened level of distress and a disruption of the person's self-organization. Let us therefore take a look at some of the phenomena that may be considered typical of the midlife transition.

Midlife often brings a remarkable shift in a person's perception and organization of life. Whereas young people typically define time in terms of years since birth, people in midlife tend to define time in years left to live (Neugarten, 1968b). In middle adulthood the future is no longer an open time frame for realizing one's goals; rather, it is now considered a limited period in which to do the things one has to do (e.g., reach goals that were perhaps neglected in the past) or still can do (e.g., accomplish a newly stated goal). This change, implying an intensified awareness of one's own mortality, creates a heightened sense of urgency, as research by Gould (1975, 1978) has suggested, a realization that time is limited and that the pursuit of goals must be begun or forever abandoned.

The sense of urgency may be accentuated by the experience of time acceleration: As people grow older, they typically feel that time is running at a higher speed and that their life may be over before they know it. This new perspective on time may result in a now-or-never attitude and is often a source of unusual creativity (reflected in +S or +HH valuations; see Chapter 4). People in midlife often accomplish more than they used to simply because they make maximal use of their inner resources. Often, in the time that remains they focus on completing a specific task as compensation for missed chances or failures in the past. With their sense of a foreshortened future, some people may completely reorganize how they spend their time (Kalish, 1977). But one can also imagine that when an unscheduled negative event (e.g., a forced change of job, financial disappointment, divorce, loss of a loved one) occurs during this period, a crisis or even depression may be experienced.

Midlife may be characterized not only by a heightened sense of urgency in the area of achievement but also by a heightened sense of obligation toward others. In most families the bonds between parents and adult children are maintained by affection, calls for assistance, and fairly frequent contact. At the same time, parents may still have their own parents to care for. When people have to care for both their own maturing children and their aging parents, they are caught in what Oppenheimer (1981) has called a life cycle squeeze. For example, many middle-aged women who report feeling greatly stressed by caring for their aging parents also report having children whose development is in some way off schedule (Hagestad, 1982)—for example, a son still without work in his late 20s or a divorced daughter who has moved back to her parents' home.

The heightened sense of urgency in the area of achievement shows a meaningful relationship to the distinction between aggression and hostility made earlier in this book. When certain achievements become urgent and certain aspirations clearly cannot be fulfilled, the striving toward these goals may assume an aggressive character or result in a transient feeling of powerlessness (see Chapter 4). In the more extreme case this aggression may become more permanent and even hostile. An example of such a dysfunction is Murray's (1962) "satanic personality," a person who has "a secret feeling of having been harshly, treacherously, unjustly, or ignominiously deprived of his deservedly large share of benefits, rewards, and glory," and "a hidden envy coupled with expressed contempt of the notable achievements of others" (p. 49). Similarly, when the self is governed by severe norms forbidding the outward expression of aggression, the person may develop a depression characterized by self-directed hostility or extreme hopelessness (Chapter 6).

The heightened sense of obligation can also be placed in the context of the present conceptual framework. When a person either feels unable to care for significant others or loses them, a *fugit amor* experience can arise and transient feelings of isolation can be expected to occur (Chapter 4). In cases where this problem cannot be resolved, prolonged grieving or a permanent state of helplessness or hopelessness may result (Chapter 6).

It would be a misunderstanding to conceive of midlife only in terms of negative experiences. Seeing midlife as a period of transition implies that there are also new chances to broaden and enrich one's life. Barnett and Baruch (1978), for example, have cited several studies indicating that the so-called empty nest has a set of undeserved negative associations. The notion, as it is usually understood, suggests that an older woman may be depressed or have identity problems because of diminishing family responsibilities. However, a woman who finds herself with an empty nest could pursue other opportunities for self-expansion, and findings from several studies (e.g., Lowenthal, 1975; Radloff, 1975) suggest that this is indeed the case: The well-being of women whose children have left home was found to be higher than in women living with young children, and the incidence of depression was found to be lower.

These results clearly indicate that we should look at the lives of women at midlife not only from the perspective of loss (i.e., with their children no longer living at home they may have less contact with the other) but also from the perspective of the self-enhancement motive (i.e., new opportunities for self-fulfillment may now present themselves). The same can be said about men: Their lives should be viewed from the perspective of both motives. Particularly during the period of middle adulthood men have, for the most part, reached the height of their career and become aware of the limits of their self-enhancement. Consequently, they look for a new balance of the S and O motives (Gutmann, 1980). Middle adulthood represents, in fact, a critical period for breaking through sex stereotypes and the barriers created by rigid sex role prescriptions. Women have new opportunities for self-expansion in this period (e.g., studying, pursuing a career, assuming civic responsibilities), and men are often able to become less involved with their careers and extend their contacts beyond family and friends (e.g., by serving as a mentor for younger colleagues, taking on civic responsibilities, engaging in a mission, supporting their wife's pursuit of a new job). In other words, midlife is a period in which men and women can come to a much more profound understanding of each other's perspectives.

LATE ADULTHOOD

No other period of life is associated with more misunderstandings, stereotypes, and incorrect expectations than late adulthood. Butler (1975), who was well aware of this, observed that popular attitudes about old age can be summed up as an odd combination of wishful thinking and stark terror. On the one hand, the elderly are described respectfully as "senior citizens" or "golden-agers." One hears of old people who have "aged well" or "aged gracefully." Old age is often considered a time of relative peace and serenity, a time when people can sit back and enjoy the fruits of their labors after the storm of the active years is over. Visions of carefree, cookie-baking grandmothers and pipe-smoking grandfathers in rocking chairs are cherished by younger generations. On the other hand, our colloquialisms reveal quite a different picture: Once we are old we are said to be "fading fast," "over the hill," "out to pasture," "down the drain," "finished," "out of date," "an old crock," or "a geezer." And all too often old age is associated with unproductivity and senility.

Such discrepant views are found not only toward old age but also toward those who are dying. As Kastenbaum (1985) has found, people's attitudes toward the elderly run in one of two different directions: Either we believe the dying should be segregated because they are hopelessly old and impaired, or we imbue them with such inspirational qualities as wisdom, saintliness, and heightened spiritual awareness. They are considered either to have a less legitimate claim to social resources than younger people or to be too pure for this imperfect earthly existence. Neither attitude encourages us to see old people and dying people as distinct individuals.

In order to arrive at a more realistic description of late adulthood, it is necessary to pay attention, from the perspective of the basic motives, not only to the losses of old age but also to the gains; moreover, we must recognize both the negative sides of death and the positive ones.

Loss and the Risk of Bereavement Overload

An important factor in late adulthood is the decline of health and the increasing rate of disease. In order to get some idea of the presence of illness in old age, it must be noted that the occurrence of acute and chronic illnesses show opposite trends during the life cycle. Once past childhood, people generally see fewer acute illnesses. Throughout adolescence, adulthood, and old age the incidence of infections, respiratory diseases, and digestive illnesses falls steadily. However, although elderly people usually have fewer bouts of acute illness than when they were younger, each illness tends to be more severe. Moreover, over the course of the life span, both the incidence and severity of chronic illness, (i.e., an illness that lasts for long periods of time, resists cure, and also tends to worsen over time) increase. Diabetes, emphysema, heart disease, and cancer are some of the chronic illnesses that plague older people. It is estimated that more than 85% of people over 65 have one or more chronic illnesses (Hickey, 1980). It should be noted, however, that the presence of chronic illness need not automatically imply that people are impeded in their activities. Although the number of limitations increases with age, the large majority (nearly two-thirds) of adults over 65 in the years 1970 to 1980 were found to be able-bodied, according to the U.S. Bureau of the Census (see Clarke-Stewart et al., 1988, p. 530).

Those who suffer from illness often become dependent on another's care (Munnichs, 1976). This new dependence may bring elderly people into conflict with the autonomy they acquired in times of good health. Knowing that others have their own problems, many an elderly person says, "I don't want to be a burden on anybody!" But the same person may also admit, "I don't want to be abandoned either!" (Kastenbaum, 1977).

Although a chronic illness may be experienced as a loss of health and may arouse nostalgia for the past, it is certainly not the only form of loss—and perhaps not even the most significant one—in old age. Late adulthood can also be marked by a combination of "role loss" and "object loss," that is, by both a disruption of one's functional relationship in society and a separation from significant others. As Averill (1968) has argued, this is a relative distinction but nevertheless useful in analyzing individual and cultural differences in bereavement behavior.

Some societies provide for role continuity in the event of the death of a significant other. This may be accomplished by providing for immediate replacement of the loss, as is done in tribes in the Ubena region of Africa, where a widow resumes her role as wife with a new mate soon after the death of her husband. Her grief is correspondingly brief, although apparently genuine (Culwick & Culwick, 1935). The elderly in our culture, however, are faced with the loss of significant others (the partner, friends, relatives) in a period during which the number of roles (parental and occupational) they fulfill is also greatly reduced. As a result, when people of this age lose a significant other, they often lack opportunities for finding meaningful compensation in other roles. This differs from the experience of loss in early and middle adulthood, for object loss and role loss typically do not coincide in these periods.

The death of a loved one can lead a person into a crisis, and this disorganization of the valuation system may or may not be followed by a reorganization. Grieving is a process of adapting to a loss. During this process there is disorganization as well as feelings of numbness, yearning, and despair; eventually, reorganization may take place (Parkes, 1972). Although these states tend to unfold in sequence, they may also blur together. People who have just learned of a death may feel shock and emotional numbness. This protective numbness eventually gives way to a yearning for contact with the other, and the individual is flooded with grief. In this stage the person may vividly imagine the deceased, expect to see or hear him or her, and interpret various sights and sounds as the deceased person's image or voice. Many grieving people feel the presence of the deceased, a feeling that may be an actual hallucination (Kalish, 1977).[11] Various feelings of longing, guilt, and anger alternate in this stage. The period of yearning is followed by despair, a disorganized state of grief in which people may grow lethargic, helpless, and hopeless. To end the grieving stage and enter a stage of reorganization, people must accept the reality of their loss and find meaning in some other way. Without this acceptance, grieving people remain depressed and may even continuously expect new losses (Clarke-Stewart et al., 1988).[12]

As Bowlby and Parkes (1970) have argued, grief is a form of adaptation in which people try to reunite themselves with the deceased person. The signs of grief are similar to signs of distress following separation from a loved one in other situations: anxious searching, crying, imagining the reappearance of the loved one, and attacking anyone who interferes. These signs call others to help and protect a vulnerable member of the group (Averill, 1968). In this period of heightened sensitivity to contact with relatives and friends, a sense of reunion with the deceased person may actually be achieved. This reunion, however, may be problematic in Western culture, where people often encourage the mourner to forget the deceased (Stroebe, Gergen, Gergen, & Stroebe, 1992).

As Kastenbaum (1977) has emphasized, the deaths of loved ones intensifies the loneliness of elderly people. The longer one lives, the greater the number of intimate companions one outlives. This may reawaken anxiety about separation and loss that has been present since early childhood; namely, the fear that the few significant people in one's life may be taken by death. Under even the most favorable circumstances, the sorrow of bereavement is usually a long and painful process. The elderly are in particular jeopardy, however, because they are likely to experience a greater number of bereavements. Before they are able to work through the death of one loved person, another may die.

The consequences for a person who is growing feeble and suffering from other age-related health problems may be quite severe: loss of appetite, insomnia, and feelings of isolation. Under these circumstances, Kastenbaum (1969) speaks of bereavement overload.[13]

Bereavement overload may make elderly people particularly susceptible to depression since the high frequency of losses experienced by them may not allow them to move from the one type of valuation (*fugit amor*) to another. Flexibility is further reduced by the impossibility of engaging in compensatory activities or roles. There is less opportunity to find distraction through work and travel (Kastenbaum, 1977) and thus (in terms of the concepts proposed in Chapter 4) less opportunity to move from a *fugit amor* experience to positive experiences of contact, success, and autonomy. One can conclude that the co-incidence of object loss and role loss for elderly people in our culture creates a high risk of depression in this population.

Schulz (1982) observes that the aged are exposed to a new class of emotion-arousing events, which he broadly identifies as losses (e.g., loss of a spouse, decreased physical mobility, reduction of income). Such events, in part because of their unfamiliarity, are likely to elicit immediate, intense, and long-lasting emotional responses of a generally negative character. Support for this notion is found in the relatively high incidence of depression among older adults.[14] However, notes Schulz, awareness of the increased probability of negative events with age may temper the degree of negative affect associated with a specific event when it occurs. That is, when events are scheduled or in some way expected, they may arouse a lesser degree of negative affect.

In summary, bereavement overload may, in combination with the burden of chronic diseases and the vacuum resulting from role loss, lead to a fixation on *fugit amor* experiences and, consequently, may impede the flexibility of the valuation system.

Life Review and Balanced Reflection

Elderly people inaugurate a process that Butler (1975) has called the life review, a process that is promoted by the realization of approaching dissolution and death. Life review is characterized by the progressive return to consciousness of past experiences, in particular, the resurgence of unresolved conflicts that can now be surveyed and perhaps reintegrated. Reviewing one's life may lead to anxiety, guilt, and depression, or it may lead to resolution of old conflicts, insight into the past, and a sense that one's life has not been in vain. The elderly not only take stock of themselves as they review their lives but also try to think through what to do with the time left. Once people have reviewed their lives, however, they tend to move on to other things and to reminisce less.

The life review is a common theme in film and fiction. Ingmar Bergman's film *Wild Strawberries* depicts an elderly physician whose dreams and reflection concerning his remoteness and selfishness in the past finally give rise to feelings of closeness and love. In *A Christmas Carol*, the classic by Charles Dickens, as the heartless and stingy Scrooge is forced to confront his past (as a schoolboy, young lover, apprentice) and then to imagine the future after his death, he realizes that his life has had little meaning and quickly turns into a cheerful, benevolent, and loving old man.[15]

It is generally accepted that aging involves a process of turning inward, of becoming more introspective, reflective, and contemplative (e.g., Bühler, 1935; Jung, 1933; Neugarten, 1968b). Elderly people may be constantly writing and rewriting the stories of their lives. Sometimes chased by the furies of guilt, they try to resurrect and come to terms with regretted actions of their past. This offers them a final opportunity to take responsibility for acts that were previously all but forgotten or ignored and, as a result, to replace significant omissions in their valuation systems with additional memories and new meanings. Reflecting on their lives, elderly people may look back on the past with feelings of gratitude and guilt and may even reconcile these feelings as an inevitable part of life. As Schulz (1982) has argued, events that in the past elicited predominantly positive affect may acquire a slightly negative loading over time and vice versa. A feeling of love, for example, may be less euphoric and more bittersweet the second, third, and fourth time around.

Whatever the result of the life review may be, elderly people are apt to be more reflective than impulsive. Having experienced a great deal and having often suffered the consequences of impulsivity, they have learned to think before acting. They are capable of differentiating between the interests of others and their own interests precisely because they, more than young people, can keep their impulses under control. Their optimism is tempered by a balanced view of the joys and sadnesses of life. They are not often overwhelmed by new ideas, for they realize how few of them are really new. And they have learned to look beyond the moment of initial enthusiasm.

These reflective qualities often make elderly people highly suited for tasks that require a balanced combination of involvement and distance. As Butler (1975) has observed, in all societies elderly people are often active in the determination of public policy and in the implementation of executive, administrative, and judicial responsibilities. For example, over 85% of the service on the Supreme Court has been rendered by people over 65. Political, religious, and business leadership is often in the hands of the aged and experienced, although any individual position may have been obtained in middle age.

To summarize, a productive life review provides new possibilities for self-reflection and for the integration of unresolved conflicts into one's self-narrative. An increased capacity for self-reflection also makes aging people well suited for tasks that require a balance of involvement and distance.

DEATH AS OPPONENT AND COMPANION

In his book *The Denial of Death* (1973), Ernest Becker vividly describes how people avoid the recognition of their own death as a basic dimension of human existence. Indeed, the personal meaning of one's own death is systematically omitted from most people's self-narratives. If it is true, as so many scholars say, that life can only be lived to its fullest when its intrinsic bond with death is recognized, this omission is a fundamental one. Late adulthood is for many the period when this omission can be redressed (Feifel, 1977). (For the term *omission*, see discussion of dissociations in Chapter 6.)

Long before one arrives at the full realization of one's definite personal end, death plays a role either in the form of a personification (e.g., death as a frightening imaginal figure) or in the form of a more abstract concept (e.g., the extinction of life in general). As Kastenbaum's (1977) review of the literature shows, it is wrong to assume that children never think of death. The games they play, the songs they sing, and the riddles they recite represent variations on the theme of death. The cry "Ashes, ashes, all fall down!" is one of the best-known examples and was enacted by children living in the shadow of the plague hundreds of years ago. The extensive list of death-related games also includes various versions of hide-and-seek, in which the players attempt to outwit the person who is "it," the person whose touch must be avoided. In some such games (such as "Dead Man Arise!") the personification of death in the person who is "it" could hardly be more obvious.

The experience of death cannot be completely avoided, and children may be confronted with the death of a grandparent, a relative, or a pet animal quite early in life. The death of an older person causes grief and sorrow for children as well as adults, but it also confirms people's expectations about the age-related nature of death and, by doing so, provides a measure of psychological security. By ascribing death to the old, younger people can create the comfortable illusion that they are a safe distance from it. When one's parents have both died, one becomes the next logical person in the family to die; in a way, a buffer, a protection, against death has been removed (Kalish, 1977). We expect death to play according to the rules and follow the "pecking order of death" (Kastenbaum, 1977), and this pecking order obviously relates to age. Most people anticipate that the oldest will be the first to die. No one wants the oldest to die, but there nevertheless tends to be a sense of rightness about this sequence. By assuming the existence of such a pecking order, young people minimize their terrifying opponent; in other words, they defend themselves against death. This can only be done by assuming a "rational death," that is, one that follows systematic and justifiable procedures. However, as soon as death shows its ugly irrational face by selecting a person low on the pecking order, as soon as an off-schedule death occurs, we see that our elaborate defenses are useless.

This protective deception regarding death—particularly in combination

with our culture's idealization of youth—can be a tremendous source of stress
for people approaching mid-life. As "in-betweeners," midlife adults may anx-
iously interpret completely characteristic age changes as signs that they are
rapidly going downhill. Growing older is akin to growing "deader" in the minds
of many of us. Kastenbaum (1977) illustrates this with the following two examples. A woman who has built her self-image on her good looks may become
alarmed when she notices that her outward appearance is beginning to fade. In
its full-blown manifestation, in fact, this anxiety over age-related physical
changes in appearance may resemble the desperation of the dying. The woman
may undertake heroic measures to halt or reverse the process; otherwise, she
may succumb to depression. A parallel experience may overcome the man who
has built much of his self-identity on exceptional physical prowess. Although
in outstanding shape when compared to his age-mates, he can no longer compete in the same way with top athletes and takes this as a serious indication of
his mortality. Mid-life is the period in which a sort of "developmental death"
("That part of my life is over, and so I am over, too") may occur (Kastenbaum,
1977). People may desperately hold on to a youthful version of the self and
thereby impede development of valuable new dimensions in their life. The
aforementioned examples suggest, moreover, that our cultural stories linking
youth with life and old age with death tend to result in defensive core valuations associated with the unrealistic ideal of staying young and foster an implicit terror of death.

Recall that many people entering middle age begin to think of their lives
not in terms of how many years they have lived but in terms of how many years
they have left (Neugarten, 1968a). People develop an increased awareness of
their finiteness, which often causes them to reorganize their lives and change
the way they spend their time. When Kalish and Reynolds (1976) asked people
what they would do if they knew they would die in 6 months, they found that
people over 60 were less likely than younger people to think of markedly changing their way of living. This result suggests that, indeed, those over 60 had
already reorganized their lives.

As Butler (1975) observed, some people avoid confronting their own aging
by retreating into the past (e.g., by rehearsing and boasting about past achievements, which should not be confused with the useful review of one's past). Others
simply deny their age and continue to be just as future-oriented as they were
earlier, although these are often people who fail to make wills, leave important
relationships unresolved, and never fully experience the present. Butler suggests that a satisfying resolution is found among those elderly people who begin to emphasize the quality of the time remaining rather than the quantity.[16]
With the prospect of death, a sense of immediacy, of here and now, of living
for the moment, tends to develop. The basics of life—children, nature, physical touching, human emotion, colors, shapes—assume greater significance as
people sort out their priorities. Butler adds, however, that this characteriza-

tion is only true today of a minority of elderly people. It is more common among those with good health and adequate financial means, and it is most frequently seen in stable persons who can rely on their inner resources, who currently have a supportive environment, and who have come to terms with the idea of their own death.[17]

According to Kastenbaum (1977), appreciation of life's finitude might well be a core aspect of the adult's development and can often occur during the middle years. More generally, Freud (1942) suggested that an awareness of the transience of life increases its value just as the knowledge that a pleasurable experience will eventually come to an end increases one's appreciation of it. A flower that blossoms only one night does not seem any less lovely to us, and although the beauty of the human form and face diminishes in the course of a lifetime, their evanescence continually lends them a fresh charm.

Elderly people may come to a point where they can not only appreciate the transient value of things but also accept the fact that death is the human condition that makes life transient. Hecht (1954) made the delicate observation that the young know about death but older adults sense death as an intimate companion in their life. As an I position in a dialogical self, such a companion represents a final integration of life and death.

For some adults this dialogical relation with death, which may increase over the years, goes together with an increased spiritual and religious awareness. As Butler (1975) reminds us, the American psychologist Stanley Hall once called religion the great psychotherapy of death. Butler found not only orthodox religious beliefs in elderly people but also idiosyncratic beliefs and various versions of the concepts of reunion and reincarnation. Some older people are deeply religious, some are agnostic, and most are somewhere in between. For those who are religious, God may be—in James's (1890) terms—the "Great Companion," or the ultimate and intimate dialogical partner of the self.

In conclusion, when death is perceived as a threatening opponent, people attempt to protect themselves in a variety of defensive ways. However, for those who tolerate an awareness of their finiteness and reorganize their lives accordingly, death may be accepted as an intimate companion.

SUMMARY: FLEXIBILITY AND THE LIFE CYCLE

Lifelong development is described in this chapter in terms of the two levels of valuation theory. From the perspective of the manifest level, people follow a developmental route whereby the various experiences in the chronological sequence of stages can be described as successive events in a life story. From the perspective of the latent level, the two basic motives are assumed to give rise to two recurrent developmental tasks: the realization of an autonomous self and the establishment of contact and union with the other. At any one period of development these two motives together constitute an organizing cycle; that is, the same two developmental tasks return at each period of development though with different manifestations. The cycle of the basic motives over the successive periods of life leads to ever-new and complex experiences, bringing these experiences within the reach of an extending self. At the same time, the basic motives go through a process of differentiation and integration, allowing for flexible movement between the self-enhancement and contact motives and between different and even opposite I positions.

Although age is always a general consideration in delineating the different global periods in life span development, the life events themselves are central to the development that takes place in these periods. Life events can be biological (including maturation,) social, or environmental. Important life events often represent new elements in a person's world and therefore require a reorganization of the valuation system. However, this reorganization may also fail. Sometimes a distressing event simply is not, or is not yet, integrated into the valuation system, resulting in a disorganization of the system (crisis) or in a blocked process (see Chapter 6). In the case of a successful reorganization, the valuations are typically of a functional nature; that is, they are adaptive and give rise to greater flexibility (see Chapter 4). For a successful reorganization two factors are assumed to be of critical importance: (1) the nature of the event itself, with an unscheduled occurrence have a more disorganizing impact than a scheduled one and (2) the flexibility achieved in earlier periods of development. A period of disorganization can, of course, eventually be followed by reorganization, suggesting that a life transition period always brings certain opportunities and dangers with it.

An important implication of this cyclic model is that there is no period in life when the valuation system of an individual can be expected to be permanently fixed. Because each event creates new possibilities, the distressing or rewarding impact of previous events does not provide for enduring and entirely stable levels of valuation. Although valuation is to a large degree socially and culturally organized and to that extent prestructured, it is nevertheless an intrinsically personal, creative process. For example, early attachment experiences may have important consequences for later years, especially when early experiences of anxiety, longing, and despair are reactivated in later periods. This does not exclude, however, the possibility of compensating for early experiences later in life.

Compensation cannot be achieved when the same type of experience reoccurs in different periods of the life cycle without other counteracting factors. For example, when a child is easily angered and aggressive early in life and this form of behavior continues without any compensating experiences of love or intimacy, the aggression may assume a traitlike character in the form of permanent hostility. The result is a high generalization of one type of valuation across time and situations such that the self assumes a rigid character

(Chapter 6). The concept of development as a cyclic process of organization and reorganization assumes the individual's capacity to move between different types of valuations and positions in response to the immediate situation. From this perspective, both positive and negative events represent new possibilities for the development of the self. Development in this sense never reaches a point of final definition; it is in principle a lifelong process of flexible valuation.

NOTES

1. Pines (1985) adds that state sharing can also be negatively experienced. Mutual gazing and mimicry can be frightening, provocative, and at times intolerably invasive. This negative intimacy corresponds to a fear of becoming too close to the other, which belongs to anxiety of the –O type (Chapter 4).

2. As Burns (1979), and Fogel (1993) have argued, the earliest self-explorations come from sensations involved in defining the boundaries of the body. Initially, infants treat body parts as though they were not part of themselves (e.g., they may bite their own fingers and then feel surprised by the pain). They examine, manipulate, twist, bite, and suck body parts in the same way they treat other objects in their environment. Nevertheless, this learning eventually leads to a rudimentary discrimination between body and not-body and sets the stage for the development of a self-boundary structure.

3. Caring acts in early childhood are, of course, preceded by the receiving of care in infancy. The successful transition from receiving care (i.e., secure attachment) to giving care is one of the first developmental indications of flexible movement within the realm of the O motive, that is, the giving and receiving of contact and union (Chapter 4).

4. Although gender differences in aggression are consistently found, the average difference is quite small—and getting still smaller as society places more emphasis on gender equality (Hyde, 1984).

5. Studies in the field of the psychology of personal constructs also indicate a growing differentiation between the individual and the other with age. For example, Adams-Webber (1985) found that Canadian children ranging in age from 8 to 18 tended to decreasingly judge others as "like self" with age. These results lend support to the general hypothesis that the extent to which children differentiate between themselves and others gradually increases with age (see also Honess, 1980, for comparable findings). This differentiation does not mean, however, that the other is simply "outside" the self. From the perspective of a multivoiced self, the two perspectives represent two increasingly autonomous positions that may be involved in dialogical relationships (Hermans & Kempen, 1993).

6. What we describe here as imagination with mythic shadings is not the only form of imagination in adolescence. Elkind and Bowen (1979) proposed the existence of an "imaginary audience" in early adolescent experience, that is, the belief of adolescents that others in their immediate vicinity are as concerned with their thoughts and behavior as they themselves are, after finding that young adolescents are relatively more self-conscious (concerned with what others think about them) than children or older adolescents.

7. Angyal (1965) described adolescent egocentrism not only in terms of homonomy

(being in love with love) but also in terms of empty autonomy, that is, a tendency to be autonomous for its own sake (e.g., "I give this opinion because I want to have my own opinion" instead of "I give this opinion because I see it this way"). Note that this adolescent egocentricism can continue into later life, like many other characteristics of this period.

8. There is evidence that occupational success does not always prevent depression. Himmelweit and Turner (1982) found a positive correlation ($r = .30$) between male occupational status and the reported incidence of nonsomatic depressive symptoms in early adulthood. They interpreted this correlation in terms of the "anomia of early success"; in reaching their goals quite early in life these young men had in fact lost their goals. The quick translation of one's aspirations into reality may lead to devaluation of these goals and the creation of ever-higher aspirations. In any case, Himmelweit and Turner's findings suggest that not success per se but, rather, the temporal organization of success is responsible for an individual's well-being.

9. A valuation in which self-enhancement and contact and union coexist is of the +HH type (Chapter 4).

10. Like the concept of midlife crisis, the belief that virtually every woman suffers from the discomforts of menopause (e.g., hot flashes, night sweats, bursts of temper and crying) is widespread. Yet Corby and Solnick (1980) found that only one-quarter of the women in a large sample said that they felt uncomfortable during menopause.

11. The reappearance of the deceased can be likened to the conjuring up of an imaginal figure to help compensate for a felt lack (Chapter 4).

12. The usual types of depression in the case of grieving are the −O and, more severe, the −LL types (see Chapter 6).

13. The distressing or depressing implications of bereavement overload may be counteracted by "anticipatory bereavement" (Kalish, 1977), a kind of psychological rehearsal of the death of a loved one. In this fashion, people work through at least some of the distress of loss and are presumably better able to handle the death when it actually occurs. In our research we often observe that people include a valuation referring to the anticipated death of a significant other in their system. With such a "buffer valuation" people prepare themselves for the coming shock.

14. Current data on affective changes indicate that when confronted with novel stress-inducing events, the aged reach a higher level of arousal as compared to the young and require more time to return to baseline (Schulz, 1982). This means that mood changes, including recovery from a depressive mood, will be slower for older people.

15. Life review is not exclusively bound to late adulthood. From adolescence on a person may think about the meaning of life. The difference is that younger people are less distanced from their own lives than elderly people and tend to more often attach their life meaning to specific goals (for a procedure for studying life meaning, see Hermans, 1989).

16. Quality of life may also be high in terminal patients. Hendrickx (1987) has described the valuation system of a 50-year-old woman who knew she had incurable cancer and was receiving palliative chemotherapy 6 years after a masectomy. The woman reported a mixture of negative valuations (e.g., pain and suffering) and positive valuations (e.g., meditating, union with relatives, contact with friends and other patients, enjoyment of plants). Without denying her death, her general feeling had high levels of S, O, and P and an intermediate level of N.

17. In a study of older women, it was found that those who were anxious about death were also more possessive of their time and more disturbed by its quick passage than those who were less anxious about death (Durlak, 1973). More generally, the normal striving for self-enhancement contains some fear of death because death represents the ultimate dissolution of one's personality. In contrast, experiences of intense contact and union with the other, for example, in receptive sexuality or in orgasm, often foster a reduced fear of death because the boundaries of the separate self have already been transcended at these moments.

CHAPTER 8

Summary and Perspective

In this final section we bring together different elements that have been extensively discussed in the preceding chapters. The conception of the self and the perspective it opens can be summarized in Figure 8.1. Let us have a look at the various components of this figure more closely. The figure consists of three circles. The middle one represents the types of valuations that characterize normal functioning (Chapter 4); the outer circle refers to the types that are characteristic of abnormal functioning (Chapter 6); and the inner circle marks the center, symbolizing the integration or synthesis of the self (Chapter 4).

In preceding chapters a distinction is made between valuation and position. The term *position* can be easily included in Figure 8.1 by substituting a position for any type of valuation. For example, instead of a valuation referring to hostility, one may imagine the position of a devil or a murderer (Chapter 5) who has its own specific valuation system, mainly filled with hostile valuations. In other words, Figure 8.1 represents not only valuations but also positions.

There are two basic types of movement. One goes from one type to another type on one and the same circle, and the other goes from one circle to another circle (from the center to the periphery and back). The first type is typically found in the flexible movement from one valuation (or position) to another in healthy functioning (Chapter 4). As we discussed extensively in Chapter 6, movement between several types of valuation in dysfunctions is not entirely excluded (e.g., from depression to mania) but the flexibility is seriously restricted. As we have argued, this involuntary restriction is an essential feature of dysfunction. This difference between function and dysfunction leads us to the second type of movement, which is represented by the opposition between centrifugal and centripetal forces. Whereas centrifugal forces go from

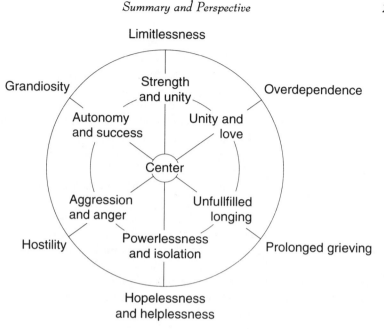

FIGURE 8.1. Summary of types of valuations and positions.

the center to the periphery of the circle, centripetal forces represent movements from the periphery to the center. In the area between the middle and outer circle, representing transitions between functional and dysfunctional valuation, centrifugal forces are dominant over centripetal ones. When centrifugal forces are no longer balanced against centripetal ones, the person deviates in one particular direction and the valuation system becomes dysfunctional. The farther the centrifugal movement deviates from the center, the weaker the integrative power of the valuation system. In the case of a multitude of positions, an exaggeration of centrifugal forces results in a monologue of fragmented positions instead of their dialogical interchange.

In the area between the middle circle and the center, centripetal forces are stronger than centrifugal ones. The more closely one approaches the center, the more integrative and flexible the valuation system becomes and the more dialogical is the relation between positions. The more a person approaches the center, the more concentrated are the different valuations and positions, and in this concentration the person is approaching what Jung (1959) described as a "coincidence of opposites," for which he used the mandala as the main symbol.

It would certainly be a naive simplification to consider centripetal forces as good and centrifugal forces as bad. Instead of an exclusive emphasis on one type only, we tend to see the two forces as complementary. During the successive phases of lifelong development (Chapter 7), child and adult are confronted with a great diversity of experiences representing centrifugal forces (successes vs. failures, friendship vs. animosity, great moments of joy vs. depressing moments of powerlessness and isolation). All these experiences are needed for balancing centripetal forces, which are activated when individuals try to understand events in their mutual relationship and influence, in sharing experiences with significant others, and in expressing them in verbal or nonverbal (e.g., painting, making music, dreaming) ways. However, an exclusive emphasis on centrifugal forces would result in a fragmented self that would not profit much from preceding experiences. Such a self would, to use an expression from Buber (1970), move as a "fluttering soul bird" (p. 93). Likewise, an exclusive emphasis on centripetal forces (on the assumption that this is possible) would deny the self the diversity of experiences that makes it acquainted with what life is and what it can be for oneself and others. In fact, a variety of different and opposite experiences, with their specific pleasures and pains, are not only the basic material of but even the challenge to the constructive energy of centripetal forces. In short, when the person fails to develop centripetal forces, the self is torn into pieces, whereas attempts to exclude or deny centrifugal forces would result in empty integration. Therefore, the concept of flexibility is a fundamental one, one that should be applied not only to the organization of valuations and positions but also to the mutual interplay of centrifugal and centripetal forces. This view reflects a dynamic self as a creator and receiver of meanings in a field of contrasting but complementary forces.

A special feature of the center of the self is that it allows the person to take a metaperspective. This part of the self is not the same kind as the other parts because it represents a perspective in which some kind of overview of the self as a whole can be achieved. Schwartz (1987) calls this center the Self, capitalized in order to distinguish it from the great variety of subparts of the self, each of which can be considered a "subself" or position. The Self offers a perspective from which one learns to see oneself as a field wherein various positions are located, each with its specific valuation. From the perspective of the Self, one identifies not rigidly with any particular part but flexibly with the interacting nature of the system as a whole. The Self can certainly be considered as an I position, but it is of a special kind. It has the capacity to juxtapose and interrelate the other positions and associated valuations, which cannot, either apart or in their incidental relationships, achieve any synthesis of the self as a whole. The Self functions as a synthesizing activity, that is, as an approximation of the self as an integrative whole, despite the existence of parts that try to maintain, or even to increase, their relative autonomy (Hermans, 1994; Hermans & Kempen, 1993).

Implicit in Figure 8.1 are collective stories that over the centuries have had much influence in shaping our culture and our selves. We have referred to many stories in Greek mythology (Chapter 5) that correspond to the various indications on the middle circle. In a similar way, it would be possible to find many examples of stories depicting dramatic figures characterized by the valuations located on the outer circle (e.g., stories about people becoming the victim of their grandiosity or hubris). One type of story, however, may highlight the relevance of the center of the circle. Across the centuries people have exchanged stories about great figures—Buddha, Christ, Mohammed, and many other great and inspiring leaders—who have achieved an extreme degree of synthesis of their Selves. As role models for millions of people, they have functioned as powerful identification figures and as beacons for moral valuations. The fact that these characters were able to synthesize strongly opposite experiences (e.g., youth vs. old age, life vs. death, happiness vs. unhappiness, sanity vs. insanity) contributes to their significance as "meaning givers" par excellence. The importance of such figures, and the stories in which they play a central role, may be understood as reflective of the Self as the most central source of valuation.

CHAPTER 9

Manual

The purpose of this manual is to provide in a condensed form a number of specific guidelines for those who want to work with the self-confrontation method in practice. These guidelines are based on our own experiences as well as on discussions with others who apply the method in their own setting as psychotherapists, counselors, or trainers. It is our intention to present a series of specific suggestions and hints that are helpful not only for those who want to apply the method in their own work setting but also for those who want to instruct trainees in the methodology discussed in this book. The presentation of the different parts of the manual corresponds with the successive parts of the self-confrontation method as presented in Chapter 3. Moreover, we give a number of guidelines for training purposes. Finally, some suggestions on how to make adaptations and extensions of the self-confrontation method are presented.

Before starting, we wish to emphasize the following points: Application of the method in practice requires a learning process that is a combination of knowledge and personal experience. The knowledge concerns the basic metaphor, the theoretical framework, and the details of the methodology. Experience can only be acquired by a theory-guided training in which psychologists learn to play the instrument of self-confrontation in practical situations. Intellectual knowledge alone can never replace actual training experience. A flexible computer program is also needed in order to assist the client in filling in the affect matrix and to calculate the relevant indices (see Chapter 3).

FORMULATION OF THE VALUATIONS

1. Reading the questions: The set of questions (e.g., referring to the past) is read as a total set before the client starts a process of self-exploration. The combination of questions affords a broader scope than does each separate question. The disadvantage of responding to each question separately is that clients may react to the questions in a stimulus–response style or as if responding to a questionnaire. It is the aim of the self-confrontation method to invite clients to a deepening self-exploration, which requires them to direct their attention to their own experiences and to forget the specific question.

2. No right or wrong answers: In the beginning of a self-investigation, clients may have some difficulties in catching the spirit of the method. After sharing their first associations in response to a set of questions they may express uncertainty by asking, in effect, "Is this a good answer to the questions?" In such cases it is helpful for the psychologist to explain that there are no right or wrong answers. Each answer is adequate if it expresses what the client finds to be significant in his or her own life. It is our experience that the process-promoting function of the method works best when clients consider the questions not simply as questions posed by the psychologist but also—and even primarily—as questions they pose to themselves.

3. Gradual introduction: When clients have great difficulty talking about their past, the psychologist then begins with another set of questions (e.g., about the present or about activities; see the extended set of questions in Appendix 1) so that a more gradual introduction to the self-investigation procedure is realized. In comparing the emotional quality of valuations elicited by different sets of questions in the self-confrontation method, Reijnen (1981) found that valuations referring to the past aroused more emotions than valuations referring to the present, which in turn aroused more emotions than valuations referring to the future. The lowest level of arousal was found for valuations referring to activities. (For the distinction between emotions and feelings, see note 3 in Chapter 6.)

4. Final sentence: The psychologist jots down short notes while listening to the client's story and makes use of these notes when reviewing the client's associations. When clients are at the end of their approximation process (see Chapter 3), the psychologist helps them formulate, in the clients' own words, the final sentence on a small index card and reads this aloud so that clients can check if they agree with the sentence. They then have the opportunity (as they continue the association process while the psychologist writes) to make a final revision of this sentence.

Some psychologists believe it is better to have the client, not the psychologist, write the final sentence on the card. This makes clients directly responsible for their final formulation. Moreover, familiarity with their own handwriting prevents clients from becoming alienated from their own formulations.

Since in the second self-investigation clients confront themselves with their own formulations from Time 1, there is a possibility that some clients may then consider these formulations as foreign if they see them in another's handwriting.

5. Overview of sentences: The use of cards permits a spatial overview at the end of the valuation construction phase. When valuations referring to past, present, and future are lying side by side in front of the client, they can be compared, classified in groups, and hierarchically ordered according to any criterion. Even without relating the valuations to the affect terms, the discussion between client and psychologist may profit from this bird's-eye view that becomes possible by the spatial juxtaposition of temporally ordered valuations. When different valuation systems are formulated (from different I positions), these systems can also be compared and dialogically related by a visual composition of different groups of cards (for the spatialization of temporal differences, see Hermans & Kempen, 1993 and Hermans, in press).

6. Ordering of events: When a client has related a particular experience or described a circumstance from the past, it is summarized in the form of a valuation (final sentence). Such a valuation may refer to a highly specific event that is considered meaningful (e.g., "When I was five years old, my mother died") or to a group of events that together form a significant unit of meaning (e.g., "The fact that our family moved frequently from one place to another resulted in my inability to feel at home anywhere"). The criterion for bringing various events together in one formulation is always the client's feeling that these events belong together as elements of a single unit of meaning. A useful question to the client is "Are you satisfied with this phrasing?" or "Does this formulation fit with your experience?"

7. More valuations than questions: Typically, each set of questions (referring to past, present, and future) elicits more than one valuation. When the client has formulated one valuation (e.g., referring to the past), the psychologist stimulates the client to formulate another by inviting him or her to tell about something relevant that is not included in the previous valuation. This means that the client starts a new round of associations ending in a second final sentence. In this way the client may formulate a variety of valuations that represent a diversity of relevant meaning units in the past. The same procedure is followed for the present and the future. Typically, clients tell more valuations for their past and present than for their future.

8. Phrasing a valuation: A valuation system is most useful when it allows for insights to be made among the valuations and, moreover, indicates the direction of the validation/invalidation process. Given this purpose, it is important that the valuations be formulated in a *specific* way. Vague and uninformative phrases like "my self-development" or "my identity" are generally not useful as valuations. Such phrases can be specified by asking additional questions like, for example, "What do you mean by 'my identity'?" or "In which situation is your identity important?" or " Could you give an example of what you intend to say?" With such additional questions, moreover, it is possible to make a narrative out of abstract phrases. When people are invited to specify a phrase in terms of a situation or to give an example, they typically locate an experience or conception in *time and space*. They may say "When I was with my husband in Europe . . ." or "When my children have problems at school . . ." The "when . . . then" formulation is a suitable grammatical structure to give experiences, circumstances, or ideas a narrative form (Bruner, 1986). Finally, the valuation should be a *personal* unit of meaning: Its formulation should reveal something that is important from the perspective of the storyteller. A useful question here is "What does this mean for you?" Meeting the criteria of specificity, location in time and space, and personal meaning is desirable but not necessary. The psychologist does not require more of clients than they can provide in this stage of construing their self-narratives.

It may happen, however, that a person will prefer to formulate a valuation in one word (e.g., "sexuality") because confusion or strong emotions prevent a more elaborate expression. This is sufficient reason for the psychologist to accept such a brief indication; the valuation may be specified at a later point (e.g., in the discussion after the investigation, in the validation/invalidation process, or in a second investigation). Note that a one-word valuation may be very informative when it is studied, via a modality analysis, in the context of the valuation system as a whole.

9. Entangled valuations and their differentiation: Sometimes clients give formulations that are entangled; that is, the sentence represents not one but two valuations that are not sufficiently distinguished. For example, a client may give the following vague formulation: "The education that I received from my parents has influenced the way I interact with other people." At some later point (e.g., during the rating of affect terms) the client may become aware that there is a clear difference in behavioral style between father and mother and that these arouse different feelings. Such a difficulty can be prevented by asking in the valuation construction phase if the valuation applies equally well to father and to mother. If this is not the case, it is better to formulate two separate valuations, one for father and another for mother. The client might then say "My father used to ridicule me when I failed" and "My mother always protected me when I was ridiculed by my father."

Some differentiation is also needed when the client refers to a significant other. When a woman uses the phrase "my husband," it is possible that this brief indication covers contrasting meaning aspects. The solution may be to make differentiations on the basis of time (i.e., before or after some event) or on the basis of space or situation (e.g., "When my husband and I are traveling" vs. "When my husband and I visit my parents"). When the relationship with a significant other typically covers a diversity of situations, it is better to distinguish these situations in terms of different valuations than to combine all these aspects in one comprehensive valuation. In this way, a global valuation is specified in terms of a subset of valuations.

10. Complex formulations: Although the psychologist may stimulate clients to express their experiences in a differentiated set of valuations, some clients offer rather complex valuations that include contrasting elements; for example: "I would like everything to stand still for 10 years so that everything, including myself, could come to rest; *continuous changes, new rules, and new laws cause me distress.*" The first part of this formulation is a wish, the latter part a complaint. In such a case the psychologist asks the client which part of the formulation is emphasized in his or her experience. The client is then invited to underline this part so that later, when the affective ratings are made, it is clear that they refer to the emphasized part of the valuation.

11. Idealizing formulations: There is nothing against the client's offering valuations that refer to ideals, certainly not when they express what the client wants to do in the future. However, idealizing formulations (e.g., "I wish I had a better relationship with Dick") may function as expressions of problems or problematic situations. In such cases it is more informative to focus on the nature of the problem than to avoid it by idealization. It is often helpful to go one step further by asking the client to include actual and ideal (or possible) experience in two separate valuations so that they can be compared.

12. Positive or negative valuations only: When a client is strongly disposed to offering negative valuations, the psychologist must be especially sensitive to the construction of positive ones. Inclusion of positive valuations in an otherwise negative system is necessary for a successful validation/invalidation process. The client learns to vacillate between negative and positive valuations, even though the positive part of the system is rather small. The same consideration applies to a system that consists of positive valuations only; in this case the psychologist pays close attention to the inclusion of negative valuations. Note that seemingly small or insignificant events may be particularly relevant when they represent an exception in the system. When the client begins to understand why he or she avoids the inclusion of such deviant valuations, this insight may be included as a new valuation in the system at a later time.

13. The presenting problem: When contacting a psychotherapist or counselor, many clients refer to a problem they want to solve or a question they want to address. It is recommended to include this first presentation as a valuation so that its relevance in the valuation system can be checked.

14. Extra questions: When the three sets of questions (concerning past, present, and future) result in a rather small number of valuations, the psychologist may use the extra questions presented in Appendix 1 in order to extend the total number of valuations. We recommend that practitioners who have not much experience with the construction of valuations use the extended list of questions. The extra questions may be used under other circumstances as well. For example, if the psychologist wishes to gradually introduce the client to the method, the set of questions listed under Activity in Appendix I may be a useful beginning. If specific positive valuations require exploration, the questions under Enjoyment may be used, and when there are reasons to investigate the meaning of significant others, the questions under Person: antagonistic, Person: unity, Group: antagonistic, and Group: unity may be used. Moreover, the client's position in society may be explored with the questions listed under Society.

15. **Time needed:** The total duration of the valuation construction phase depends on the number of valuations and the depth of exploration of the valuation system. The construction of 20 valuations takes between 1 and 2 hours. The total number of valuations may vary greatly and depends on the number and nature of the questions, the extension and complexity of the person's self-narrative, his or her need for expression, and the level of detail aimed for in the investigation. Therefore, a good investigation may consist of 20 valuations, but it may also consist of 50 valuations.

AFFECTIVE EXPLORATION AND ANALYSES

1. **Check of affect terms:** Before the client starts rating the valuations with a list of affect terms, the psychologist first makes certain that the client knows and understands the affect terms by perusing the list with him or her. When a particular term is unfamiliar, the psychologist should explain the term and allow the client to give an approximation of the original in his or her own words; the new term is written in brackets after the original term (e.g., "feeling respect for myself" may be the client's rewording of "self-esteem"). An additional advantage of this check is that it prevents the affect terms from "wandering" through the valuation system; that is, there is a tendency for clients to give divergent meanings to a particular affect term depending on the nature of the valuations. The initial perusal and check of the affect list gives the terms a certain stability and specificity so that their meaning is not lost during the rating process. Note that there is always some variation in the meaning of an affect term, despite this procedure, when it is applied to different valuations. The affect terms are broad categories that always permit a certain range of meaning variations. For example, *joy* in relation to being active in a sport is to some extent different from *joy* in relation to reading an interesting book. Nevertheless, the term *joy* covers both situations.

2. **Computer facilities:** Although paper and pencil may be used to fill in the affect matrix, experience to date suggests that computer facilities provide the means for an optimal procedure. After working with various versions of the self-confrontation method, we have concluded that the best procedure is for the client to formulate in direct contact with the psychologist a set of valua-

tions that serve as input for a computer program that is devised to guide the rating of affect terms. This program proceeds in such a way that the first valuation is presented on the screen in combination with the first affect term of the standard list. The client indicates the degree to which the affect applies to the valuation ("not at all," to some extent," etc.) by choosing the corresponding symbol. All other affect terms are combined with the first valuation in the same way. Next, the second valuation is presented on the screen, and the list of affect terms is successively presented again. In this way all valuations, including the general and ideal feeling, are affectively characterized. Finally, the computer calculates all relevant indices.

3. **Extended list of affect terms:** The number of affect terms included in the list may vary. The list of 16 affect terms used for the examples in this book has the advantage that it is not very long and yet allows for a variety of indices. It can be easily used for instruction purposes (as we have done in this book) and for research. For clinical, counseling, or therapeutic purposes it may be too limited. Especially in the positive (P) and negative (N) domain, the number of affect terms (four in each) may be insufficient to fulfill a client's need for affective expression. If a client says, "I experience more positive and negative feelings than those mentioned in the list," the psychologist may use the extended list of Appendix 2 (or any other list that has been devised on the basis of theoretical and psychometric analyses).

4. **Idiosyncratic list:** In special cases, psychologist and client may decide to compose an idiosyncratic list of affect terms. In this case a specific list is composed with terms that are familiar to the client. This procedure has the advantage that the client finds it easy to apply these terms to the valuations. One should, however, be aware of the following disadvantages: Composing a new list is time consuming, and people generally have a larger passive than active vocabulary, certainly in the realm of affect. Most people can talk more easily about their valuations than about the affect involved. Moreover, when clients are provided with a list of carefully selected affect terms, they not only learn to focus on the affective component of their valuations but become sensitive to feeling aspects they would otherwise have neglected. For example, clients who are generally focused on self-enhancement are invited to view all their valuations from the perspective of such affective notions as tenderness, love and other O feelings. In this way their attention is drawn to those affective aspects that heretofore have been neglected or avoided in their lives. Similar remarks can be made with respect to positive versus negative affect.

5. **Pool of affect terms:** Instead of working with a standard or idiosyncratic list of affect terms, the psychologist can select a large pool of affect terms on the basis of theoretical relevance, check these on psychometric properties, divide them into subgroups of S, O, P, and N terms, and present them to the client, who now has the freedom to choose those terms that are most appropriate to him or her. The client is then asked to choose an equal number of affect

terms from the various subgroups (i.e., the number of S items equals the number of O items, and the number of P items and the number of N items are equal).

6. Inclusion of strong affect terms: Depending on the purpose of the investigation, the client population, and the setting, the list may include or exclude affect terms with strong emotional qualities (e.g., revenge, hate, panic, passion). Similarly, for some clients the terms selected for O affect may be too strong. In that case, the psychologist may replace them with, for example, terms like, *sympathy, warmth, solidarity,* and *respect.* More generally, the psychologist prepares for an investigation by selecting those affect terms that are understood and used by the client population.

7. Meaning of zero level: When clients do not see any relationship between a particular affect and a specific valuation, they are instructed to give a score of zero. For practical purposes we assume that when the client perceives no relationship between the two elements, no affect aroused by the valuation. In fact, these two notions are not identical. One may hold that the perception "This feeling has nothing to do with this valuation [e.g., intimacy in relation to an exam]" is different from the perception "This feeling has certainly something to do with this valuation, but unfortunately it is not there [e.g., intimacy in relation to a friend]." It is certainly possible to make an explicit distinction between the two notions (relationship and level of arousal), but this would result in a rather complex scoring scheme. Note also that it is common for clients to not see a relationship between a particular affect term and a particular valuation in a first investigation but to do so in a second investigation as the result of attending to their own affective reactions.

8. Missing affect terms: Sometimes clients say that a particular affect that is important to them is missing in the affect list provided. Two options are available here: (1) One of the affect terms of the standard list (perceived by the client as not relevant) is replaced by a new affect term that is seen as relevant, or (2) the new affect that is of personal relevance is added to the standard list. When many clients in a specific setting refer to the same affect term as missing, the psychologist may include this term in the standard list. The psychometric properties of any new affect term can be investigated by correlating this affect term with all the other affect terms on the list (correlations between the columns of the matrix) and by comparing the mean score of the affect term with mean scores of other affect terms (comparison between means of rows of the matrix).

9. Past or present: When rating a valuation referring to the past, some clients wonder if they should give their affect as they perceived it in the past or as they perceive it in the present. The answer to this question depends on the formulation of the valuation. When the formulation explicitly refers to the past (e.g., "At table conversations my father used to compare me with my older brother"), the person may indicate how he or she felt at that time. When, however, the formulation puts an emphasis on the present (e.g., "When I compare

myself with ten years ago, I find myself now . . ."), the affective ratings focus
on the present situation. Note that the formulation and affective ratings of
valuations that refer to the past may have a strong generalization in the system. Although the person is speaking in the past tense, the experiences referred
to may be highly influenced by his or her present view.

   10. Experiential quality: When there is reason to bring the affect terms
more closely to the person's I, or to increase the experiential quality, one may
use I-formulations for the affect terms (e.g., "I feel anxious" or "I feel happy").
The experiential quality may be further increased in the discussion phase (see
next section) by focusing on one particular affect and inviting the client to
imagine this affect as vividly as possible. The selection of an affect to focus on
(see also Gendlin, 1978) may be based on the analysis of the affective properties of the valuation system as a whole (e.g., the affect with the highest mean or
the one with the lowest mean).

   11. Numbers or verbal indications: Some people do not like to indicate the level of an affect with a scale. This aversion to "quantifying feelings"
applies primarily to the paper-and-pencil procedure, in which numbers are
added to a matrix. This problem is avoided when the computer program is used,
since the client selects phrases that are presented on the screen ("not at all,"
"to some extent," etc.), not numbers. The computer program then transforms
the verbal indications into numbers.

   12. Returning to raw data: Although affect terms are used for the investigation of affective profiles, it must never be forgotten that each separate score
represents a more or less relevant aspect of the person's experiences. Skilled
use of the self-confrontation method implies that the psychologist returns to
the raw data at any moment in the process. This can be done when psychologist and client want to have a check on the calculations of the indices or when
they are interested in special characteristics of the profiles.

   13. Exceptional scores: The raw data may show peculiarities that are
not (or not easily) seen in the quantitative indices. For example, when in a row
of zero scores there is only one exception, say, a score of 1 or 2, this deviating
score may be highly relevant as it indicates an exceptional aspect in the person's
affective experience of this valuation. The deviance may be reason enough for
the psychologist to ask the person in the discussion phase to concentrate on
this exception and to make its meaning explicit. In other words, a score of 1 in
one valuation may be more relevant than a score of 5 in another valuation.

   14. Focusing on *own* feelings: The instruction should emphasize that
clients are invited to focus on their own feelings, not on the feelings of other
people. Moreover, clients are requested to indicate their actual feelings, not
their ideal feelings, unless the valuation has been formulated in an ideal way.

   15. Main processes involved: Rating one's valuations with a set of affect terms is not simply a registration, but, rather, an investigative action. Four
processes are involved: (1) The affective properties of a valuation that are usu-

ally implicit are made explicit so that the valuation is better understood (*affective explication*), (2) clients view their valuations from a broader range of affective states than they normally do (*affective extension*), (3) they make fine distinctions between a variety of affective states and between several levels within each state (*affective differentiation*), and (4) they concentrate on a selection of affects that have a particular meaning for a particular valuation or for the valuation system as a whole (*affective focusing*).

16. **Discrepancy, dissociation, rationalization, differentiation:** The processes mentioned in the previous guideline may be helpful in discerning notable phenomena that may be found in self-investigations. For example, some people show an apparent discrepancy between the explicit formulation of their valuations and the structure of their affective profiles (e.g., more N than P with the valuation "I respect my parents for the things they have given me"). Such a discrepancy can be made explicit by asking the client to tell about the meaning of the affect that deviates from the formulation. The client then becomes more conscious of aspects in the relation with the parents that were heretofore neglected or dissociated. Another example is the person who assigns a zero to many of the affects measured against one or more valuations, which may be a sign of affective ignorance or dissociation (subduing); that is, the person simply does not know which are the affective characteristics of the valuation or has emotional reasons to dissociate the corresponding affect. (Before reaching this conclusion, the psychologist should be certain that the list of affect terms used fits the client). In this case it may be important for the client to learn to extend his or her affective realm (the psychologist should check the number of zero levels in the second investigation!). Finally, the psychologist may be confronted by the phenomenon of rationalization: Some clients do not have much contact with their feelings or are afraid of them and then answer with a systematic but poor structure of equalized levels (e.g., 0, 4, 0, 0, 4, 4, 4, etc.). By using two levels only, they resort to a "safe" pattern. Other clients rationalize their affect by systematically giving high levels to positive affect and low levels for negative affect. For clients who rationalize, it may be a challenge to use more differentiation in a second investigation after they have had the opportunity to explore and deepen their affective life.

17. **Implicit meanings:** During the rating procedure various affective aspects of a valuation are touched upon, and some of them may be striking. Some valuation–affect patterns reveal unexpected or hitherto implicit insights, which the client may want to know. Or on discovering that a particular valuation is associated with a certain affect, a client's attention may be drawn to implicit meanings. All these possibilities reflect the dynamic nature of the self-confrontation method. It is helpful, therefore, for clients to make notes on their memories, thoughts, and ideas during the affective rating procedure so that these notes can be discussed later with the psychologist. The notes are, moreover, a means for expressing the emotions that may be aroused during the rating process.

18. Assisting the client: Because the affective rating is done by the client in the absence of the psychologist, it is important that the client be well prepared for this task. In order to become accustomed to this procedure, the client does one row, or part of it, in the presence of the psychologist; thus, the client gets a feel for the task and may pose any question that arises. Once clients have finished the first row, they usually are well prepared to fill in the rest of the matrix. It is, however, recommended that the psychologist be available in case of additional questions (when the client is doing the rating process at home, there should be a possibility for telephone contact).

19. Special assistance: In special cases the entire rating procedure can be done in the presence of the psychologist. In self-investigation with children or when an investigation concerns a delicate topic—Sandfort's (1984) research with young people involved in a pedophiliac relationship is an example of this— the psychologist should be present during the entire rating task.

20. Clients' reactions to the rating procedure: The rating procedure evokes a variety of reactions in clients. For some it is an emotional experience; others feel confused by the huge amount of valuation–affect patterns that loosen or even shake their fixed self-conceptions. Some clients find it a boring task whereas others consider it a form of meditation. Most people, however, find it a very involving task that requires a lot of energy. When a client becomes tired during the task, it may be a good idea to suggest a short break to relax (during which time the process of self-reflection often continues). It is recommended, however, that the task be completed in one day. Extending the process over several days should be avoided to prevent a weakening of the relationship between valuation construction and affective rating.

21. Difference between sum scores: Part of the goal of affective analysis is to compare the different sum scores. A simple procedure is to take a difference of at least 6 scale points for comparing S with O, and P with N (e.g., when $S = 14$ and $O = 8$, we say that S is higher than O. When the difference is less than 6 scale points, S and O are considered equal. The choice of a minimum difference depends on the total number of affect terms included in the index. For example, when the extended list of affect terms is used (including 8 P and 8 N terms; see Appendix 2), a mimimum difference score between P and N of at least 12 scale points can be taken. The general rule is that the difference is at least .3 × the maximum number of scale points. Note that the choice of such minimum scores is quite arbitrary. More sophisticated rules for differences can be developed when not only the total number of affect terms but also the reliability (e.g., Cronbach's alpha) is taken into account.

22. Reliability of indices: Computer programs written for computation of the indices of the self-confrontation method usually contain the calculations of the reliability coefficients (e.g., Cronbach's alpha) for the various sum scores (the term *homogeneity* is perhaps more precise in this case than *reliability*). Usually these reliability coefficients are around .80 when four affect terms are included in the index. Homogeneity coefficients are sensitive to the number of items included in the index and the extent of the correlations between these items.

23. Differentiation between S and O: The correlations between the different sum scores gives information on the extent of differentiation beween S and O, and between P and N. When, for example, the correlation between S and O is very high (e.g., .90), this means that the client does not make much differentiation between S and O across the valuations of the system. When, however, the correlation is low (e.g., .30), such clients make finer discriminations between S and O in affectively characterizing their valuations. (The psychologist should also take the distribution of the sum scores into account). A high correlation between S and O may be an indication that the person is not able or does not want to make a distinction between the two groups of affect terms. Why not? The reason may be that the person feels safe only when S and O are kept together, and unsafe when O is high and S is low or when S is high and O is low. When the person is systematically doing this, the number of valuation types (see Figure 4.1) in the system is seriously reduced (with an emphasis on +HH and −LL valuations).

However, even when a correlation is high, there may be deviant scoring patterns that give relevant information. A correlation of, say, .90 or higher does not exclude the possibility that the client has a difference of more than 6 scale points for one or more valuations; however, such a difference is an exception because in the total system there is not much differentiation, as indicated by the high correlation between S and O. The fact that this exception exists suggests that this person is able to make a differentiation between S and O for some parts of the system but does not extend this differentiation to large parts of it. In that case, a profound analysis of the content and organization of the system is required to explain this phenomenon.

24. Means on S, O, P, and N: Whereas the sum scores S, O, P, and N are calculated for each valuation separately, it is also possible to compute the means of the S, O, P, and N sum scores across all valuations. These overall means give an impression of the valuation system as a whole. When, for example, these overall means are high S, low O, high P, and low N, this may be an indication that the system as a whole is expressing successful self-enhancement.

25. Means on separate affects: It is recommended that means be computed for each column of the matrix. Comparison of these column means gives an impression of which affect is most typical of the valuation system as a whole. An appropriate computer program orders these means from high to low. Is the highest mean an S, O, P, or N affect? When it is a negative affect, for example, which affect precisely is it? When one compares the affect with the highest mean with the affect with the lowest mean, the affective extremities between which the system is stretched become visible. Apparently, the affect with the lowest mean has not been used much to characterize the valuations; perhaps it is even avoided. When, for example, anxiety has the lowest mean, two quite different interpretations are possible: Either anxiety is not a relevant affect in the system of this person in this period of life, or the person has formulated a valuation system whose function is to avoid or dissociate anxiety. Deciding on one of these possibilities requires (1) an analysis of the content of the valuation system as a whole and (2) discussion of this possibility with the client. When clients have systematically avoided or dissociated this affect, it is relevant not only to see how they react to the finding that anxiety has the lowest mean but also to give them the opportunity to contribute to a shared insight.

26. Combination of affect means: Particular attention should be given to the combination of affect means (column means). One should not only take into account the affect term with the highest mean but also the ones that are next highest. For example, a combination of high anger with high energy represents an affective organization that is quite different from high anger with high powerlessness. In the first case, anger may be a force that motivates the person to do things; in the second case the same affect, anger, may cause the person to perceive himself or herself as a passive victim of the situation.

27. Affective emphasis: The usual scoring procedure requires the connection of a list of affect terms with a set of valuations. When a particular valuation is taken as a starting point, one may ask to what extent the affect terms apply to the valuation as a whole? Although people usually give their affective reactions to the valuation as a Gestalt, one specific part of the valuation often evokes more affect than another part. When, for example, someone says, "I try to prepare the children to find their way in a hard society in which they should live as an individual," it makes a difference if affect is focused on the words "hard society" or on the words "live as an individual." In the first case, one expects more negative than positive feelings, in the second case more positive than negative feelings. We use the term *affective emphasis* to indicate the part of the valuation that attracts most of the affective ratings. The simplest way to determine the affective emphasis is to ask the client to underline the part of the sentence that evokes the most affect. A more systematic way is to ask the client, after the rating procedure, to indicate to which part of the sentence each affect is related. It may be found that one part corresponds to O affect and another part to N affect (e.g., "I loved my father very much, but I lost him when I was 13"). Finally, it is possible to break a complex sentence into parts and to rate each of the parts as a separate valuation. Then each of the parts, as a separate valuation, has its own emphasis.

28. Features of affective emphasis: It is possible to discern several features of the affective emphasis of a valuation: breadth, pregnancy, structure, complexity, and locus. The *breadth* of the emphasis is usually indicated by the relative number of words the emphasis receives as part of a sentence. The broader the emphasis, the greater the proportion of words in the sentence that are affect laden. The *pregnancy* is determined by the number and level of affects the emphasized part receives. When the emphasis is very pregnant, it attracts many affects and each is at a high level. The *structure* concerns the pattern of affect as expressed in the S, O, P, and N indices. Kinds of structure correspond with types of valuation (Chapter 4). Usually the affective pattern of the emphasis reflects the affective pattern of the valuation as a whole. This is, however, not always true. An emphasis may be atypical in the sense that it expresses a particular affective pattern, but the same affective pattern is not representative of the valuation as a whole (i.e., the same pattern is not found in the other parts of the valuation). The *complexity* refers to the number of parts that are emphasized in a particular valuation. The emphasis is complex when the person tends to underline several parts of the valuation as most significant. When these different emphases also have different patterns (i.e., reflecting different or even opposed types), the rating procedure is a very difficult one to perform (and can even become impossible). The simplest solution to this problem is to reformulate the complex valuation into two or more valuations of a simpler structure. Finally, the *locus* of the emphasis can be internal or external. Usually it is internal, but sometimes the client rates affect that is implicit or even dissociated from the valuation. When the emphasis is external, there is often an apparent discrepancy between the explicitly formulated valuation and its affective rating. The existence of external emphasis may mark a conflict between conscious and unconscious aspects of a valuation. Note that all these complex relationships between affective patterns and corresponding valuations offer relevant information that can be used to explore and deepen the valuation system as a whole.

29. "Unfolding" a valuation into parts: Breaking or "unfolding" a valuation into parts can also be used as a procedure for attending to elements of a valuation that are suppressed by other, more dominating, elements. For example, Hermans and Hermans-Jansen (1992) discussed the following valuation from a promiscuous client: "With father's death and mother's work I missed out on parental guidance and had to find my own way." This valuation was unfolded into four parts: (1) "My father's death," (2) "My mother's work," (3) "I missed parental guidance," and (4) "I had to find my own way." It was found that the first part represented a −O valuation and was strongly generalizing in the system whereas the other parts were in the direction of the −S type and lacked generalizing influence. The valuation as a whole was also of the −S type and had no generalizing influence. The conclusion was that the first part, representing a *fugit amor* theme, was suppressed by the other dominating parts of the valuation, which were erected to cover a painful experience. This organization suggests a failing attempt to fill an existential gap stemming from the early loss of a father.

30. Time needed: The total duration of the rating procedure depends, of course, on the total number of valuations, the number of affect terms included in the list, and the speed of the client. In the case of 20 valuations and a list of 16 affect terms, the duration is typically between 1 and 2 hours.

DISCUSSION WITH THE CLIENT

1. Aim: The general aim of the discussion with the client is to arrive at an overview of the data of the self-investigation in such a way that the relationship among the valuations is made explicit and a transition to the validation/invalidation process is prepared and facilitated.

2. Preparation: The discussion is prepared by the psychologist, who has studied the results of the self-investigation as an organized data base. This preparation, however, should not develop into simply a report of the data. The psychologist's role is to get the client to interact with the information from the first investigation in such a way that the client can develop (through the validation/invalidation process) the valuations of the second investigation. Therefore, the client must affirm that the psychologist's evaluation of the data from the first investigation is on the mark; the psychologist needs to be open to, and must elicit, changes the client wishes to make in the results of the first investigation. A central element in the preparation of the discussion is the selection of some valuations as starting points for modality analyses. When the psychologist is well prepared, he or she is able to give reasons to the client for selecting a particular valuation as a pivot. When the client has a preference for another valuation as pivot, both analyses should be performed. In this way both client and psychologist contribute to the process. More generally, well-founded selections can be made on the basis of the direction the discussion with the client takes. The notion of "open knowledge" implies that this direction is never fixed in advance.

Computer programs compute a total intercorrelation matrix such that any of the valuations can be chosen as a pivot. It may be advisable to choose not only a negative (unpleasant) pivot but also a positive (pleasant) one in order to balance out the discussion with positive and negative experiences.

3. Sitting side by side: As in the valuation construction phase, psychologist and client sit at a table side by side, or at right angles to each other (i.e., never facing each other), their positions symbolizing a cooperative working relationship.

4. Starting the discussion: The best way to start the discussion is to invite clients to tell how they experienced the self-investigation and what they thought, felt, or did as a reaction to it. Their response often gives useful information about the way they have digested the investigation to this point. Does the client remember significant aspects of the investigation? Has the client started to relate the valuations formulated in the investigation to the events of daily life? Are there any indications that the client has begun a process of attending to his or her own experiences and if so, does the client do this differently than before? Such questions are important to pose because they give the psychologist relevant information about a period (between investigation and discussion) in which the validation/invalidation process may have received its first impetus. Dissociations may become apparent. Has the client "forgotten" significant parts of the self-investigation or perhaps the total valuation system formulated the week before? In this context a simple but revealing question may be "What strikes you most when you think about your self-investigation?" The following points (5–12) are the likeliest and most preferable steps the discussion might take.

5. **Learning the indices:** An instructive way to continue the discussion is to ask the client to indicate those affects on the list of affect terms that seem to express S, O, P, and N (after the psychologist has briefly explained the nature of these concepts in the context of the investigation as a whole). In this way clients are challenged to become actively involved in the discussion. Moreover, they learn in a playful way the nature of the indices and the included affect terms, on which further discussion will be based.

6. **Valuations with extreme positions on indices:** The affective indices serve as criteria for the selection of valuations that have extreme positions on these indices. That is, the valuation with the highest score for S is compared with the valuation lowest in S. Similarly, the valuations that are highest and lowest on each of the other indices are compared. In this way clients are made familiar with the opposites in their valuation system. Moreover, this information may be highly relevant to clients, particularly when the results contradict their expectations. Note that there are some clients for whom simply nothing is unexpected, striking, or new. They seem to know everything, *after* the psychologist has presented them with the findings. A simple but effective procedure is to ask clients to estimate specific results *before* the psychologist shows the data. Mostly, their estimations are wrong. In this way clients may become aware that there is something to learn.

7. **General and ideal feeling:** The affective patterning of the general feeling and the ideal feeling and their comparison may be discussed. For example, psychologist and client may discuss the extent to which the S index is lower for the general feeling than for the ideal feeling? Similar questions can be posed for the other indices. A special case in point is the ideal feeling. Usually, S, O, and P have very high levels on the ideal feeling whereas N has a very low level. There are, however, significant exceptions. Some people give pride or some other S affect a low score on the ideal feeling because they associate these feelings with selfishness or recklessness. Similarly, some clients score a feeling of love at a low level on the ideal feeling. When asked to tell more about this, they may explain that they have closed themselves off from this feeling as a protection against disappointments. Such a finding emerging from the discussion is a relevant piece of information that is kept with the intention of including it in the revised valuation system at Time 2.

8. **Generalization, idealization, affective correspondence:** The extent of generalization and idealization of the different valuations is also discussed. The valuations with the highest and lowest position on these indices are most

relevant. The psychologist may ask clients to explain why they think a particular valuation is so high in generalization. Clients may be stimulated to make short notes about the findings they find significant.

Because generalization, idealization, and affective correspondence between the affective modalities of valuations are expressed in correlations, some explanation of this index to the client is required. Of course, it is not the intention to fatigue the client with technical explanations, but the notion of correlation—that is, "the similarity between two profiles of scores"—is easily explained. A suitable metaphor is the chord. Each valuation is associated with a musical chord representing an affective profile. When two valuations have a high correlation, their affective chords are similar. The positive or negative quality of a valuation, moreover, corresponds with major and minor scales. The advantage of a musical metaphor is that it is closer to clients' experience than the technical term *correlation.*

9. **Affects with highest and lowest means:** The affects with the highest and lowest column means can also be presented. This information typically gives some overview because the column means are calculated across *all* valuations. Here also one can ask clients in advance which affect they think is most typical and which least typical of their valuation system as a whole.

10. **Interpretation by the client:** After this general information, the discussion should focus on one or more valuations that are selected for modality analyses. In accordance with the description of this procedure in Chapter 3, the client is invited to interpret the highest correlation. If necessary, client and psychologist may return to the raw scores. The client can then see how fluctuations of affect within one valuation go together with fluctuations in any other valuation. (Returning to the raw ratings has also the advantage that clients see that the correlations are based on the ratings they themselves have filled in.)

11. **Selection of a valuation for modality analysis:** It is very difficult to formulate criteria for selection of a valuation for a modality analysis. The selection of a particular valuation as the starting point for a modality analysis is based on an enormous amount of information. The complexity of this task is evident: There are many valuations, each with its specific formulations, each associated with a multitude of affects. Moreover, the fact that these elements all hang together as parts of an organized and multifaceted system, whose nature may be further elucidated by remarks from the client, means that the psychologist is confronted with a most difficult task.

Nevertheless, it is possible to give some crude guidelines that may be helpful in this selection. Most clients come with a problem that has motivated them to seek the assistance of a therapist or counselor. This problem is addressed in the valuation construction phase, and the resulting valuation may be selected as a pivot in a modality analysis. Note, however, that clients sometimes present a superficial problem as their reason for coming to a psychologist; this may be reason enough *not* to take this valuation as pivot. Another possibility is to take as pivot the valuation with the highest level of negative affect, because there must be a reason for so much affect. The valuation with the highest degree of generalization is another criterion for selection. Since this valuation has such an important influence on the client's well-being, its broader affective context is worth exploring.

12. **Importance of summary:** When clients have formulated a summary of their modality analysis (see Chapter 3), it is recommended that they give special attention to this formulation in their daily lives. Some clients give it shape as an artistically written piece, and others hang it above their bed. Apart from encouraging clients to give the summary special emphasis as a powerful impetus to the validation/invalidation process, it is recommended that the psychologist provide clients with some kind of client manual that contains relevant information and an overview of the results. This manual should at least include (1) an explanation of the basic motives and the indices, (2) a diagram of the types of valuations (e.g., the circle in Figure 4.1), (3) an overview of the results of the analysis (e.g., by marking in the circle which types of valuations are frequent in the client's system and which are not).

13. **Contrasting valuations:** The case study reported in Chapter 3 is an example of a modality analysis that was based on positive correlations only. A more extensive analysis can be realized when negative correlations are also taken into account. Contrasting experiences are then included in the interpretation. When, for example, some valuations have a commonality centering around −LL experiences, the contrasting valuations refer to +HH experiences. In a similar way, polar opposites on other axes in Figure 4.1 may characterize a person's valuation system. Generally, a modality analysis working with opposite experiences stimulates the person's capacity for integration.

14. **Synthesizing valuations:** A special technique for stimulating the integration of opposite experiences is to provide a client with two opposite valuations (i.e., showing a minus correlation with one another) and invite him or her to formulate a third valuation in which the two original ones are synthesized. This technique is extensively discussed in the context of Jungian psychology (see Hermans, 1993).

15. **Content of valuations:** Note that a modality analysis, and correlations in general, are not the only way of exploring relationships in the client's valuation system. There may be relationships between valuations, including similarities and contrasts, in the *content* of the formulations that are not expressed in the correlations (correlations are computed among affective modalities).

16. **Time needed:** A profound discussion with the client takes approximately 2 hours. When there are many subjects to explore or additional modality analyses have been performed, more than one session is devoted to the discussion. In fact, there should be a smooth transition between the discussion and the following validation/invalidation process.

THE VALIDATION/INVALIDATION PROCESS

1. Plans and goals: A gradual transition between the discussion and the validation/invalidation process can be realized by taking the summary resulting from the modality analysis as a starting point. This summary leads to the formulation of additional, more specific, plans and goals to guide the validation/invalidation process. In the following sessions the client's experiences with these plans and goals are discussed, specified, corrected, changed, and evaluated.

2. Attending, creating, anchoring: When we speak of plans and goals, these terms should be understood in a broad sense. They refer to a variety of actions that play a constructive role in the three phases of the validation/invalidation process: attending, creating, and anchoring (ACA cycle). In the attending phase, for example, clients may be focused on perceiving exceptions to a basic but generalized insight formulated in the summary. In the creating phase, clients may formulate specific plans to realize small but meaningful changes in their own behavior in order to contribute to the generalization of these exceptions. In the anchoring phase, clients may concentrate on various actions that function to generalize the new behaviors in a variety of situations.

3. Diary: The sensitivity of attending can be stimulated by having the client make daily notes (of specific details, for example, when, where, with whom?) in a diary or logbook. These notes can then be discussed with the psychologist at the next session. Clients may be invited not only to describe the events of their daily lives but also to relate these events to the summary and the valuations with their associate affects.

4. Learning to apply S and O concepts: The learning process can be stimulated by applying the already familiar affect terms in the attending, creating, and anchoring phases. Clients attend to the affect that is associated with their own behavior and with their responses to the behaviors of others. They learn to ask—and answer—such questions as the following: "In which situations do I experience feelings of self-esteem and in which situations not?" "What kind of actions are taking place, on my side and on the side of others?" "In which situations am I able to make a movement from S affect to O affect, and what kind of behavior takes place?" "What is the significance of this movement for me?" "When the situation becomes difficult and causes feelings of hopelessness and isolation, what do I do to cope with this situation?" In this way clients train themselves to understand and organize their daily experiences from an affective and motivational point of view. Moreover, this practice stimulates the ACA cycle.

5. Evaluation of change: Part of the validation/invalidation process is to evaluate this process in such a way that the meaning of changes or the meaning of their absence becomes evident. After some weeks or months the client is instructed to focus on (1) the validation/invalidation process itself and to formulate some valuations that refer to significant aspects of the learning process or (2) aspects that have functioned as obstacles in this process.

6. Formulating significant learning experiences: Significant learning experiences or obstacles hindering such experiences are formulated as a limited set of valuations, which are then rated with the standard list of affect terms. First of all, the content of such valuations deserve attention. Is the content a repetition, perhaps in different words, of certain valuations already formulated in the original self-investigation, or does it refer to new experiences or behavior? When the valuations include new elements, do these changes originate with the client or with someone or something in the situation that is beyond the control of the client? Is the valuation expressed in dynamic terms, suggesting meaningful change (e.g., "I am beginning to feel . . .") or in static terms ("I can't . . .")? Second, the affective indices give information about the direction of the change from the perspective of the basic motives: Is the valuation associated with a certain degree of S affect? Does this S affect coexist with P affect (type +S)? When the valuation represents type −LL, what are the obstacles? When and where do they occur? When the valuation is of type −S, is this a sign of aggressive feelings? If so, how can this aggression be expressed in such a way that it does not become destructive? When the general and ideal feeling are included in this investigation, additional questions may be posed: When the change is going in a positive direction, does it have a generalizing influence? Is the discrepancy between general and ideal feeling still as large as it was in the original self-investigation, or is it smaller? All these questions may be posed as a result of a limited evaluation. The results may give the validation/invalidation process a corrective impulse, or they may convince psychologist and client that they are on the right track.

7. Relationship between new and old valuations: A very specific way to evaluate is to correlate the new valuations (resulting from the validation/ invalidation process) with all valuations of the original self-investigation. Suppose the new valuation correlates highly (e.g., .88) with, say, Valuation 12 of the original investigation. This means that the new valuation is associated with a modality, an "affective track," that was originally present. It is, of course, interesting to consider the content of this valuation that functions as an affective precursor to succeeding valuations. Has it a dynamic or static content? What affective type does it represent? When the evaluation consists of more than one valuation, do the other valuations also use the same affective track? If so, then the change process apparently selects a specific affective track, which suggests the existence of a latent route for a variety of manifest changes. In this case, it is too simplistic to conclude that the old is continued in the new. Rather, there is a reorganization of the valuation system as a whole. The old track is made deeper and filled with new material (valuations); that is, it becomes more generalizable.

8. Difference between counseling and psychotherapy: Counseling and psychotherapy differ in the speed and nature of the validation/invalidation process. In counseling, the process takes a clear direction more quickly. Generally, the following differences exist: (1) In counseling there is an easier transition from attending to creating. (2) In psychotherapy there is often an emphasis on valuations of type −LL, so that the movement toward +S and +HH types takes a large part of the invalidation process. (3) In counseling settings there is a higher probability of finding valuation systems with a greater variety of valuation types; this means that types +S and +HH, so typical of a successful validation/invalidation process, are more within the client's reach. (4) In counseling settings one may develop more than one valuation referring to purposes and goals, meaning that the client can work on these simultaneously, whereas in psychotherapy simultaneous working on several goals would easily disturb the client's concentration on the first attempts on the ladder of increasing difficulty (see Chapter 3).

9. New actions rooted in previous valuations: In the self-confrontation method the validation/invalidation process is neither simply practicing new behavior nor developing new insights. Rather, it is a self-instigated action device in which each new behavior is rooted in a previously formulated valuation that resounds at every step the client makes during the change process. The previously formulated system gives a broad background that feeds the change process with meaning and direction. On the other hand, the initiatives the client takes in the validation/invalidation process may modify parts of the original system or may even lead to its reorganization as a whole.

10. Method is open and structured: The psychologist is challenged to address elements of assessment, change, and evaluation during the valuation process as a whole. The self-confrontation method is a procedure that is both systematic and open. It is the open character that invites psychologists (and other professionals) to adapt the method to the individual client.

11. Time needed: It is difficult to give a time estimate for the validation/invalidation process because it differs not only for different clients but also for different settings and purposes (e.g., psychotherapy or counseling). In fact, the time needed for a significant change of the valuation system varies from a few weeks to several years—a few weeks for clients who are able to work quite independently and who need only one self-investigation to make significant alterations in their situation but several years for clients with a dysfunctional valuation system (e.g., a depression of type −LL).

THE SECOND SELF-INVESTIGATION

1. Evaluation of validation/invalidation process: While evaluations are of a limited kind during the validation/invalidation process (see Chapter 3), they are more extensive in the second self-investigation. Whereas the shorter evaluations may be spread out over the course of the validation/invalidation process, the second full self-investigation typically takes place after several months or half a year, when psychologist and client have the feeling that relevant parts of the valuation system have been changed since the first self-investigation.

2. **Familiarity with the procedure:** The construction of valuations often goes faster in the second than in the first self-investigation because the client is familiar with the method and the psychologist's way of working.

3. **New set of valuations:** Part of the procedure is to confront the client with the valuations constructed at Time 1. Some clients, however, feel they are fixed to their old valuations and do not feel free enough to modify them or to construct new ones. In that case, it is better not to show the valuations from Time 1 but to read the questions (Table 3.2) as if they were being read for the first time. The new set of valuations are compared with those from the first self-investigation so that it can be determined which valuation from Time 1 has developed into which valuation from Time 2. This comparison may also be used to supplement the second investigation with valuations from the first one.

4. **Including changes and obstacles:** The valuations referring to the changes and felt obstacles in the validation/invalidation process are also included in the second self-investigation. They may be included as modifications or supplementations of the valuations at Time 1.

5. **Types of change:** To study the change process in detail, it is recommended that the changes be labeled according to the classification presented in Chapter 3 (modification, substitution, elimination, and supplementation).

6. **Number of valuations:** The second investigaton may include more or fewer valuations than the first investigation. There are fewer valuations when the client becomes aware of the fact that several valuations are related or represent a common factor and, as a result, prefers to formulate broader units of meaning that cover a large number of events. This is typical of the client who is especially motivated to focus on the central elements of the valuation system.

7. **Comparing two systems:** When the findings of the first and second self-investigations are compared, clients are often surprised that more has been changed than they expected. When two investigations from different moments in time are juxtaposed so that the two pictures can be considered simultaneously, they often exhibit unexpected and conspicuous differences. This is similar to the feeling of discontinuity and shock that is evoked when one is confronted by two photographs of a person that were taken at two widely separated points in time (Hermans & Kempen, 1993).

8. **Self-investigation as process, not product:** Knowledge of the changes that mark the period between Time 1 and Time 2 is certainly not available

before starting the second self-investigation. Rather, the construction of the valuations themselves makes the client conscious of what has happened. In other words, a self-investigation is not a product but a process.

GUIDELINES FOR THE LEARNING PSYCHOLOGIST

   1. Required skills: It is essential that any psychologist or professional who wants to apply the self-confrontation method for psychotherapeutic or counseling purposes be able to do the following: (1) open himself or herself to the story and experiences of others; (2) listen actively in silence; (3) remain faithful to the client's words and intentions when paraphrasing; (4) seek clarification when the client's meaning is insufficiently understood; (5) draw the client's attention, in the discussion phase, to insights and relationships that he or she does not see and check the relevance of this by asking the client; (6) avoid abstract statements and ask for specifics in time and space; (7) give interpretations if they contribute to the client's own interpretations; (8) inform the client of findings resulting from the investigation and of aspects of the self-confrontation procedure; and (9) advise when the client needs advice and is ready to use it. Note that these skills on the part of the psychologist represent a scale (Figure 9.1) ranging from responsive behavior (e.g., opening and listening) to initiating behavior (e.g., informing and advising). Different phases in the self-confrontation procedure require emphasis on different skills. In the valuation construction phase, for example, opening and listening are most important whereas in the discussion with the client informing (e.g., giving results) and advising (e.g., on possibilities for invalidation of particular valuations) are the necessary skills. Note that we are referring here to a relative emphasis; in reality, all skills are required in all phases.

   2. Pitfalls: Every psychologist or professional who is assisting a person in performing a self-investigation, should be aware that there are a number of pitfalls that often mark the beginning of a learning process. The main pitfalls in the self-confrontation method are the following. Psychologists may (1) allow

Opening	Listening	Para-phrasing	Clarifying	Drawing attention	Specifying	Inter-preting	Informing	Advising

FIGURE 9.1. The range of skills required by professionals who use the self-confrontation method for psychotherapeutic or counseling purposes.

their own valuations to interfere with the client's valuations (in the sense that they may, for example, be afraid to touch a delicate subject or may give a subject inappropriate attention); (2) be tempted to offer solutions (i.e., may feel they know the solution to the client's problem and should therefore give the "right advice"; (3) feel uneasy and restless (often owing to feelings of uncertainty or to the implicit demands they put on themselves that cannot be fulfilled); (4) have lapses in attention (often resulting from overconcentration or a faulty economy of energy); (5) attach labels to their clients (diagnostic labels, in particular, may distract their concentration from the story a particular client has to tell); (6) hesitate to continue questioning (e.g., may be afraid of intruding on the client's privacy); (7) may prematurely formulate a valuation (before the client has an opportunity to explore his or her experience in depth; (8) leave the client alone (i.e., may neglect the significance of the dialogical nature of the valuation construction phase); (9) neglect relevant information (psychologists should make notes so that they can remember and combine the client's utterings); (10) make interpretations in the formulation phase (interpretations should be postponed because they may constrain the psychologist's perspective and openness prematurely and, moreover, may distract the client from self-reflection; (11) make normative statements (normative expressions may block the client's openness and bend the process in a particular direction); (12) accept superficiality (psychologists should listen and attend carefully and ask for the personal meaning when the client gives a short and superficial reaction); (13) accept impersonal statements (psychologists should ask the client for I-formulations unless they feel the client is unable to give these); (14) lose patience and attempt to stop a client who becomes long-winded or is getting sidetracked); (15) feel unable to stop the client's verbalizations (this can be avoided if psychologists tell their clients *in advance* that they will stop them when they consider it necessary for the process); (16) attempt to make amusing conversation with the client (there is no objection to a lighthearted moment or to occasional laughter, but these should not encourage a flight from deep self-reflection).

3. **Psychologist's self-investigation:** Before using the self-confrontation method for counseling or psychotherapeutic purposes, it is required that the psychologist perform a full self-investigation on himself or herself with the assistance of a supervisor who is experienced in the application of the method and familiar with its underlying theory. It is recommended that specific pitfalls (i.e., those relevant to the trainee) be part of this self-investigation and that they be included in the validation/invalidation process.

4. **Psychologist's learning process:** Training is based on the notion that science and practice interact to their mutual benefit (Hoshmand & Polkinghorne, 1992). It proceeds in two phases. First, trainees study valuation theory and learn how to apply the method, first on themselves and then on others. Second, this initial training is followed by continued self-training during which

psychologists expand their experiences and skills and consolidate their learning process. In fact, psychologists-in-training run through a professional ACA cycle themselves as they (1) attend to their own experience and behavior in assisting clients with the self-confrontation method, (2) learn new behaviors so that they can work with the method in a creative way, and (3) anchor these learning experiences through continued self-training.

5. Psychologist's own valuations: In the initial training phase particular attention is paid to the relationship between the psychologist's own valuations and the client's valuations. The phenomenon called "countertransference" in psychoanalytic circles can be investigated by exploring how the psychologist's own valuations facilitate or interfere with the client's valuation process during all phases of the self-confrontation procedure, an exploration that proceeds in the following sequence: (1) Trainees perform a full self-investigation on themselves with the assistance of an experienced supervisor. (2) As a form of practice, they assist another trainee who performs a self-investigation on himself or herself. (3) The interaction between helper and client is observed by a trainer (videotaping may be useful). (4) The trainer gives feedback to the trainee with respect to the aforementioned pitfalls. (5) The trainee makes notes about these observations and expresses their meaning in a limited number of valuations (an example of a valuation referring to interference might be "I tend to break the silence in a conversation in order to avoid confronting my own feelings" while an example of a facilitating valuation might be "A certain distancing helps me keep my objectivity without losing my sensitivity." (6) These valuations may be added to the trainee's first self-investigation (or in a second self-investigation) so that the correspondence with the other valuations (including those referring to significant others in the past) may be explored and discussed with a supervisor.

6. Prejudices against the self-confrontation method: Any training should address the main prejudices against the self-confrontation method, namely, the notions that this method is only for people who are capable of self-reflection and have a high intellectual level, is very time-consuming, and is quantitative and technical. The first objection seems to see people from a static trait perspective, rather than from a dynamic perspective. In fact, the method is a learning experience for many people; they *become* more explicit about their lives, differentiate and deepen their affect, and change their behavior. A relevant observation here is that an adapted version of the self-confrontation method has long been used with groups of adolescent delinquents (at various levels of intelligence) who are preparing themselves for release (Janssen, Van der Molen, & Van Steen, 1980; Van Assen, 1985). On the other hand, people who are overly self-reflective may learn to transform their reflections into actions (validation/invalidation). The second objection seems to implicitly compare the method with a standardized test or with a common session in psychotherapy or counseling. Note that one profound self-investigation may have more implications for a person's insight and behavior than a long series of short therapeutic conversations. Moreover, a specific feature of this method is that it allows an overview of experiences and their mutual relationships, which simply cannot be achieved in a series of sessions dispersed over time. The third objection equates the method with quantitative analysis only and does not recognize that the quantitative profiles are only a means for arriving at underlying affective commonalities and contrasts.

ADAPTATIONS AND EXTENSIONS OF THE SELF-CONFRONTATION METHOD

1. **General rule:** The self-confrontation method allows a variety of adaptations, depending on purpose, setting, and client population. The general rule is that adaptations should be in accordance with the basic metaphor, the theoretical underpinnings, and the spirit of the method.

2. **Career counseling:** A special adaptation of the self-confrontation method for career counseling was developed by Van de Loo (1992). Factor analysis of affect terms in a group of 169 applicants (143 men and 26 women) for a variety of jobs resulted in three groups of affect terms that were labeled self-enhancement (S), contact and union with the other (O), and stress. Factor S included "self-esteem," "self-confidence," "meaningfulness," and "self-expansion." Factor O included "sympathy," "union," "togetherness," and "affection." Factor stress included "nervousness," "tension," "restlessness," and "hurried." Coefficients alpha for the S, O, and stress indices were .60, .77, and .80, respectively. The product–moment correlation between S and O was .36, between S and stress −.17, and between O and stress −.05. Adding stress to the affect terms opens extra possibilities for affective analysis. Does a high level of S coexist with a high level of stress or with a low level of stress? Is S more sensitive for stress than O, or is the picture reversed? Note that for some people stress is not a negative experience. This makes stress different from index N. For a person who cannot cope with stress, a high positive correlation (computed across all valuations within the valuation system) between stress and N is expected. However, for people who are used to stress or even find it stimulating, the correlation between stress and N is low or even negative.

3. **Types of behavior:** The self-confrontation can be expanded by also taking behavior into account. The basic idea is that self-narratives tell about the actions of actors and valuations imply action tendencies (Hermans, 1981). From this point of view, Van de Loo (1992) examined sets of behaviors and factor analyzed the data from the group of applicants mentioned in the preceding paragraph. This resulted in three factors S, O, and stress, the same factors that had already been found in the analysis of affect terms. The items of factor S (behavior) were "taking initiatives," "taking the lead," "achieving," and

"creating something new." The items of factor O were "helping," "expressing understanding," "taking the trouble for somebody," and "presenting myself as team-oriented." The stress items were "hurrying," "rushing," "being busy," and "working myself into a lather." Coefficients alpha of S, O, and stress were .71, .72, and .78, respectively. The product–moment correlation between S and O was .42, between S and stress .18, and between O and stress .20. The symmetrical factorial structure of affect and behavior in Van de Loo's study permits comparisons between affective and behavioral aspects of valuations and thus gives extra information on the valuation system as a whole. The following questions are relevant: Is S affect expressed in S behavior? Can people exhibit O behavior they do not feel? Is a discrepancy of this type true for some valuations or for most valuations of the system? Can stress be high in the affective realm but not expressed in behavior? These and other questions referring to the symmetry or asymmetry between affect and behavior point to the relevance of the organization of the valuation system. The inclusion of indices of general behavior and ideal behavior as counterparts of the general feeling and ideal feeling indices suggests the possibility of computing not only correlations among affective profiles but also among profiles of behavior. Note that extra questions may be posed that are relevant from a counseling point of view. For example, for career counseling it may be informative to include the general feeling about one's career and the general behavior about one's career; these general profiles can then be correlated with specific valuations so that highly generalizing valuations can be identified that may be relevant to a person's career decisions.

4. **Adaptation of questions:** The sets of questions may also be adapted. Taking the specific demands of career counseling into account, Van de Loo (1992) used questions referring to past, present, and future but adapted them so that they referred specifically to career experiences (e.g., "Which experiences in your work or study do you remember that have made a special impression on you?" or "Which plans or perspectives do you have with reference to your career in the long run?"). Moreover, Van de Loo supplemented these questions with questions that probed career applicants' view of their capacities, their present work situation, and their nonwork activities.

5. **Young people:** Special applications of the self-confrontation method are required for children. Studying the valuation of fear of failure of 13-to-15-year-old children in school, Poulie (1991) used the following affect terms for S: "strong," "self-confident," "certain of myself," and "I can manage." For O were terms such as "feeling accepted," "sympathy," "feeling open," and "feeling a bond"; for P were "glad," "happy," "at ease," and "enjoy"; and for N were "powerless," "worry," "inferior," and "disappointed." Coefficients alpha, calculated separately for each pupil in a group of 22, were all between .70 and .99, with two exceptions that were lower than .70. The correlation between S and O, calculated across 22 pupils on the basis of the general feeling, was .58 for the first self-investigation and .48 for the second self-investigation; the corre-

lation between P and N was −.53 for the first and −.08 for the second self-investigation. Poulie also adapted the sets of questions in order to explore the negative and positive aspects of pupils' fear of failure in several school situations.

6. Consultant and consultee: Meijer (1991) combined an adapted version of the self-confrontation method with Caplan's (1964) consultation method. Consultation in Caplan's view is a temporary cooperation between a consultant (a specialist helper) and a consultee, a key person to clients (e.g., a teacher working with a class of pupils), with the aim of optimizing consultee functioning toward a particular client. In this version a self-investigation was not performed by the troublesome pupil but by a teacher who had serious problems with the pupil in the classroom. The consultant assisted the consultee in performing a self-investigation, with the troublesome pupil being introduced as a valuation in the consultee's system.

7. Types of power: When the self-confrontation method is used to explore the relationship between two or more people (e.g., counseling or therapy for partner relationships), it may be revealing to distinguish three forms of power: direct, indirect, and passive power (Hermans, 1981). The items used for direct power were "threatening," "using violence," "forcing," and "ridiculing"; for indirect power "misleading," "keeping on a string," "abusing," and "betraying"; and for passive power "neglecting," "ignoring," "dropping," and "letting down." The point in making these distinctions is to counteract the naive supposition that equates power with direct power only. In fact, people use other forms of power (indirect and passive) with great frequency and in a great variety of situations. For example, if a person's requests are systematically ignored or neglected, he or she may then react with direct power. In that case the ignored or neglected person is accused of using power although the ignoring or neglecting person is not. People who use ignoring or neglecting strategies are often not aware that they too are using power and that they themselves are involved in an interactional process from the beginning. By exploring valuations in terms of the three types of power, the power pattern for each separate valuation and for the system as a whole can be assessed. The same can be done for the system of a significant other so that two or more people involved in an interaction can compare themselves. Two procedures are to be distinguished: (1) All valuations can be rated with a list of behavioral terms concentrating on the relationship with a significant other that is implicitly or explicitly included in a valuation, with the formulation of the valuation serving as the immediate context for guiding the rating process. (2) A limited number of significant others or groups may be selected from the valuations and rated systematically from two directions (e.g., "how I behave toward the other" and "how the other behaves toward me"). Other interactions may be rated in a similar way. Moreover, two people involved in interaction in their daily lives may both complete the rating process so that they can examine their interactions on power patterns. When this is done, it is recommended that a set of positive behavioral terms be included in order to avoid a focusing on negative behavior only.

8. Self-directed behavior: Special use can be made of the rating of "self-directed behavior," that is, the way the person behaves toward himself or herself. When self-directed behavior is compared with behavior one uses toward others or receives from others, it may be found that a particular person directs more negative behavior toward himself or herself than toward any other person. In that case it is informative to investigate the power pattern of this self-directed behavior. Which of the three types of power has the highest mean score? Analysis of this behavioral pattern may stimulate the person's awareness that he or she is, for example, neglecting, misleading, or deliberately ridiculing himself or herself. Moreover, correlations between self-directed behavior and behavior in relation to others show which interactions have the highest similarity with self-directed behavior. For example, the client may be led to ask, "Is my self-directed behavior similar to the behavior of my father toward me, or does it bear greater similarity to the behavior I use with my children?" The supposition underlying these analyses is that people who use a particular pattern of behavior with others can use the same pattern with themselves.

9. Dyads and small groups: Application of the self-confrontation method in dyads or groups (e.g., in marital therapy or management development) is possible by having members exchange valuations (and their associated affective and/or behavioral patterns) that have been previously assessed. A special extension of the method is when exchanges are followed by a commonly subscribed valuation; that is, the several members of a dyad or group formulate, as a result of these exchanges, a valuation that is felt as common to the dyad or group. Ideally, each of the members of the dyad or group contributes to the common valuation so that each recognizes himself or herself in the end result. Verstraeten (1978, 1983) used common valuations in the context of psychotherapeutic assistance of couples, and Hermans (1981) experimented with teams of psychotherapists in order to explore the nature of team valuations. Note that the construction of common valuations is difficult and time-consuming in all those dyads or groups in which individuals have divergent views on significant topics. The problem of individual differences may be tackled by combining individual valuations and common valuations so that people involved in the construction of a common valuation have an outlet for their particular views in the individualized part of the investigation.

10. Specific topics: An individual self-investigation is usually performed in order to construct a valuation system as a whole (with the use of the questions presented in Chapter 3, which can be supplemented by the extended set of questions of Appendix 1). Another possibility is to perform a "specified self-investigation," that is, one directed at the investigation of a specific topic. Usually, a specific topic requires an adapted set of questions—and often also an adapted set of affective or behavioral terms. The investigation may focus on such divergent topics as the significance of religious symbols (Van Loon, 1992), the content and organization of one's career perspective (Van de Loo, 1992), the experiences of young people involved in pedophiliac relationships (Sandfort, 1984), and fear of failure in children at school (Poulie, 1991).

11. **Content analysis:** Qualitative analysis can profit from content analysis, or the rating of valuations by external judges from the perspective of pre-formulated content categories. For example, Bonke (1984) chose the categories "supporting versus adapting" and "protecting versus exposing" in his research on interactions between parents and children. With these general categories Bonke could observe particular phenomena across specific valuations within a particular system and across the systems of different individuals. Similarly, in his research on those who practice transcendental meditation, Gelderloos (1987) applied such categories as "unifying," "autonomy," and "spirituality" in order to investigate the changes in their valuation system over the course of time. Interrater reliability coefficients (coefficient alpha) of raters (three to five) in these types of studies are typically between .70 and .85.

12. **Proportion indices:** Additional *quantitative* indices can be developed to further the purpose of an investigation. Proportion indices may be used, for example, the proportion of positive affect in the total of positive plus negative affect. This index may be calculated for each of the valuations separately, as well as for the general and ideal feeling. Three classes of well-being can be distinguished: low well-being (< 40%), ambivalent well-being (40–60%), and high well-being (> 60%). In a similar way, a proportion index can be constructed for the relationship between S and P. Such proportion indices are particularly useful for a quick overview of data in an individual case and for comparison of groups of subjects in research.

Extended Set of Questions

Sometimes the three basic sets of questions of the Self-Confrontation Method (concerning the past, present, and future; see Table 3.2) result in an insufficient number of usable valuations. The following are extra questions that can be used to extend the total number of valuations. These should be especially useful for inexperienced practitioners. And it should be noted that these questions can be modified as the situation warrants (see item 14 of Formulation of the Valuations in the Manual).

Activity
What is the main activity (work, study, or else) in which you are engaged? Please, describe the situation that is most relevant to you.

What is normally your main occupation? Could you describe the situation in which this occupation is most relevant to you?

Enjoyment
What is the main thing in your life from which you derive great enjoyment. When and where do you experience this enjoyment?

What more than anything else causes you moments of great enjoyment? When and where does this happen?

Thinking
Is there something which you think about a great deal? Could you specify the situation that you have in mind?

Is there something which frequently exercises your mind? At which moments and in what situations?

Person: antagonistic
Which person particularly arouses antagonistic feelings in you? When and where does this happen?

Which person in your life are you particularly at odds with? When and where?

Group: antagonistic
What group of people or what type of people particularly arouses antagonistic feelings in you? Could you specify the situation in which this takes place?

What group of people or what type of people do you feel particularly compelled to defy? When and where does this happen?

Person: unity
With which person in your life do you identify most easily? When and where does this typically happen?

Is there someone who is important in your life and to whom you feel closely allied? In which situation do you have this feeling?

Group: unity
With which group of people or what kind of people do you particularly feel at one with? When and where?

Is there a group of people or a type of people that is important to your life and to whom you feel closely allied? In which situation?

Society
Is there an aspect of society which is of importance or influential for you? Can you describe the situation that you have particularly in mind?

What do you think of your position in society? Please, describe your situation in society.

Extended List of Affect Terms

For clinical, counseling, and therapeutic work, we recommend the use of an extended list of affect terms. In comparison with the list of 16 affect terms (see Table 3.3) used throughout the book, the extended list provides a more differentiated picture in the positive (P) and negative (N) domain. Moreover, it allows clients to express a broader range of affect in relation to their valuation. Here is a key to the letters in parentheses: S, affect reflects self-enhancement; O, affect reflects desire for contact with others; P, positive affect; N, negative affect. The S and O affect terms are the same as those in Table 3.3, but the P and N terms are different (see item 3 of Affective Exploration and Analysis in the Manual).

1. Joy (P)
2. Powerlessness (N)
3. Self-Esteem (S)
4. Anxiety (N)
5. Satisfaction (P)
6. Strength (S)
7. Shame (N)
8. Enjoyment (P)
9. Care (O)
10. Love (O)
11. Self-Alienation (N)
12. Tenderness (O)
13. Guilt (N)
14. Self-Confidence (S)
15. Loneliness (N)
16. Trust (P)
17. Inferiority (N)
18. Intimacy (O)
19. Safety (P)
20. Anger (N)
21. Pride (S)
22. Energy (P)
23. Inner calm (P)
24. Freedom (P)

Information for Those Interested in Learning This Method

Foundation and Aim

In 1992 the Valuation Theory and the Self-Confrontation Method (SCM) Foundation was established in The Netherlands with the aim of preserving and extending the body of knowledge associated with this theory and method. The foundation does this by developing training programs for psychologists and other social scientists interested in becoming qualified users of the valuation approach at all levels: theory, method, and practice. An approach that explicitly integrates theory and practice, this method advocates a two-way cooperation between researchers and practitioners.

Training Program

The full training program consists of two parts: basic training and advanced training. The basic program is a series of sessions spread across a first year. Between the sessions participants study the relevant literature. In the sessions they learn the method by practicing it on themselves and on each other, in direct collaboration with specialized trainers. The advanced program continues with a series of sessions spread across a second year and permits a choice of three areas of specialization: mental health, personnel management, and education. In the intervals between these sessions, the participants continue to study the literature and apply the theory and method in settings of their own, receiving supervisory assistance from experienced and specialized trainers. Another option is for a participant to take the full training program in a limited number of intensive courses (e.g., two summer courses) with practical applications, supervision, and study of the literature in between.

Intensive Courses and Workshops

Training facilities and trainers for both curricula (basic and advanced) are available in The Netherlands. Intensive courses and workshops are sometimes also held in other countries. (Interested persons should contact the Foundation to find out where these will be taking place.) Workshops and training programs can be modified according to the needs of interested persons and organizations.

Certification

Upon successful completion of a full training program (long-term or intensive) participants are included on an international list of SCM consultants. This guarantees that the person has the requisite knowledge and skills in the application of valuation theory and the self-confrontation method.

Videotape and Computer Resources

A one-hour videotape of a psychologist working with a client is available to enable viewers to see the self-confrontation procedure in action. Computer programs are also available that enable quick and easy computation of the numerical values of the valuation survey.

Research Program

The Foundation cooperates with the research program Valuation and Motivation at the University of Nijmegen. This program, which was described as "excellent" in 1994 by the Review Committee on Psychology, part of the Association of Universities in The Netherlands, includes research projects on the theory and practice of the valuation approach, and the results of these studies have been published in a variety of internationally recognized scientific and professional journals. The research program has been a cooperative effort by researchers from several countries.

Addresses

Valuation Theory and Self-Confrontation Method Foundation, Hubert J. M. Hermans, Chairman, Bosweg 18, 6571 CD Berg en Dal, The Netherlands. e-mail HHermans @psych.kun.nl.
Hubert J. M. Hermans, Professor of Psychology and Director of the Valuation and Motivation research program, Psychological Laboratory, Montessorilaan 3, 6525 HR Nijmegen, The Netherlands. Fax: +31.80.615594.

References

Abraham, K. (1909). Dreams and myths. In H. C. Abraham (ed.), *Clinical papers and essays in psychoanalysis* (pp. 153–209). New York: Basic Books.

Abraham, K. (1942). *Selected papers on psychoanalysis*. London: Hogarth Press.

Adams-Webber, J. (1985). Self–other contrasts and the development of personal constructs. *Canadian Journal of Behavioral Science, 17,* 303–314.

Adler, A. (1922). *Über den nervösen Charakter* (3e Auflage). Munich, Germany: Bergmann.

Adorno, T. W., Frenkel-Brunswik, E., Levinson, D. J., & Sanford, R. N. (1950). *The authoritarian personality*. New York: Harper.

Ainsworth, M. D. S. (1973). The development of infant–mother attachment. In B. M. Caldwell & H. N. Ricciuti (eds.), *Review of child development research* (Vol. 3, pp. 1–94). Chicago: University of Chicago Press.

Ainsworth, M. D. S., Blehar, M. C., Waters, E., & Wall, S. (1978). *Patterns of attachment: A psychological study of the strange situation*. Hillsdale, NJ: Lawrence Erlbaum.

Allport, G. W. (1960). *Personality and social encounter*. Boston: Beacon Press.

Alschuler, C. F., & Alschuler, A. S. (1984). Developing healthy responses to anger: The counselor's role. *Journal of Counseling and Development, 63,* 26–29.

American Psychiatric Association. (1994). *Diagnostic and statistical manual of mental disorders* (4th ed.). Washington, DC: Author.

Angyal, A. (1965). *Neurosis and treatment: A holistic theory*. New York: Wiley.

Arend, R., Gove, F. L., & Sroufe, L. A. (1979). Continuity of individual adaptation from infancy to kindergarten: A predictive study of ego-resiliency and curiosity in preschoolers. *Child Development, 50,* 950–959.

Aries, E. J., & Olver, R. R. (1985). Sex differences in the development of a separate sense of self during infancy: Directions for future research. *Psychology of Women Quarterly, 9,* 515–532.

Averill, J. R. (1968). Grief: Its nature and significance. *Psychological Bulletin, 70,* 721–748.

Bakan, D. (1966). *The duality of human existence.* Chicago: Rand-McNally.

Bakhtin, M. (1973). *Problems of Dostoevsky's poetics* (2nd ed.; R. W. Rotsel, Trans.). Ann Arbor, MI: Ardis. (First edition published in 1929 under the title *Problemy tvorchestva Dostoevskogo* [Problems of Dostoevsky's art].)

Baltes, P. B. (1979). Life-span developmental psychology: Some converging observations on history and theory. In P. B. Baltes & O. G. Brim (eds.), *Life-span development and behavior* (Vol. 2, pp. 255–279). New York: Academic Press.

Baltes, P. B. (1987). Theoretical propositions of life-span developmental psychology: On the dynamics between growth and decline. *Developmental Psychology, 23,* 611–626.

Baltes, P. B., & Willis, S. L. (1978). Life-span developmental psychology, cognitive functioning, and social policy. In M. White Riley (ed.), *Aging from birth to death: Interdisciplinary perspectives* (pp. 15–46). Boulder, CO: Westview Press.

Barlow, D. H., Hayes, S. C., & Nelson, R. (1984). *The scientist practitioner: Research and accountability in clinical and educational settings.* New York: Pergamon Press.

Barnett, R. C., & Baruch, G. K. (1978). Women in the middle years: A critique of research and theory. *Psychology of Women Quarterly, 3,* 187–197.

Baruch, G., & Barnett, R. C. (1986). Role quality, multiple role development, and psychological well-being in midlife women. *Journal of Personality and Social Psychology, 51,* 578–585.

Beane, J. A., & Lipka, R. P. (1980). Self-concept and self-esteem: A construct differentiation. *Child Study Journal, 10,* 1–6.

Beck, A. T. (1967). *Depression: Clinical, experimental, and theoretical aspects.* New York: Harper.

Becker, E. (1971). *The birth and death of meaning: An interdisciplinary perspective on the problem of man.* New York: Free Press.

Becker, E. (1973). *The denial of death.* New York: Free Press.

Belar, C. D., & Perry, N. W. (1992). National conference on scientist-practitioner education and training for the professional practice of psychology. *American Psychologist, 47,* 71–75.

Benn, R. K. (1985). *Factors associated with security of attachment in dual career families.* Paper presented at the biennial meeting of the Society for Research in Child Development, Toronto.

Bergmann, M. S. (1984). The legend of Narcissus. *American Imago, 41,* 383–411.

Berndt, T. J. (1978, August). *Children's conceptions of friendship and the behavior expected of friends.* Paper presented at the annual meeting of the American Psychological Association, Toronto.

Berndt, T. J., & Hoyle, S. G. (1985). Stability and change in childhood and adolescent friendships. *Developmental Psychology, 21,* 1007–1015.

Bigelow, B. J. (1977). Children's friendship expectations: A cognitive developmental study. *Child Development, 48,* 246–250.

Binswanger, L. (1963). *Being-in-the-world: Selected papers of Ludwig Binswanger*. New York: Basic Books.

Blurton Jones, N. (1972). Categories of child–child interaction. In N. Blurton Jones (ed.), *Ethological studies of child behaviour* (pp. 97–127). Cambridge, UK: Cambridge University Press.

Bonke, P. (1984). *Opvoedingsproblemen als waarderingsconflicten* [Educational problems as valuation conflicts]. Lisse, The Netherlands: Swets & Zeitlinger.

Bowerman, W. R. (1978). Subjective competence: The structure, process, and function of self-referent causal attributions. *Journal for the Theory of Social Behavior, 8*, 45–57.

Bowlby, J. (1969). *Attachment and loss: Vol. I. Attachment*. New York: Basic Books.

Bowlby, J. (1980). *Attachment and loss: Vol. III. Sadness and depression*. New York: Basic Books.

Bowlby, J., & Parkes, C. M. (1970). Separation and loss within the family. In E. J. Anthony & C. Koupernik (eds.), *The child in his family* (Vol. 1, pp. 197–216). New York: Wiley.

Boyatzis, R. E. (1973). Affiliation motivation. In D. C. McClelland & R. S. Steele (eds.), *Human motivation* (pp. 252–276). Morristown, NJ: General Learning Press.

Breger, L. (1969). Children's dreams and personality development. In J. Fisher & L. Breger (eds.), *California Mental Health Research Symposium* (No. 3). Sacramento: California Department of Mental Hygiene.

Brim, O. G., Jr., & Ryff, C. D. (1980). On the properties of life events. In P. B. Baltes & O. G. Brim, Jr. (eds.), *Life-span development and behavior* (Vol. 3, pp. 367–388). New York: Academic Press.

Bronson, G. W. (1972). *Infants' reactions to unfamiliar persons and novel objects*. Chicago: University of Chicago Press.

Bronson, G. W. (1978). Aversive reactions to strangers: A dual process interpretation. *Child Development, 49*, 495–499.

Bruner, J. S. (1986). *Actual minds, possible worlds*. Cambridge, MA: Harvard University Press.

Buber, M. (1970). *I and Thou: A new translation with a prologue "I and You" and notes by Walter Kaufmann*. Edinburgh: T. & T. Clark.

Buehler, C. A., Hogan, M. J., & Robinson, B. E. (1985). The parental divorce transition: Divorce-related stressors and well-being. *Journal of Divorce, 9*, 61–81.

Bühler, C. (1935). The curve of life as studied in biographics. *Journal of Applied Psychology, 19*, 405–409.

Burgoon, J. K., & Jones, S. B. (1976). Toward a theory of personal space expectations and their violations. *Human Communication Research, 2*, 131–146.

Burns, R. B. (1979). *The self concept: In theory, measurement, development, and behaviour*. London: Longman.

Butler, R. N. (1975). *Why survive? Being old in America*. New York: Harper & Row.

Campbell, J. D. (1975). Illness is a point of view: The development of children's conceptions of illness. *Child Development, 46*, 92–100.

Caplan, G. (1964). *Principles of preventive psychiatry*. New York: Basic Books.

Caughey, J. L. (1984). *Imaginary social worlds: A cultural approach*. Lincoln: University of Nebraska Press.

Chomsky, N. (1968). *Language and the mind*. New York: Harcourt, Brace & World.

Clarke-Stewart, A., Perlmutter, M., & Friedman, S. (1988). *Lifelong human development*. New York: Wiley.

Clausen, J. A. (1972). The life course of individuals. In M. Riley, M. Johnson, & A. Foner (eds.), *Aging and society: A sociology of the age stratification* (Vol. 3, pp. 457–514). New York: Russell Sage.

Clausen, J. A. (1981). Men's occupational careers in the middle years. In D. H. Eichorn, J. A. Clausen, N. Haan, M. P. Honzik, & P. Mussen (eds.), *Present and past in middle life* (pp. 321–351). New York: Academic Press.

Cohler, B. J. (1982). Personal narrative and life course. In P. B. Baltes & O. G. Brim (eds.), *Life-span development and behavior* (Vol. 2, pp. 205–241). New York: Academic Press.

Corbin, H. (1972). Mundus imaginalis or the imaginary and the real. *Spring 1972*. Zürich: Spring publications.

Corby, N., & Solnick, R. L. (1980). Psychosocial and physiological influences on sexuality in the older adult. In J. E. Birren & R. B. Sloane (eds.), *Handbook of mental health and aging* (pp. 893–921). Englewood Cliffs, NJ: Prentice-Hall.

Corsini, J. (ed.). (1987). *Concise encyclopedia of psychology*. New York: Wiley.

Crites, S. (1986). Storytime: Recollecting the past and projecting the future. In T. R. Sarbin (ed.), *Narrative psychology: The storied nature of human conduct* (pp. 152–173). New York: Praeger.

Culwick, A. T., & Culwick, G. M. (1935). *Ubena of the rivers*. London: Allen and Unwin.

Davison, G. C., & Neale, J. M. (1990). *Abnormal psychology* (5th ed.). New York: Wiley.

Deal, T. E., & Kennedy, A. A. (1982). *Corporate cultures. The rites and rituals of corporate life*. Reading, MA: Addison-Wesley.

Decary, T. G. (1974). *The infant's reaction to strangers*. New York: International Universities Press.

Deikman, A. J. (1971). Bimodal consciousness. *Archives of General Psychiatry, 25*, 481–489.

De Laet, E. (1979). *Ovidius metamorphosen* [Metamorphoses of Ovid]. Amsterdam: Standaard Uitgeverij.

De Rougemont, D. (1956). *Love in the Western world*. New York: Pantheon Books.

Diener, E. (1984). Subjective well-being. *Psychological Bulletin, 95*, 542–575.

Domino, G. (1976). Compensatory aspects of dreams: An empirical test of Jung's theory. *Journal of Personality and Social Psychology, 34*, 658–662.

Durlak, J. (1973). Relationship between attitudes toward life and death among elderly women. *Developmental Psychology, 8*, 146.

Dusek, J. B., & Flaherty, J. F. (1981). The development of the self-concept during adolescent years. *Monographs of the Society for Research in Child Development, 46*, 191.

Eigen, M. (1983). On time and dreams. *The Psychoanalytic Review, 70*, 211–220.

Elder, G. (1974). *Children of the great depression.* Chicago: University of Chicago Press.

Elder, G. (1979). Historical change in life patterns and personality. In P. B. Baltes & O. G. Brim, Jr. (eds.), *Life-span development and behavior* (Vol. 2, pp. 117–159). New York: Academic Press.

Eliade, M., Adams, C. J., Kitagawa, J. M., Marty, M. E., McBrien, R. P., Needleman, J., Schimmel, A., Seltzer, R. M., & Turner, V. (eds.). (1987). *The encyclopedia of religion.* New York: Macmillan.

Elkind, D., & Bowen, R. (1979). Imaginary audience behavior in children and adolescents. *Developmental Psychology, 15,* 38–44.

Erikson, E. H. (1963). *Childhood and society* (rev. ed.). New York: Norton.

Erikson, E. H. (1968). Identity, psychosocial. *International Encyclopedia of Social Sciences, 7,* 61–65.

Falbo, T., & Peplau, L. A. (1980). Power strategies in intimate relationships. *Journal of Personality and Social Psychology, 38,* 618–628.

Farber, M. L. (1967). Suicide and hope. *Proceedings of the Fourth International Conference on Suicide Prevention* (pp. 297–306). Los Angeles: International Association for Suicide Prevention.

Farberow, N. L., & Shneidman, E. S. (eds.). (1961). *The cry for help.* New York: McGraw Hill.

Feifel, H. (1977). Death in contemporary America. In H. Feifel (ed.), *New meanings of death* (pp. 3–14). New York: McGraw-Hill.

Fischoff, B. (1978). Attribution theory and judgment under uncertainty. In J. H. Harvey, W. J. Ickes, & R. F. Kidd (eds.), *New directions in attribution research* (Vol. 1, pp. 421–452). New York: Wiley.

Fisher, S., & Cleveland, S. E. (1958). *Body image and personality.* New York: D. Van Nostrand.

Fogel, A. (1993). *Developing through relationships.* New York: Harvester Wheatsheaf.

Foulkes, D. (1967). Dream of the male child: Four case studies. *Journal of Child Psychology and Psychiatry, 8,* 81–97.

Foulkes, D. (1971). Longitudinal studies of dreams in children. In J. Masserman (ed.), *Science and psychoanalysis* (pp. 48–71). New York: Grune & Stratton.

Foulkes, D. (1978). *A grammar of dreams.* Sussex, UK: Harvester Press.

Foulkes, D., Larson, J. D., Swanson, E., & Rardin, M. (1969). Two studies of childhood dreaming. *American Journal of Orthopsychiatry, 39,* 627–643.

Fowler, J. (1981). *Stages of faith.* New York: Harper & Row.

Frank, J. (1991). *The idea spatial form.* New Brunswick, NJ and London: Rutgers University Press. (Original work published 1945)

Freud, S. (1953). The interpretation of dreams. In J. Strachey (Ed. & Trans.), *The standard edition of the complete psychological works of Sigmund Freud* (Vols. 4 & 5). London: Hogarth Press, 1953. (Original work published 1900)

Freud, S. (1942). On transience. *International Journal of Psycho-Analysis, 23,* 84–85.

Frye, N. (1957). *Anatomy of criticism.* Princeton, NJ: Princeton University Press.

Garvey, C. (1984). *Children's talk.* Cambridge, MA: Harvard University Press.

Gelderloos, P. (1987). *Valuation and transcendental meditation.* Lelystad, Netherlands: Soma Scientific.

Gendlin, E. T. (1978). *Focusing* (1st ed.). New York: Everest House.

Gergen, K. J. (1980). The emerging crisis in theory of life-span development. In P. Baltes & O. Brim, Jr. (eds.), *Life-span development and behavior* (Vol. 3, pp. 31–63). New York: Academic Press.

Gergen, K. J., & Gergen, M. M. (1988). Narrative and the self as relationship. *Advances in Experimental Social Psychology, 21,* 17–56.

Gilligan, C. (1982). *In a different voice: Psychological theory and women's development.* Cambridge, MA: Harvard University Press.

Glaser, B. G., & Strauss, A. L. (1966). *Awareness of dying.* Chicago: Aldine.

Glaser, B. G., & Strauss, A. L. (1967). *The discovery of grounded theory: Strategies for qualitative research.* Chicago: Aldine.

Goldin, F. (1967). *The mirror of Narcissus in the courtly love lyric.* Ithaca, NY: Cornell University Press.

Gould, R. L. (1975). Adult life stages: Growth toward self-tolerance. *Psychology Today, 8,* 74–78.

Gould, R. L. (1978). *Transformations: Growth and change in adult life.* New York: Simon & Schuster.

Gregg, G. S. (1991). *Self-representation: Life narrative studies in identity and ideology.* New York: Greenwood Press.

Grünbaum, A. A. (1925). *Hersschen und Lieben als Grundmotive der philosophischen Weltanschauungen* [Ruling and loving as basic motives of philosophical world views]. Bonn, Germany: Friedrich Cohen.

Gutmann, D. L. (1980). The post-parental years: Clinical problems and developmental possibilities. In W. H. Norman & T. J. Scaramella (eds.), *Mid-life: Developmental and clinical issues* (pp. 38–52). New York: Brunner/Mazel.

Haan, N. (1981). Common dimensions of personality development: Early adolescence to middle life. In D. H. Eichorn, J. A. Clausen, N. Haan, M. P. Honzik, & P. H. Mussen (eds.), *Present and past in middle life* (pp. 117–153). New York: Academic Press.

Hagestad, G. O. (1982). Parent and child: Generations in the family. In T. M. Field, A. Husaton, H. C. Quey, L. Twel, & G. E. Finley (eds.), *Review of human development* (pp. 485–499). New York: Wiley-Interscience.

Haney, D. Q. (1984, October 28). Boys found more likely to phantasize than girls. *Los Angeles Times,* Part 8, p. 10.

Hart, J. (1981). The significance of William James' ideas for modern psychotherapy. *Journal of Contemporary Psychotherapy, 12,* 88–102.

Hartup, W. W. (1974). Aggression in childhood: Developmental perspectives. *American Psychologist, 29,* 336–341.

Havener, P. H., & Izard, C. E. (1962). Unrealistic self-enhancement in paranoic schizophrenics. *Journal of Consulting Psychology, 26,* 65–68.

Havighurst, R. J. (1972). *Developmental tasks and education.* New York: McKay.

Hecht, B. (1954). *A child of the century.* New York: Simon & Schuster. (Reprinted New York: Ballantine Books, 1970)

Hendrickx, M. (1987). *De ervaring kanker* [The experience of cancer]. Unpublished doctoral dissertation, University of Nijmegen, Nijmegen, The Netherlands.

Hermans, H. J. M. (1981). *Persoonlijkheid en waardering* [Personality and valuation] (Vols. 1–3). Lisse, The Netherlands: Swets & Zeitlinger.

Hermans, H. J. M. (1986). Stability and change in the process of valuation: An idiographic approach. In A. Angleitner, A. Furnham, & G. van Heck (eds.), *Personality psychology in Europe: Current trends and controversies* (pp. 23–43). Lisse, The Netherlands: Swets & Zeitlinger.

Hermans, H. J. M. (1987a). Self as organized system of valuations: Toward a dialogue with the person. *Journal of Counseling Psychology, 34,* 10–19.

Hermans, H. J. M. (1987b). The dream in the process of valuation: A method of interpretation. *Journal of Personality and Social Psychology, 53,* 163–175.

Hermans, H. J. M. (1988). On the integration of idiographic and nomothetic research method in the study of personal meaning. *Journal of Personality, 56,* 785–812.

Hermans, H. J. M. (1989). The meaning of life as an organized process. *Psychotherapy, 26,* 11–22.

Hermans, H. J. M. (1992a). Telling and retelling one's self-narrative: A contextual approach to life-span development. *Human Development, 35,* 361–375.

Hermans, H. J. M. (1992b). Unhappy self-esteem: A meaningful exception to the rule. *Journal of Psychology, 126,* 555–570.

Hermans, H. J. M. (1992c). The person as an active participant in psychological research. *American Behavioral Scientist, 36,* 102–113.

Hermans, H. J. M. (1993). Moving opposites in the self: A Heraclitean approach. *Journal of Analytical Psychology, 38,* 437–462.

Hermans, H.J.M. (1994). Buber on mysticism, May on creativity, and the dialogical nature of the self. *Studies in Spirituality, 4,* 279–305.

Hermans, H. J. M. (in press). Voicing the self: From information processing to dialogical interchange. *Psychological Bulletin.*

Hermans, H. J. M., & Hermans-Jansen, E. (1976). De methode van zelfconfrontatie in de practijk: De procesbevordering van Charlotte [The method of self-confrontation in practice: The process promotion of Charlotte]. Amsterdam: Swets & Zeitlinger.

Hermans, H. J. M., & Hermans-Jansen, E. (1978). Het aforisme als middel tot herkenning [Proverbs as means of recognition]. *Nederlands Tijdschrift voor de Psychologie, 33,* 473–481.

Hermans, H. J. M., & Hermans-Jansen, E. (1992). The personal valuation of promiscuity: A method of investigation. *Psychotherapy Patient, 1/2,* 121–140.

Hermans, H. J. M., Hermans-Jansen, E., & Van Gilst, W. (1985a). *De grondmotieven van het menselijk bestaan: Hun expressie in het persoonlijk waarderingsleven* [The basic motives of human existence: Their expression in personal valuation]. Lisse, The Netherlands: Swets & Zeitlinger.

Hermans, H. J. M., Hermans-Jansen, E., & Van Gilst, W. (1985b). Does the medium change the message? De computer in het waarderingsonderzoek. *De Psycholoog*, 3, 122–125.

Hermans, H. J. M., & Kempen, H. J. G. (1993). *The dialogical self: Meaning as movement*. San Diego: Academic Press.

Hermans, H. J. M., Kempen, H. J. G., & Van Loon, R. J. P. (1992). The dialogical self: Beyond individualism and rationalism. *American Psychologist*, 47, 23–33.

Hermans, H. J. M., Rijks, T. I., & Kempen, H. J. G. (1993). Imaginal dialogues in the self: Theory and method. *Journal of Personality*, 61, 207–236.

Hermans, H. J. M., & Van Gilst, W. (1991). Self-narrative and collective myth: An analysis of the Narcissus story. *Canadian Journal of Behavioural Science*, 23, 423–440.

Hermans, H. J. M., & Van Loon, R. J. P. (1991). The personal meaning of symbols. *Journal of Religion and Health*, 30, 241–261.

Hickey, T. (1980). *Health and aging*. Monterey, CA: Brooks/Cole.

Higgins, E. T. (1987). Self-discrepancy: A theory relating self and affect. *Psychological Review*, 94, 319–340.

Himmelweit, H. T., & Turner, Ch. (1982). Social and psychological antecedents of depression: A longitudinal study from adolescence to early adulthood of a non-clinical population. In P. B. Baltes & O. G. Brim (eds.), *Life-span development and behavior* (Vol. 4, pp. 315–344). New York: Academic Press.

Hintikka, J. (1968). The varieties of information and scientific explanation. In N. van Rootselaar & R. Staal (eds.), *Logic, methodology, and the philosophy of science* (pp. 311–331). Amsterdam: North-Holland.

Honess, T. (1980). Self-reference in children's description of peers: Egocentricity or collaboration. *Child Development*, 51, 476–480.

Horner, M. S. (1972). Toward an understanding of achievement-related conflicts in women. *Journal of Social Issues*, 28, 157–175.

Horner, T. M. (1983). On the formation of personal space and self-boundary structures in early human development: The case of infant stranger reactivity. *Developmental Review*, 3, 148–177.

Hoshmand, L. T., & Polkinghorne, D. E. (1992). Redefining the science–practice relationship and professional training. *American Psychologist*, 47, 55–66.

Hultsch, D. F., & Plemons, J. K. (1979). Life events and life-span development. In P. B. Baltes & O. G. Brim, Jr. (eds.), *Life-span development and behavior* (Vol. 2, pp. 1–36). New York: Academic Press.

Hyde, J. S. (1984). How large are gender differences in aggression? A developmental meta-analysis. *Developmental Psychology*, 20, 722–736.

James, W. (1890). *The principles of psychology* (Vol. 1). London: Macmillan.

Janssen, W., Van der Molen, P., & Van Steen, F. (1980). Zelfonderzoek binnen de gevangenis [Self-investigation in prison]. In H. J. M. Hermans & D. Verstraeten (eds.), *Zelfonderzoek: Waarderingen van mensen in diverse toepassingsvelden* [Self-investigation: Valuations from people in diverse settings] (pp. 47–48). Deventer, The Netherlands: Van Loghum Slaterus.

Jenkins, C. D., Rosenman, R. H., & Zyzanski, S. (1974). Prediction of clinical coronary heart disease by a test for the coronary-prone behavior pattern. *New England Journal of Medicine, 23,* 1271–1275.

Jung, C. G. (1933). *Modern man in search of a soul.* New York: Harcourt.

Jung, C. G. (1959). Mandalas. In *Collected works* (Vol. 9, Part 1). Princeton, NJ: Princeton University Press.

Jung, C. G. (1967). *Die Dynamik des Unbewussten* [The dynamics of the unconscious]. Zürich: Rascher Verlag.

Kagan, J. (1980). Perspectives on continuity. In O. G. Brim & J. Kagan (eds.), *Constancy and change in human development* (pp. 26–74). Cambridge, MA: Harvard University Press.

Kagan, S., & Madsen, M. C. (1971). Cooperation and competition of Mexican and Anglo-American children of two ages under four instructional sets. *Developmental Psychology, 5,* 32–39.

Kalish, R. A. (1977). Dying and preparing for death: A view of families. In H. Feifel (ed.), *New meanings of death* (pp. 215–232). New York: McGraw-Hill.

Kalish, R. A., & Reynolds, D. K. (1976). Phenomenological reality and post-death contract. *Journal for the Scientific Study of Religion, 12,* 209–221.

Kastenbaum, R. (1969). Death and bereavement in later life. In A. H. Kutscher (ed.), *Death and bereavement* (pp. 28–54). Springfield, IL: Thomas.

Kastenbaum, R. (1977). Death and development through the lifespan. In H. Feifel (ed.), *New meanings of death* (pp. 17–45). New York: McGraw-Hill.

Kastenbaum, R. (1985). Death and dying: A lifespan approach. In J. E. Birren & K. W. Schaie (eds.), *Handbook of the psychology of aging* (2nd ed., pp. 619–643). New York: Van Nostrand Reinhold.

Keller, A., Ford, L. H., & Meacham, J. A. (1978). Dimensions of self-concept in preschool children. *Developmental Psychology, 14,* 483–489.

Kelly, G. A. (1955). *The psychology of personal constructs.* New York: Norton.

Klages, L. (1948). *Charakterkunde* (Characterology). Zürich: Hirzel.

Koestler, A. (1967). *The ghost in the machine.* London: Hutchinson.

Kohlberg, L. (1969). Stage and sequence: The cognitive-developmental approach to socialization. In D. A. Goslin (ed.), *Handbook of socialization theory and research* (pp. 347–480). Chicago: Rand McNally.

Kramer, M. (1982). The psychology of the dream: Art or science? *Psychiatric Journal of the University of Ottawa, 7,* 87–100.

Kuhn, D., Nash, S. C., & Brucken, L. (1978). Sex role concepts of two- and three-year-olds. *Child Development, 49,* 445–451.

Lacan, J. (1966). *Ecrits.* Paris: Editions du Seuil.

Larson, R., Csikszentmihalyi, M., & Graef, R. (1980). Mood variability and the psychosocial adjustment of adolescents. *Journal of Youth and Adolescence, 9,* 469–490.

Lester, D. (1972). *Why people kill themselves: A summary of research findings on suicidal behavior.* Springfield, IL: Thomas.

Levine, R. (1966). *Dreams and deeds: Achievement motivation in Nigeria.* Chicago: University of Chicago Press.

Levinson, D. J., Darrow, C. M., Klein, E. B., Levinson, M. H., & McKee, B. (1978). *The seasons of a man's life*. New York: Knopf.

Lewis, M., Feiring, C., McGuffog, C., & Jaskir, J. (1984). Predicting psychopathology in six-year-olds from early social relations. *Child Development, 55,* 123–136.

Linell, P. (1990). The power of dialogue dynamics. In I. Marková & K. Foppa (eds.), *The dynamics of dialogue* (pp. 147–177). New York: Harvester Wheatsheaf.

Loevinger, J. (1976). *Ego development*. San Francisco: Jossey-Bass.

Lowenthal, M. F. (1975). Psychosocial variations across the adult life course: Frontiers for research and policy. *Gerontologist, 15,* 6–12.

Maddi, S. R. (1972). *Personality theories: A comparative analysis*. Homewood, IL: Dorsey Press.

Madsen, M. C. (1971) Developmental and cross-cultural differences in the cooperative and competitive behavior of young children. *Journal of Cross-Cultural Psychology, 2,* 365–371.

Madsen, M. C., & Shapiro, A. (1970). Cooperative and competitive behavior of urban Afro-American, Anglo-American, Mexican-American, and Mexican village children. *Developmental Psychology, 3,* 16–20.

Maher, B. (ed.). (1969). *Clinical psychology and personality: The selected papers of G. A. Kelly*. New York: Wiley.

Mahler, M. S., Pine, F., & Bergman, A. (1975). *The psychological birth of the human infant: Symbiosis and individuation*. New York: Basic Books.

Mahoney, M. J. (1989, January 15). *The future of scientific psychology*. Paper presented to the American Association for the Advancement of Science, San Francisco.

Main, M., & Goldwyn, R. (1984). Predicting rejection of her infant from mother's representation of her own experience: Implications for the abused–abusing intergenerational cycle. *Child Abuse & Neglect, The International Journal, 8,* 203–217.

Mair, M. (1989). Kelly, Bannister, and a story-telling psychology. *International Journal of Personal Construct Psychology, 2,* 1–14.

Maloney, H. N. (1992). Response to Vitz: The search for method. *Journal of Psychology and Theology, 1,* 34–38.

Manosevitz, M., Prentice, N. M., & Wilson, F. (1973). Individual and family correlates of imaginary companions in preschool children. *Developmental Psychology, 8,* 72–79.

Marková, I. (1987). On the interaction of opposites in psychological processes. *Journal for the Theory of Social Behavior, 17,* 279–299.

Markus, H. R., & Kitayama, S. (1991). Culture and the self: Implications for cognition, emotion, and motivation. *Psychological Review, 98,* 224–253.

Markus, H. R., & Wurf, E. (1987). The dynamic self-concept: A social psychological perspective. *Annual Review of Psychology, 38,* 299–337.

Maslow, A. H. (1970). *Religions, values, and peak experiences*. New York: Viking.

Mathes, E. W., Adams, H. E., & Davies, R. M. (1985). Jealousy: Loss of relationship rewards, loss of self-esteem, depression, anxiety, and anger. *Journal of Personality and Social Psychology, 48,* 1552–1561.

May, R. (1966). *Psychology and the human dilemma*. Princeton, NJ: Van Nostrand.

McAdams, D. P. (1985). *Power, intimacy, and the life story: Personological inquiries into identity.* Chicago: Dorsey Press. (Reprinted 1988 by Guilford Press)

McClelland, D. C. (1961). *The achieving society.* Princeton, NJ: Van Nostrand.

McClelland, D. C., Atkinson, J. W., Clark, R. A., & Lowell, E. L. (1953). *The achievement motive.* New York: Appleton-Century-Crofts.

McClelland, D. C., Koestner, R., & Weinberger, J. (1989). How do self-attributed and implicit motives differ? *Psychological Review, 96,* 690–702.

McCrae, R. R., & Costa, P. T., Jr. (1982). Aging, the life course, and models of personality. In T. M. Field, A. Huston, H. C. Quay, L. Troll, & G. E. Finley (eds.), *Review of human development* (pp. 602–613). New York: Wiley-Interscience.

Mead, G. H. (1934). *Mind, self, and society.* Chicago: University of Chicago Press.

Meijer, R. W. J. (1991). *Konsultatie voor leerkrachten* [Consultation for teachers]. Unpublished doctoral dissertation, Free University, Amsterdam.

Merleau-Ponty, M. (1945). *Phénoménologie de la perception* [Phenomenology of perception]. Paris: Gallimard. (Translated into English by Smith, C. [1962]. *Phenomenology of perception.* London: Routledge & Kegan Paul.)

Milton, T. (1981). *Disorders of personality: DSM III, Axis II.* New York: Wiley-Interscience.

Mintz, R. S. (1968). Psychotherapy of the suicidal patient. In H. L. P. Resnik (ed.), *Suicidal behaviors: Diagnosis and management* (pp. 271–297). Boston: Little, Brown.

Munnichs, J. M. A. (1976). Dependency, interdependency, and autonomy: An introduction. In J. M. A. Munnichs & W. J. A. van den Heuvel (eds.), *Dependency or interdependency in old age* (pp. 3–8). The Hague, The Netherlands: Martinus Nijhoff.

Murray, H. A. (1938). *Explorations in personality.* New York: Oxford University Press.

Murray, H. A. (1962). The personality and career of Satan. *Journal of Social Issues, 28,* 36–54.

Neugarten, B. L. (1968a). Adult personality: Toward a psychology of the life cycle. In B. L. Neugarten (ed.), *Middle age and aging* (pp. 137–147). Chicago: University of Chicago Press.

Neugarten, B. L. (ed.). (1968b). *Middle age and aging.* Chicago: University of Chicago Press.

Neugarten, B. L. (1970a). Adaptation and the life cycle. *Journal of Geriatric Psychiatry, 4,* 71–87.

Neugarten, B. L. (1970b). Dynamics of transition of middle age to old age: Adaptation and the life cycle. *Journal of Geriatric Psychiatry, 4,* 71–87.

Newcomb, A. F., & Brady, J. E. (1982). Mutuality in boys' friendship relations. *Child Development, 53,* 392–395.

Norton, D. L., & Kille, M. F. (eds.). (1983). *Philosophies of love.* Totowa, NJ: Rowman and Allanheld.

Nuttin, J. (1965). *La structure de la personnalité* [The structure of personality]. Paris: Presses Universitaires de France.

Oppenheimer, V. K. (1981). The changing nature of life-cycle squeezes: Implication for the socioeconomic position of the elderly. In R. W. Fogel, E. Hatfield, S. B. Kiesler, & E. Shanes (eds.), *Aging: Stability and change in the family* (pp. 47–81). New York: Academic Press.

Ortega, Y., & Gasset, J. (1957). *On love: Aspects of a single theme.* New York: Meridian Books.

Parkes, C. M. (1972). *Bereavement: Studies of grief in adult life.* New York: International Universities Press.

Pepper, S. (1942). *World hypotheses.* Berkeley: University of California Press.

Perls, F. S. (1969). *Gestalt therapy verbatim.* Moab, Utah: Real People Press.

Pervin, L. A. (1993). *Personality* (4th ed.). New York: Wiley.

Pines, M. (1985). Mirroring and child development. *Psychoanalytic Inquiry, 5,* 211–231.

Pitcher, E. G., & Schultz, L. H. (1984). *Boys and girls at play: The development of sex roles.* New York: Praeger.

Polkinghorne, D. (1988). *Narrative knowing and the human sciences.* Albany: State University of New York Press.

Poulie, M. F. (1991). *Meer licht op faalangst: De waardering van het individu* [More light on fear of failure: The valuation of the individual]. Unpublished doctoral dissertation, University of Nijmegen, Nijmegen, The Netherlands.

Radloff, L. (1975). Sex differences in depression: The effects of occupation and marital status. *Sex Roles, 1,* 249–265.

Raimy, V. C. (1950). *Training in clinical psychology.* New York: Prentice-Hall.

Reijnen, P. (1981). *Het verschil tussen gevoelens en emoties* [The difference between feelings and emotions]. Unpublished doctoral dissertation, University of Nijmegen, Nijmegen, The Netherlands.

Rheingold, H. L., & Emery, G. N. (1986). The nurturant acts of very young children. In D. Olweus, J. Block, & M. Radke-Yarrow (eds.), *Development of antisocial and prosocial behavior: Research, theories, and issues* (pp. 75–96). Orlando, FL: Academic Press.

Riegel, K. (1975). Adult life-crises: A dialectical interpretation of development. In N. Datan & L. Ginsberg (eds.), *Life-span developmental psychology: Normative life-crises* (pp. 99–128). New York: Academic Press.

Robinson, J. A., & Hawpe, L. (1986). Narrative thinking as a heuristic process. In T. R. Sarbin (ed.), *Narrative psychology: The storied nature of human conduct* (pp. 111–125). New York: Praeger.

Rogers, C. R. (1951). *Client-centered therapy.* Boston, MA: Houghton Mifflin.

Roscher, W. H. (1965). *Ausführliches Lexikon der griechischen und römischen Mythologie* (Comprehensive lexicon of Greek and Roman mythology). Leipzig, Germany: Teubner Verlag, 1897–1902. Hildesheim, Germany: Georg Olms Verlag.

Rosenberg, M. (1979). *Conceiving the self.* New York: Basic Books.

Rowan, J. (1990). *Subpersonalities: The people inside us.* London: Routledge.

Rubin, J. Z., Provenzano, F. J., & Luria, Z. (1974). The eye of the beholder: Parents' view on sex of newborns. *American Journal of Orthopsychiatry, 44,* 512–519.

Rychlak, J. F. (1988). *The psychology of rigorous humanism* (2nd ed.). New York: New York University Press.

Sampson, E. E. (1985). The decentralization of identity: Toward a revised concept of personal and social order. *American Psychologist, 11,* 1203–1211.

Sampson, E. E. (1993). *Celebrating the other: A dialogic account of human nature.* Boulder, CO: Westview Press.

Sandfort, T. G. M. (1984). Sex in pedophiliac relationships: An empirical investigation among a nonrepresentative group of boys. *Journal of Sex Research, 20*, 123–142.

Sarbin, T. R. (1986). The narrative as a root methaphor for psychology. In T. R. Sarbin (ed.), *Narrative psychology: The storied nature of human conduct* (pp. 3–21). New York: Praeger.

Savin-Williams, R. C., & Demo, D. H. (1984). Developmental change and stability in adolescent self-concept. *Developmental Psychology, 20*, 1100–1110.

Schmoll, J. A. (1978). *Auguste Rodin*. Herrsching am Ammersee, Germany: Schuler Verlag.

Schön, D. (1983). *The reflective practitioner: How professionals think in action.* New York: Basic Books.

Schön, D. (1987). *Educating the reflective practitioner.* San Francisco: Jossey-Bass.

Schulz, R. (1982). Emotionality and aging: A theoretical and empirical analysis. *Journal of Gerontology, 37*, 42–51.

Schuyler, D., & Katz, M. M. (1973). *The depressive illnesses: A major public health problem.* Washington, DC: U.S. Government Printing Office.

Schwartz, R. (1987, March/April). Our multiple selves: Applying systems thinking to the inner family. *The Family Therapy Networker*, pp. 25–83.

Seligman, M. E. P. (1973). Fall into helplessness. *Psychology Today, 7*, 43–48.

Seligman, M. E. P. (1974). Depression and learned helplessness. In R. J. Friedman & M. M. Katz (eds.), *The psychology of depression: Contemporary theory and research* (pp. 83–125). Washington, DC: Winston-Wiley.

Selman, R. L. (1981). The child as a friendship philosopher. In S. R. Asher & J. M. Gottman (eds.), *The development of children's friendships* (pp. 242–272). Cambridge, UK: Cambridge University Press.

Selman, R. L., & Selman, A. (1979). Children's ideas about friendship: A new theory. *Psychology Today*, pp. 70–80.

Shapiro, A., & Madsen, M. C. (1969). Cooperative and competitive behavior of kibbutz and urban children in Israel. *Child Development, 40*, 609–617.

Shavelson, R. J., Hubner, J. J., & Stanton, G. C. (1976). Self-concept: Validation of construct interpretations. *Review of Educational Research, 3*, 407–441.

Shneidman, E. S. (1987). A psychological approach to suicide. In G. R. VandenBos & B. K. Bryant (eds.), *Cataclysms, crises, and catastrophes: Psychology in action* (pp. 147–183). Washington, DC: American Psychological Association.

Sluzki, C. E. (1992). Transformations: A blueprint for narrative changes in therapy. *Family Process, 31*, 217–230.

Spence, J. T. (1985). Achievement American style: The rewards and costs of individualism. *American Psychologist, 40*, 1285–1295.

Spence, J. T., & Helmreich, R. L. (1983). Achievement-related motives and behavior. In J. T. Spence (ed.), *Achievement and achievement motives: Psychological and sociological approaches* (pp. 7–74). San Francisco: Freeman.

Sroufe, L. A. (1977). Wariness of strangers and the study of infant development. *Child Development, 48*, 731–746.

Sroufe, L. A. (1983). Infant–caregiver attachment and patterns of adaptation in preschool:

The roots of maladaptation and competence. In M. Perlmutter (ed.), *Development and policy concerning children with special needs: Vol. 16. Minnesota Symposium in Child Psychology* (pp. 41–83). Hillsdale, NJ: Lawrence Erlbaum.

Staub, E. A. (1975). *The development of prosocial behavior of children.* Morristown, NJ: General Learning Press.

Staub, E. A. (1986). A conception of the determinants and development of altruism and aggression: Motives, the self, and the environment. In C. Zahn-Waxler, E. M. Cummings, & R. Iannotti (eds.), *Altruism and aggression: Biological and social origins* (pp. 135–164). Cambridge, UK: Cambridge University Press.

Stern, D. (1983). The early development of schemas of self, other and self with other. In J. D. Lichtenberg & S. Kaplan (eds.), *Reflections on self psychology* (pp. 49–84). Hillsdale, NJ: Analytic Press.

Stone, A. A. (1960). A syndrome of serious suicidal intent. *Archives of General Psychiatry, 3,* 331–339.

Straus, E. W. (1958). Aesthesiology and hallucinations. In R. May, E. Angel, & H. F. Ellenberger (eds.), *Existence: A new dimension in psychiatry and psychology* (pp. 139–169). New York: Basic Books.

Stroebe, M., Gergen, M. M., Gergen, K. J., & Stroebe, W. (1992). Broken hearts or broken bonds: Love and death in historical perspective. *American Psychologist, 47,* 1205–1212.

Super, D. E. (1957). *The psychology of careers.* New York: Harper & Row.

Tart, C. T. (ed.). (1969). *Altered states of consciousness.* New York: Wiley.

Thigpen, C. H., & Cleckley, H. (1954). A case of multiple personality. *Journal of Abnormal and Social Psychology, 49,* 135–151.

Thomae, H. (1988). *Das Individuum und Seine Welt* [The individual and his world] (2nd ed.). Göttingen, Germany: Hogrefe.

Toch, H. (1969). *Violent men.* Chicago: Aldine.

Turner, R. H., & Vanderlippe, R. N. (1958). Self-ideal consequence as an index of adjustment. *Journal of Abnormal and Social Psychology, 57,* 202–206.

Vaillant, G. E. (1977). *Adaptation to life: How the best and brightest came of age.* Boston: Little, Brown.

Van Assen, K. (1985). *Zelfwaardering en verzet* [Self-valuation and opposition]. Doctoral dissertation. Lisse, The Netherlands: Swets & Zeitlinger.

Van Dassel, Y. (1985). *Atypische rouw en de zelf-konfrontatiemethode* [Atypical mourning and the self-confrontation method]. Unpublished master's thesis, University of Nijmegen, Nijmegen, The Netherlands.

Van de Loo, R. (1992). *Verheldering van loopbaanperspectief: Ontwikkeling en toepassing van een programma voor loopbaanoriëntatie op basis van de zelfkonfrontatiemethode* [Clarification of career perspective: Development and application of a program for career orientation on the basis of the self-confrontation method]. Doctoral dissertation. Assen, The Netherlands: Van Gorcum.

Van Gennip, A. (1909). *Les rites de passage: Étude systématique des rites* [Rites of passage: Systematic study of rites]. Paris: Librairie critique Emile Nourry.

Van Gilst, W., & Hermans, H. J. M. (1988). *Computerprogrammatuur bij de zelfkonfrontatie methode* [Computer programs with the self-confrontation method]. Lisse, The Netherlands: Swets & Zeitlinger.

Van Loon, R. J. P. (1992). Way symbolism in personal life: Illustrated and explained from a Taoist perspective. In P. Mischel (ed.), *Symbolik von Weg und Reise. Schriften zur Symbolforschung* [Symbolism of way and travel. Documents of symbol research] (Vol. 8, pp. 299–325). Bern: Peter Lang.

Verstraeten, D. (1978). Waarderingsonderzoek in het kader van partnerrelatietherapie [Valuation research within the framework of partner-relation therapy]. *Nederlands Tijdschrift voor de Psychologie, 33,* 441–452.

Verstraeten, D. (1983). Waardering en welbevinden in partnerrelaties [Valuation and well-being in partner relationships]. *Gedrag, 6,* 269–309.

Vitz, P. C. (1990). The use of stories in moral development: New psychological reasons for an old education method. *American Psychologist, 45,* 709–720.

Warren, L. (1983). Male intolerance of depression: A review with implications for psychotherapy. *Clinical Psychology Review, 3,* 147–156.

Watkins, M. (1986). *Invisible guests: The development of imaginal dialogues.* Hillsdale, NJ: Erlbaum.

Webb, W. B., & Cartwright, R. D. (1978). Sleep and dreams. *Annual Review of Psychology, 29,* 223–252.

Weber, R. A., Levitt, M. J., & Clark, M. C. (1986). Individual variation in attachment security and strange situation behavior: The role of maternal and infant temperament. *Child Development, 57,* 56–65.

Weston, D. R., & Richardson, E. (1985, April). *Children's world views: Working models and quality of attachment.* Paper presented at the biennial meeting of the Society for Research in Child Development, Toronto.

Winget, C., Kramer, M., & Whitman, R. (1972). Dreams and demography. *Canadian Psychiatric Association Journal, 17,* 203–208.

Winnicott, D. W. (1971). *Playing and reality.* London: Tavistock.

Winter, D. G. (1973). *The power motive.* New York: Free Press.

Wylie, R. C. (1974). *The self-concept* (rev. ed.). Lincoln: University of Nebraska Press.

Yalom, I. D. (1980). *Existential psychotherapy.* New York: Basic Books.

Zahn-Waxler, C., & Radke-Yarrow, M. (1979). *A developmental analysis of children's responses to emotions in others.* Paper presented at the biennial meeting of the Society for Research in Child Development, San Francisco.

Zahn-Waxler, C., Radke-Yarrow, M., & Brady-Smith, J. (1977). Perspective-taking and prosocial behavior. *Developmental Psychology, 13,* 87–88.

Zimeth, C. H. (1982). *De zelfkonfrontatiemethode als diagnostisch middel bij de hulpverlening aan voortijdige schoolverlaters* [The method of self-confrontation as an assessment tool for the professional help of school dropouts]. Unpublished master's thesis, University of Amsterdam.

Index